THE NATURE READER

Daniel Halpern is the author of seven collections of poetry, most recently *Foreign Neon and Selected Poems*, and is editor-in-chief of The Ecco Press. He has edited numerous anthologies, including *Plays in One Act*, *Writers on Artists* and *The Art of the Tale: An International Anthology of Short Stories*.

Dan Frank, Editorial Director of Pantheon Books, has edited books on natural history for over ten years and helped launch the Penguin Nature Library during his tenure at Viking Penguin.

THE

NATURE READER

edited by DANIEL HALPERN *and* DAN FRANK

PICADOR

First published 1996 by The Ecco Press, new Jersey

This edition published 2001 by Picador
an imprint of Pan Macmillan Ltd
Pan Macmillan, 20 New Wharf Road, London N1 9RR
Basingstoke and Oxford
Associated companies throughout the world
www.panmacmillan.com

ISBN 0 330 37444 3

CONTENTS

PREFACE

I INTRODUCTORY

Seamus Heaney *Death of a Naturalist* 3
John Hay *The Nature Writer's Dilemma* 5

II AN HISTORICAL OVERVIEW

Derek Walcott *The Sea Is History* 11
Noel Perrin *Forever Virgin: The American View of America* 14
Ann Zwinger *A World of Infinite Variety* 24
Edward Hoagland *In Praise of John Muir* 35
Julia Blackburn *St. Helena's* 49
Italo Calvino *Man, the Sky and the Elephant: On Pliny's* Natural History 59

III NATURAL PHENOMENA

Louise Glück *All Hallows* 71
Leslie Marmon Silko *Landscape, History, and the Pueblo Imagination* 72
Keith H. Basso *"Stalking with Stories": Names, Places, and Moral Narratives among the Western Apaches* 84
Richard K. Nelson *The Gifts* 106
David Abram *The Ecology of Magic* 121
John Fowles *The Green Man* 132
Gary Nabhan *Enduring Seeds: The Sacred Lotus and the Common Bean* 140
Annie Dillard *Total Eclipse* 148
Gretel Ehrlich *Spring* 160
Edward O. Wilson *Storm over the Amazon* 170
William Langewiesche *The Physics of Blown Sand* 173

IV AMERICAN DIRECTIVES

Robert Hass *The Apple Trees at Olema* 181
Gary Snyder *The Rediscovery of Turtle Island* 183
Edward Abbey *The Moon-eyed Horse* 192
Barry Lopez *The Stone Horse* 204
Jim Harrison *Passacaglia on Getting Lost* 214
John Haines *Shadows and Vistas* 220
Joyce Carol Oates *Against Nature* 226

V CREATURES

Ted Hughes *Hawk Roosting* 237
Peter Matthiessen *The Cranes of Hokkaido* 238
David Quammen *Rattlesnake Passion* 248
Guy de la Valdéne *Quail Farm* 255
Jennifer Ackerman *Five Fathoms* 261
John McPhee *Under the Snow* 266
Terry Tempest Williams *To Be Taken* 272

VI FICTION

Elizabeth Bishop *The Map* 283
Bruce Chatwin *The Drought* 284
Paul Bowles *The New Day* 286
David Malouf *An Imaginary Life* 288
Cormac McCarthy *The Mountain* 291
Gabriel García Márquez *To the Sea* 293
Richard Ford *Hunters* 295
John Berger *Goats* 298
Jim Crace *The Prospect from the Silver Hill* 301

VII NATURAL HISTORY: AN ANNOTATED BOOKLIST

W.S. Merwin, *The Last One* 311

Annie Dillard 315

Gretel Ehrlich 321

John Hay 323

Edward Hoagland 325

Barry Lopez 326

David Quammen 329

Terry Tempest Williams 333

Jim Harrison 336

CONTRIBUTORS 339

PREFACE

Nature likes to hide.
—Heraclitus

Some of the writing here was originally gathered in a special issue of *Antaeus* called *On Nature*, published in 1986 and brought out in hardcover by the North Point Press in 1987. We have used that anthology as a seedbed and an opportunity to create a richer, more diverse habitat—one that reflects the veritable renaissance of writing on nature that has taken place in the decade since the first collection appeared.

Among other things, John Hay's essay "The Nature Writer's Dilemma" identifies the traditional Western assumption about nature that has finally come under serious scrutiny: the idea that we are both apart from, and superior to, the natural world. The phrase "natural resources" is indicative of our old empiricist point of view, in which the natural world is an exploitable raw material, subject to technological manipulation and "improvement" as humankind sees fit, endlessly forgiving of our depredations.

Yet the counter-idea, that we may restore nature to some pristine, Edenic state—untrammelled by human use or definition, uncorrupted even by our presence—is a quixotic one, as writers as disparate as Simon Schama and William Cronin have pointed out.

In both instances we have been hemmed in by the perception that we are separate from nature. In our enlightenment, however, we may say *of course we are part of nature* without having much idea of what this might mean—how we are in nature, how nature expresses itself through us, as it expresses itself through a flower, say, or a shark. Our lives spent in rooms, our imaginations and outlooks framed by windows—by concepts, logic, language—most of us continue to think of nature as a place to visit, wearing sunscreen and suitable protective clothing. Visitors in the museum of the great outdoors.

We have succeeded in externalizing the natural world. Today, it is fashionable to think of nature as a mental or historical construct: Nature is only an ideal envisioned by each particular age, each particular society, and our vision of it reflects only our desires and limitations. How then do we turn the ugly specter of subjectivity and relativism away from the palace gates?

We are a part of nature, yet we stand apart from nature. Perhaps our focus should be upon how we have attempted, over the centuries, to balance that opposition. We might say that the history of nature is in part a quest for our right relation to it. We belong, and yet we are just visitors.

Among the most astute observers of our relation to the natural world and our effort to hold that relation in balance have been writers—not only writers of natural history, but poets and novelists as well. As diverse as the visions gathered here are, it seems to us that there is a common strand that unites them: the quest for a right relation to the natural world is also the quest to understand our own nature. This connection was recognized by the pre-Socratic thinker Heraclitus, who also identified a few signposts for that quest. Two seem particularly worth noting: the trail will be trackless, and it will yield the unexpected. These two markers are the starting points for many of the pieces that we have collected here. They are points of departure, but they are not bad places to end, either.

THE NATURE READER

I

INTRODUCTORY

Seamus Heaney

Death of a Naturalist

All year the flax-dam festered in the heart
Of the townland; green and heavy-headed
Flax had rotted there, weighted down by huge sods.
Daily it sweltered in the punishing sun.
Bubbles gargled delicately, bluebottles
Wove a strong gauze of sound around the smell.
There were dragonflies, spotted butterflies,
But best of all was the warm thick slobber
Of frogspawn that grew like clotted water
In the shade of the banks. Here, every spring
I would fill jampotfuls of the jellied
Specks to range on window-sills at home,
On shelves at school, and wait and watch until
The fattening dots burst into nimble-
Swimming tadpoles. Miss Walls would tell us how
The daddy frog was called a bullfrog
And how he croaked and how the mammy frog
Laid hundreds of little eggs and this was
Frogspawn. You could tell the weather by frogs too
For they were yellow in the sun and brown
In rain.

      Then one hot day when fields were rank
With cowdung in the grass the angry frogs
Invaded the flax-dam; I ducked through hedges
To a coarse croaking that I had not heard
Before. The air was thick with a bass chorus.
Right down the dam gross-bellied frogs were cocked
On sods; their loose necks pulsed like sails. Some hopped:

The slap and plop were obscene threats. Some sat
Poised like mud grenades, their blunt heads farting.
I sickened, turned, and ran. The great slime kings
Were gathered there for vengeance and I knew
That if I dipped my hand the spawn would clutch it.

John Hay

The Nature Writer's Dilemma

You might think, after many years of teaching a class called "Nature Writers," that I would know what nature meant, but I do not. Perhaps this is of little importance. The word comes from the Latin, *to be born*, which is fundamental enough, and puts it under the heading of abiding mystery. Then we have the essential character of something, like a rock, or a child; plus physical power, according to the dictionary, causing the phenomena of the material world; or for one grand definition, the sum of the surrounding universe. When I hear it said in caustic tones that "Everyone knows man is a part of nature," I have only the vaguest idea of what that means either. The last time I heard such a remark, it came from a teacher of philosophy who did not seem to be particularly interested in what is often referred to as "the lower forms of life." There is reason to suspect the assumptions of the human brain when it becomes too elevated from the earth that nurtured it.

The dictionary also includes "the state of nature," which was long considered to be unregenerate, the opposite of grace, with the heathen and the wolves. The Judeo-Christian ethic has been blamed for putting man above nature in God's name. In this view, technology, ravaging industrialism, the will to exploit are an extension of overweening Christian arrogance. It is certainly true that most people still believe in their superiority to nonhuman life, though this may now be tempered by the idea that both of us share in an equality of inheritance, and that consciousness may not be man's exclusive property.

Are we unique? The ethologist Niko Tinbergen says it is difficult to prove scientifically. The question of why we need to feel unique might be more useful. How does the human spirit stand and survive in relation to the surrounding universe?

I find further difficulties in coming to grips with this subject because of my society, which sees the natural world not as a range of correlated lives and communities but as a province for plunder. The terms it appropriates, such as *ecology*, *the environment*, or *conservation*, may be politically useful to the cause, but they hardly guarantee an intimacy with its sources. Someone might go into a woodland area saying: "Great ecology you got here!" and care less about the trees.

For all our human claiming of the right to possess and dominate the earth, we have lost a great deal of our sense of it. A relationship which was once as direct as the food we put into our mouths has become abstract. We seldom know where the food comes from. If you approach certain publishers with writing which deals with nature, in other words, the world of life, the water we could not live without, the air we breathe, you might very well be advised to "put more people into it." But if you can't find nature, where will the people live? The subject is only au courant if backpacking, canoeing, sailing, and other acceptable activities make it so, added, of course, to writings with the authority of science, the accepted interpreter of all natural phenomena. We could identify very little without it. At the same time, the priesthood that can take us beyond Jupiter to black holes and quarks seems to alter common nature into a detached state most people can't take in.

So the contemporary nature writer can be forgiven if he is not quite sure on which shelf he is to end up. It may give him some confidence that his subject derives from the Latin *nasci*, "to be born," and so is the most important one he could possibly have, but he is subject, like all the race, to confusion. It may be better to hang loose and respect your capacity to receive unknown surprises than to wait on terms and categories, from whatever important direction they come.

John Muir, who was a religious man in spite of his rejection of his Scots Calvinist upbringing, said that he took a walk and decided to stay out past sundown, to conclude that going out is really going in. His wilderness has now become the cause for a more translated religion, so that those who want it saved but have never entered it, and might not like it if they did, talk about it as if it were some paradisal refuge at the end of the mind. Things are getting pretty desperate when you can no longer move out into the substance of where you ought to be.

A practical culture wants to know what things are, how they work, even, for almost anything under the sun, "What good is it?" Existence for its own sake—life forms that flow in the beauty of the wind, like a flock of sanderlings—becomes subordinated to labels. The facts may help us to feel sure about our control of circumstances, but they are a poor substitute for the deeper equations of earth and human life.

The American Indian saw the Word behind all manifested things, the primal, creative power. The Word was invoked through silence and dreams, through chants in healing ceremonies, and hypnotic poetry that mirrored the sounds of nature. Knud Rasmussen wrote down the words of a song which came spontaneously to a woman Eskimo from her "helping spirit," as Margot Astrov records it in her anthology, *The Winged Spirit*. The song went like this:

> The great sea
> Has sent me adrift,
> It moves me as the weed in a great river,
> Earth and the great weather move me,
> Have carried me away,
> And move my inward parts with joy.

Now, if a Western reader should read this as a poem for the first time, he might find it pleasing, fragmentary, even moving, but the depth and spontaneity which occasioned it would certainly pass him by, as, I am afraid, much of the Indian experience has passed us by. Rasmussen said that she was repeating these verses incessantly during a gathering in a big snow house; and that she was intoxicated with joy, a joy that everyone else in the house felt too. They began to state all "their misdeeds, as well as those of others, and those who felt themselves accused and admitted their offenses obtained release from these by lifting their arms and making movements as if to fling away all evil, all that was false and wicked was thrown away. . . ."

We do not often get catharsis of the soul, I am afraid, out of what goes under the general heading of Nature Writing, but one senses through this example just how narrow our view of the subject is forced to be. The earth's great weather is too often put down in terms of climatology, meteorology, predictable fronts, and clouds, such as cirrus, nimbus, and cumulus, which have little to do with tears or joy.

Writers who go beyond scientific nomenclature to talk about their thoughts and feelings, with nature as their foil, are invariably compared with Thoreau, as if he were the only writer we had who belonged in that classification. Thoreau tested the ideals of experience against the elements of his country world, and certainly derived much joy from it. That he was a poet and a literary craftsman, rather than an educator in outdoor living, may have put him in the nature-writer category by default, but there are a great many others who belong there with him. Wasn't Emily Dickinson invoking the Word behind natural phenomena? Surely *Moby-Dick*, a great mythic saga, belongs there, and would it be demeaning to Shakespeare, with his incomparable human range, to call him a nature writer, or to hear profoundly natural rhythms in Beethoven?

Clearly, the term *Nature Writers* is totally inadequate to start with if it only implies an interest in landscapes peopled by plants and animals but otherwise isolated from central human experience. We give the novelists charge of our demented psyches, our quirks and foibles, but the depth of human character seldom seems anchored in the known earth and its surrounding waters. Man is still on one side, Nature on the other.

If I am to stick solely to the discipline of natural history I suppose I have no right to bring in poetry, music, drama, and other arts, but the implication is that our subject may be starved for want of room. That diverse human experience should be kept out of it does not bode well for our earth relationship. (Naturalists are often thought of in terms of whether or not they like people, which assumes that their concerns with the natural world leave little room for human sympathy. It is a chilly gap, but I doubt that the naturalists created it.)

A writer like Edward Abbey, in his *Desert Solitaire*, defended Moab, Utah, and its beautiful environs with savage irony and sympathy, as if he felt he was going to be accused of bias. Too often the acceptable norm is natural history in its tamest and most factual form. You cannot go wrong if you are backed up by accurate nomenclature. Thus Gilbert White's *The Natural History of Selborne* is praised as much for its early use of precise observation and the scientific method as for the wonderful sense of peace and rooted continuity that pervades the book. We think of nature as a source of information we are entitled to have.

Nature is also a place, like Florida, to escape to (except that Florida appears to have become denaturalized) and it implies the danger, discomfort, and inconvenience which a whole civilization works to overcome; but as reality, as a part and parcel of this volatility, this deep turmoil, this trouble and delight we call existence, the term has lost credit. But we will come back to its truth through our own inadequacy, if nothing else. Primal law demands it. In the meantime, though I am obliged to an economy and a readership that insists on categories, I think I will stick with my confusion and the mystery of things, as if human domination never existed. How else are we to be born again? There is no help but to continue on this tack until I reach the far side of the horizon, if the food holds out. Nature undefined is what I know in myself. What better, more incalculable, capricious, and impossible guide could I have than that! This voyage is going to be interesting.

II

AN HISTORICAL OVERVIEW

Derek Walcott

The Sea Is History

Where are your monuments, your battles, martyrs?
Where is your tribal memory? Sirs,
in that grey vault. The sea. The sea
has locked them up. The sea is History.

First, there was the heaving oil,
heavy as chaos;
then, like a light at the end of a tunnel,

the lantern of a caravel,
and that was Genesis.
Then there were the packed cries,
the shit, the moaning:

Exodus.
Bone soldered by coral to bone,
mosaics
mantled by the benediction of the shark's shadow,

that was the Ark of the Covenant.
Then came from the plucked wires
of sunlight on the sea floor

the plangent harps of the Babylonian bondage,
as the white cowries clustered like manacles
on the drowned women,

and those were the ivory bracelets
of the Song of Solomon,
but the ocean kept turning blank pages

looking for History.
Then came the men with eyes heavy as anchors
who sank without tombs,

brigands who barbecued cattle,
leaving their charred ribs like palm leaves on the shore,
then the foaming, rabid maw

of the tidal wave swallowing Port Royal,
and that was Jonah,
but where is your Renaissance?

Sir, it is locked in them sea-sands
out there past the reef's moiling shelf,
where the men-o'-war floated down;

strop on these goggles, I'll guide you there myself.
It's all subtle and submarine,
through colonnades of coral,

past the gothic windows of sea-fans
to where the crusty grouper, onyx-eyed,
blinks, weighted by its jewels, like a bald queen;

and these groined caves with barnacles
pitted like stone
are our cathedrals,

and the furnace before the hurricanes:
Gomorrah. Bones ground by windmills
into marl and cornmeal,

and that was Lamentations—
that was just Lamentations,
it was not History;

then came, like scum on the river's drying lip,
the brown reeds of villages
mantling and congealing into towns,

and at evening, the midges' choirs,
and above them, the spires
lancing the side of God

as His son set, and that was the New Testament.

Then came the white sisters clapping
to the waves' progress,
and that was Emancipation—

jubilation, O jubilation—
vanishing swiftly
as the sea's lace dries in the sun,

but that was not History,
that was only faith,
and then each rock broke into its own nation;

then came the synod of flies,
then came the secretarial heron,
then came the bullfrog bellowing for a vote,

fireflies with bright ideas
and bats like jetting ambassadors
and the mantis, like khaki police,

and the furred caterpillars of judges
examining each case closely,
and then in the dark ears of ferns

and in the salt chuckle of rocks
with their sea pools, there was the sound
like a rumour without any echo

of History, really beginning.

Noel Perrin

Forever Virgin: The American View of America

If there is one novel that nearly all educated Americans have read, it's F. Scott Fitzgerald's *The Great Gatsby*. If there's a single most famous passage in that novel, it's the one on the last page where Fitzgerald talks about Gatsby's belief in the green light ahead. He has in mind two or three kinds of green light at once. There's the literal green dock-identification light that Gatsby can see from his Long Island mansion, glimmering across the bay where Daisy lives. There's the metaphorical green traffic light: the future is open, the future is GO. And finally there's the green light that nature produces: the reflection from trees, and especially from a whole forest, a forest crowding right up to the shore of Long Island Sound.

In that famous last passage, the narrator of the book is standing in front of Gatsby's mansion at night—a summer night. He is looking across the bay, just as Gatsby used to do. There is a bright moon. As he looks, "the inessential houses began to melt away until gradually I became aware of the old island here that flowered once for Dutch sailors' eyes—a fresh, green breast of the new world. Its vanished trees, the trees that had made way for Gatsby's house, had once pandered in whispers to the last and greatest of all human dreams; for a transitory enchanted moment man must have held his breath in the presence of this continent . . . face to face for the last time in history with something commensurate to his capacity for wonder."

Fitzgerald says in this passage that it was just for a moment that men and women beheld the new world as a fresh, untouched place, a virgin world, a place where the future is open and green. But, of course, it wasn't. We still see it that way—or most of us do most of the time. Certainly that was how Jay Gatsby saw it sixty years ago. In the narrator's vision, there on the last page, that is how he, too, sees it: Long Island with the houses invisible in the moonlight, the island like a green breast, the breast of Mother Nature, inexhaustibly nourishing. As I am going to try to show in a little while, that is how most Americans still perceive the country now: morning in America, a green light ahead, nature glad and strong and free. Or at least we do in our dominant mood, and that's why the majority of us don't really worry much about acid rain, or recycling, or any of that. We have a consciousness below knowledge that the big country can handle all that.

But there are two things I want to do before I come to the relationship between human beings and nature in America in the 1980s: a short thing and a long thing. The short one is simply to make clear what I mean by nature. And the long one is to give some of the history of the encounter between us and nature since we got here. Because of course I am not claiming we feel exactly the same as Henryk Hudson's sailors did in 1609. We have changed, and the country has changed since then. A lot. All I'm claiming is that we still see the green light.

First, what nature is. Among other things, it's a word that if you look it up turns out to have twelve meanings, plus eight more sub-meanings. They vary so widely that Robert Frost could and did once write a poem on the subject. In the poem, he and an anonymous college official are arguing about what the word means in the epitaph that the Victorian poet Walter Savage Landor wrote for himself. Landor summed up his life thus:

> I strove with none, for none was worth my strife.
> Nature I loved, and next to Nature, Art.
> I warm'd both hands before the fire of life;
> It sinks, and I am ready to depart.

Frost and the administrator can't agree on what it was that Landor loved, and the result is a mocking little poem that begins

> Dean, adult education may seem silly.
> What of it, though? I got some willy-nilly
> The other evening at your college deanery.
> And grateful for it (let's not be facetious!)
> For I thought Epicurus and Lucretius
> By Nature meant the Whole Goddam Machinery
> But you say that in college nomenclature
> The only meaning possible for Nature
> In Landor's quatrain would be Pretty Scenery.

Well, what I mean by nature is more than pretty scenery, but slightly less than the whole goddam machinery. I mean everything that exists on this planet (or elsewhere) that was not made by man. It's what most people mean. Only the minute you look closely, it turns out to be very hard to decide what was made by man and what wasn't. A plastic bag or a beer can is easy: Both were made by man—though of course out of natural materials, since that's all there are. But what about a garden? Nature made the carrot, but man modified it, planted it, grew it. There are two wills in collaboration here—the will of the carrot to be orange and to taste carroty and so forth—and the will of human beings to have it be a large carrot that travels well, keeps in cold storage, and so forth. What about a lake that exists because someone has built a dam, a so-called man-made or artificial lake? What about a tree? Only God—or nature—can make them, as Joyce Kilmer pointed out. But then, there are hybrid poplars: designed, planted, shaped by human beings. Again, a collaboration. Almost the entire surface of England is such a collaboration, and most of the United States, too. Only a wilderness area is not at least partly a collaboration. Lots of the prettiest scenery *is*.

So what I'm going to call nature is everything on this planet that is at least partially under the control of some other will than ours. Pure nature is of course what exists entirely without our will. In terms of landscape, there isn't much of it.

That still leaves one big question unanswered. Is man himself part of nature? Our remote ancestors certainly were: They evolved without planning to. But we ourselves? Well, I think we're partly in and partly out of nature—and the balance varies from age to age. But for the moment I'm going to say we're outside of nature. Certainly we thought of ourselves that way when we came to America. The Dutch sailors did, the pioneer settlers did. The authors of the Bible did.

Now let me drop back a little, and talk history. Not as far back as 1609—the Dutch sailors didn't leave much record of what they thought when they saw Long Island—but back to the eighteenth century and to a book called *Letters From an American Farmer*, which was written in the 1770s (though not published until 1782), and which was one of the very early American best-sellers. Basically, it's a report to Europeans on conditions in America just before the Revolution. Most of it is about what it's like to come be a farmer in one of the thirteen colonies, though there is one long section on what it's like to live on Nantucket and be a sailor.

At that time "America" was a strip of land about 300 miles wide, going south from Maine to Georgia. In the absence of airplanes, satellites, and so forth, no one knew exactly how much more land there was west of the frontier.

But the general feeling was that for all practical purposes this continent was infinite. As Hector St. John de Crevecoeur says in *Letters From an American Farmer*, "Many ages will not see the shores of our great lakes replenished with inland nations, nor the unknown bounds of North America entirely peopled. Who can tell how far it extends?"

St. John was wrong, of course. It did not take many ages to start inland nations on the shores of our Great Lakes. It took about two generations. Fifty years after he wrote the book, the inland nation of Illinois came into being. Another fifty years and Chicago was a large city, another forty and it had two million people. But he couldn't know that. He and everyone else in 1770 thought we would still have a frontier in, say, the twenty-fifth century, and that the still-growing country could absorb all the immigrants who might ever wish to come, that it, in fact, would always *need* more. "There is room for everybody in America," he wrote. And, remember, America had already existed for a century and a half when he wrote that: The image was firmly fixed that this was an infinite country.

The other thing that St. John took for granted was that pure nature is an appalling thing. He saw no beauty in wilderness whatsoever. Trackless forests did not appeal to him, and he considered frontiersmen corrupt and degenerate barbarians. What he liked, what he thought beautiful was the collaboration between man and nature that a farm is, and he considered that the best possible use of a person's time lay in taming wild nature.

> To examine how the world is gradually settled, how the howling swamp is converted into a pleasing meadow, the rough ridge into a fine field; and to hear the cheerful whistling, the rural song, where there was no sound heard before save . . . the screech of the owl or the hissing of the snake—

that, says St. John, gives him enormous pleasure. He explains to his European audience how the first thing an American does when he comes into a new piece of wilderness is to build a bridge over whatever creek or little river runs through it, and the second is to take his axe and chop down as many acres of trees as he has energy to do that year, and the third is to start draining swamps and other wetlands. And perfectly reasonable, too, since the woods, the swamps, and the rivers are infinite. But St. John's assumptions are that nature is not in any way sacred, or precious, or to be treasured just because it exists; on the contrary it is badly in need of collaboration with man, and only under our governance can it become the beautiful thing it should be. And he also assumes, as the Bible told him to, that nature has no other important function than to serve us. He even thinks that God intended the wolves, the bears, the snakes, and the Indians themselves to give way before us. He doesn't worry about their becoming extinct, because the continent is infinite — but I think if you pressed him, he'd say that had to be their eventual fate.

One other observation of St. John's demands mention, even though it has little to do with nature, only nurture. I mentioned that one long section of the book is about Nantucket, a place St. John greatly admired. It was a Quaker community, and already deep into whaling — the people St. John met there were the great-grandfathers of the people Melville wrote about in *Moby-Dick*. St. John also admired the women of Nantucket, who ran the farms while their husbands were off whaling — and whom he regarded as the most spirited, independent, and, incidentally, good-looking women in America — which for him means they were the most spirited, independent, and good-looking women in the world. But, he says, "a singular custom prevails here among the women, at which I was greatly surprised. . . . They have adopted these many years the Asiatic custom of taking a dose of opium every morning, and so deeply rooted is it that they would be at a loss how to live without this indulgence; they would rather be deprived of any necessary than forego their favorite luxury." Nantucket men, St. John says, didn't touch opium.

Now I want to move ahead to 1804, which was the year that President Jefferson sent Captains Meriwether Lewis and William Clark of the U.S. Army across the continent on foot, the first human beings, so far as I know, to make that entire trip across what is now the United States. It took them and their party of twenty-five enlisted men and a couple of guides two years to get to the Pacific ocean and back again. Plus, as usual, rather more money than the government had anticipated. President Jefferson budgeted the two-year trip for thirty people, including boats, a newly invented airgun to impress the Indians, all supplies, at $2,500. The actual cost of the expedition was nearly $5,000. But it did reach the Pacific.

After Lewis and Clark, no one could think that North America was infinite. They returned with maps and mileage estimates. The shrinking process had begun. But it was still huge — a place that takes you a year to cross in each direction — and it was still largely pure nature.

Lewis and Clark did not see the wilderness quite the way St. John did — partly because the region he knew was all woods, and a great deal of their time was spent crossing the Great Plains, the grassy open plains with herds of antelope and buffalo. What struck them was that nature had already made the center of America into a garden, just waiting for the settlers to come cultivate it. In fact, some of it God or nature had already cultivated for us. On July 10, 1804, going up the Missouri River, they passed a piece of bottom-land: 2,000 acres covered with wild potatoes. At any time, there were hordes of deer, wild turkeys, elk, just waiting to be killed. Lewis gave it as his professional army captain's opinion that two hunters could keep a regiment supplied with meat. On August 5, 1804, Captain Clark noticed how abundant the fresh fruit was. "Great quantities of grapes on the banks. I observe three kinds, at this time ripe." On August 16, 1804, Captain Lewis and twelve men spent the morning fishing. Here's the report: "Caught upwards of 800 fine fish: 79 pike, 8 salmon resembling trout, 1 rock, 1 flat back, 127 buffalo and red horse, 4 bass, 490 cats, with many small silver fish and shrimp."

Sometimes, when the captains climbed a hill for the view, a whole section of what is now Iowa or Nebraska would remind them of a giant stock farm back in Virginia. Lewis described one view in which there was a forest of wild plum trees on one side — "loaded with fruit and now ripe" — and on the other twenty miles of open grassland, smooth as a bowling green. "This scenery," he says, "already rich, pleasing, and beautiful, was still further heightened by immense herds of buffalo, deer, elk, and antelopes, which we saw in every direction. . . . I do not think I exaggerate when I estimate the number of buffalo which could be comprehended at one view to be 3,000." The wolves prowling around the edge of each herd even reminded him of the sheepdogs back in Virginia.

Again, the sense is that nature is so bounteous that we could never possibly run short of anything. Nor was this some special white prejudice. The Indians felt the same. Lewis and Clark watched several times while a small tribe of Plains Indians drove a whole herd of buffalo over a cliff, took the tongues and humps of a couple of dozen to eat, and left all the rest to rot. Why not? There was no more need to be frugal with buffalo than we feel the need to be frugal with, say, ice cubes. Don't think I'm blaming either Lewis and Clark or the Indians. Their behavior made perfect sense at the time.

Nature wasn't all bounty, though. For example, the whole region was swarming with grizzly bears: eating plums, waiting at the bottoms of cliffs for someone to drive a herd of buffalo over, and just generally enjoying life. They were not a bit afraid of American soldiers. And in fact a soldier with a single-shot rifle was in no way a match for a grizzly. By experience, Lewis and Clark found that about six soldiers equaled one grizzly. If all six shot, they were pretty likely to kill the bear with no one being hurt or chased up a tree. If fewer shot, there was apt to be trouble.

There was other trouble, too. When the expedition reached the Rocky Mountains, they found the peaks terrifying. Not beautiful (except snow-capped from a distance), not fun to be in. Instead, a place where you were very apt to starve to death, freeze to death, fall off a cliff. A typical campsite was by the mountain stream they called Hungry Creek — "at that place we had nothing to eat" — where they spent the night of September 18, 1805. A typical adventure occurred the next morning when Private Robert Frazer's packhorse, bought from the Indians, lost its footing and rolled a hundred yards down a precipice.

Most of the year, the only food you were going to find in the Rockies was what you carried in on your back, and when you ran out of that, there was no store to buy more at, nor could you decide to quit and hitch a ride back to Virginia, much less catch a plane to Denver. In short, not only was nature huge, but man was weak. Clever — clever enough to have invented axes and to drive stupid buffalo off cliffs — but weak. Nature, Mother Nature, was a worthy opponent as well as a worthy partner. In fact, let me make a sort of metaphor out of the grizzly and the buffalo, the two of them standing for wild nature. Both are physically stronger than men, and can run faster. One, the grizzly, is untameable, and more or less useless to us. So the thing to do is kill them, and that's a heroic and dangerous task: one part of subduing the wilderness. The other, the buffalo, is partially tameable, and very useful to us. Kill them, too, but not all of them, because we want them around to eat. Or else replace them with cattle, which are completely tameable. That's another part of subduing the wilderness — less heroic, maybe, but still a big job, and still nature offers plenty of resistance to the changes we make. The collaboration is not entirely on our terms, but partly on hers.

In sum, for the first two centuries that Europeans lived in North America, they saw the continent as a giant wilderness or desert — they used the two words interchangeably — the motto of Dartmouth College, *Vox clamantis in deserto*, translates to "A voice crying in the wilderness." They saw a vast, powerful, and immensely rich wilderness, which it would be the bounden duty of their descendants to turn into farms and gardens and alabaster cities, but which we would never entirely do, because the country was so damned big and the power of the axe and plow so limited.

All that began to change in the nineteenth century with the growth of technology. Railroads and steamboats were, of course, the first major manifestations. They made the wilderness accessible and the continent (relatively) small. In so doing, they produced the first few converts to a new point of view. Henry David Thoreau was one. Thoreau lived right next to the Fitchburg Railroad. He saw quite clearly the threat steam posed to untamed nature. Steam engines are bigger and faster than grizzlies. Steam saws can cut trees up far more quickly than forests can grow them. Steam shovels can drain an everglade.

Wilderness threatened became wilderness desirable — for the handful of converts. Thoreau was, as far as I know, the first American who publicly concluded that wilderness as wilderness — that is, pure nature — was a good thing to have around. In the 1850s he made a proposal that each town in Massachusetts save a 500-acre piece of woods which would be forever wild: no lumbering, no changes at all. Needless to say, he got nowhere, not even in Concord itself. It was still too much like going down to McDonald's and suggesting to the manager that he put 500 ice cubes in permanent deep freeze, against the time when ice may be scarce.

John Muir was a slightly later convert. It's a coincidence, but a nice coincidence, that the year in which he began to describe the western mountains as wonderful places, sacred ground, God's outdoor temples, was the same year in which the transcontinental railroad was completed. That was 1869. Henceforth the Lewis and Clark journey of a year could be done in a few days. Muir, like Thoreau before him, sensed the growth of man's power against nature, though in 1869 nature was still stronger. And, of course, Muir could be romantic about mountains in part because by now the country had been so much tamed that within one day's walk of most of his camping places in the Sierras he could borrow or buy flour to make bread with, sometimes even go to a regular store. He could even be worried about the ecological harm that overgrazing by sheep was doing in the Sierras, and eventually have some success in banning sheep from portions.

Ever since then, human power has grown at an almost geometric rate, while the forces of nature have remained static. The ascending line was bound eventually to cross the level one. It's not possible to pinpoint the year in which this happened, but it *is* possible to suggest a decade. I think the 1950s represent the swing point in man's relationship to nature, certainly in the United States, and probably in the whole world. During that decade we became stronger than our surroundings. Certainly not in all ways—such physical phenomena as earthquakes and hurricanes and volcanoes remain quite beyond our power to control. But in most ways. The biggest river isn't even difficult for us to bridge, or to dam. No other living creature can seriously dispute us, certainly not on a one-to-one basis. In Melville's day, six men in a whaleboat were generally a match for one whale—but not always; sometimes the whale won. By the 1950s, one man with a harpoon gun could do in any number of whales. There's not even any thrill to it.

More important than any of this, by the 1950s our science and our engineering enabled us to produce new substances and to distribute old substances on a scale equal to nature's own. For example, we can put sulfur dioxide in the air at a rate faster than the volcanoes do. One single refinery in Sudbury, Ontario, became the source of 5 percent of all the sulfur dioxide that entered the air of the entire planet, there to become sulfuric acid and to come down again as acid rain and snow. One fleet of jet airplanes could seriously affect the ozone layer.

We have earth-moving machinery that can rearrange a whole landscape. We have new chemical compounds that can affect the whole chain of life. Nature cannot easily absorb the effect of DDT or of Sevin; nature is no longer resilient. We can nearly eliminate whales, sort of half-meaning to, and we can all but extinguish peregrine falcons as an unintended by-product of raising crops. We really are what our ancestors only claimed to be: the masters of nature—or at least we're the dominant partner in the collaboration. To use one more metaphor, we are like goldfish who have been living in an aquarium for as long as we can remember; and being clever goldfish, we have discovered how to manipulate the controls of the aquarium: put more oxygen in the water, get rid of the pesky turtle we never liked anyway, triple the supply of goldfish food. Only once we realize we're partly running the aquarium, it scares some of us. What if we make a mistake, and wreck the aquarium entirely? We couldn't live outside it.

That has been the actual position since the 1950s, and it is what our rational minds clearly report. The green light has turned yellow, and there is a real possibility it will go to red. But it is not what our emotions tell us. Emotionally, almost all of us still believe what the Dutch sailors thought: that here is an inexhaustible new world, with plenty of everything for everybody.

And because of that emotion, which I, too, share, we have had a double response since the 1950s. One is to do our damndest to keep part of our continent still virgin—pure nature, wilderness. That's the nature-lover's response, the Sierra Club response, and sometimes the environmentalist's response. It's almost uniquely American. I have a friend, for example, who is a Spanish environmentalist, and I know from him that there is exactly one national park in Spain, the former hunting forest of the dukes of Medina, and even that is by no means a wilderness area. Spain is not virgin country. At the moment, about 2 percent of the United States is official wilderness, just about the same amount that is paved. And in a country this big, 2 percent is quite a lot: something like 60,000 square miles, twelve times as big as the state of Connecticut.

In terms of our whole population, to be sure, it's less impressive: If you put all of us in the wilderness at once, we'd each have a fifth of an acre. But it's enough to give a comforting illusion that pure nature is still going, independent of us. And most people who seek that illusion also want to downplay their separateness from nature, and to say that we have no right to meddle, our collaboration is deadly. We goldfish should stand back and let the aquarium run itself as it always has.

The other response involves a much greater illusion—or I think it does, anyway. And that is simply to deny that anything has changed significantly since the days of Hector St. John de Crevecoeur and Lewis and Clark. This is the response, for example, of the present United States government. We're still just collaborators with nature, people who hold this view say, more effective collaborators than we used to be, certainly; and if we do our part, nature will do its. Nature is still resilient; it can still absorb anything we do. Besides, we were meant to rule the planet—this aquarium was designed specially for us—and what we do was pretty much all allowed for in the original design.

One group wants to re-create the world the Dutch sailors saw, and the other denies that it has ever ceased to exist. If I have to choose, of course I choose to be one of the re-creators—to try to protect as much wilderness as possible. I'd like to get the proportion of untouched land up to 3 percent. I've even dreamt of 4 percent.

But neither group, I think, is right. Neither has really dealt with the fact that a generation ago the green light turned to yellow. If there is anything that is really, really worth doing in the rest of this century, I think, it's to find a third and better way of dealing with the relationship between man and nature.

Ann Zwinger

A World of Infinite Variety

I find myself in the midst of an index to the letters of John Xantus, written from Baja California where he was a tidal observer for the U.S. Coast Survey between 1859 and 1861, to Spencer F. Baird at the Smithsonian, for whom he collected. Xantus, a Hungarian, fled the 1848 revolution in his country and ended up in the United States Army, as unsympathetic a profession for this well-educated, thin-skinned, arrogant personality as one could imagine. Fortunately, through a combination of being in the right place at the right time and his knowledge of natural history, he came to be a collector for Baird, then Assistant Secretary of the Smithsonian, who was interested in building an unparalleled collection for the United States Museum of Natural History.

Unlike modern specialist collectors, Xantus snagged specimens from ocean to mountain, finny as well as feathered, four-legged hoppers, six-legged crawlers, eight-legged lurkers, flutterers and slinkers, as well as plants, minerals, and fossils. His letters record the breadth of his collecting activities, and the index reflects, in truncated form, that exhilarating variety. The index begins with Abalone and ends with *Zonotrichia*. Gila River comes before Gill, Theodore; three lights of the nineteenth-century natural history world are cheek by jowl in the index: George Lawrence, John LeConte, and Joseph Leidy; Ophurian comes before Oregon and Orioles; Rattlesnake precedes the schooner *Raymond*; the Smithsonian Institution follows Captain Charles B. Smith; and toward the end it's Whalers, Whimbrels, Whipsnakes, and Whistling-ducks.

The range of entries, characteristic of Xantus's activities, is also the range characteristic of the breadth of natural history. Where else can one range so widely and wander so happily into archaeology and anthropology, biology and botany, geology and history, taxonomy and zoology? And that only skims the surface of the subjects in my note cards. Which is precisely what makes natural history the far-ranging, fascinating discipline that it is for its practitioners — those batty people who like to tie together yesterday and tomorrow within the framework of today's natural world in which man walks, crab scuttles, lizard leaps, jack rabbit bounds, and beetle trundles.

It is impossible to write natural history without getting involved in history history, and especially so in a book of historical letters. Through Xantus's descriptive carping but observant letters, I have stepped back in time and space and come to walk in a natural world that I can never otherwise have known.

No wonder he bridled whenever Baird praised other collectors; Xantus was an alien in an alien world, and collecting was his definition of self. No wonder he never missed carping about an expense—he was nearly penniless because of penurious Coast Survey practices and the Smithsonian's own close-to-the-vest financing. No wonder his natural acquisitiveness endlessly found new species—not only was the nineteenth century a time of splitting rather than lumping, but there were so many new species to be named. To be credited with discovering a new species, or even more wonderful, to have one named after you, was a ticket to immortality.

A few years ago, when I stood on the beach at Cape San Lucas where Xantus had mounted his tidal gauge, it was not hard to imagine myself back in the nineteenth century. It was not difficult at all to read away the thin veneer of civilization that modern-day tourist-oriented Cabo San Lucas sports, and even less difficult when one gets away from the populated fringe back into the countryside on some of the remote ranches. I stepped back to 1860 and smelled the endless heat in July, watched the same vultures soar in the cool upper air, watched the same lizards scatter between bushes and the same kestrels peer, sharp-eyed and hungry, from the spire of a cardon cactus.

Another carryover is the collector's instinct. While ornithologists no longer go around shooting at everything that flies to get a specimen, as they did in Xantus's day, netting insects and pressing plants is still a very current concern of entomologists and botanists. An amateur in both, I respond to Xantus's enthusiasm when he first netted fish out of San Lucas Bay: "The first time I tried my large seine, we capture about 3000 pounds in a few pulls, and my heart bursted nearly when I had to throw them away, so beautiful they were." I felt the same way when I first saw a king angelfish and a Moorish idol.

The mid-nineteenth century was a prime time for naturalists in the United States. By that time, any city of any size was opening its own natural science institutions and building up its collections, from the New York Lyceum for Natural History on the East Coast to The California Academy of Sciences on the West. There was a wonderfully chaotic expansiveness about those early natural history societies, a sense of discovery around every corner that I, as a child of the twentieth century, rather envy.

Most naturalists of the time were generalists, fascinated by stars and starfish, *Chelonius* and *Chaenactis*, Gila monsters and *Gilia*, enthralled by lepidoptera and *Lepidium*, ponderosa and *Pondetaria*, and whether you can make a silk purse out of a pig's ear as someone at the Academy of Natural Sciences of Philadelphia did. Dr. Elliott Coues may have been an ornithologist but he wrote definitively on mammals. Baird was primarily a mammalogist but wrote up the birds *and* the reptiles for the Pacific Railroad Reports.

The spontaneity and diversity of these institutions is fascinating. They are not only interesting in themselves, but several were the forerunners of more sophisticated educational institutions such as The California Academy and The American Museum of Natural History.

Among the most venerable of the early natural history associations was The Academy of Natural Sciences in Philadelphia, an august body into which John Xantus was inducted on the strength of his collection of flora and fauna from Fort Tejon, California.

The Academy's early *Proceedings* are handsome leather-bound volumes complete with marbled end papers. In the very first volume, March–April 1841, with the president "in the Chair," the Academy acknowledged contributions received and papers given, and presented a treasurer's report — unique in that there was not a single figure given. That year the Academy received from contributors, and gave papers on, everything from owls, sugar cane, and the micaceous oxides of iron, to shells taken at 75 fathoms off the coast of Maine as well as off the coast of West Africa.

Two hippopotamus skulls were logged in, and William Gambel, after whom our delightful western quail is named, contributed a grebe. One paper compared old soil from the Nile Valley, dug three feet above the river, with newly laid sediments — an item which might be of interest to present-day ecologists since the Nile no longer floods below the Aswan Dam.

The wonderful variety of interests continued. Sixteen years later, in 1857, the Academy published a list of its members, italicizing the names of those who had passed on to the greater Academy in the sky — in other words, once a member always a member (like the Cook County voting list). There are over 350 names in that membership list, and included are some of the most prestigious naturalists and scientists of the day: Spencer F. Baird, then Assistant Secretary of the Smithsonian Institution and a life member of the Academy; Dr. Joseph Leidy, the great paleontologist; John L. LeConte, who wrote up the innumerable species of coleoptera coming into the Academy; and John Cassin, a successful publisher who catalogued the 26,000 birds in the collection of the Academy and wrote widely on taxonomy—in his spare time. Among those who sent him birds was John Xantus.

Also members of the Academy were many military men and members of major surveys. In addition to their duties, the Pacific Railroad Survey and Boundary Survey teams collected plants and animals. Baird exhorted the many surgeons at Western posts to "collect, collect, collect." These surgeons had an almost unlimited resource of enlisted men for various jobs and produced very well-prepared specimens. Dr. Elliot Coues contributed impressively in Western ornithology, as well as mammalogy and history. Dr. William Hammond, stationed with the United States Army at Fort Riley, Missouri (during the Civil War he gave distinguished service as Surgeon General of the United States), sent forty species of reptiles from that area. He was later immortalized in Hammond's flycatcher, a new species taken by his protégé, John Xantus, while he was stationed with the Army in California.

The Academy extended its member resource through a list of "Correspondents," outlanders which included such drop-dead names as John James Audubon and Thomas Jefferson. There were Correspondents from England and Brazil, Argentina and Sweden, Germany and Italy, including Alfred Malherbe of France and William M'Gillivray of Edinburgh. M. Malherbe wrote a distinguished treatise on woodpeckers, and Mr. M'Gillivray's name is associated with a charming warbler. The list even includes such foreigners as those living in New York and Maine.

In that same year of 1857 the Academy's *Proceedings* noted that Dr. A. Heermann sent thirty new species of reptiles from Texas; Heermann is better known for the somber-plumaged Heermann's gull. The Academy welcomed a collection of plants from lichenologist Tuckerman, a name familiar to hikers of Mt. Washington.

The 1857 volume is elegantly illustrated "on stone by Wm E. Hitchcock," and these lithographs, on heavy paper, carefully printed, distinguish many natural history publications, a thread which runs felicitously through much natural history publishing. This year's [1986] recipient of the John Burroughs Medal for Natural History Writing, *Gathering the Desert*, is as handsomely illustrated as it is written.

Early scientific illustrators were unparallelled for their portrayals of detail and their understanding of the natural world. For a wonderful afternoon, spend it looking at the illustrations in the Pacific Railroad Surveys. They are of the highest quality—exquisite, precise, and informative.

Because the Academy was so well-known, it drew contributions like a magnet. A single year suffices to show the range of scholarly and descriptive papers. In 1856 Dr. Leidy produced papers on topics ranging from tapeworms to extinct mammals, fish, and reptiles. Dr. Charles Girard, who assisted Baird at the Smithsonian, gave four papers on West Coast fish, and Edward Hallowell seven on reptiles. Robert Kennicott, who would become one of Baird's most famous collectors, described a new snake from Illinois. Lieutenant Beale described the first crossing of the American desert with the Camel Corps and recommended the beasts highly for their performance and weight-carrying ability (the Civil War and the ensuing railroads terminated this practical venture in cross-country transportation).

Also included in the 1856 *Proceedings* is a paper by a gentleman from Indiana, Rufus Haymond, who sent in a collection of and wrote a paper on "Birds of Southern Indiana." Another Haymond wrote on bats. Since I grew up in Indiana, the daughter of William T. Haymond, I felt a warm albeit tenuous connection with the Academy through one of their far-flung correspondents.

Although the Pacific Railroad Survey Reports were within the purview of the Smithsonian, Assistant Secretary Baird maintained close ties with the Philadelphia Academy. In their *Proceedings* he published the initial reports of many of the findings that would later be worked up in the larger, more definitive Smithsonian reports. For example, Baird published the first list of new species of North American mammals collected by Major W. H. Emory on the United States–Mexican Boundary Survey in the Academy *Proceedings* of 1857.

In the main, the important natural history associations were East Coast institutions. Besides the New York Lyceum there was the Boston Society of Natural History. Thomas Brewer was associated with the latter, and collectors all over the country, like Xantus, learned to collect eggs and nests, to blow, package, and ship them to him as he prepared a monumental publication of Oölogy for the Smithsonian—a publication, alas, that was never finished for the oldest publishing reason in the world: the plates cost too much.

I have the impression that in order to be encyclopedic these societies accepted, higgledy-piggledy, objects ranging from the bizarre to the sublime and the important to the ridiculous. One year the Boston Society of Natural History logged in everything from the "dried and inflated lungs of a snapping-turtle, and a frog intermediate between the imperfect and perfect animal" plus "two teeth of the sperm whale" along with a noddy tern, a gecko egg, and a section of an elephant's tusk with a musket-ball imbedded in it!

Natural historians have been known to express themselves quite pungently. The son of the president of the Boston Society, William Greene Binney, migrated West from the sedate halls of Boston. He later published a natural history journal and wrote a definitive treatise on land snails (he named *Bulimulus xantusi* after a specimen collected by Xantus near Cabo San Lucas). As an editor he was evidently plagued by a Mr. Orcutt who sent him minuscule shells to be identified. After what must have been a particularly exasperating incursion on his time and energies, Binney wrote one of my favorite paragraphs:

> The San Diego Pupa does not seem to me arizonensis, and I cannot spare eyes to determine it. In my books are enlarged views of the described species of Pupa, by means of which and a pocket lens you can readily make this out. I detest Pupa and Succinea above all things Conchological. I give you a camera lucida drawing of the outline of your shell — the aperture was still unfinished when the tube of my microscope slid down on the shell and smashed it, much to my delight.

The California Academy of Sciences was founded April 4, 1853. Unlike the Academy of Philadelphia's imposing and proper *Proceedings*, their first publication is a scant three-eighths inch thick, bound in paper — they've made up for any difference between the two institutions in the magnificence of their current museum and superb library.

There were only fifty-seven members in 1857 and, in true Western hospitality, the membership included men from all over the United States and Mexico — from Boston, Cambridge, Philadelphia, and New York — and included Louis Agassiz, Spencer Baird, Dr. Charles Girard, John Torrey, and Dr. Asa Gray, the most prominent botanists in the United States, and Theodore Gill, a felicitously named Smithsonian employee who wrote widely on fish, among them those that Xantus collected in Baja California. Alexander Bache, then head of the U.S. Coast Survey, was a member. Some members of the Academy served as tidal observers for the Survey on the West Coast.

There were forty-one resident members, among them William Gabb of the California Geological Survey, John Cooper who founded the Cooper Ornithological Society, and Dr. John B. Trask who went West with Audubon's son and became curator of the Academy's geology and mineralogy collections, and eventually its president.

In 1857 they discussed the boracic acid in Pacific sea water and published drawings and descriptions of new plants such as *Fritillaria*, *Abies*, *Ledum*, and *Penstemon* with the appropriate engraved illustrations.

At the annual meeting in 1864 there were fifteen members present. The financial report indicated that $815.35 was received from various sources, and that expenditures were $903.75, ending the year with $52.82 in the treasury, an expense sheet a modern natural history society might view with disbelief. Such modest expenses took their toll. Although fifty books and three hundred shell species were added, other collections remained static. The botany acquisitions were noted, but the collections were deemed "not in good condition for want of suitable cases." Things had not improved in five years. In 1859, when he was in San Francisco learning how to run the tide gauge before shipping out to Cabo San Lucas, Xantus noted that the Academy was

> in a deplorable condition, they have only 11 . . . members, and each of them has to pay about $300 a year to defray the expenses of the society. Their once beautiful collection is entirely eaten up by the miriads of mice & rats, they even destroyed the labels of all the Rocks & fossil.

At their meeting of July 3, 1865, only eight members were present, but what members! Dr. John Torrey, Robert Kennicott, W. H. Dall (Baird's biographer), and Horace Mann made up half the group. The minutes closed with this quintessential natural history line:

> This evening, at 7 o'clock, a magnificent rainbow was observed, the colors of which were unusually vivid.

Many early natural scientists were medical doctors, although many of them never practiced medicine. At that time a medical education was the best and in some cases the only scientific education available. Although they may have had special fields of interest, they tended to be competent in many, with a curiosity fired by all the unfamiliar species turning up in the newly opened West. By default they were primarily collectors and namers, and it is no accident that the names of so many familiar species in the West are those of these gentlemen who often found, studied, and identified the species.

Most maintained a faithful correspondence with each other. Spencer Baird estimated that one year he wrote three thousand letters. Longhand. Edwin Way Teale, in the Foreword to *The American Seasons*, when asked what naturalists do, replied with some spirit and perhaps a little exasperation, "They write *letters!*" As Joseph Kastner, in *A Species of Eternity*, described naturalists of the previous century in Europe:

> The world . . . was a small place and every prominent person knew all the others. Naturalists who never laid eyes on each other became intimate friends by virtue of the long and faithful letters they wrote to each other, year in and year out, until death ended their exchanges.

Quite obviously, being an old-fashioned naturalist involved energy, devotion, and enthusiasm. One followed the naturalist's path for the love of doing and the joy of learning, not for the profit. As an avocation, it enriched without impinging on the necessities of making a living. It provided intellectual challenges and aesthetic pleasures and pleasant friendships.

The picture, rightly or wrongly, that I have of old-fashioned naturalists is tinged with dilettanteism, of professionally amateur status. There is good reason that Jacob Bronowski called it "that quaint Victorian profession." Compared to the professions that are taken more seriously, a naturalist is rather a dabbler. Naturalists are wanderers and wonderers, and perhaps there is not time for that in the highly paced world in which we live.

Just when I felt comfortably ensconced in the long naturalist tradition that goes back to Aristotle and was happily following my avocation of nature writer, I got a nasty turn. Edwin Way Teale, the epitome of the old-fashioned naturalist, gave me a biography of William Beebe. Beebe was a scientist at The American Museum of Natural History and a prolific and well-known natural history writer.

His biographer, Robert Welker, found that natural science was fast becoming obsolete, and its practitioners with it. Welker felt that there was no longer room for a botanist or an entomologist, a limnologist or an ecologist in the research team concept in large universities and museums. He concluded:

> And of all such people, the naturalist is surely the oddest, a figure not merely old-fashioned but antique. A naturalist studies nothing less than the living world, perhaps out of love for it; and for such a man or woman, where is there a meaningful place?

I can cope with allergies and absent-mindedness, but to be an anachronism is too much. Was there no space for the naturalist's profession in a fast-moving, computerized, scientific world? I felt like an endangered species. Had I become the wafting cranefly, left behind on the evolutionary ladder, to be replaced by the lethally efficient assassin fly?

I began looking about in some desperation for others of my ilk. I expected to find, and did, that in the expanding frontiers of science, more and more scientists pursue more and more esoteric and restricted lines of research. As research becomes narrower, so the language becomes more and more precise. Oftentimes such scientists can speak to and be understood by only the few others in their field. This focusing down may be a necessary prerequisite for the kind of solid scientific knowledge upon which our continued existence as a viable genus depends, and this work may hold for the specialist the same joys and challenges as that of being a generalist naturalist holds for me, but their communication with an interested public, one of the glories of natural history, is limited. One of the things natural historians have done over the decades is to put into words an appreciation of the natural world and by so doing, lead others to care.

Fortunately, I also got some good news. Dr. Kenneth Norris is a Professor of Natural History at the University of California at Santa Cruz. Walking out in the desert, looking for the little night lizard *Xantusia vigilis*, we talked about the naturalist's trade. Dr. Norris considers himself first a naturalist, then a herpetologist (which he was) or a geologist (with his brother he did a definitive paper on the Algodones Dunes in California) or a mammalogist (which he is), a point of view more typical of a naturalist-generalist thinker who looks for big connections than a researcher (which he also is). He later wrote:

> By the way naturalists are definitely not extinct. People in my

field keep realizing, sometimes with a kind of surprise, that eye-to-eye contact with nature is the truest of experiences, and the simplest way to understand. I noted recently that people studying ultra high pressure phenomena, such as occur in the core of the earth, do so through pressure vises whose jaws are diamonds through which they can see that which they squeeze.

And imagine my delight when I discovered that there actually were courses in "Natural History" at respected colleges like Carleton College, where students get up at the crack of dawn to go look at birds and limestone cliffs and ponder what is growing there and why, who competently discuss soil development on alluvial fans in the Mojave deserts and how that correlates with the plants that grow there, and why the horned lark is singing in springtime by the third creosote bush from the right and where to look for algae on a quartz pebble.

I find this downright exhilarating because in my bones I feel there is a place for the old-fashioned naturalist in today's world. Whether these students become economists or diplomats, musicians or historians, they have discovered something that will give them sustenance and pleasure for the rest of their lives. And that is precisely what a college *should* teach: what to do with your tomorrows.

As I finger through page proofs and deal with Xantus's archaic nomenclature and his peregrinations through a place I know and love, it is with a comforting sense of connection. I index *Hylocharis xanti*, the white-eared hummingbird George Lawrence named after Xantus, and the tiny leaf-toed gecko, *Phyllodactylus xantii*, with an appreciation for Xantus's contribution to natural history, keenly aware that for the naturalist there is always something to be interested in: the tiny crab that hangs by one claw on the side of a tide pool, swaying with the gentle currents of tide out and tide in; the bouquets of pink *Malacothrix xantii* blooming across the sea cliffs.

It is no leap of the imagination but a personal reality to walk the same shores and watch the Sally Lightfoots scuttle out of sight like lightning, to delight in the brilliant origami-like tide-pool fish, to listen to the empty landsnail crunch under foot in a cool arroyo, to inhale the spicy odor of elephant tree bark and taste the frolicking freshness of sea air.

Xantus found a reason for living in the formal patterns of cactus spines, in the way in which a darkling beetle left parenthetical tracks in the sand. For him, as for me over a hundred years later, as for any naturalist, there is the joy of discovery and the sense of wonder. Xantus's specimens range from *Aphelocoma* to *Xanthodes xantusii* and come to imbue the index with a life of its own as a witness to a world of infinite variety and richness, of proven sense and reassuring order — the world of an old-fashioned naturalist.

Edward Hoagland

In Praise of John Muir

We must go halfway with John Muir. He was more of an explorer than a writer, more confident of his abilities in botany and geology than of what he could do with the eagle-quill pens he liked to use, while encouraging a friend's year-old baby to scramble about the floor, lending liveliness to the tedium of a writer's room. He was a student of glaciers, cloud shapes and skyscapes — a lover of Sitka spruce one hundred and fifty feet tall, of big sequoias, tiny woods orchids and great waterfalls. He put together his books late in life — he was fifty-six before *The Mountains of California*, his first book, was published — from magazine articles, most of which had themselves been reconstructed well after the events described, from notes jotted down in the field with wildfire enthusiasm but little thought of eventually publishing them. Though he was a wonderful talker, he was never entirely respectful of the written word and was surprised to find that there was an audience willing to read him, amazed he could earn a living by writing. Being one of those people "who give the freest and most buoyant portion of their lives to climbing and seeing for themselves," he wished more of his readers preferred to hike on their own two feet into the fastnesses he had described.

Henry David Thoreau lived to write, but Muir lived to hike. "I will touch naked God," he wrote once, while glacier-climbing. And, on another jaunt, lunching on his customary dry crust of bread: "To dine with a glacier on a sunny day is a glorious thing and makes common feasts of meat and wine ridiculous. The glacier eats hills and sunbeams." Although he lacked the coherent artistic passion of a professional writer, he was Emersonianism personified. There is a time-freeze, a time-warp to a river of ice, as if God had been caught still alive, in the act and at work. And because Muir's passions were religious and political instead of artistic, Muir, unlike Thoreau — who in comfortable Concord only speculated that his Transcendental intuitions were right — put his life and his legs on the line in continual tests of faith in the arduous wilderness of the High Sierras. He believed that if his intuitions were wrong, he would fall, but he didn't ask himself many questions about what was happening, as Thoreau would have, and didn't believe that such exalted experiences could be conveyed to the page, anyway.

Thoreau welded together one of the enduring prose styles of the nineteenth century. He may be America's paramount stylist, and also established in his spare time a famously disobedient stance toward the institutionalized cruelties of the world that later was to help Gandhi and, through Gandhi, Martin Luther King in formulating mass-movement nonviolent campaigns, before dying at only forty-four, in 1862. Of course, in addition he was what we would call a conservationist, but not a militant, innovative one, like Muir. Muir (1838–1914) was the founding president of the Sierra Club and chief protector of Yosemite Park. Thoreau, on the other hand, anathematized American imperial conduct in the Mexican War and got still more exercised about slavery, angrily championing the early "terrorist" John Brown. Muir — who was all in all a more conventional soul in his politics — even after the end of the Civil War commented approvingly during a trek through Georgia that "the Negroes here have been well-trained and are extremely polite. When they come in sight of a white man on the road, off go their hats, even at a distance of forty to fifty yards, and they walk bare-headed until he is out of sight."

It's important to recognize that such contrasts were not merely due to the fact that Muir was born twenty-one years after Thoreau and thus lived through the ambiguities of Reconstruction. Thoreau sought out the company of Indians on his trips to Maine and respectfully studied their customs, whereas Muir generally disparaged the Indians of California as ignoramuses and children, dirty and cultureless wretches. Not until his adventurous travels to Alaska in middle age — three trips during his forties, two in his fifties, and one tour to the Bering Sea by steamer at sixty-one — did he admit a semblance of tolerance into his view of Indians. And though as a conservationist he was highly "advanced," a Vermonter named George Perkins Marsh, born back in 1801, proves to have sounded as modernist a tocsin as Muir's in a widely read book called *Man and Nature*, which came out in 1864. Thirty years before *The Mountains of California*, Marsh counterposed to the Biblical theory that Nature was a wilderness which mankind should "subdue and rule" the idea that "Man has too long forgotten that the earth was given to him for usufruct alone, not for consumption, still less for profligate waste . . . We are, even now, breaking up the floor and wainscoting and doors and window frames of our dwelling . . . The earth is fast becoming an unfit home for its noblest inhabitant, and another era of equal human crime and human improvidence . . . would reduce it to such a condition of impoverished productiveness . . . as to threaten the depravation, barbarism, and perhaps even extinction of the species."

Marsh was a complex personality who served four terms in Congress and twenty years as U.S. Ambassador to Italy, but he was a quiet visionary and public servant in the style of a New England Brahmin — not a public figure, not the man of mounting celebrity that Muir became. Muir as lecturer, as Westerner, as "John o' the Mountains," learned, like Walt Whitman and Longfellow, to wear a public sort of beard. Living to the ripe old age of seventy-six, he enjoyed three active decades that were denied to Thoreau, and changed a good deal during the course of them. Although a far "wilder" naturalist, he had lived nearly as celibately as Thoreau for nearly as long. However, with no undue enthusiasm, he did marry, a week short of being forty-two. He then had two daughters — whom he deeply loved — and turned himself into a substantial, successful landowner and grape-farmer as well as a well-known writer and a force to be reckoned with in Sacramento and occasionally in Washington, D.C. International lecture tours, friendship with Teddy Roosevelt, honorary degrees from Harvard and Yale — in these extra years he knew rewards that Thoreau had never aspired to, yet remained an adventurer to the end, traveling to Africa, South America and Asia late in life. Only Jack London and John James Audubon among American artists come to mind as adventurers with a spirit to compare with his, and for both of them adventuring was more closely tied to ambition.

Thoreau, less and less a thinker and more and more a naturalist after he turned forty, was also changing in personality before he died. Supporting himself as a professional surveyor and by reorganizing his family's pencil business, he was making elaborate mathematical calculations in his journal and sending zoological specimens to Louis Agassiz. But though he didn't know it, he was already on the point of winning a considerable readership. Being in a small way a professional lecturer too, he might have capitalized on that development eventually, just as Muir did. In his last year he traveled to Minnesota to try to repair his health; and with the love that he felt for the big woods of Maine, he might well have given up his previous insistence that it was enough to have "traveled a good deal in Concord," if he'd lived on. Perhaps his best work was behind him, but there would have been some interesting darkening of the tints and rounding of the details, if he had blossomed as a generalist and an essayist again.

It's doubtful, nevertheless, that Thoreau, given another thirty years, would have become as touching an individual as Muir. He was always a less personal man—less vulnerable, vociferous, strenuous, emotional. He would never have married; and not having gone through a childhood as miserable, a youth as risky and floundering as Muir's, he wouldn't have burgeoned in such an effusion of relief when fame and financial security blessed him.

Yet, really, no amount of worldly acclaim made Muir half as happy as being in remote places. Muir is touching just because he was so immensely gleeful in wild country—happier than Thoreau, Audubon, London, Whitman, Mark Twain, James Fenimore Cooper, Francis Parkman and other figures one thinks of as being happy out-of-doors. He was a genteel and ordinary man in most of his opinions, and his method of lobbying politically for his beloved Yosemite was to ally himself with rich men such as the railroad magnate E. H. Harriman, who had the power to sway events Muir's way if the whim seized them. He was no nay-sayer on social questions and never would have conceived of putting himself in jail overnight to register a protest, as Thoreau had done. He would have agreed with Thoreau's now famous phrase "In wildness is the preservation of the world"; but Muir emphasized a wilderness of joy. And that, after all, is what the 1872 law creating Yellowstone—the first of the national parks—had stipulated. "The region is hereby . . . set aside as a public park and pleasuring ground for the enjoyment of the people . . ."

Muir was not a hypocrite, and he once let Harriman hear of his saying to some scientist friends that he didn't regard Harriman as truly rich: "He has not as much money as I have. I have all I want and Mr. Harriman has not." Muir, indeed, devoted only seven years of his life to the primary aim of making money. ("The seven lost years," his wife called them, when he was managing full-time the fruit ranch she inherited from her father.) But he valued money and respectability and held few views on any subject to alarm a "bully" president like Roosevelt or a tycoon like Harriman. Like Audubon, Muir was proud of being foreign-born. He nurtured the strong streak of business acumen, the religious if disputatious temperament, the Spartan understatement and resilience, and the excellent mechanical aptitudes that he considered to be part of his Scottish heritage. His mix of idealism and innocence with the hard-mannered Scotch burr—a familiar, respected accent in the immigrant stream of a hundred years ago—charmed at the same time as it reassured such men. ("Frenchiness" would not have been nearly as useful.)

Although Harriman's Southern Pacific Railroad had no stake in what happened to Yosemite Valley, he responded charitably and fancifully to Muir's particular pleas for help in 1905, when the valley's fate was being decided in the state senate, with a confidential telegram to his chief agent in San Francisco. The vote was whisker-close, but to the astonishment of the logging and livestock industries, several legislators that Southern Pacific "owned" suddenly swung their votes behind a bill to give this spectacular scenery to the federal government. The next year, Harriman wrote with the same potent effect to the Speaker of the U.S. House and to Senate leaders to have Yosemite included in a national park. And after Teddy Roosevelt's presidency had ended, Muir's odd appeal worked upon William Howard Taft, a much tougher nut among presidents.

Muir as an advocate was a johnny-one-note, but, oh, that note! "When California was wild, it was one sweet bee-garden throughout its entire length," he wrote with yearning. "Wherever a bee might fly within the bounds of this virgin wilderness . . . throughout every belt and section of climate up to the timber line, bee-flowers bloomed in lavish abundance." Wistfully he proposed that all of the state might be developed into a single vast flower palace and honey-hive to the continent, its principal industry the keeping, herding and pasturing of bees.

When California was wild! Luckily he'd seen it then. He had arrived by ship seven years after Mark Twain had appeared by stagecoach in Nevada, on the other side of the Sierras, to transcribe the experience of *Roughing It.* Both Muir and Twain originally had harbored the hope of lighting out for the Amazon, but Twain got sidetracked into piloting Mississippi riverboats and Muir got seriously sick in Florida and Cuba en route to South America. Muir—who had reveled in one of the best adventures of his life in walking south from Louisville to Georgia—sailed to New York City to recuperate. However, disliking the city, he caught a packet immediately for San Francisco, landing in March of 1868, a month before his thirtieth birthday.

Unlike Twain, he hadn't come west as a writer; not till he was thirty-seven did he resolve to be one. This was "the wild side of the continent," he said, which was reason enough. Yet he invariably soft-pedaled its dangers and hardships. Twain, quite the opposite, and quintessentially "American," celebrated the badmen and primitive conditions in marvelously exploitative tall tales, boasting of how his knees knocked. Twain used the mountains as a theatrical prop, having abandoned his *manqué* career as a silver miner as soon as he obtained a job as a newspaperman in Virginia City. The mountains themselves had small fascination for him, and he sought companionship with writerly acquisitiveness at every opportunity, whereas Muir at that time was grasping at solitude, avoiding "the tyrant of creation," as Audubon had once described mankind.

But the reason Muir so seldom speaks about the cold rains, the icebite and exhaustion he met with in the mountains, the terror of an avalanche, of breaking through ice in crossing a waterway, or of the many deer he must have observed starving to skin and bones after a series of snows, is not simply Scottish diffidence and asceticism. He loved most of nature's violence — "the jubilee of waters," as he called one particular winter storm. In the earthquake of 1872, for instance, "disregarding the hard fist of fear in his stomach, he ran out into the moonlit meadows," according to Linnie Marsh Wolfe, his biographer. "Eagle Rock, high on the south wall of the valley, was toppling. . . . All fear forgotten, he bounded toward the descending mass," shouting exuberantly in the shower of dust and falling fragments, leaping among the new boulders before they had finished settling into their resting places on the valley floor.

Besides, when he got around to organizing the journals of his early wanderings, he had become sharply political. He had been jotting plant identifications and geological evidence of glaciation, but now was gleaning memories from the same pages, meaning to write to save the wilderness from obliteration — and not just by the timber and mining companies. More pervasive a threat at the turn of the century was the injunction in Genesis that any wilderness was a wasteland until tilled, that man was made in the likeness of God and in opposition to wilderness and its multitudinous creatures, which were not. It seems a very old pronouncement; yet it was the revolutionary edict of a new religion attacking established spiritual values — monotheism on the offensive against polytheism which revered or at least incorporated the realities of the wilderness. Furthermore, later texts and preachers went beyond the objection that certain mountains, forests, springs and animal races had been considered gods, to decry the wilderness as actually Devil-ridden, inimical to the salvation of men.

Muir, like the eastern Transcendentalists, was not advocating polytheism. Nor was he secular. He believed that wilderness, like man, was an expression of one God; that man was part of nature; that nature, fount of the world, remained his natural home, under one God. Like Emerson and Thoreau—like Twain and Whitman and Melville and Hawthorne—Muir had found Christianity to be a stingy religion in matters vital to him. In his case, it wasn't the Church's vapid response to the issue of slavery or to the mysterious ambiguities of evil or the imperatives of love that swung him toward the perilous experiment of inventing his own religion (for Twain, this became atheism). Polytheism was long dead, yet the wilderness was still perceived as inimical, and so Muir didn't want to increase by even a little the lore that had contributed to such a misreading.

His father had been a free-lance Presbyterian preacher, when not working on their Wisconsin farm—a hellfire Presbyterian, fierce with the one flock given into his care, who were his children. The family had emigrated to America when John was eleven, and from then on he worked like an adult, dawn to dusk in the summer, with many beatings. At fifteen, he was set the task of digging a well in sandstone by the light of a candle. Daily for months, except on Sundays, he was lowered alone in a bucket, and once at the eighty-foot level passed out from lack of oxygen. Though he was only just rescued in time, the next morning his father punctually lowered him to the bottom all over again. Not till he was ninety feet down did he hit water.

This amok Presbyterianism helped to estrange him from Christianity but not from religion, and paradoxically made Muir gentler toward everyone but himself. He had encountered kinder treatment from some of the neighbors, and despite his deficiencies in schooling, was welcomed to the university in Madison, where a science professor and Emerson and Agassiz disciple named Ezra Carr (and especially Mrs. Carr) drew him into their household like a son. His education was so hard-won that he seems to have got more out of his two and a half years at college in terms of friendships and influences than Thoreau did at Harvard, although both learned to keep an assiduous notebook and to insist that America had a great intellectual role to play in the world.

Muir was one of those people who believe in the rapture of life but who must struggle to find it. He wasn't always blissful in the woods. During the Civil War, when he was twenty-six, he fled to Canada, partly in order to evade the draft, and wandered the environs of the Great Lakes for eight months in intermittent torment. He had already aspired to be a doctor, had then leaned toward natural science, had exhibited a phenomenal knack for inventing machine tools and implements — the kind of talent that has founded family dynasties — and had won his independence from his father without bruising his mother and sisters and brothers unduly. He had had fine friends, had been in love; yet still he wanted to leave "the doleful chambers of civilization, the beaten charts" and search for "the Law that governs the relations between human beings and Nature." There was one indispensable lesson he had gained from the brutal schedule of labors of his boyhood. During the next couple of decades when it was essential that he explore, laze, gaze, loaf, muse, listen, climb and nose about, he was free of any puritan compulsion to "work." After the North-woods sojourn he put in another two years as millwright and inventor for wages (not drudgery, because he enjoyed it), before a frightening injury to his right eye in the carriage factory in which he worked bore in upon him the realization that life was short.

Once, finding himself in the metropolis of Chicago, he had passed the five hours between trains by botanizing in vacant lots; and now as he struck off like one of his heroes, Alexander von Humboldt, for the valley of the Amazon, he set a compass course directly through Louisville so as not to notice the city too much. Beginning this, his earliest journal extant, he signed himself with ecstatic curlicues "John Muir, Earth-planet, Universe." Later on, in California, he would set off into the radiant high country of "the Range of Light" — as he called the Sierra Nevadas — with his blanket roll and some bread and tea thrown into a sack tossed over his shoulder like "a squirrel's tail." He might scramble up a Douglas fir in spiked boots in a gale to cling to it and ride the wind "like a bobolink on a reed," smelling the flower fields far away and the salt of the sea. "Heaven bless you all," he exclaimed, in his first summer journal from the Sierras — meaning all California's citizenry, including its lizards, grasshoppers, ants, bighorn sheep, grizzly bears, bluebottle flies (who "make all dead flesh fly") — "our horizontal brothers," as he was apt to describe the animal kingdom.

On the giddy cliffs and knife-edges he was not out to test his courage, like the ordinary outdoorsman, but was set upon proving the beneficence of God. More than Thoreau, though less than Emerson, he skewed the evidence. God *was* in the mountains, as he knew from his own sense of joy; and as he gradually discovered that his intuitions were tied in with compass directions, storms brewing, the migration of ice, and the movements of bears, he was preparing to preach the goodness of God to us as well as himself. In even the mildest Christian theology, nature was simply handed over in servitude to man, and the Transcendentalists were trying to bypass not only this destructive anthropocentrism, as they perceived it, but also the emphasis that Christianity placed upon an afterlife at the expense of what seemed a proper reverence for life on earth. Such stress upon salvation appeared to isolate people from one another as well, because each person's fate was to be adjudicated separately. The Transcendentalists believed in universal links, and while never denying the possibilities of an afterlife, chose to emphasize the miraculous character, the healing divinity of life here and now.

Emerson admired and communed with Muir during a visit to Yosemite and afterwards encouraged him by correspondence. Other intellectual doyens—Asa Gray, Agassiz, Joseph Le Conte—took up his banner, and he was offered professorships in science in California and Massachusetts, which he turned down. From the start he had seemed a marked man. Like his father's neighbors, his college instructors and factory mentors, Muir's first employer in the Sierras, a sheep-owner named Delaney, predicted that he was going to be famous and "facilitated and encouraged" his explorations, Muir said. Some of the Mormons, too, appear to have noticed him favorably when he descended from the Wasatch Range on one of his larks to hobnob a bit near Salt Lake City. Ardent, outspoken, eloquent in conversation, he wore his heart on his sleeve throughout his life, but although more driven, more energetic than Thoreau, he lacked Thoreau's extraordinary gift of self-containment and single-mindedness. He had more friendships—an intricacy of involvements—and was a "problem-solver," as we say nowadays, a geyser of inventiveness. The trajectory of his career carried him finally to the winsome, wise figure leading day hikes for the Sierra Club or posed on his ample front porch in a vest and watch fob with his high-collared daughters and black-garbed wife, Muir quarreling publicly and condescendingly with the Hudson River naturalist John Burroughs, Muir as a visiting fireman in London, or elected to the American Academy of Arts and Letters in 1909. Yet, for all these amenities and the freedom he won to do as he liked in the world, he never achieved anything like Thoreau's feeling of mastery over it—that easy-wheeling liberty to analyze, criticize, anatomize and summarize society's failings with roosterly pleasure: "the mass of men lead lives of quiet desperation." Compared to Thoreau's spiky commentaries on his neighbors and other townsfolk, on politics, culture, labor, industry, civilization, "Boston," Muir's admonitory remarks sound aloof, stiff and hostile, as if directed at targets with which he had no firsthand familiarity. For, despite all his friendships, Muir sought the glory of God far from other people; and just as he had had to reinvent Transcendentalism for himself way out on a kind of rim of the world, he devised his own brand of glaciology to explain the landforms of Yosemite — notions at first ridiculed by the academic geologists, then vindicated, though he had taken no account of previous and contemporaneous studies, mainly because he was unacquainted with them. We need to remember that one reason he roamed so high and far was to measure living glaciers and inspect virgin evidence, but he was both too religious and too idiosyncratic rightly to pursue a scientific career, and moved on to become a rhapsodist, a polemicist and a grandfather whitebeard.

He had seen the last of the Wisconsin, Appalachian and California frontiers. Like twenty-one-year-old Francis Parkman on the Oregon Trail in 1846, like twenty-six-year-old Sam Clemens jolting into Fort Bridger in 1861, he had gone West for adventure. But he stayed in the West, stayed exhilarated, witnessing nature on a scale never presented on the Atlantic seaboard. Volcanoes, landslides, glaciers calving, oceans of flowers, forests of devil's-club and Alaskan hemlock. He was thick-skinned to criticism like Mark Twain but more personally peaceable, as exuberant in Alaska as Jack London, but indifferent to gold rushes and desperadoes. His favorite bird was the water ouzel, an agile, inoffensive creature living in mountain watercourses, not the golden eagle, and his favorite animals were squirrels.

"The Douglas squirrel is by far the most interesting and influential of the California *sciuridae*, surpassing every other species in force of character . . . Though only a few inches long, so intense is his fiery vigor and restlessness, he stirs every grove with wild life, and makes himself more important than even the huge bears that shuffle through the tangled underbrush beneath him. Every wind is fretted by his voice, almost every bole and branch feels the sting of his sharp feet. How much the growth of the trees is stimulated by this means is not easy to learn, but . . . Nature has made him master forester and committed most of her coniferous crops to his paws. . . ." This is not the author of *White Fang* talking.

But, like Audubon, Muir was often painfully lonely in wild places and was later pursued by rumors of romantic misconduct. Our nature writers tend to be damned if they do and damned if they don't, with regard to sex. A special prurience attaches to inquiries as to whether Thoreau really fell in love with Emerson's wife, why Audubon was abruptly exiled from Oakley Plantation in West Feliciana Parish, Louisiana, where he had been tutoring "my lovely Miss Pirrie," or whether poor Mrs. Hutchings, wife of Muir's sawmill employer in Yosemite Valley, left her husband as a result of her winter's companionship with Muir when her husband went East. Furthermore, *did* Muir sleep with the Honorable Mrs. Thérèse Yelverton, a divorcée celebrity who visited Yosemite in 1870 and made him the hero of a novel? Or with Mrs. Jeanne Carr, his early benefactress at the University of Wisconsin? Still, it's true that most of our preeminent nature interpreters didn't recognize that the nexus of the sexes could become a natural adjunct of what is lately called "the wilderness experience," and something faintly ludicrous attaches to their infirmity. They differed in this respect from he-men like London, from the internationally minded Audubon, and certain British explorers like Sir Richard Burton and Sir Samuel Baker (not to mention innumerable mountainmen-squawmen).

As seems to be the case with many wounded-hearts who make a decisive leap away from wherever they were wounded, joy eventually became Muir's strong suit. His joy in the bee-meadows under sun-shot granite and ice, the fir trees and river willows, the tiny water ouzels diving into cold rapids and running on the bottom after insects, ruddering themselves in the current with their half-open wings, was so tactile that he repeatedly experienced episodes of mental telepathy. He lived recklessly and efficiently enough that he did as much ambling, clambering, trekking and roaming as he could sensibly have done, but at the age of seventy still had published just two books. His most delicious volumes — *A Thousand Mile Walk to the Gulf* and *My First Summer in the Sierra* — were reconstructed from his youthful journals only after that, journals by then forty years old. His true story of the brave loyal mongrel "Stickeen," which may be the best of all dog stories, took seventeen years to see print in a magazine after the night that they shared on a glacier. And he postponed work on what might have been his finest book, *Travels in Alaska*, until the last year of his life, when his energies were not up to the task. He died of pneumonia in a Los Angeles hospital with his Alaska notes beside his bed; a collaborator had to finish jiggling them into narrative form.

Although Muir helped to invent the conservation movement, he was a tender soul, not merely a battling activist, and lived with the conviction that God was in the sky. Yet the Transcendentalists, in revering the spark of life wherever it occurred, were groping toward a revolutionary concept of survival for Western man: that we must live together with the rest of nature or we will die together with the rest of nature. Centrist churchmen over the years had issued apologias for Inquisitions, wars of racial and sectarian extermination, slavery, child labor and so on, and their ethics were proving inadequate once again. And because Muir is such an endearing individual, to grow to care for him is all the sadder because the crusade failed. We lead a scorched-earth existence; so much of what he loved about the world is nearly gone. Naturalists themselves are turning into potted plants, and mankind is re-creating itself quite in the way that a born-again Fundamentalist does, who once went to school and learned some smattering of geology, biology and human history, but who abruptly shuts all that out of his mind, transfixed instead by the idea that the Earth is only six thousand years old, that practically every species that ever lived is right here with us now for our present service and entertainment. So it is with our preternatural assumption that the world was invented by Thomas Edison and Alexander Graham Bell.

Thoreau's optimism is out of fashion, but not Thoreauvian combativeness and iconoclasm. The whole theater of orchards, ponds, back fields, short woods, short walks in which *Walden* was staged remains accessible to anyone who wants to recapitulate the particulars of what he did and saw. Muir, however, is not the same. Less thoughtful, less balanced to begin with, he hooked himself to the wide world of wilderness for support, and now that that world is shattering all around, it's hard to imagine where he would tie his lifeline. Except as a tactician and a man of good will, he has no current solutions to offer us. More than Thoreau, in other words, he is a sort of historical embodiment, like some knight of Chivalry, or leader of the Wobblies from 1919. Frank Norris employed him as the mystic Vanamee in his 1901 novel *The Octopus*, opposed to unbridled industrial power.

"Instinct with deity" was how Muir described the elements of nobility he recognized among the Tlingits of southeastern Alaska, who were the only Indians he ever took to. His own "instinct with deity" was gushier, vaguer, more isolated in character, being linked to no central traditions, no hereditary culture, no creation myths or great-grandfather tales. Muir, not born to it, blundering and fumbling as he sought to create a religion in reaction to his savage foe from childhood, Presbyterianism, left out a lot that the Indians put in. There were no carrion smells beneath his landslides, no half-eaten elk in his glacial basins, no parched nestlings fallen from his spruce and aspens. More than Thoreau, he let his philosophy dictate which observations he put in. But though his embrace of nature is not to be confused with the more intimate, inherent conjugality that animist tribal peoples on all continents have had, his was sufficiently headlong that we would find it almost impossible to duplicate today.

We have disacknowledged our animalness. Not just American Indians spoke affectionately to turtles, ravens, eagles and bears as "Uncle" and "Grandfather," but our ancestors as well. The instant cousinhood our children feel for animals, the way they go toward them directly, with all-out curiosity, is a holdover from this. Even now, to visit the Tlingit villages on Admiralty, Chichagof and other islands of the Alexander Archipelago where Muir kayaked and boated is to meet with a thicket of animal life — whales in the channels, bears ashore — from which the native clans trace their origins and which therefore were seldom hunted. Bears still have accepted territorial spheres of influence on these islands, and the roofs in the villages belong to the ravens as much as the streets do to the people, while eagles bank as closely as seagulls overhead.

In looking on my bookshelves for a contemporary writer who has the same earthy empathy and easy knowledgeability for what is going on out-of-doors as Muir's, the nearest kindred spirits I could find were the Craighead brothers, Frank and John, who are old hawk, owl and grizzly experts and the co-authors of a field guide to Rocky Mountain wildflowers which was first published over twenty years ago. It's too unorthodox and informal a book to be especially popular now, but I love thumbing through it. The fact that brothers wrote it is appealing. Like the Murie brothers, Olaus and Adolph, who ten years earlier had studied elk and wolves and waterfowl and wildlife tracking, the Craigheads possess an old-fashioned air of blood alliance and clannish loyalty. And, writing about the Rockies — whose climatic zones vary too much for ecological cycles to be described simply by dates on a calendar — they say that wild violets come into bloom when wood ducks are building nests and crows are sitting on their eggs; that vetch vines flower at the same time as moose are having calves; that chokecherries blossom when prairie falcons are about to fledge; fireweed when bald eagles are making their first flights from the nest; and primroses when young goshawks leave for good. Coyote pups depart from their dens at about the time blueberry plants have fully bloomed. Bearberries start to flower when tree swallows return from the south, are in full blossom when Canada goose eggs begin to hatch, and the berries themselves, although still green, have formed by the time young chipmunks are to be seen scampering about. The life schedules of wild licorice and lodgepole lupine are linked to the flight lessons of ruffed grouse; meadowsweet to long-eared owls; balsamroot and serviceberries to bighorn ewes; harebells and silverweed to mallard ducklings; long-plumed avens to bison calves and Swainson's hawks.

On and on these virtuosos go. Since the book is about flowers, they are limited to events of the spring and summer, but we know that this inventory of lore could spin around the larger cycle of the year as no ecologist of a younger generation would conceive of trying to do. The Craigheads and the Muries did not age into crusaders on the order of John Muir, and were too late to enjoy Muir's faith in God. But in their various modest books the same joy is there, and the feel of an encyclopedic synthesis of experience and observation on a scale Muir had and few outdoorsmen will ever be permitted again.

Julia Blackburn

St. Helena's

From the place where we rode, which was
on the northwest side, there is hardly
such another Ragged, steepy, stony, high,
Cragged, rocky, barren, Desolate, and
Comfortless coast to be seen. But above,
the ground is of excellent Mold.
                    —The Voyage of Peter Mundy

St. Helena is further away from anywhere than anywhere else in all the world. It is a dot in the middle of the South Atlantic, situated just below the line of the Equator; eighteen hundred miles from the coast of Brazil in South America, and twelve hundred miles from the port of Alexander in Angolan Africa. Even its nearest neighbour, pale grey and brittle Ascension Island, is separated from it by seven hundred miles of deep ocean waters.

St. Helena is ten and a half miles long and six miles wide, but it seems much bigger because it is so jagged and mountainous. It came into existence some sixty million years ago, towards the end of what is called the Tertiary Period, when the continents of the world split off from each other, and the earth's crust folded and buckled and molten rock erupted onto its outer surface. My young son has a book which illustrates this process on one large and colourful page. On the right-hand side prehistoric monsters are being hurtled to their death by a huge tidal wave, and on the left-hand side a rippling line of volcanoes is spitting out fire and brimstone. St. Helena is part of such a volcanic chain which stretches from Tristan da Cunha in the south, up through Ascension, Cape Verde and the Canaries. Were it not for the Atlantic Ocean, these mountains would look similar to the Andes of South America, but as it is only their tips stick out above the water.

Because St. Helena was so isolated, only certain forms of life could ever reach it and establish themselves here. The seeds of plants and trees could be carried on the waves or lodged in a broken branch and deposited somewhere along the coast, while the smallest seeds could be transported by the feet of sea birds. The eggs of certain insects, land snails and spiders could also have a chance of surviving a long and haphazard journey across the Atlantic. Slowly St. Helena became colonised by vegetation, and a quantity of insignificant creatures without backbones. The island is so buffeted by wind and saturated by rain that the temperature is never extreme; warm, damp summers are followed by warm, damp winters. And so, in spite of the steepness of the rock and the lack of any true soil, the seeds that found a place to root themselves flourished to an extraordinary degree, transforming St. Helena into one entire forest. Trees fixed their roots into the steepest ravines, into the sheer faces of rock jutting out over the sea, and covered even the highest peaks of the mountains. There were gumwood, redwood and scrubwood trees, and he-cabbage palms, and she-cabbage palms, fern trees and umbrella trees, and many others that have never been given a Latin name or a botanical description. The most magnificent of all the trees were the black-hearted coromandel ebonies, that grew as slowly as oaks and stretched out their awkward rigid branches like vast candelabra. There were no grasses, but in the small clearings between the trees there were flowering shrubs and bushes; fat-leaved yellow samphire along the cliffs, wild celery and watercresses near the little streams and springs.

Feeding on the plants and the trees were at least one hundred and twenty-nine species of beetle. All of them but one were unique to this island, and most of them were small, dull-coloured members of the weevil family, with long hard noses well suited for tunnelling runways and nesting chambers under the bark of trees. There were also ten varieties of spiders that lived on beetles, and a number of large land snails that fed on leaves and stalks. At some stage in the island's early history a single species of bird made this place its home. It is a small, nervous, unremarkable, dapple-grey creature, related to the plover family and called the wirebird because of its long, spindly legs.

Apart from the one bird, and the colonies of beetles, snails and spiders, the island was without inhabitants; a silent greenness, inaccessible and almost without sound or movement. But around its steep cliffs there was often intense activity. Seals, and the ungainly vegetarian sea cows, used to rest on the scattered rocks that were the remnants of the southern rim of the volcano's crater. The water was shallow here, and rich in many varieties of fish: congers and soldiers, old wives and bulls' eyes, and the rare coal fish. Turtles came to lay their eggs in the sands of the little bay that is now the port of Jamestown. Seabirds in their thousands nested on the cliffs, and a rock called Shore Island was so thickly covered with their white droppings that it could easily be mistaken for a ship in full sail.

Until the beginning of the sixteenth century, nobody knew of the existence of this little green island. But St. Helena lies in the direct line of the south-east Trade Winds, and that meant that once the early navigators had rounded the Cape of Good Hope, and gained access to the South Atlantic, they were bound to come across it sooner or later. The Portuguese were the first. Admiral da Nova, in command of three warships, was returning to Portugal from India, and on 21 May 1502 he sighted a dark hump of land in an otherwise blank expanse of ocean. The date of this discovery was the birthday of Helena, the mother of the Emperor Constantine the Great.

Da Nova circled the island until he found a place, about the only place, where it was possible to anchor the boats and come ashore without scaling the cliffs. He and his sailors spent several days there. They explored the greenness of the great forests, and collected fresh water from the many springs. They caught quantities of fish that leapt up to swallow the shining bait of a bent nail tied to a piece of twine. They tasted the unsavoury flesh of the seabirds which sat in gregarious crowds and watched the sailors coming amongst them with clubs, making no attempt to fly away because they did not understand the danger they were in.

Before setting off on his journey, Da Nova ordered his men to release a few goats. It was a usual thing to do at that time; a way of providing a source of fresh meat for any subsequent visitors who came here. The goats on St. Helena had plenty of food and no predators and they soon multiplied and became very fat and large. When Captain Cavendish came to the island thirty years later he had never seen goats of such a size before, and thinking that they must be a native species he named them *caprus Hellenicus*. He wrote a description of the descendants of Da Nova's original small band:

> you shall see one or two hundred of them together, and sometimes you may behold them going in a flock almost a mile long. Some of them are as big as an ass, with a mane like a horse and a beard hanging down to the very ground. They will climb up the cliffs which are so steep that a man would think it a thing impossible for any living thing to go there.
>
> We took and killed many of them for all their swiftness, for there be thousands upon the mountains. (Quoted in Gosse, p. 18)

A place can be haunted by the people who knew it long ago and who stared at the stones under their feet, the leaves on the trees, and out at the far distances and horizons that encircled them. Something about St. Helena's isolation seems to concentrate this sense of the land being haunted, soaked to the bone with the lives of people who were once here and are now long since dead. It is as if the island's own loneliness creates a feeling of kinship that stretches back to everyone who has ever stood on this little platform, which seems to be balanced on the very edge of the world.

I have been told that when the children of St. Helena are asked who they consider to be central to their island's history, they do not think of mentioning Napoleon—he has become the property of historians and curious foreign visitors—but turn instead to the story of a Portuguese nobleman called Fernando Lopez. More than anyone else who has become embedded in this place, he stands out as the most vivid personality.

Fernando Lopez arrived here in 1515. Because of a crime he had committed he had no right hand, no left thumb, no nose and no ears, and the hair of his head, his eyebrows and his beard had been plucked out—a practice that was known as 'scaling the fish'. According to one account the fingers of his left hand had also been removed.

Lopez spent thirty years on the island. For most of that time he was entirely on his own, and for stretches of uninterrupted years he spoke to no one and was seen by no one, and went and hid in the greenness of the forest whenever a ship approached the harbour. On one occasion he did make a brief visit to Portugal, but then his only wish was to be allowed to return to his solitary home.

The story of this man with his grotesquely wounded face and his maimed hands is told by three early writers on Portuguese history. One of them saw him on the island, although it seems that he only caught sight of him from a distance and never managed to speak with him, and the other two wrote about him not long after his death. These accounts were written very simply, without comment or emotion, but just the idea of how this man must have looked serves to give him a complex personality, and it is easy to understand how the last years of his life were absorbed into the heart of the island, until man and place were in some ways indistinguishable.

Lopez was a Portuguese nobleman who left his home and his family and went with a group of soldiers under the leadership of General D'Alboquerque in search of new lands to conquer and claim for the Portuguese Empire. In 1510 they crossed the Indian Ocean from Arabia, and arrived in Goa on the south-west coast of India. After a brief battle they captured the ancient fortress town and claimed the ownership of the land that they stood on, and the vast unknown continent that lay beyond it. Because they had not got enough military strength to push their claim, D'Alboquerque set sail for Portugal to fetch more warships and more fighting men while Lopez and some of the soldiers were left behind to guard the fortress and to wait for the return of their general. D'Alboquerque was away for two years, and when he finally came back, bristling with reinforcements, he found that the men he had left behind had betrayed his trust in them, and had adopted the Muslim faith and the way of life of the local people. The traitors were rounded up without any resistance and brought before him, and since he had promised to be lenient they were not killed, although more than half of their number died during the three days that they were punished 'by black torturers and young men'. Lopez received the heaviest punishment because he was of noble birth and had been made responsible for the whole group. When it was all over, he and the others who had survived were released from the ropes and chains that bound them, and were set free to go wherever they chose. They all went and hid themselves somewhere in the countryside, so that neither their terrible wounds nor their shame could be seen.

Three years later D'Alboquerque was dead, and Lopez emerged out of hiding and took a passage on a ship bound for Portugal. He was planning to return to the wife and children he had not seen for so long, and to return to his house, his people, his language and his homeland. After many days at sea the ship stopped at the island of St. Helena to replenish its supplies of water, and it was then that he realised he could not bring himself to complete his journey. He went ashore and hid himself deep in the forest. When the boat was ready to leave the sailors searched for him but could not find him, so they left some provisions on the shore and went on their way.

Lopez dug himself a hole in the ground in which to sleep. He had been provided with a barrel of biscuits and a few strips of dried meat, a tinder box and a saucepan. There were many edible herbs and fruits to be found, and it would not have been difficult for him to catch fish or nesting birds, or even one of the goats. The island was extremely benevolent; there were no wild animals here to harm him, no insects or reptiles to bite him, no diseases to sap his strength. In spite of the wind and the rain, the weather was always mild, and the trees were thick with sheltering leaves. A year went by before another ship appeared and dropped anchor in the bay that is now the port of Jamestown.

> The crew was amazed when they saw the grotto and a straw bed on which he slept . . . and when they saw the clothing they agreed it must be a Portuguese man.
> So they took in their water and did not meddle with anything, but

left biscuits and cheeses and things to eat, and a letter telling him not to hide himself next time a ship came to the island, for no one would harm him.

Then the ship set off, and as she was spreading her sails a cockerel fell overboard, and the waves carried it to the shore and Fernando Lopez caught it and fed it with some rice which they had left behind for him. (Hakluyt Society, No. 62)

The cockerel was the first living creature to share the man's solitude. At night it roosted above his head and during the day it pattered after him and came to him when he called it. Time went on and Lopez learnt to be less afraid; slowly he grew into the habit of appearing when a ship was at anchor, coming to talk to the men who came ashore. Everyone who met him must have been moved by a sense of pity and of horror, and since Lopez refused to be separated from his island, the sailors treated him as if he was a sort of saint, a man carrying on his shoulders a huge weight of human suffering and estrangement. And since they could not take him with them and give him the freedom of their own way of life, they offered him gifts; they inundated him with anything they could find which they thought might please him. They gave him the seeds of vegetables and flowers; they gave him young palm trees and banana trees, pomegranates and lemons, oranges and limes. They also gave him living creatures: ducks and hens, pheasants and partridges, guinea fowl with their shrill warning shouts, peacocks with their harsh screams, turkeys, bullocks and cows, pigs, dogs and cats, even more goats, and, accidentally, a certain number of rats which came ashore when no one was looking. And so Lopez became a gardener and a keeper of livestock. With his single hand he worked tirelessly and relentlessly, planting and clearing, digging and tending, until under his care whole stretches of the landscape were utterly transformed. Among the ebony, the redwood and the gumwood trees he created gardens, vineyards and orchards, and because of the rain, the wind and the fertility of the soil, the seeds of many of the plants took root and flourished in parts of the island where he was not tending them, and because it was impossible to keep such a quantity of birds and animals in captivity, they also learnt to roam freely across the steep green landscape.

And this is how the island of St. Helena became fused in people's minds with the idea of a rich garden growing on a rock in a distant ocean, a place of natural and yet unnatural perfection, fruitful throughout the year, cultivated and yet wild and without any human disturbances. It was hardly surprising that everyone who came here talked about this place that they had seen and the man who ruled over it like a king without subjects. In time the story was told to the king and queen of Portugal, and they summoned Lopez to appear before them at their royal palace in Lisbon. He came, unwillingly but obediently, and when he was offered anything he might desire, he asked simply to be taken to see the Pope in Rome so that he could confess his sins, and when he had seen the Pope, he begged permission to be taken back to the island he had come from. After this brief incursion into the world of men, Lopez was again visited by his old fears, and he stayed in hiding in the forest whenever he saw a ship approaching, and agreed to show himself only once it was promised in the king's name that no one would try a second time to carry him away.

And Fernando Lopez felt assured, so that he no longer used to hide himself, and spoke with those who came here, and gave them the produce of the island, which yielded in great abundance. And in the island he died, after living there a long time, which was in the year 1546. (Hakluyt Society, No. 62)

The extraordinary oasis that one man had created survived relatively unchanged for some years after his death. Portuguese sailors and soldiers who were too ill to continue on their journey would be left here to convalesce and gather their strength. A wooden chapel was built near the harbour, along with a few simple houses, but there were never more than a few men here at any one time, and there was no permanent settlement. The groves of citrus trees, the date palms and banana trees, the pineapples and pomegranates, all flourished, especially in the sheltered valley that rose up steeply from the harbour, and in a valley further to the east that came to be known as Lemon Valley. The wild domestic animals, the wild domestic birds and the rats ranged over the entire surface of the island, eating what they needed and multiplying. It was said that no matter what the season there was always enough fruit to fill the holds of six ships and there were wonderful herbs that could cure the scurvy within eight days. A man armed with a stick need not go far or exert himself much before he had secured the carcass of some plump bird or a large, well-fed and familiar animal.

On all sides the ancient forests stood as silent witnesses to the changes that were being brought about. The pigs, dogs, goats, cats and cattle were moving across the landscape like heavy earthbound locusts, but it would be a while before the effects of their presence were felt. The goats could eat the low branches and the young saplings of the trees, but they could not damage the bark of the old ebonies and gumwoods. The pigs could dig up the roots from the rich but shallow soil, but as long as the trees remained standing, that soil would be held fast, and no amount of rain or wind could sweep it away. So, in spite of the newly imported inhabitants, the island still had its strange and fertile beauty, with the old world and the new flourishing in apparent harmony.

The first book that attempted to provide a thorough and accurate account of St. Helena was called the *General Description of Africa*. It was published in 1573, although the text seems to have been based on reports from travellers who visited the island during the 1550s. It explains that St. Helena is an earthly paradise, a place where a man can refresh his soul as well as his body, where the climate is always mild, the food is plentiful, there is no sickness and not a single wild creature that could cause any harm. But by the time that the book was published, the island was already beginning to change character and its gentle benevolence was being shaken. Huge poisonous spiders, as big as a clenched fist, had arrived from Africa and settled in the banana trees, and there was a species of stinging fly the size of a grasshopper whose origins were unknown. Vicious battles were being fought between the colonies of dogs, cats and rats, and the rats were in the ascendancy and had taken to nesting in the high trees where they disrupted the roosting peacocks and other birds.

In 1581 the battle for mastery and power moved from the animal into the human realm. An English pirate captain called James Fenton came across St. Helena accidentally, and determined to chase out the Portuguese so that he might possess the island and 'there be proclaimed Kyng'. This scheme came to nothing but in the following year another Englishman, Captain Cavendish, discovered the island while returning from a voyage round the world. He stayed there for twelve days, and he explored it, mapped it, wrote about it, and charted its position very exactly in the middle of the Atlantic Ocean. From then onwards the secret was broken, and a succession of ships from various countries arrived to examine the land and fight over its ownership. They developed the habit of collecting fruit by cutting down whole lemon trees and taking the trunk with its richly decorated branches on board ship with them when they were ready to leave. Sometimes they would uproot or trample on the produce of the wild gardens and orchards when they had no use for it themselves; it was a simple way of denying it to anyone who happened to arrive after them.

By 1610 only a few lemon trees were left and they were hard to find. There were none remaining on the hills close to the harbour, but there was still a grove big enough to provide 14,000 lemons at one picking at Lemon Valley, further along the coast. By 1634 it was said that there were less than forty lemon trees on the whole island: twenty in Lemon Valley and the rest scattered all over the place. However, the native trees were still growing thickly across most of the island's surface, and there was 'an abundance of Hoggs, store of little speckled guinea Henns, partridges and Pigeons, also doggs, and Catts (runne away) of whome the Companie killed divers'. (Gosse, pp. 29–30).

Maybe because it was so very far away and although many people had heard of it few had actually seen it, or maybe because human beings cannot bear very much reality and often prefer to see what they imagine rather than what lies before their eyes, whatever the reason, the written descriptions of St. Helena were hardly altered in spite of the passage of time and the changes that time was bringing with it. By the late eighteenth century, when the island was almost naked, stripped of its covering of earth, plants and trees everywhere except in the higher regions and in cultivated gardens, the *Portable Geographer's Gazetteer*, a standard reference work which was available in a number of editions in French and in English, was able to explain confidently:

> The hills are for the most part covered with verdure and large species of tree such as ebony etc. The valleys are very fertile in all kinds of excellent fruits, vegetables, etc. The fruit trees there bear at the same time flowers, green fruit and ripe fruit. The forests are full of orange, lemon and citrus trees. There are game birds in quantity, poultry and wild cattle. No savage or hurtful animal is found there, and the sea is full of fish. (Quoted in Masson, p. 98)

When Napoleon was a young man studying at the military academy at Auxonne he had filled a notebook with information about the lands that were at that time under British rule, and on the top line of an otherwise empty page he had written in his restless handwriting, 'St. Helena, a small island'. In 1804 he even considered capturing this small island that could be so useful as a military base in the middle of the South Atlantic: '1,200 to 1,500 men will be required . . . The English are in no wise expecting this expedition and it will be a simple matter to surprise them' (Masson, p. 97). The expedition never materialised, but he did prepare himself by finding out all he could about the nature of St. Helena. He was bound to have read the *Portable Geographer's Gazetteer* in its French edition, as well as the other descriptive books that were available at the time; they all echoed each other in their accounts of this green oasis where fruits were ripe all the year round.

The island of St. Helena is a witness to the changes it has seen and is still the same place, even though it has been put to many uses by the succession of people who have made claims to it and have adapted it to suit one purpose and then another. If you stare at the strangely naked landscape you can easily see what it must have lost, and you are close to knowing how it once was.

Italo Calvino

Translated from the Italian by Patrick Creagh

Man, the Sky, and the Elephant:
On Pliny's Natural History

In Pliny the Elder's *Natural History*, for the sheer pleasure of reading, I would advise concentrating on three books: the two that contain the main lines of his philosophy, which are the second (on cosmography) and the seventh (on man), and — as an example of his jumping back and forth between erudition and fantasy — the eighth (on the animals of the earth). We can of course find extraordinary pages everywhere. For example, in the books on geography (III and VI), on aquatic zoology, entomology, and comparative anatomy (IX and XI), botany, agronomy, and pharmacology (XII and XXXII), or on metals, precious stones, and the fine arts (XXXIII and XXXVII).

Pliny has, I think, always been used chiefly for reference, both to find out what the ancients knew or thought they knew on any particular subject, and to pick up oddities and eccentricities. From this point of view one cannot neglect book I, the summary of the whole work, the interesting thing about which is the wealth of unexpected juxtapositions: "Fish that have a pebble in their heads; Fish that hide in winter; Fish that feel the influence of the stars; Extraordinary prices paid for certain fish." Or "Concerning the rose: 12 varieties, 32 drugs; 3 varieties of lily: 21 drugs; a plant born from one of its own tears; 3 varieties of narcissus: 16 drugs; a plant one dyes the seeds of so that it produces colored flowers; Saffron: 20 drugs; Where the best flowers grow; Which flowers were known at the time of the Trojan War; clothing that rivals flowers." Or yet again: "The nature of metals; Concerning gold; The amount of gold possessed by the ancients; The equestrian order and the right to wear gold rings; How many times has the equestrian order changed names?"

But Pliny is also a writer who deserves to be read at length for the calm movement of his prose, animated as it is by admiration for everything that exists and respect for the infinite variety of things.

We might perhaps distinguish a poetical-philosophical Pliny, with his feeling for the universe and his love of knowledge and mystery, from the Pliny who was a neurotic collector of data, an obsessive compiler who seems to think only of not wasting a single jotting in his mastodonic notebook. (In using written sources he was omnivorous and eclectic, but not without a critical sense. There were some things he accepted at face value, others that he simply recorded, and still others that he rejected as obvious fantasies. It is just that his method of evaluation appears to be very unstable and unpredictable.) But once we have recognized these two faces of Pliny, we have to admit immediately that he is always one and the same man, exactly as the world he aims to describe in all its variety of form is one and the same world. To achieve this aim, he did not hesitate to plunge into the endless number of existing forms, multiplied by the endless number of existing ideas about these forms, because forms and ideas had for him equal right to be part of natural history and to be examined by anyone looking into them for an indication of a higher "reason" that he was convinced they must contain.

The world is the eternal and uncreated sky, whose spherical, rotating face covers all terrestrial things (II. 2), but it is difficult to distinguish the world from God, who for Pliny (and the Stoic culture to which he belonged) is one God, not to be identified with any single portion or aspect of him, or with the crowd of characters on Olympus, though perhaps with the sun, the soul or mind or spirit of the sky (II. 13). At the same time, the sky is made of stars as eternal as he is; the stars weave the sky and yet are part of the celestial fabric: *aeterna caelestibus est natura intexentibus mundum intextuque concretis* (II. 30). But it is also air (both below and above the moon) that looks empty and diffuses the spirit of life here below, and produces clouds, thunder, hail, lightning, and storms (II. 102).

When we speak of Pliny, we never know to what extent we should attribute the ideas he expresses to the author himself. He is in fact scrupulous about inserting as little of himself as possible and sticking to what his sources tell him. This conforms to his impersonal concept of knowledge, which excludes individual originality. To try to understand what his sense of nature really is, and how much of it consists of the arcane majesty of principles and how much of the materiality of the elements, we have to cling to what is undeniably his own: the expressive substance of his prose. Look, for example, at the pages concerning the moon, where the tone of heartfelt gratitude for this "supreme heavenly body, the most familiar to those who live on earth, the remedy of darkness" ("*novissimum sidus, terris familiarissimum et in tenebrarum remedium*" [II. 41]), and for all that it teaches us with the rhythm of its phases and eclipses, combines with the agile functionality of the sentences to express this mechanism with crystal clarity. It is in the pages on astronomy in book II that Pliny shows himself to be something more than the compiler with an imaginative flair that he is usually taken for, and reveals himself as a writer possessing what was destined to be the chief quality of all great scientific prose: that of expounding the most complex subject with perfect clarity, while deriving from it a sense of harmony and beauty.

He does this without ever leaning toward abstract speculation. Pliny always sticks to the facts (what he considers to be facts or what others have considered to be such). He does not hold with an infinite number of worlds because the nature of this world is already hard enough to understand, and infinity would scarcely simplify the problem (II. 4). Nor does he believe in the music of the spheres, either as a din out of earshot or as inexpressible harmony, because "for us who are in it, the world glides around both day and night in silence" (II. 6).

Having stripped God of the anthropomorphic characteristics attributed by mythology to the immortals of Olympus, Pliny is forced by the rules of logic to bring God closer to man by means of the limits necessarily imposed on His powers. In fact, God is less free than man in one case, because He could not kill Himself even if He wanted to. Nor does He have any power over the past, over the irreversibility of time (II. 27). Like Kant's God, He cannot come into conflict with the independence of reason (He cannot prevent two plus two from equaling four), but to define Him in these terms would lead us astray from the natural immanence of his identification with the forces of nature (*"per quae declaratur haut dubie naturae potentia idque quod deum vocemus* [II. 27]).

The lyrical or lyrical-philosophical tones dominant in the earlier chapters of book II correspond to a vision of universal harmony that does not take long to fall to pieces. A considerable part of that book is devoted to celestial prodigies. Pliny's science oscillates between the intent to recognize an order in nature and the recording of what is extraordinary or unique: and the second aspect of it always wins out. Nature is eternal and sacred and harmonious, but it leaves a wide margin for the emergence of inexplicable prodigious phenomena. What general conclusion ought we to draw from this? That we are concerned with a monstrous order entirely composed of exceptions to the rule? Or else a set of rules so complex it eludes our understanding? In either case, for every fact an explanation must exist, even if for the time being this explanation is unknown to us: "All things of explanation that is uncertain and hidden in the majesty of nature" (II. 101), and, a little farther on, "*Adeo causa non deest*" (II. 115), "it is not the causes that are lacking"—a cause can always be found. Pliny's rationalism exalts the logic of cause and effect and at the same time minimizes it, for even if you find the explanation for facts, that is no reason for the facts to cease to be marvelous.

This last maxim concludes a chapter on the mysterious origin of the winds: the folds of mountains, the hollows of valleys that hurl back blasts of wind after the manner of an echo, a grotto in Dalmatia where one need only drop a light object to unleash a storm at sea, a rock in Cyrenaica that only has to be touched to raise a sandstorm. Pliny gives us many of these catalogues of strange facts unrelated to one another: on the effects of lightning on man, with its cold wounds (among plants, lightning spares only the laurel; among animals, the eagle, according to II. 146), on extraordinary rains (of milk, blood, meat, iron, or sponges of iron, wool, and bricks, according to II. 147).

And yet Pliny clears the ground of a lot of old wives' tales, such as comets as omens (for example, he refutes the belief that a comet appearing between the pudenda of a constellation—was there anything the ancients did not see in the skies?—foretells an era of moral laxity: "*obscenis autem moribus in verendis partibus signorum*" [II. 93]). Still, each prodigy presents itself to him as a problem of nature, insofar as it is the reverse side of the norm. Pliny holds out against superstitions but cannot always recognize them, especially in book VII, where he deals with human nature. Even concerning easily observable facts he records the most abstruse beliefs. Typical is the chapter on menstruation (VII. 63–66), but it must be said that Pliny's views all accord with the most ancient religious taboos regarding menstrual blood. There is a whole network of traditional analogies and values that does not clash with Pliny's rationalism, almost as if the latter were based on the same foundations. Thus he is sometimes inclined to construct analogical explanations of the poetic or psychological type: "The corpses of men float face upward, those of women face down, as if nature wished to respect the modesty of dead women" (VII. 77).

On rare occasions Pliny reports facts vouched for by his own personal experience: "On guard duty at night in front of the trenches I have seen star-shaped lights shining on the soldiers' spears" (II. 101); "during the reign of Claudius we saw a centaur which he had had brought from Egypt, preserved in honey" (VII. 35); "I myself in Africa once saw a citizen of Tisdrus changed from a woman to a man on her wedding day" (VII. 36).

But for a tireless seeker such as he, a protomartyr of experimental science, destined to die asphyxiated by the fumes during the eruption of Vesuvius, direct observations occupy a minimal place in his work, and are on exactly the same level of importance as information read in books—and the more ancient these were, the more authoritative. All the same, to forestall criticism, he declares: "However, for most of these facts I would not vouch, preferring to go back to the sources to whom I turn in all doubtful cases, without ceasing to follow the Greeks, who are the most precise in their observations, as well as the most ancient" (VII. 8).

After this preamble Pliny feels free to launch into his famous review of the "prodigious and incredible" characteristics of certain foreign peoples, a passage that was to be so popular in the Middle Ages and even later, and to transform geography into a fairground of living phenomena. There are echoes of it in later accounts of *real* travels, such as those of Marco Polo. That the unknown lands on the fringes of the world should contain beings on the fringes of humanity should be no cause for wonder: the Arimaspi with a single eye in the middle of their foreheads, who contest the gold mines with the griffins; the inhabitants of the forest of Abarimon, who run extremely swiftly on feet that point backward; the androgynous people of Nasamona, who assume alternate sexes during intercourse; the Tibii, who have two pupils in one eye and the image of a horse in the other. But the great Barnum presents his most spectacular acts in India, where one can find a people of mountain hunters who have the heads of dogs, and a race of jumping people with one leg only, who when they want to rest in the shade lie down and raise their single foot above their heads like a parasol. There is also a nomadic people with legs like snakes, and there are the Astomoi, who have no mouths and live by sniffing odors. Mixed in with these are pieces of information we now know to be true, such as the description of the Indian fakirs (whom he calls "gymnosophist philosophers"), or else things such as still provide us with those mysterious events we read about in the newspapers (where he talks about immense footprints, he could be referring to the Yeti or Abominable Snowman of the Himalayas). Then there are legends destined to continue down through the centuries, such as that of the curing power of kings (King Pyrrhus, who cured disorders of the spleen by touching the patient with his big toe).

What emerges from all this is a dramatic notion of human nature as something precarious and insecure. The form and the destiny of man hang by a thread. Quite a number of pages are devoted to the unpredictability of childbirth, with the exceptional cases and the dangers and difficulties. This, too, is a frontier zone, for everyone who exists might very well not exist, or might be different, and it is *there* that it is all decided.

> In pregnant women everything—for example, the manner of walking—has an influence on childbirth. If they eat oversalted food they will give birth to a child without nails; if they cannot hold their breath they will have more trouble in delivering; during childbirth even a yawn can be fatal, as a sneeze during coitus can cause a miscarriage. Compassion and shame come over one who considers how precarious is the origin of the proudest of living beings: often the smell of a lately extinguished lamp is enough to cause a miscarriage. And to think that from such a frail beginning a tyrant or a butcher may be born! You who trust in your physical strength, who embrace the gifts of fortune and consider yourself not their ward but their son, you who have a domineering spirit, you who consider yourself a god as soon as success swells your breast, think how little could have destroyed you! [VII. 42–44]

One can understand why Pliny was so popular in the Christian Middle Ages: "To weigh life in a just balance one must always remember human fragility."

The human race is a zone of living things that should be defined by tracing its confines. Pliny therefore records the extreme limits reached by man in every field, and book VII becomes a kind of *Guinness Book of World Records.* They are chiefly quantitative records, such as strength in carrying weights, speed at running, acuteness of hearing or of memory, and so on, down to the size and extent of conquered territories. But there are also purely moral records—in virtue, generosity, and goodness. Nor is there a lack of curiosities—Antonia, wife of Drusus, who never spat; or the poet Pomponius, who never belched (VII. 80); or the highest price ever paid for a slave (the grammarian Daphnis cost seven hundred thousand sesterces, according to VII. 128).

Only about one aspect of human life does Pliny not feel inclined to quote records or attempt measurements or comparisons: happiness. It is impossible to say who is happy and who is not, since this depends on subjective and debatable criteria. (*"Felicitas cui praecipua fuerit homini, non est humani iudicii, cum prosperitatem ipsam alius alio modo et suopte ingenio quisque determinet"* [VII. 130]). If one is to look truth straight in the face, no man can be called happy, and here Pliny's anthropological survey reviews a whole rank of illustrious destinies (drawn mostly from Roman history) to show that the men most favored by fortune had to suffer unhappiness and mischance.

In the natural history of man it is impossible to include the variable that is destiny. This is the message of the pages Pliny devotes to the vicissitudes of fortune, to the unpredictability of the length of life, to the uselessness of astrology, and to sickness and death. The separation between the two forms of knowledge that astrology lumped together — the objectivity of calculable and predictable phenomena and the sense of individual existence as having an uncertain future — a separation that modern science takes for granted, can be found in these pages, but as a question not yet finally decided, so that exhaustive documentation is called for. In producing these examples Pliny seems to flounder a bit. Every event that has occurred, every biography, every anecdote can go to show that, if looked at from the point of view of someone living, life is not subject to either qualitative or quantitative judgment, and cannot be measured or compared with other lives. Its value is interior, all the more so because hopes and fears of another life are illusory. Pliny shares the opinion that after death begins a nonexistence equivalent to and symmetrical with that which came before birth.

This is why Pliny's attention is focused on the things of this world, the territories of the globe, heavenly bodies, animals, plants, and stones. The soul, to which any sort of survival is denied, can only enjoy being alive in the present if it withdraws into itself. *"Etenim si dulce vivere est, cui potest essere vixisse? At quanto facilius certiusque sibi quemque credere, specimen securitas antegenitali sumere experimento!"*: "To mold one's own peace of mind on the experience of before birth!" (VII. 190). In other words, we must project ourselves into our own absence, the only certain thing before we came into this world or after death. Hence the pleasure of recognizing the infinite variety of what is other than us, all of which the *Natural History* parades before our eyes.

If man is defined by his limitations, should he not also be defined by the points at which he excels? In book VII Pliny feels bound to include the praise of man's virtues and the celebration of his triumphs. Turning to Roman history as the exemplar of every virtue, he gives way to the temptation to reach a pompous conclusion in praise of the Empire by finding the zenith of human perfection in the person of Caesar Augustus. In my opinion, however, the characteristic note in his treatment is not this, but the hesitant, limitative, and disenchanted note, which best suits his temperament.

Here we can discern the questions that arose when anthropology was becoming a science. Should anthropology attempt to escape from a "humanistic" point of view to attain the objectivity of a science of nature? Do the men of book VII matter more, the more they are "other" and different from us, and perhaps most if they are no longer or not yet men at all? And is it really possible that man can emerge from his own subjectivity to the point of taking himself as an object of scientific knowledge? The moral that echoes back and forth in Pliny suggests caution and reservation: no science can illuminate us concerning happiness or fortune, the distribution of good and bad, or the values of existence. Each individual, when he dies, takes his secrets with him.

On this cheerless note Pliny might well have ended his dissertation, but he prefers to add a list of discoveries and inventions, both historical and legendary. Anticipating those modern anthropologists who maintain that there is continuity between biological evolution and technological evolution, from Paleolithic tools to electronics, Pliny implicitly admits that what man has added to nature becomes part of human nature. To demonstrate that man's true nature is his culture is only a step away. But Pliny, who has no time for generalizations, looks for what is specifically human in inventions and customs that might be considered universal. According to Pliny (or his sources) there are three cultural matters on which all peoples have reached a tacit agreement ("*gentium consensus tacitus*" [VI. 210]). These are the alphabet (both Greek and Latin), the shaving of men's beards, and the measurement of time by means of a sundial.

This triad could scarcely be more bizarre, given the incongruity between the three terms—alphabet, barber, and sundial—or, for that matter, more debatable. The fact is that not all peoples have similar ways of writing, nor is it true that everyone shaves; and as for the hours of the day, Pliny himself launches into a brief history of the various ways of subdividing time. But here we wish to stress not the "Eurocentric" viewpoint, which is not peculiar to Pliny or to his own age, but, rather, the direction he is taking. For the attempt to put a finger on the elements that are constantly repeated in the most diverse cultures, in order to define what is specifically human, was destined to become one of the principles of modern ethnology. And having established this point of *gentium consensus tacitus*, Pliny can conclude his treatise on the human race and pass on to other animate creatures.

Book VIII, which makes a general survey of the animals of the world, begins with the elephant, to which the longest chapter is devoted. Why is priority given to the elephant? Because it is the largest of the animals, certainly (Pliny's treatment proceeds according to an order of importance that often coincides with physical size), but also and above all because, spiritually, it is the animal "closest to man"! *"Maximum est elephas proximumque humanis sensibus"* is the opening of book VIII. In fact, the elephant—he explains immediately afterward—recognizes the language of his homeland, obeys orders, remembers what he learns, knows the passion of love and the ambition of glory, practices virtues "rare even among men," such as probity, prudence, and equity, and has a religious veneration for the sun, the moon, and the stars. Not one word (apart from that single superlative, *maximum*) does Pliny spend on describing this animal (which is, however, accurately portrayed in Roman mosaics of the time). He simply relates the legendary curiosities that he had found in books. The rites and customs of elephant society are represented as those of a people with a culture different from ours, but nonetheless worthy of respect and understanding.

In the *Natural History* man is lost in the middle of the multiform world, the prisoner of his own imperfection; yet, on the one hand, he has the relief of knowing that even God is limited in His powers (*"Imperfectae vero in homine naturae praecipus solacia, ne deum quidem posse omnia"* [II. 27]), while, on the other hand, his next-door neighbor is the elephant, who can serve him as a model on the spiritual plane. Between these two vast presences, both imposing and benign, man certainly appears cut down to size, but not crushed.

After the elephant, as in a childhood visit to the zoo, the review of the world's animals passes on to the lion, the panther, the tiger, the camel, the giraffe, the rhinoceros, and the crocodile. Then, following an order of decreasing dimensions, he goes on to the hyena, the chameleon, the porcupine, the animals that live in burrows, and even snails and lizards. The domestic animals are all lumped together at the end of book VIII.

Pliny's main source is Aristotle's *Historia animalium*, but he also goes to more credulous or fanciful authors for legends that the Stagirite rejected, or reported only to confute them. This is the case both with information about the better-known animals and with the mention of imaginary animals, the catalogue of which is interwoven with that of the real ones. Thus, while speaking of elephants, he makes a digression informing us about dragons, their natural enemies; in connection with wolves (though criticizing the credulity of the Greeks), he records the legends of the werewolf. It is in this branch of zoology that we find the amphisbaena, the basilisk, the catoblepa, the crocoti, the corocoti, the leukocroti, the leontophont, and the manticore, all destined to go on from these pages to populate the bestiaries of the Middle Ages.

The natural history of man is extended into that of animals throughout book VIII, and this not only because the knowledge recorded is to a large extent concerned with the rearing of domestic animals and the hunting of wild ones, as well as the practical use man makes of the one and the other, but also because what Pliny is doing is taking us on a guided tour of the human imagination. An animal, whether real or imaginary, has a place of honor in the sphere of the imagination. As soon as it is named it takes on a dreamlike power, becoming an allegory, a symbol, an emblem.

It is for this reason that I recommend to the reader who is wandering through these pages to pause not only at the most "philosophical" books (II and VII), but also at VIII, as the most representative of an idea of nature that is expressed at length in all the thirty-seven books of the work: nature as external to man, but not to be separated from what is most intrinsic to his mind — the alphabet of dreams, the code book of the imagination, without which there is neither thought nor reason.

III

NATURAL PHENOMENA

Louise Glück

All Hallows

Even now this landscape is assembling.
The hills darken. The oxen
sleep in their blue yoke,
the fields having been
picked clean, the sheaves
bound evenly and piled at the roadside
among cinquefoil, as the toothed moon rises:

This is the barrenness
of harvest or pestilence.
And the wife leaning out the window
with her hand extended, as in payment,
and the seeds
distinct, gold, calling
Come here
Come here, little one

And the soul creeps out of the tree.

Leslie Marmon Silko

Landscape, History, and the Pueblo Imagination

FROM A HIGH ARID PLATEAU IN NEW MEXICO

You see that after a thing is dead, it dries up. It might take weeks or years, but eventually if you touch the thing, it crumbles under your fingers. It goes back to dust. The soul of the thing has long since departed. With the plants and wild game the soul may have already been borne back into bones and blood or thick green stalk and leaves. Nothing is wasted. What cannot be eaten by people or in some way used must then be left where other living creatures may benefit. What domestic animals or wild scavengers can't eat will be fed to the plants. The plants feed on the dust of these few remains.

The ancient Pueblo people buried the dead in vacant rooms or partially collapsed rooms adjacent to the main living quarters. Sand and clay used to construct the roof make layers many inches deep once the roof has collapsed. The layers of sand and clay make for easy grave-digging. The vacant room fills with cast-off objects and debris. When a vacant room has filled deep enough, a shallow but adequate grave can be scooped in a far corner. Archaeologists have remarked over formal burials complete with elaborate funerary objects excavated in trash middens of abandoned rooms. But the rocks and adobe mortar of collapsed walls were valued by the ancient people. Because each rock had been carefully selected for size and shape, then chiseled to an even face. Even the pink clay adobe melting with each rainstorm had to be prayed over, then dug and carried some distance. Corn cobs and husks, the rinds and stalks and animal bones were not regarded by the ancient people as filth or garbage. The remains were merely resting at a midpoint in their journey back to dust. Human remains are not so different. They should rest with the bones and rinds where they all may benefit living creatures — small rodents and insects — until their return is completed. The remains of things — animals and plants, the clay and the stones — were treated with respect. Because for the ancient people all these things had spirit and being.

The antelope merely consents to return home with the hunter. All phases of the hunt are conducted with love. The love the hunter and the people have for the Antelope People. And the love of the antelope who agree to give up their meat and blood so that human beings will not starve. Waste of meat or even the thoughtless handling of bones cooked bare will offend the antelope spirits. Next year the hunters will vainly search the dry plains for antelope. Thus it is necessary to return carefully the bones and hair, and the stalks and leaves to the earth who first created them. The spirits remain close by. They do not leave us.

The dead become dust, and in this becoming they are once more joined with the Mother. The ancient Pueblo people called the earth the Mother Creator of all things in this world. Her sister, the Corn Mother, occasionally merges with her because all succulent green life rises out of the depths of the earth.

Rocks and clay are part of the Mother. They emerge in various forms, but at some time before, they were smaller particles or great boulders. At a later time they may again become what they once were. Dust.

A rock shares this fate with us and with animals and plants as well. A rock has being or spirit, although we may not understand it. The spirit may differ from the spirit we know in animals or plants or in ourselves. In the end we all originate from the depths of the earth. Perhaps this is how all beings share in the spirit of the Creator. We do not know.

FROM THE EMERGENCE PLACE

Pueblo potters, the creators of petroglyphs and oral narratives, never conceived of removing themselves from the earth and sky. So long as the human consciousness remains *within* the hills, canyons, cliffs, and the plants, clouds, and sky, the term *landscape*, as it has entered the English language, is misleading. "A portion of territory the eye can comprehend in a single view" does not correctly describe the relationship between the human being and his or her surroundings. This assumes the viewer is somehow *outside* or *separate from* the territory he or she surveys. Viewers are as much a part of the landscape as the boulders they stand on. There is no high mesa edge or mountain peak where one can stand and not immediately be part of all that surrounds. Human identity is linked with all the elements of Creation through the clan: you might belong to the Sun Clan or the Lizard Clan or the Corn

Clan or the Clay Clan.* Standing deep within the natural world, the ancient Pueblo understood the thing as it was—the squash blossom, grasshopper, or rabbit itself could never be created by the human hand. Ancient Pueblos took the modest view that the thing itself (the landscape) could not be improved upon. The ancients did not presume to tamper with what had already been created. Thus *realism*, as we now recognize it in painting and sculpture, did not catch the imaginations of Pueblo people until recently.

The squash blossom itself is *one thing*: itself. So the ancient Pueblo potter abstracted what she saw to be the key elements of the squash blossom—the four symmetrical petals, with four symmetrical stamens in the center. These key elements, while suggesting the squash flower, also link it with the four cardinal directions. By representing only its intrinsic form, the squash flower is released from a limited meaning or restricted identity. Even in the most sophisticated abstract form, a squash flower or a cloud or a lightning bolt became intricately connected with a complex system of relationships which the ancient Pueblo people maintained with each other, and with the populous natural world they lived within. A bolt of lightning is itself, but at the same time it may mean much more. It may be a messenger of good fortune when summer rains are needed. It may deliver death, perhaps the result of manipulations by the Gunnadeyahs, destructive necromancers. Lightning may strike down an evil-doer. Or lightning may strike a person of good will. If the person survives, lightning endows him or her with heightened power.

Pictographs and petroglyphs of constellations or elk or antelope draw their magic in part from the process wherein the focus of all prayer and concentration is upon the thing itself, which, in its turn, guides the hunter's hand. Connection with the spirit dimensions requires a figure or form which is all-inclusive. A "lifelike" rendering of an elk is too restrictive. Only the elk *is* itself. A *realistic* rendering of an elk would be only one particular elk anyway. The purpose of the hunt rituals and magic is to make contact with *all* the spirits of the Elk.

The land, the sky, and all that is within them—the landscape—includes human beings. Interrelationships in the Pueblo landscape are complex and fragile. The unpredictability of the weather, the aridity and harshness of much of the terrain in the high plateau country ex-

*Clan—*A social unit composed of families sharing common ancestors who trace their lineage back to the Emergence where their ancestors allied themselves with certain plants or animals or elements.*

plain in large part the relentless attention the ancient Pueblo people gave the sky and the earth around them. Survival depended upon harmony and cooperation not only among human beings, but among all things — the animate and the less animate, since rocks and mountains were known to move, to travel occasionally.

The ancient Pueblos believed the Earth and the Sky were sisters (or sister and brother in the post-Christian version). As long as good family relations are maintained, then the Sky will continue to bless her sister, the Earth, with rain, and the Earth's children will continue to survive. But the old stories recall incidents in which troublesome spirits or beings threaten the earth. In one story, a malicious ka'tsina, called the Gambler, seizes the Shiwana, or Rainclouds, the Sun's beloved children.* The Shiwana are snared in magical power late one afternoon on a high mountain top. The Gambler takes the Rainclouds to his mountain stronghold where he locks them in the north room of his house. What was his idea? The Shiwana were beyond value. They brought life to all things on earth. The Gambler wanted a big stake to wager in his games of chance. But such greed, even on the part of only one being, had the effect of threatening the survival of all life on earth. Sun Youth, aided by old Grandmother Spider, outsmarts the Gambler and the rigged game, and the Rainclouds are set free. The drought ends, and once more life thrives on earth.

THROUGH THE STORIES WE HEAR WHO WE ARE

All summer the people watch the west horizon, scanning the sky from south to north for rain clouds. Corn must have moisture at the time the tassels form. Otherwise pollination will be incomplete, and the ears will be stunted and shriveled. An inadequate harvest may bring disaster. Stories told at Hopi, Zuni, and at Acoma and Laguna describe drought and starvation as recently as 1900. Precipitation in west-central New Mexico averages fourteen inches annually. The western pueblos are located at altitudes over 5,600 feet above sea level, where winter temperatures at night fall below freezing. Yet evidence of their presence in the high desert plateau country goes back ten thousand years. The ancient Pueblo people not only survived in this environment, but many

*Ka'tsina — *Ka'tsinas are spirit beings who roam the earth and who inhabit kachina masks worn in Pueblo ceremonial dances.*

years they thrived. In A.D. 1100 the people at Chaco Canyon had built cities with apartment buildings of stone five stories high. Their sophistication as sky-watchers was surpassed only by Mayan and Inca astronomers. Yet this vast complex of knowledge and belief, amassed for thousands of years, was never recorded in writing.

Instead, the ancient Pueblo people depended upon collective memory through successive generations to maintain and transmit an entire culture, a world view complete with proven strategies for survival. The oral narrative, or "story," became the medium in which the complex of Pueblo knowledge and belief was maintained. Whatever the event or the subject, the ancient people perceived the world and themselves within that world as part of an ancient continuous story composed of innumerable bundles of other stories.

The ancient Pueblo vision of the world was inclusive. The impulse was to leave nothing out. Pueblo oral tradition necessarily embraced all levels of human experience. Otherwise, the collective knowledge and beliefs comprising ancient Pueblo culture would have been incomplete. Thus stories about the Creation and Emergence of human beings and animals into this World continue to be retold each year for four days and four nights during the winter solstice. The "humma-hah" stories related events from the time long ago when human beings were still able to communicate with animals and other living things. But, beyond these two preceding categories, the Pueblo oral tradition knew no boundaries. Accounts of the appearance of the first Europeans in Pueblo country or of the tragic encounters between Pueblo people and Apache raiders were no more and no less important than stories about the biggest mule deer ever taken or adulterous couples surprised in cornfields and chicken coops. Whatever happened, the ancient people instinctively sorted events and details into a loose narrative structure. Everything became a story.

Traditionally everyone, from the youngest child to the oldest person, was expected to listen and to be able to recall or tell a portion, if only a small detail, from a narrative account or story. Thus the remembering and retelling were a communal process. Even if a key figure, an elder who knew much more than others, were to die unexpectedly, the system would remain intact. Through the efforts of a great many people, the community was able to piece together valuable accounts and crucial information that might otherwise have died with an individual.

Communal storytelling was a self-correcting process in which listeners were encouraged to speak up if they noted an important fact or detail omitted. The people were happy to listen to two or three different versions of the same event or the same humma-hah story. Even conflicting versions of an incident were welcomed for the entertainment they provided. Defenders of each version might joke and tease one another, but seldom were there any direct confrontations. Implicit in the Pueblo oral tradition was the awareness that loyalties, grudges, and kinship must always influence the narrator's choices as she emphasizes to listeners this is the way *she* has always heard the story told. The ancient Pueblo people sought a communal truth, not an absolute. For them this truth lived somewhere within the web of differing versions, disputes over minor points, outright contradictions tangling with old feuds and village rivalries.

A dinner-table conversation, recalling a deer hunt forty years ago when the largest mule deer ever was taken, inevitably stimulates similar memories in listeners. But hunting stories were not merely after-dinner entertainment. These accounts contained information of critical importance about behavior and migration patterns of mule deer. Hunting stories carefully described key landmarks and locations of fresh water. Thus a deer-hunt story might also serve as a "map." Lost travelers, and lost piñon-nut gatherers, have been saved by sighting a rock formation they recognize only because they once heard a hunting story describing this rock formation.

The importance of cliff formations and water holes does not end with hunting stories. As offspring of the Mother Earth, the ancient Pueblo people could not conceive of themselves within a specific landscape. Location, or "place," nearly always plays a central role in the Pueblo oral narratives. Indeed, stories are most frequently recalled as people are passing by a specific geographical feature or the exact place where a story takes place. The precise date of the incident often is less important than the place or location of the happening. "Long, long ago," "a long time ago," "not too long ago," and "recently" are usually how stories are classified in terms of time. But the places where the stories occur are precisely located, and prominent geographical details recalled, even if the landscape is well-known to listeners. Often because the turning point in the narrative involved a peculiarity or special quality of a rock or tree or plant found only at that place. Thus, in the case of many of the Pueblo narratives, it is impossible to determine which came first: the incident or the geographical feature which begs to be brought alive in a story that features some unusual aspect of this location.

There is a giant sandstone boulder about a mile north of Old Laguna, on the road to Paguate. It is ten feet tall and twenty feet in circumference. When I was a child, and we would pass this boulder driving to Paguate village, someone usually made reference to the story about Kochininako, Yellow Woman, and the Estrucuyo, a monstrous giant who nearly ate her. The Twin Hero Brothers saved Kochininako, who had been out hunting rabbits to take home to feed her mother and sisters. The Hero Brothers had heard her cries just in time. The Estrucuyo had cornered her in a cave too small to fit its monstrous head. Kochininako had already thrown to the Estrucuyo all her rabbits, as well as her moccasins and most of her clothing. Still the creature had not been satisfied. After killing the Estrucuyo with their bows and arrows, the Twin Hero Brothers slit open the Estrucuyo and cut out its heart. They threw the heart as far as they could. The monster's heart landed there, beside the old trail to Paguate village, where the sandstone boulder rests now.

It may be argued that the existence of the boulder precipitated the creation of a story to explain it. But sandstone boulders and sandstone formations of strange shapes abound in the Laguna Pueblo area. Yet most of them do not have stories. Often the crucial element in a narrative is the terrain—some specific detail of the setting.

A high dark mesa rises dramatically from a grassy plain fifteen miles southeast of Laguna, in an area known as Swanee. On the grassy plain one hundred and forty years ago, my great-grandmother's uncle and his brother-in-law were grazing their herd of sheep. Because visibility on the plain extends for over twenty miles, it wasn't until the two sheepherders came near the high dark mesa that the Apaches were able to stalk them. Using the mesa to obscure their approach, the raiders swept around from both ends of the mesa. My great-grandmother's relatives were killed, and the herd lost. The high dark mesa played a critical role: the mesa had compromised the safety which the openness of the plains had seemed to assure. Pueblo and Apache alike relied upon the terrain, the very earth herself, to give them protection and aid. Human activities or needs were maneuvered to fit the existing surroundings and conditions. I imagine the last afternoon of my distant ancestors as warm and sunny for late September. They might have been traveling slowly, bringing the sheep closer to Laguna in preparation for the approach of colder weather. The grass was tall and only beginning to change from green to a yellow which matched the late-afternoon sun shining off it. There might have been comfort in the warmth and the sight of the sheep fattening on good pasture which lulled my ancestors into their fatal inattention. They might have had a rifle whereas the Apaches had only bows and arrows. But there would have been four or five Apache raiders, and the surprise attack would have canceled any advantage the rifles gave them.

Survival in any landscape comes down to making the best use of all available resources. On that particular September afternoon, the raiders made better use of the Swanee terrain than my poor ancestors did. Thus the high dark mesa and the story of the two lost Laguna herders became inextricably linked. The memory of them and their story resides in part with the high black mesa. For as long as the mesa stands, people within the family and clan will be reminded of the story of that afternoon long ago. Thus the continuity and accuracy of the oral narratives are reinforced by the landscape — and the Pueblo interpretation of that landscape is *maintained*.

THE MIGRATION STORY: AN INTERIOR JOURNEY

The Laguna Pueblo migration stories refer to specific places — mesas, springs, or cottonwood trees — not only locations which can be visited still, but also locations which lie directly on the state highway route linking Paguate village with Laguna village. In traveling this road as a child with older Laguna people I first heard a few of the stories from that much larger body of stories linked with the Emergence and Migration.* It may be coincidental that Laguna people continue to follow the same route which, according to the Migration story, the ancestors followed south from the Emergence Place. It may be that the route is merely the shortest and best route for car, horse, or foot traffic between Laguna and Paguate villages. But if the stories about boulders, springs, and hills are actually remnants from a ritual that retraces the creation and emergence of the Laguna Pueblo people as a culture, as the people they became, then continued use of that route creates a unique rela-

*The Emergence — *All the human beings, animals, and life which had been created emerged from the four worlds below when the earth became habitable.*
The Migration — *The Pueblo people emerged into the Fifth World, but they had already been warned they would have to travel and search before they found the place they were meant to live.*

tionship between the ritual-mythic world and the actual, everyday world. A journey from Paguate to Laguna down the long incline of Paguate Hill retraces the original journey from the Emergence Place, which is located slightly north of the Paguate village. Thus the landscape between Paguate and Laguna takes on a deeper significance: the landscape resonates the spiritual or mythic dimension of the Pueblo world even today.

Although each Pueblo culture designates a specific Emergence Place — usually a small natural spring edged with mossy sandstone and full of cattails and wild watercress — it is clear that they do not agree on any single location or natural spring as the one and only true Emergence Place. Each Pueblo group recounts its own stories about Creation, Emergence, and Migration, although they all believe that all human beings, with all the animals and plants, emerged at the same place and at the same time.*

Natural springs are crucial sources of water for all life in the high desert plateau country. So the small spring near Paguate village is literally the source and continuance of life for the people in the area. The spring also functions on a spiritual level, recalling the original Emergence Place and linking the people and the spring water to all other people and to that moment when the Pueblo people became aware of themselves as they are even now. The Emergence was an emergence into a precise cultural identity. Thus the Pueblo stories about the Emergence and Migration are not to be taken as literally as the anthropologists might wish. Prominent geographical features and landmarks which are mentioned in the narratives exist for ritual purposes, not because the Laguna people actually journeyed south for hundreds of years from Chaco Canyon or Mesa Verde, as the archaeologists say, or eight miles from the site of the natural springs at Paguate to the sandstone hilltop at Laguna.

The eight miles, marked with boulders, mesas, springs, and river crossings, are actually a ritual circuit or path which marks the interior journey the Laguna people made: a journey of awareness and imagination in which they emerged from being within the earth and from everything included in earth to the culture and people they became, differen-

---

*Creation — *Tse'itsi'nako, Thought Woman, the Spider,* thought about it, and everything she thought came into being. First she thought of three sisters for herself, and they helped her think of the rest of the Universe, including the Fifth World and the four worlds below. The Fifth World is the world we are living in today. There are four previous worlds below this world.

tiating themselves for the first time from all that had surrounded them, always aware that interior distances cannot be reckoned in physical miles or in calendar years.

The narratives linked with prominent features of the landscape between Paguate and Laguna delineate the complexities of the relationship which human beings must maintain with the surrounding natural world if they hope to survive in this place. Thus the journey was an interior process of the imagination, a growing awareness that being human is somehow different from all other life — animal, plant, and inanimate. Yet we are all from the same source: the awareness never deteriorated into Cartesian duality, cutting off the human from the natural world.

The people found the opening into the Fifth World too small to allow them or any of the animals to escape. They had sent a fly out through the small hole to tell them if it was the world which the Mother Creator had promised. It was, but there was the problem of getting out. The antelope tried to butt the opening to enlarge it, but the antelope enlarged it only a little. It was necessary for the badger with her long claws to assist the antelope, and at last the opening was enlarged enough so that all the people and animals were able to emerge up into the Fifth World. The human beings could not have emerged without the aid of antelope and badger. The human beings depended upon the aid and charity of the animals. Only through interdependence could the human beings survive. Families belonged to clans, and it was by clan that the human being joined with the animal and plant world. Life on the high arid plateau became viable when the human beings were able to imagine themselves as sisters and brothers to the badger, antelope, clay, yucca, and sun. Not until they could find a viable relationship to the terrain, the landscape they found themselves in, could they *emerge*. Only at the moment the requisite balance between human and *other* was realized could the Pueblo people become a culture, a distinct group whose population and survival remained stable despite the vicissitudes of climate and terrain.

Landscape thus has similarities with dreams. Both have the power to seize terrifying feelings and deep instincts and translate them into images — visual, aural, tactile — into the concrete where human beings may more readily confront and channel the terrifying instincts or powerful emotions into rituals and narratives which reassure the individual while reaffirming cherished values of the group. The identity of the individual as a part of the group and the greater Whole is strengthened, and the terror of facing the world alone is extinguished.

Even now, the people at Laguna Pueblo spend the greater portion of social occasions recounting recent incidents or events which have occurred in the Laguna area. Nearly always, the discussion will precipitate the retelling of older stories about similar incidents or other stories connected with a specific place. The stories often contain disturbing or provocative material, but are nonetheless told in the presence of children and women. The effect of these inter-family or inter-clan exchanges is the reassurance for each person that she or he will never be separated or apart from the clan, no matter what might happen. Neither the worst blunders or disasters nor the greatest financial prosperity and joy will ever be permitted to isolate anyone from the rest of the group. In the ancient times, cohesiveness was all that stood between extinction and survival, and, while the individual certainly was recognized, it was always as an individual simultaneously bonded to family and clan by a complex bundle of custom and ritual. You are never the first to suffer a grave loss or profound humiliation. You are never the first, and you understand that you will probably not be the last to commit or be victimized by a repugnant act. Your family and clan are able to go on at length about others now passed on, others older or more experienced than you who suffered similar losses.

The wide deep arroyo near the Kings Bar (located acoss the reservation borderline) has over the years claimed many vehicles. A few years ago, when a Viet Nam veteran's new red Volkswagen rolled backwards into the arroyo while he was inside buying a six-pack of beer, the story of his loss joined the lively and large collection of stories already connected with that big arroyo. I do not know whether the Viet Nam veteran was consoled when he was told the stories about the other cars claimed by the ravenous arroyo. All his savings of combat pay had gone for the red Volkswagen. But this man could not have felt any worse than the man who, some years before, had left his children and mother-in-law in his station wagon with the engine running. When he came out of the liquor store his station wagon was gone. He found it and its passengers upside down in the big arroyo. Broken bones, cuts and bruises, and a total wreck of the car. The big arroyo has a wide mouth. Its existence needs no explanation. People in the area regard the arroyo much as they might regard a living being, which has a certain character and personality. I seldom drive past that wide deep arroyo without feeling a familiarity with and even a strange affection for this arroyo. Because as treacherous as it may be, the arroyo maintains a strong connection between human beings and the earth. The arroyo demands from us the caution and attention that constitute respect. It is this sort of respect the old believers have in mind when they tell us we must respect and love the earth.

Hopi Pueblo elders have said that the austere and, to some eyes, barren plains and hills surrounding their mesa-top villages actually help to nurture the spirituality of the Hopi *way*. The Hopi elders say the Hopi people might have settled in locations far more lush where daily life would not have been so grueling. But there on the high silent sandstone mesas that overlook the sandy arid expanses stretching to all horizons, the Hopi elders say the Hopi people must "live by their prayers" if they are to survive. The Hopi way cherishes the intangible: the riches realized from interaction and interrelationships with all beings above all else. Great abundances of material things, even food, the Hopi elders believe, tend to lure human attention away from what is most valuable and important. The views of the Hopi elders are not much different from those elders in all the Pueblos.

The bare vastness of the Hopi landscape emphasizes the visual impact of every plant, every rock, every arroyo. Nothing is overlooked or taken for granted. Each ant, each lizard, each lark is imbued with great value simply because the creature is there, simply because the creature is alive in a place where any life at all is precious. Stand on the mesa edge at Walpai and look west over the bare distances toward the pale blue outlines of the San Francisco peaks where the ka'tsina spirits reside. So little lies between you and the sky. So little lies between you and the earth. One look and you know that simply to survive is a great triumph, that every possible resource is needed, every possible ally — even the most humble insect or reptile. You realize you will be speaking with all of them if you intend to last out the year. Thus it is that the Hopi elders are grateful to the landscape for aiding them in their quest as spiritual people.

Keith H. Basso

"Stalking with Stories":
Names, Places, and Moral Narratives
Among the Western Apache

Shortly before his death in 1960, Clyde Kluckhohn made the following observation in a course he gave at Harvard University on the history of anthropological thought: "The most interesting claims people make are those they make about themselves. Cultural anthropologists should keep this in mind, especially when they are doing fieldwork." This essay focuses on a small set of spoken texts in which members of a contemporary American Indian society express claims about themselves, their language, and the lands on which they live. Specifically, I shall be concerned here with a set of statements that were made by men and women from the Western Apache community at Cibecue, a dispersed settlement of 1100 people that has been inhabited by Apaches for centuries and is located near the center of Fort Apache Indian Reservation in east-central Arizona (see Figure 1). The statements that interest me, which could be supplemented by a large number of others, are the following.

1. The land is always stalking people. The land makes people live right. The land looks after us. The land looks after people. [Mrs. Annie Peaches, age 77, 1977]
2. Our children are losing the land. It doesn't go to work on them anymore. They don't know the stories about what happened at these places. That's why some get into trouble. [Mr. Ronnie Lupe, age 42; Chairman, White Mountain Apache Tribe, 1978]
3. We used to survive only off the land. Now it's no longer that way. Now we live only with money, so we need jobs. But the land still looks after us. We know the names of the places where

Figure 1. Map showing location of the community of Cibecue on the Fort Apache Indian Reservation, Arizona.

everything happened. So we stay away from badness. [Mr. Nick Thompson, age 64, 1980]

4. I think of that mountain called "white rocks lie above in a compact cluster" as if it were my maternal grandmother. I recall stories of how it once was at that mountain. The stories told to me were like arrows. Elsewhere, hearing that mountain's name, I see it. Its name is like a picture. Stories go to work on

you like arrows. Stories make you live right. Stories make you replace yourself. [Mr. Benson Lewis, age 64, 1979]

5. One time I went to L.A., training for mechanic. It was no good, sure no good. I start drinking, hang around bars all the time. I start getting into trouble with my wife, fight sometimes with her. It was *bad*. I forget about this country here around Cibecue. I forget all the names and stories. I don't hear them in my mind anymore. I forget how to live right, forget how to be strong. [Mr. Wilson Lavender, age 52, 1975]

If the texts of these statements resist quick and easy interpretation, it is not because the people who made them are confused or cloudy thinkers. Neither is it because, as one unfortunate commentator would have us believe, the Western Apache are "mystically inclined and correspondingly inarticulate." The problem we face is a semiotic one, a barrier to constructing appropriate sense and significance. It arises from the obvious circumstance that all views articulated by Apache people are informed by their experience in a culturally constituted world of objects and events with which most of us are unfamiliar. What sort of world is it? Or, to draw the question into somewhat sharper focus, what is the cultural context in which Apache statements such as those presented above find acceptance as valid claims about reality?

More specifically, what is required to interpret Annie Peaches's claim that the land occupied by the Western Apache is "always stalking people" and that because of this they know how to "live right"? And how should we understand Chairman Lupe's assertion that Apache children sometimes misbehave because the land "doesn't go to work on them anymore"? Why does Nick Thompson claim that his knowledge of place-names and historical events enables him to "stay away from badness"? And why does Benson Lewis liken place-names to pictures, stories to arrows, and a mountain near the community of Cibecue to his maternal grandmother? What should we make of Wilson Lavender's recollection of an unhappy time in California when forgetting place-names and stories caused him to forget "how to be strong"? Are these claims structured in metaphorical terms, or, given Western Apache assumptions about the physical universe and the place of people within it, are they somehow to be interpreted literally? In any case, what is the reasoning that lies behind the claims, the informal logic of which they are simultaneously products and expressions? Above all, what makes the claims make sense?

I address these and other questions through an investigation of how Western Apaches talk about the natural landscape and the importance they attach to named locations within it. Accordingly, my discussion focuses on elements of language and patterns of speech, my purpose being to discover from these elements and patterns something of how Apache people construe their land and render it intelligible. Whenever Apaches describe the land — or, as happens more frequently, whenever they tell stories about incidents that have occurred at particular points upon it — they take steps to constitute it in relation to themselves. Which is simply to say that in acts of speech, mundane and otherwise, Apaches negotiate images and understandings of the land which are accepted as credible accounts of what it actually is, why it is significant, and how it impinges on the daily lives of men and women.

"LEARN THE NAMES"

Nick Thompson is, by his own admission, an old man. It is possible, he told me once, that he was born in 1918. Beneath snow-white hair cut short, his face is round and compact, his features small and sharply molded. His large, black, and very bright eyes move quickly, and when he smiles he acquires an expression that is at once mischievous and intimidating. I have known him for more than 20 years, and he has instructed me often on matters pertaining to Western Apache language and culture. A man who delights in play, he has also teased me unmercifully, concocted humorous stories about me that are thoroughly apocryphal, and embarrassed me before large numbers of incredulous Apaches by inquiring publicly into the most intimate details of my private life. Described by many people in Cibecue as a true "Slim Coyote" (*ma' ts'ósé*), Nick Thompson is outspoken, incorrigible, and unabashed.[1] He is also generous, thoughtful, and highly intelligent. I value his friendship immensely.

As I bring my Jeep to a halt on the road beside the old man's camp, I hear Nick complaining loudly to his wife about the changing character of life in Cibecue and its regrettable effects on younger members of the community. I have heard these complaints before and I know they are deeply felt. But still, on this sunny morning in June

---

1. *A prominent figure in Western Apache oral literature, Slim Coyote is appreciated by Apache people for his keen and crafty intelligence, his complex and unpredictable personality, and his penchant for getting himself into difficult situations from which he always manages to extract himself, usually with humorous and embarrassing results.*

1977, it is hard to suppress a smile, for the image Nick presents, a striking example of what can be achieved with sartorial *bricolage*, is hardly what one would expect of a staunch tribal conservative. Crippled since childhood and partially paralyzed by a recent stroke, the old man is seated in the shade of a cottonwood tree a few yards from the modest wooden cabin where he lives with his wife and two small grandchildren. He is smoking a mentholated Salem cigarette and is studying with undisguised approval the shoes on his feet — a new pair of bright blue Nike running shoes trimmed in incandescent orange. He is also wearing a pair of faded green trousers, a battered brown cowboy hat, and a white T-shirt with "Disneyland" printed in large red letters across the front. Within easy reach of his chair, resting on the base of an upended washtub, is a copy of the *National Enquirer*, a mug of hot coffee, and an open box of chocolate-covered doughnuts. If Nick Thompson is an opponent of social change, it is certainly not evident from his appearance. But appearances can be deceiving, and Nick, who is an accomplished singer and a medicine man of substantial reputation, would be the first to point this out.

The old man greets me with his eyes. Nothing is said for a minute or two, but then we begin to talk, exchanging bits of local news until enough time has passed for me to politely announce the purpose of my visit. I explain that I am puzzled by certain statements that Apaches have made about the country surrounding Cibecue and that I am anxious to know how to interpret them. To my surprise, Nick does not ask what I have been told or by whom. He responds instead by swinging out his arm in a wide arc. "Learn the names," he says. "Learn the names of all these places." Unprepared for such a firm and unequivocal suggestion (it sounds to me like nothing less than an order), I retreat into silence. "Start with the names," the old man continues. "I will teach you like before. Come back tomorrow morning." Nodding in agreement, I thank Nick for his willingness to help and tell him what I will be able to pay him. He says the wage is fair.

A few moments later, as I stand to take my leave, Nick's face breaks suddenly into a broad smile and his eyes begin to dance. I know that look very well and brace myself for the farewell joke that almost always accompanies it. The old man wastes no time. He says I look lonely. He urges me to have prolonged and abundant sex with very old women. He says it prevents nosebleeds. He says that someday I can write a book about it. Flustered and at a loss for words, I smile weakly and shake my head. Delighted with this reaction, Nick laughs heartily and reaches for his coffee and a chocolate-covered doughnut. Our encounter has come to an end.

I return to the old man's camp the following day and start to learn Western Apache place-names. My lessons, which are interrupted by mapping trips with more mobile Apache consultants, continue for the next ten weeks. In late August, shortly before I must leave Cibecue, Nick asks to see the maps. He is not impressed. "White men need paper maps," he observes. "We have maps in our minds."

Located in a narrow valley at an elevation of 1507 m, the settlement at Cibecue (from *deeschii' bikoh*, "valley with elongated red bluffs") is bisected by a shallow stream emanating from springs that rise in low-lying mountains to the north. Apache homes, separated by horse pastures, agricultural plots, and ceremonial dancegrounds, are located on both sides of the stream for a distance of approximately 8 km. The valley itself, which is bounded on the east and west by a broken series of red sandstone bluffs, displays marked topographic diversity in the form of heavily dissected canyons and arroyos, broad alluvial flood plains, and several clusters of prominent peaks. Vegetation ranges from a mixed Ponderosa Pine-Douglas Fir association near the headwaters of Cibecue Creek to a chaparral community, consisting of scrub oak, cat's-claw, agave, and a variety of cactus species, at the confluence of the creek with the Salt River. In between, numerous other floral associations occur, including dense riparian communities and heavy stands of cottonwood, oak, walnut, and pine.

Together with Michael W. Graves, I have mapped nearly 104 km² in and around the community at Cibecue and within this area have recorded the Western Apache names of 296 locations; it is, to say the least, a region densely packed with place-names. But large numbers alone do not account for the high frequency with which place-names typically appear in Western Apache discourse. In part, this pattern of regular and recurrent use results from the fact that Apaches, who travel a great deal to and from their homes, habitually call on each other to describe their trips in detail. Almost invariably, and in sharp contrast to comparable reports delivered by Anglos living at Cibecue, these descriptions focus as much on *where* events occurred as on the nature and consequences of the events themselves. This practice has been observed in other Apachean groups as well, including, as Harry Hoijer (personal communication, 1973) notes, the Navajo: "Even the most minute occurrences are described by Navajos in close conjunction with their physical settings, suggesting that unless narrated events are *spatially anchored* their significance is somehow reduced and cannot be properly assessed." Hoijer could just as well be speaking of the Western Apache.

Something else contributes to the common use of place-names in Western Apache communities, however, and that, quite simply, is that Apaches enjoy using them. For example, several years ago, when I was stringing a barbed-wire fence with two Apache cowboys from Cibecue, I noticed that one of them was talking quietly to himself. When I listened carefully, I discovered that he was reciting a list of place-names — a long list, punctuated only by spurts of tobacco juice, that went on for nearly ten minutes. Later, when I ventured to ask him about it, he said he frequently "talked names" to himself. Why? "I like to," he said. "I ride that way in my mind." And on dozens of other occasions when I have been working or traveling with Apaches, they have taken satisfaction in pointing out particular locations and pronouncing their names — once, twice, three times or more. Why? "Because we like to," or "Because those names are good to say." More often, however, Apaches account for their enthusiastic use of place-names by commenting on the precision with which the names depict their referents. "That place looks just like its name," someone will explain, or "That name makes me see that place like it really is." Or, as Benson Lewis (example 4) states so succinctly, "Its name is like a picture."

Statements such as these may be interpreted in light of certain facts about the linguistic structure of Western Apache place-names. To begin with, it is essential to understand that all but a very few Apache place-names take the form of complete sentences. This is made possible by one of the most prominent components of the Western Apache language: an elaborate system of prefixes that operates most extensively and productively to modify the stems of verbs. Thus, well-formed sentences can be constructed that are extremely compact yet semantically very rich. It is this combination of brevity and expressiveness, I believe, that appeals to Apaches and makes the mere pronunciation of place-names a satisfying experience.

"ALL THESE PLACES HAVE STORIES"

When I return to Cibecue in the spring of 1978, Nick Thompson is recovering from a bad case of the flu. He is weak, despondent, and uncomfortable. We speak very little and no mention is made of place-names. His wife is worried about him and so am I. Within a week, however, Nick's eldest son comes to my camp with a message: I am to visit his father and bring with me two packs of Salem cigarettes and a dozen chocolate-covered doughnuts. This is good news.

When I arrive at the old man's camp, he is sitting under the cottonwood tree by his house. A blanket is draped across his knees and he is wearing a heavy plaid jacket and a red vinyl cap with white fur-lined earflaps. There is color in his cheeks and the sparkle is back in his eyes. Shortly after we start to converse, and apropos of nothing I can discern, Nick announces that in 1931 he had sexual intercourse eight times in one night. He wants to know if I have ever been so fortunate. His wife, who has brought us each a cup of coffee, hears this remark and tells him that he is a crazy old man. Nick laughs loudly. Plainly, he is feeling better.

Eventually, I ask Nick if he is ready to resume our work together. "Yes," he says, "but no more on names." What then? "Stories," is his reply. "All these places have stories. We shoot each other with them, like arrows. Come back tomorrow morning." Puzzled once again, but suspecting that the old man has a plan he wants to follow, I tell him I will return. We then discuss Nick's wages. He insists that I pay him more than the year before as it is necessary to keep up with inflation. I agree and we settle on a larger sum. Then comes the predictable farewell joke: a fine piece of nonsense in which Nick, speaking English and imitating certain mannerisms he has come to associate with Anglo physicians, diagnoses my badly sunburned nose as an advanced case of venereal disease.[2] This time it is Nick's wife who laughs loudest.

The next day Nick begins to instruct me on aspects of Western Apache storytelling. Consulting on a regular basis with other Apaches from Cibecue as well, I pursue this topic throughout the summer of 1978.

WESTERN APACHE HISTORICAL TALES

If place-names appear frequently in ordinary forms of Western Apache discourse, their use is equally conspicuous in oral narratives. It is here,

2. *Jokes of this type are intended to poke fun at the butt of the joke and, at the same time, to comment negatively on the interactional practices of Anglo-Americans.*

in conjunction with stories Apaches tell, that we can move closer to an interpretation of native claims about the symbolic importance of geographical features and the personalized relationships that individuals may have with them. The people of Cibecue classify "speech" (*yat'i'*) into three major forms: "ordinary talk" (*yat'i'*), "prayer" (*'okąąhí*), and "narratives" or "stories" (*nagoldi'é*). Narratives are further classified into four major and two minor genres. The major genres include "myths" (*godiyįhgo nagoldi'*; literally, "to tell the holiness"), "historical tales" (*'ágodzaahí* or *'ágodzaahí nagoldi'*; literally, "that which has happened" or "to tell of that which has happened"), "sagas" (*nlt'éégo nagoldi'*; literally, "to tell of pleasantness"), and stories that arise in the context of "gossip" (*ch'idii*). The minor genres, which do not concern us here, are "Coyote stories" (*ma' highaalyú' nagoldi'*; literally "to tell of Coyote's travels") and "seduction tales" (*binííma' nagoldi'*; literally, "to tell of sexual desires").

Western Apaches distinguish among the major narrative genres on two basic semantic dimensions: time and purpose. Values on the temporal dimension identify in general terms when the events recounted in narratives took place, while values on the purposive dimension describe the objectives that Apache narrators typically have in recounting them (see Figure 2). Accordingly, "myths" deal with events that occurred "in the beginning" (*'godiyaaná'*), a time when the universe and all things within it were achieving their present form and location. Performed only by the medicine men and medicine women, myths are

Narrative Category	Temporal Locus of Events	Purposes
godiyįhgo nagoldi' ("myth")	*godiyaaná'* ("in the beginning")	to enlighten; to instruct
'ágodzaahí ("historical tale")	*doo 'ánííná'* ("long ago")	to criticize; to warn; to "shoot"
nlt'éégo nagoldi' ("saga")	*dííjįįgo* ("modern times")	to entertain; to engross
ch'idii ("gossip")	*k'ad* ("now")	to inform; to malign

Figure 2. Major categories of Western Apache narrative distinguished by temporal locus of events and primary purposes for narration.

presented for the primary purpose of enlightenment and instruction: to explain and reaffirm the complex processes by which the known world came into existence. "Historical tales" recount events that took place "long ago" (*doo 'ániiná*) when the Western Apache people, having emerged from below the surface of the earth, were developing their own distinctive ways and customs. Most historical tales describe incidents that occurred prior to the coming of the white man, but some of these stories are set in postreservation times, which began for the Western Apache in 1872. Like myths, historical tales are intended to edify, but their main purpose is to alarm and criticize social delinquents (or, as the Apache say, to "shoot" them), thereby impressing such individuals with the undesirability of improper behavior and alerting them to the punitive consequences of further misconduct.

Although sagas deal with historical themes, these narratives are chiefly concerned with events that have taken place in "modern times" (*dííjiigo*), usually within the last 60 or 70 years. In contrast to historical tales, which always focus on serious and disturbing matters, sagas are largely devoid of them. Rather than serving as vehicles of personal criticism, the primary purpose of sagas is to provide their listeners with relaxation and entertainment. Stories of the kind associated with gossip consist of reports in which persons relate and interpret events involving other members of the Western Apache community. These stories, which embrace incidents that have occurred "now" or "at present" (*k'ad*), are often told for no other reason than to keep people informed of local developments. Not uncommonly, however, narratives in gossip are also used to ridicule and malign the character of their subjects.

Nowhere do place-names serve more important communicative functions than in the context of historical tales. As if to accentuate this fact, stories of the *'ágodzaahí* genre are stylistically quite simple. Historical tales require no specialized lexicon, display no unusual syntactical constructions, and involve no irregular morphophonemic alternations; neither are they characterized by unique patterns of stress, pitch, volume, or intonation. In these ways *'agodzaahí* narratives contrast sharply with myths and sagas, which entail the use of a variety of genre-specific stylistic devices. Historical tales also differ from myths and sagas by virtue of their brevity. Whereas myths and sagas may take hours to complete, historical tales can usually be delivered in less than five minutes. Western Apache storytellers point out that this is both fitting and effective, because *'ágodzaahí* stories, like the "arrows" (*k'aa*) they are commonly said to represent, work best when they move swiftly. Finally, and most significant of all, historical tales are distinguished from all other forms of Apache narrative by an opening and closing line that identifies with a place-name where the events in the narrative occurred. These lines frame the narrative, mark it unmistakably as belonging to the *'agodzaahí* genre, and evoke a particular physical setting in which listeners can imaginatively situate everything that happens. It is hardly surprising, then, that while Apache storytellers agree that historical tales are "about" the events recounted in the tales, they also emphasize that the tales are "about" the sites at which the events took place.

If the style of Western Apache historical tales is relatively unremarkable, their content is just the opposite. Without exception, and usually in very graphic terms, historical tales focus on persons who suffer misfortune as the consequence of actions that violate Apache standards for acceptable social behavior. More specifically, *'ágodzaahí* stories tell of persons who have acted unthinkingly and impulsively in open disregard for "Apache custom" (*ndee bi 'at'ee'*) and who pay for their transgressions by being humiliated, ostracized, or killed. Stories of the *'agodzaahí* variety are morality tales pure and simple. When viewed as such by the Apaches—as compact commentaries on what should be avoided so as to deal successfully and effectively with other people—they are highly informative. For what these narratives assert—tacitly, perhaps, but with dozens of compelling examples—is that immoral behavior is irrevocably a community affair and that persons who behave badly will be punished sooner or later. Thus, just as *'ágodzaahí* stories are "about" historical events and their geographical locations, they are also "about" the system of rules and values according to which Apaches expect each other to organize and regulate their lives. In an even more fundamental sense, then, historical tales are "about" what it means to *be* a Western Apache, or, to make the point less dramatically, what it is that being an Apache should normally and properly entail.

To see how this is so, let us consider the texts of three historical tales and examine the manner in which they have been interpreted by their Apache narrators.

    1. It happened at "big cottonwood trees stand spreading here and there."

          Long ago, the Pimas and Apaches were fighting. The Pimas were carrying long clubs made from mesquite wood; they were also heavy and hard. Before dawn the Pimas arrived at Cibecue and attacked the Apaches there. The Pimas attacked while the Apaches were still asleep. The Pimas killed the Apaches with their clubs. An old woman woke up; she heard the Apaches crying out. The old woman thought it was her son-in-law because he often picked on her daughter. The old woman cried out: "You pick on my child a lot. You should act pleasantly toward her." Because the old woman cried out, the Pimas learned where she was. The Pimas came running to the old woman's camp and killed her with their clubs. A young girl ran away from there and hid beneath some bushes. She alone survived.

It happened at "big cottonwood trees stand spreading here and there."

Narrated by Mrs. Annie Peaches, this historical tale deals with the harmful consequences that may come to persons who overstep traditional role boundaries. During the first year of marriage it is customary for young Apache couples to live in the camp of the bride's parents. At this time, the bride's mother may request that her son-in-law perform different tasks and she may also instruct and criticize him. Later, however, when the couple establishes a separate residence, the bride's mother forfeits this right and may properly interfere in her son-in-law's affairs only at the request of her daughter. Mrs. Peaches explains that women who do not abide by this arrangement imply that their sons-in-law are immature and irresponsible, which is a source of acute embarrassment for the young men and their wives. Thus, even when meddling might seem to serve a useful purpose, it should be scrupulously avoided. The woman on whom this story centers failed to remember this — and was instantly killed.

2. It happened at "coarse-textured rocks lie above in a compact cluster."

Long ago, a man became sexually attracted to his stepdaughter. He was living below "coarse-textured rocks lie above in a compact cluster" with his stepdaughter and her mother. Waiting until no one else was present, and sitting alone with her, he started to molest her. The girl's maternal uncle happened to come by and he killed the man with a rock. The man's skull was cracked open. It was raining. The girl's maternal uncle dragged the man's body up above to "coarse-textured rocks lie above in a compact cluster" and placed it there in a storage pit. The girl's mother came home and was told by her daughter of all that had happened. The people who owned the storage pit removed the man's body and put it somewhere else. The people never had a wake for the dead man's body.

It happened at "coarse-textured rocks lie above in a compact cluster."

Narrated by Mr. Benson Lewis, this historical tale deals with the theme of incest, for sexual contact with stepchildren is considered by Western Apaches to be an incestuous act. According to Mr. Lewis, the key line in the story is the penultimate one in which he observes, "The people never had a wake for the dead man's body." We may assume, Mr. Lewis says, that because the dead man's camp was located near the storage pit in which his body was placed, the people who owned the pit were also his relatives. This makes the neglect with which his corpse was treated all the more profound, since kinsmen are bound by the strongest of obligations to care for each other when they die. That the dead man's relatives chose to dispense with customary mortuary ritual shows with devastating clarity that they wished to disown him completely.

3. It happened at "men stand above here and there."

Long ago, a man killed a cow off the reservation. The cow belonged to a Whiteman. The man was arrested by a policeman living at Cibecue at "men stand above here and there." The policeman was an Apache. The policeman took the man to the head Army officer at Fort Apache. There, at Fort Apache, the head Army officer questioned him. "What do you want?" he said. The policeman said, "I need cartridges and food." The policeman said nothing about the man who had killed the Whiteman's cow. That night some people spoke to the policeman. "It is best to report on him," they said to him. The next day the policeman returned to the head Army officer. "Now what do you want?" he said. The policeman said, "Yesterday I was going to say HELLO and GOOD-BYE but I forgot to do it." Again he said nothing about the man he arrested. Someone was working with words on his mind. The policeman returned with the man to Cibecue. He released him at "men stand above here and there."

It happened at "men stand above here and there."

This story, narrated by Nick Thompson, describes what happened to a man who acted too much like a white man. Between 1872 and 1895, when the Western Apache were strictly confined to their reservations by U.S. military forces, disease and malnutrition took the lives of many people. Consequently, Apaches who listen to this historical tale find it perfectly acceptable that the man who lived at "men stand above here and there" should have killed and butchered a white man's cow. What is not acceptable is that the policeman, another Apache from the same settlement, should have arrested the rustler and contemplated taking him to jail. But the policeman's plans were thwarted. Someone used witchcraft on him and made him stupid and forgetful. He never informed the military officer at Fort Apache of the real purpose of his visit, and his second encounter with the officer—in which he apologized for neglecting to say "hello" and "good-bye" the previous day—revealed him to be an absurd and laughable figure. Although Western Apaches find portions of this story amusing, Nick Thompson explains that they understand it first and foremost as a harsh indictment of persons who join with outsiders against members of their own community and who, as if to flaunt their lack of allegiance, parade the attitudes and mannerisms of white men.

Thus far, my remarks on what Western Apache historical tales are "about" have centered on features of textual content. This is a familiar strategy and certainly a necessary one, but it is also incomplete. In addition to everything else—places, events, moral standards, conceptions of cultural identity—every historical tale is also "about" the person at whom it is directed. This is because the telling of a historical tale is always prompted by an individual having committed one or more social offenses to which the act of narration, together with the tale itself, is intended as a critical and remedial response. Thus, on those occasions when 'agodzaahí stories are actually told—by real Apache storytellers, in real interpersonal contexts, to real social offenders—these narratives are understood to be accompanied by an unstated message from the storyteller that may be phrased something like this: "I know that you have acted in a way similar or analogous to the way in which someone acted in the story I am telling you. If you continue to act in this way, something similar or analogous to what happened to the character in the story might also happen to you." This metacommunicative message is just as important as any conveyed by the text of the storyteller's tale. For Apaches contend that if the message is taken to heart by the person at whom the tale is aimed—and if, in conjunction with lessons drawn from the tale itself, he or she resolves to improve his or her be-havior—a lasting bond will have been created between that individual and the site or sites at which events in the tale took place. The cultural premises that inform this powerful idea will be made explicit presently; but first, in order to understand more clearly what the idea involves, let us examine the circumstances that led to the telling of a historical tale at Cibecue and see how this narrative affected the person for whom it was told.

In early June 1977, a 17-year-old Apache woman attended a girls' puberty ceremonial at Cibecue with her hair rolled up in a set of over-sized pink plastic curlers. She had returned home two days before from a boarding school in Utah where this sort of ornamentation was con-sidered fashionable by her peers. Something so mundane would have gone unnoticed by others were it not for the fact that Western Apache women of all ages are expected to appear at puberty ceremonials with their hair worn loose. This is one of several ways that women have of showing respect for the ceremonial and also, by implication, for the people who have staged it. The practice of presenting oneself with free-flowing hair is also understood to contribute to the ceremonial's effectiveness, for Apaches hold that the ritual's most basic objectives, which are to invest the pubescent girl with qualities necessary for life as an adult, cannot be achieved unless standard forms of respect are faithfully observed. On this occasion at Cibecue, everyone was follow-ing custom except the young woman who arrived wearing curlers. She soon became an object of attention and quiet expressions of disap-proval, but no one spoke to her about the large cylindrical objects in her hair.

Two weeks later, the same young woman made a large stack of tortillas and brought them to the camp of her maternal grandmother, a widow in her mid-60s who had organized a small party to celebrate the birthday of her eldest grandson. Eighteen people were on hand, myself included, and all of us were treated to hot coffee and a dinner of boiled beef and potatoes. When the meal was over casual conversation began to flow, and the young woman seated herself on the ground next to her younger sister. And then—quietly, deftly, and totally without warn-ing—her grandmother narrated a version of the historical tale about the forgetful Apache policeman who behaved too much like a white man. Shortly after the story was finished, the young woman stood up, turned away wordlessly, and walked off in the direction of her home. Uncertain of what had happened, I asked her grandmother why she had departed. Had the young woman suddenly become ill? "No," her grandmother replied. "I shot her with an arrow."

Approximately two years after this incident occurred, I found myself again in the company of the young woman with the taste for distinctive hairstyles. She had purchased a large carton of groceries at the trading post at Cibecue, and when I offered to drive her home with them she accepted. I inquired on the way if she remembered the time that her grandmother had told us the story about the forgetful policeman. She said she did and then went on, speaking in English, to describe her reactions to it. "I think maybe my grandmother was getting after me, but then I think maybe not, maybe she's working on somebody else. Then I think back on that dance and I know it's me for sure. I sure don't like how she's talking about me, so I quit looking like that. I threw those curlers away." In order to reach the young woman's camp, we had to pass within a few hundred yards of *ndee dah naazįįh* ("men stand above here and there"), the place where the man had lived who was arrested in the story for rustling. I pointed it out to my companion. She said nothing for several moments. Then she smiled and spoke softly in her own language: "I know that place. It stalks me every day."

The comments of this Western Apache woman on her experience as the target of a historical tale are instructive in several respects. To begin with, her statement enables us to imagine something of the sizable psychological impact that historical tales may have on the persons to whom they are presented. Then, too, we can see how *'ágodzaahí* stories may produce quick and palpable effects on the behavior of such individuals, causing them to modify their social conduct in quite specific ways. Lastly, and most revealing of all, the young woman's remarks provide a clear illustration of what Apaches have in mind when they assert that historical tales may establish highly meaningful relationships between individuals and features of the natural landscape.

To appreciate fully the significance of these relationships, as well as their influence on the lives of Western Apache people, we must explore more thoroughly the manner in which the relationships are conceptualized. This can be accomplished through a closer examination of Apache ideas about the activity of storytelling and the acknowledged power of oral narratives, especially historical tales, to promote beneficial changes in people's attitudes toward their responsibilities as members of a moral community. These ideas, which combine to form a native model of how oral narratives work to achieve their intended effects, are expressed in terms of a single dominant metaphor. By now it should come as no surprise to learn that the metaphor draws heavily on the imagery of hunting.

"STALKING WITH STORIES"

Nick Thompson is tired. We have been talking about hunting with stories for two days now and the old man has not had an easy time of it. Yesterday, my uneven control of the Western Apache language prevented him from speaking as rapidly and eloquently as he would have liked, and on too many occasions I was forced to interrupt him with questions. At one point, bored and annoyed with my queries, he told me that I reminded him of a horsefly buzzing around his head. Later, however, when he seemed satisfied that I could follow at least the outline of his thoughts, he recorded on tape a lengthy statement which he said contained everything he wanted me to know. "Take it with you and listen to it," he said. "Tomorrow we put it in English." For the last six hours that is what we have been trying to do. We are finished now and weary of talking. In the weeks to come I will worry about the depth and force of our translation, and twice more I will return to Nick's camp with other questions. But the hardest work is over and both of us know it. Nick has taught me already that hunting with stories is not a simple matter, and as I prepare to leave I say so. "We know," he says, and that is all. Here is Nick Thompson's statement:

> This is what we know about our stories. They go to work on your mind and make you think about your life. Maybe you've not been acting right. Maybe you've been stingy. Maybe you've been chasing after women. Maybe you've been trying to act like a Whiteman. People don't *like* it! So someone goes hunting for you — maybe your grandmother, your grandfather, your uncle. It doesn't matter. Anyone can do it.
>
> So someone stalks you and tells a story about what happened long ago. It doesn't matter if other people are around — you're going to know he's aiming that story at you. All of a sudden it *hits* you! It's like an arrow, they say. Sometimes it just bounces off — it's too soft and you don't think about anything. But when it's strong it goes in *deep* and starts working on your mind right away. No one

says anything to you, only that story is all, but now you know that people have been watching you and talking about you. They don't like how you've been acting. So you have to think about your life.

Then you feel weak, real weak, like you are sick. You don't want to eat or talk to anyone. That story is working on you now. You keep thinking about it. That story is changing you now, making you want to live right. That story is making you want to replace yourself. You think only of what you did that was wrong and you don't like it. So you want to live better. After a while, you don't like to think of what you did wrong. So you try to forget that story. You try to pull that arrow out. You think it won't hurt anymore because now you want to live right.

It's hard to keep on living right. Many things jump up at you and block your way. But you won't forget that story. You're going to see the place where it happened, maybe every day if it's nearby and close to Cibecue. If you don't see it, you're going to hear its name and see it in your mind. It doesn't matter if you get old — that place will keep on stalking you like the one who shot you with the story. Maybe that person will die. Even so, that place will keep on stalking you. It's like that person is still alive.

Even if we go far away from here to some big city, places around here keep stalking us. If you live wrong, you will hear the names and see the places in your mind. They keep on stalking you, even if you go across oceans. The names of all these places are good. They make you remember how to live right, so you want to replace yourself again.

After stories and storytellers have served this beneficial purpose, features of the physical landscape take over and perpetuate it. Mountains and arroyos step in symbolically for grandmothers and uncles. Just as the latter have "stalked" delinquent individuals in the past, so too particular locations continue to "stalk" them in the present. Such surveillance is essential, Apaches maintain, because "living right" requires constant care and attention, and there is always a possibility that old stories and their initial impact, like old arrows and their wounds, will fade and disappear. In other words, there is always a chance that persons who have "replaced themselves" once — or twice, or three times — will relax their guard against "badness" and slip back into undesirable forms of social conduct. Consequently, Apaches explain, individuals need to be continuously reminded of why they were "shot" in the first place and how they reacted to it at the time. Geographical sites, together with the crisp mental "pictures" of them presented by their names, serve admirably in this capacity, inviting people to recall their earlier failings and encouraging them to resolve, once again, to avoid them in the future. Grandmothers and uncles must perish but the landscape endures, and for this the Apache people are deeply grateful. "The land," Nick Thompson observes, "looks after us. The land keeps badness away."

It should now be possible for the reader to interpret the Western Apache texts at the beginning of this essay in a manner roughly compatible with the Apache ideas that have shaped them. Moreover, we should be able to appreciate that the claims put forward in the texts are reasonable and appropriate, culturally credible and "correct," the principled expressions of an underlying logic that invests them with internal consistency and coherent conceptual structure. As we have seen, this structure is supplied in large part by the hunting metaphor for Western Apache storytelling. It is chiefly in accordance with this metaphor—or, more exactly, in accordance with the symbolic associations it orders and makes explicit—that the claims presented earlier finally make sense.

Thus, the claim of Annie Peaches—that the land occupied by the Western Apache "makes the people live right"—becomes understandable as a proposition about the moral significance of geographical locations as this has been established by historical tales with which the locations are associated. Similarly, Wilson Lavender's claim—that Apaches who fail to remember place-names "forget how to be strong"—rests on an association of place-names with a belief in the power of historical tales to discourage forms of socially unacceptable behavior. Places and their names are also associated by Apaches with the narrators of historical tales, and Benson Lewis's claim—that a certain mountain near Cibecue is his maternal grandmother—can only be interpreted in light of this assumption. The hunting metaphor for storytelling also informs Ronnie Lupe's claim that Western Apache children who are not exposed to historical tales tend to have interpersonal difficulties. As he puts it, "They don't know the stories of what happened at these places. That's why some of them get into trouble." What Mr. Lupe is claiming, of course, is that children who do not learn to associate places and their names with historical tales cannot appreciate the utility of these narratives as guidelines for dealing responsibly and amicably with other people. Consequently, he believes, such individuals are more likely than others to act in ways that run counter to Apache social norms, a sure sign that they are "losing the land." Losing the land is something the Western Apache can ill afford to do, for geographical features have served the people for centuries as indispensable mnemonic pegs on which to hang the moral teachings of their history.

The Apache landscape is full of named locations where time and space have fused and where, through the agency of historical tales, their intersection is made visible for human contemplation. It is also apparent that such locations, charged as they are with personal and social significance, work in important ways to shape the images that Apaches have—or should have—of themselves. Speaking to people like Nick Thompson and Ronnie Lupe, to Annie Peaches and Benson Lewis, one forms the impression that Apaches view the landscape as a repository of distilled wisdom, a stern but benevolent keeper of tradition, an ever-vigilant ally in the efforts of individuals and whole communities to put into practice a set of standards for social living that are uniquely and distinctively their own. In the world that the Western Apache have constituted for themselves, features of the landscape have become symbols of and for this way of living, the symbols of a culture and the enduring moral character of its people.

We may assume that this relationship with the land has been pervasive throughout Western Apache history; but in today's climate of accelerating social change, its importance for Apache people may well be deepening. Communities such as Cibecue, formerly isolated and very much turned inward, were opened up by paved roads less than 20 years ago, and the consequences of improved access and freer travel—including, most noticeably, greatly increased contact with Anglo-Americans—have been pronounced. Younger Apaches, who today complain frequently about the tedium of village life, have started to develop new tastes and ambitions, and some of them are eager to explore the outside world. To the extent that the landscape remains not merely a physical presence but an omnipresent moral force, young Apaches are not likely to forget that the "Whiteman's way" belongs to a different world.

A number of American Indian authors, among them Vine Deloria, Jr. (Sioux), Simon Ortiz (Acoma), Joy Harjo (Creek), and the cultural anthropologist Alfonso Ortiz (San Juan), have written with skill and insight about the moral dimensions of Native American conceptions of the land. No one, however, has addressed the subject with greater sensitivity than N. Scott Momaday (Kiowa). The following passages, taken from his short essay entitled "Native American Attitudes to the Environment" (1974), show clearly what is involved, not only for the Western Apache but for other tribes as well.

> You cannot understand how the Indian thinks of himself in relation to the world around him unless you understand his conception of what is appropriate; particularly what is morally appropriate within the context of that relationship. [1974:82]

> The native American ethic with respect to the physical world is a matter of reciprocal appropriation: appropriations in which man invests himself in the landscape, and at the same time incorporates the landscape into his own most fundamental experience. . . . This appropriation is primarily a matter of imagination which is moral in kind. I mean to say that we are all, I suppose, what we imagine ourselves to be. And that is certainly true of the American Indian. . . . [The Indian] is someone who thinks of himself in a particular way and his idea comprehends his relationship to the physical world. He imagines himself in terms of that relationship and others. And it is that act of imagination, that moral act of imagination, which constitutes his understanding of the physical world. [1974:80]

The summer of 1980 is almost gone and soon I must leave Cibecue. I have walked to Nick's camp to tell him good-bye. This is never easy for me, and we spend most of the time talking about other things. Eventually, I move to thank him for his generosity, his patience, and the things he has taught me. Nick responds by pointing with his lips to a low ridge that runs behind his home in an easterly direction away from Cibecue Creek. "That is a good place," he says. "These are all good places. Goodness is all around."

POSTSCRIPT

If the thoughts presented here have a measure of theoretical interest, recent experience has persuaded me that they can have practical value as well. During the last six years, I have authored a number of documents for use in litigation concerning the settlement of Western Apache water rights in the state of Arizona. Until a final decision is reached in the case, I am not permitted to describe the contents of these documents in detail, but one of my assignments has been to write a report dealing with Apache conceptions of the physical environment. That report contains sections on Western Apache place-names, oral narratives, and certain metaphors that Apache people use to formulate aspects of their relationship with the land.

Preliminary hearings resulted in a judgment favorable to Apache interests, and apparently my report was useful, mainly because it helped pave the way for testimony by native witnesses. One of these witnesses was Nick Thompson; and according to attorneys on both sides, the old man's appearance had a decisive impact. After Nick had taken his place on the stand, he was asked by an attorney why he considered water to be important to his people. A man of eminent good sense, Nick replied, "Because we drink it!" And then, without missing a beat, he launched into a historical tale about a large spring not far from Cibecue — *tú nchaa halį́į́'* ("much water flows up and out") — where long ago a man drowned mysteriously after badly mistreating his wife. When Nick finished the story he went on to say: "We know it happened, so we know not to act like that man who died. It's good we have that water. We need it to live. It's good we have that spring. We need it to live right." Then the old man smiled to himself and his eyes began to dance.

Richard K. Nelson

The Gifts

Cold, clear, and calm in the pale blue morning. Snow on the high peaks brightening to amber. The bay a sheet of gray glass beneath a faint haze of steam. A November sun rises with the same fierce, chill stare of an owl's eye.

I stand at the window watching the slow dawn, and my mind fixes on the island. Nita comes softly down the stairs as I pack gear and complain of having slept too late for these short days. A few minutes later, Ethan trudges out onto the cold kitchen floor, barefoot and half asleep. We do not speak directly about hunting, to avoid acting proud or giving offense to the animals. I say only that I will go to the island and look around; Ethan says only that he would rather stay at home with Nita. I wish he would come along so I could teach him things, but know it will be quieter in the woods with just the dog.

They both wave from the window as I ease the skiff away from shore, crunching through cakes of freshwater ice the tide has carried in from Salmon River. It is a quick run through Windy Channel and out onto the freedom of the Sound, where the slopes of Mt. Sarichef bite cleanly into the frozen sky. The air stings against my face, but the rest of me is warm inside thick layers of clothes. Shungnak whines, paces, and looks over the gunwale toward the still-distant island.

Broad swells looming off the Pacific alternately lift the boat and drop it between smooth-walled canyons of water. Midway across the Sound a dark line of wind descends swiftly from the north, and within minutes we are surrounded by whitecaps. There are two choices: either beat straight up into them or cut an easier angle across the waves and take the spray. I vacillate for a while, then choose the icy spray over the intense pounding. Although I know it is wrong to curse the wind, I do it anyway.

A kittiwake sweeps over the water in great, vaulting arcs, its wings flexed against the touch and billow of the air. As it tilts its head passing over the boat, I think how clumsy and foolish we must look. The island's shore lifts slowly in dark walls of rock and timber that loom above the apron of snow-covered beach. As I approach the shelter of Low Point, the chop fades and the swell is smaller. I turn up along the lee, running between the kelp beds and the surf, straining my eyes for deer that may be feeding at the tide's edge.

Near the end of the point is a narrow gut that opens to a small, shallow anchorage. I ease the boat between the rocks, with lines of surf breaking close on either side. The waves rise and darken, their sharp edges sparkle in the sun, then long manes of spray whirl back as they turn inside out and pitch onto the shallow reef. The anchor slips down through ten feet of crystal water to settle among the kelp fronds and urchin-covered rocks. On a strong ebb the boat would go dry here, but today's tide change is only six feet. Before launching the punt I meticulously glass the broad, rocky shore and the sprawls of brown grass along the timber's edge. A tight bunch of rock sandpipers flashes up from the shingle and an otter loops along the windrows of drift logs, but there is no sign of deer. I can't help feeling a little anxious, because the season is drawing short and our year's supply of meat is not yet in. Throughout the fall, deer have been unusually wary, haunting the dense underbrush and slipping away at the least disturbance. I've come near a few, but these were young ones that I stalked only for the luxury of seeing them from close range.

Watching deer is the same pleasure now that it was when I was younger, when I loved animals only with my eyes and judged hunting to be outside the bounds of morality. Later, I tried expressing this love through studies of zoology, but this only seemed to put another kind of barrier between humanity and nature—the detachment of science and abstraction. Then, through anthropology, I encountered the entirely different views of nature found in other cultures. The hunting peoples were most fascinating because they had achieved deepest intimacy with their wild surroundings and had made natural history the focus of their lives. At the age of twenty-two, I went to live with Eskimos on the arctic coast of Alaska. It was my first year away from home, I had scarcely held a rifle in my hands, and the Eskimos—who call themselves the Real People—taught me their hunter's way.

The experience of living with Eskimos made very clear the direct, physical connectedness between all humans and the environments they draw existence from. Some years later, living with Koyukon Indians in Alaska's interior, I encountered a rich new dimension of that connectedness, and it profoundly changed my view of the world. Traditional Koyukon people follow a code of moral and ethical behavior that keeps a hunter in right relationship to the animals. They teach that all of nature is spiritual and aware, that it must be treated with respect, and that humans should approach the living world with restraint and humility. Now I struggle to learn if these same principles can apply in my own life and culture. Can we borrow from an ancient wisdom to structure a new relationship between ourselves and the environment? Or is Western society irreversibly committed to the illusion that humanity is separate from and dominant over the natural world?

A young bald eagle watches nervously from the peak of a tall hemlock as we bob ashore in the punt. Finally the bird lurches out, scoops its wings full of dense, cold air, and soars away beyond the line of trees. While I trudge up the long tide flat with the punt, Shungnak prances excitedly back and forth hunting for smells. The upper reaches are layered and slabbed with ice; slick cobbles shine like steel in the sun; frozen grass crackles underfoot. I lean the punt on a snow-covered log, pick up my rifle and small pack, and slip through the leafless alders into the forest.

My eyes take a moment adjusting to the sudden darkness, the deep green of boughs, and the somber, shadowy trunks. I feel safe and hidden here. The entire forest floor is covered with deep moss that should sponge gently beneath my feet. But today the softness is gone: frozen moss crunches with each step and brittle twigs snap, ringing out in the crisp air like strangers' voices. It takes a while to get used to this harshness in a forest that is usually so velvety and wet and silent. I listen to the clicking of gusts in the high branches and think that winter has come upon us like a fist.

At the base of a large nearby tree is a familiar patch of white — a scatter of deer bones — ribs, legs, vertebrae, two pelvis bones, and two skulls with half-bleached antlers. I put them here last winter, saying they were for the other animals, to make clear that they were not being thoughtlessly wasted. The scavengers soon picked them clean, the deer mice have gnawed them, and eventually they will be absorbed into the forest again. Koyukon elders say it shows respect, putting animal bones back in a clean, wild place instead of throwing them away with trash or scattering them in a garbage dump. The same obligations of etiquette that bind us to our human community also bind us to the natural community we live within.

Shungnak follows closely as we work our way back through a maze of windfalls, across clear disks of frozen ponds, and around patches of snow beneath openings in the forest canopy. I step and wait, trying to make no sound, knowing we could see deer at any moment. Deep snow has driven them down off the slopes and they are sure to be distracted with the business of the mating season.

We pick our way up the face of a high, steep scarp, then clamber atop a fallen log for a better view ahead. I peer into the semi-open understory of twiggy bushes, probing each space with my eyes. A downy woodpecker's call sparks from a nearby tree. Several minutes pass. Then a huckleberry branch moves, barely twitches, without the slightest noise . . . not far ahead.

Amid the scramble of brush where my eyes saw nothing a few minutes ago, a dim shape materializes, as if its own motion had created it. A doe steps into an open space, deep brown in her winter coat, soft and striking and lovely, dwarfed among the great trees, lifting her nose, looking right toward me. For perhaps a minute we are motionless in each other's gaze; then her head jerks to the left, her ears twitch back and forth, her tail flicks up, and she turns away in the stylized gait deer always use when alarmed.

Quick as a breath, quiet as a whisper, the doe glides off into the forest. Sometimes when I see a deer this way I know it is real at the moment, but afterward it seems like a daydream.

As we work our way back into the woods, I keep hoping for another look at her and thinking that a buck might have been following nearby. Any deer is legal game and I could almost certainly have taken her, but I would rather wait for a larger buck and let the doe bring on next year's young. Shungnak savors the ghost of her scent that hangs in the still air, but she has vanished.

Farther on, the snow deepens to a continuous cover beneath smaller trees, and we cross several sets of deer tracks, including some big prints with long toe drags. The snow helps to muffle our steps, but it is hard to see very far because the bushes are heavily loaded with powder. The thicket becomes a latticed maze of white on black, every branch hung and spangled in a thick fur of jeweled snow. We move through it like eagles cleaving between tumbled columns of cloud. New siftings occasionally drift down when the treetops are touched by the breeze.

Slots between the trunks up ahead shiver with blue where a muskeg opens. I angle toward it, feeling no need to hurry, picking every footstep carefully, stopping often to stare into the dizzying crannies, listening for any splinter of sound, keeping my senses tight and concentrated. A raven calls from high above the forest, and as I catch a glimpse of it an old question runs through my mind: Is this only the bird we see, or does it have the power and awareness Koyukon elders speak of? It lifts and plays on the wind far aloft, then folds up and rolls halfway over, a strong sign of luck in hunting. Never mind the issue of knowing; we should assume that power is here and let ourselves be moved by it.

I turn to look at Shungnak, taking advantage of her sharper hearing and magical sense of smell. She lifts her nose to the fresh but nebulous scent of several deer that have moved through here this morning. I watch her little radar ears, waiting for her to focus in one direction and hold it, hoping to see her body tense as it does when something moves nearby. But so far she only hears the twitching of red squirrels on dry bark. Shungnak and I have very different opinions of the squirrels. They excite her more than any other animal because she believes she will catch one someday. But for the hunter they are deceptive spurts of movement and sound, and their sputtering alarm calls alert the deer.

We approach a low, abrupt rise, covered with obscuring brush and curtained with snow. A lift of wind hisses in the high trees, then drops away and leaves us in near-complete silence. I pause to choose a path through a scramble of blueberry bushes and little windfalls ahead, then glance back at Shungnak. She has her eyes and ears fixed off toward our left, almost directly across the current of breeze. She stands very stiff, quivering slightly, leaning forward as if she has already started to run but cannot release her muscles. I shake my finger at her as a warning to stay.

I listen as closely as possible, but hear nothing. I work my eyes into every dark crevice and slot among the snowy branches, but see nothing. I stand perfectly still and wait, then look again at Shungnak. Her head turns so slowly that I can barely detect the movement, until finally she is looking straight ahead. Perhaps it is just another squirrel. . . . I consider taking a few steps for a better view.

Then I see it.

A long, dark body appears among the bushes, moving deliberately upwind, so close I can scarcely believe I didn't see it earlier. Without looking away, I carefully slide the breech closed and lift the rifle to my shoulder, almost certain that a deer this size will be a buck. Shungnak, now forgotten behind me, must be contorted with the suppressed urge to give chase.

The deer walks easily, silently, along the little rise, never looking our way. Then he makes a sharp turn straight toward us. Thick tines of his antlers curve over the place where I have the rifle aimed. Koyukon elders teach that animals will come to those who have shown them respect, and will allow themselves to be taken in what is only a temporary death. At a moment like this, it is easy to sense that despite my abiding doubt there is a shared world beyond the one we know directly, a world the Koyukon people empower with spirits, a world that demands recognition and exacts a price from those who ignore it.

This is a very large buck. It comes so quickly that I have no chance to shoot, and then it is so close that I haven't the heart to do it. Fifty feet away, the deer lowers his head almost to the ground and lifts a slender branch that blocks his path. Snow shakes down onto his neck and clings to the fur of his shoulders as he slips underneath. Then he half-lifts his head and keeps coming. I ease the rifle down to watch, wondering how much closer he will get. Just now he makes a long, soft rutting call, like the bleating of a sheep except lower and more hollow. His hooves tick against dry twigs hidden by the snow.

In the middle of a step he raises his head all the way up, and he sees me standing there—a stain against the pure white of the forest. A sudden spasm runs through his entire body, his front legs jerk apart, and he freezes all akimbo, head high, nostrils flared, coiled and hard. I can only look at him and wait, my mind snarled with irreconcilable emotions. Here is a perfect buck deer. In the Koyukon way, he has come to me; but in my own he has come too close. I am as congealed and transfixed as he is, as devoid of conscious thought. It is as if my mind has ceased to function and I only have eyes.

But the buck has no choice. He suddenly unwinds in a burst of ignited energy, springs straight up from the snow, turns in mid-flight, stabs the frozen earth again, and makes four great bounds off to the left. His thick body seems to float, relieved of its own weight, as if a deer has the power to unbind itself from gravity.

The same deeper impulse that governs the flight of a deer governs the predator's impulse to pursue it. I watch the first leaps without moving a muscle. Then, not pausing for an instant of deliberation, I raise the rifle back to my shoulder, follow the movement of the deer's fleeing form, and wait until it stops to stare back. Almost at that instant, still moving without conscious thought, freed of the ambiguities that held me before, now no less animal than the animal I watch, my hands warm and steady and certain, acting from a more elemental sense than the ones that brought me to this meeting, I carefully align the sights and let go the sudden power.

The gift of the deer falls like a feather in the snow. And the rifle's sound has rolled off through the timber before I hear it.

I walk to the deer, now shaking a bit with swelling emotion. Shungnak is beside it already, whining and smelling, racing from one side to the other, stuffing her nose down in snow full of scent. She looks off into the brush, searching back and forth, as if the deer that ran is somewhere else, still running. She tries to lick at the blood that trickles down, but I stop her out of respect for the animal. Then, I suppose to consummate her own frustrated predatory energy, she takes a hard nip at its shoulder, shuns quickly away, and looks back as if she expects it to leap to its feet again.

As always, I whisper thanks to the animal for giving itself to me. The words are my own, not something I have learned from the Koyukon. Their elders might say that the words we use in prayer to spirits of the natural world do not matter. Nor, perhaps, does it matter what form these spirits take in our own thoughts. What truly matters is only that prayer be made, to affirm our humility in the presence of nurturing power. Most of humanity throughout history has said prayers to the powers of surrounding nature, which they have recognized as their source of life. Surely it is not too late to recover this ancestral wisdom.

It takes a few minutes before I settle down inside and can begin the other work. Then I hang the deer with rope strung over a low branch and back twice through pulley-loops. I cut away the dark, pungent scent glands on its legs, and next make a careful incision along its belly, just large enough to reach the warm insides. The stomach and intestines come easily and cleanly; I cut through the diaphragm, and there is a hollow sound as the lungs pull free. Placing them on the soft snow, I whisper that these parts are left here for the other animals. Shungnak wants to take some for herself but I tell her to keep away. It is said that the life and awareness leaves an animal's remains slowly, and there are rules about what should be eaten by a dog. She will have her share of the scraps later on, when more of the life is gone.

After the blood has drained out, I sew the opening shut with a piece of line to keep the insides clean, and then toggle the deer's forelegs through a slit in the hind leg joint, so it can be carried like a pack. I am barely strong enough to get it up onto my back, but there is plenty of time to work slowly toward the beach, stopping often to rest and cool down. During one of these stops I hear two ravens in an agitated exchange of croaks and gurgles, and I wonder if those black eyes have already spotted the remnants. No pure philanthropist, the raven gives a hunter luck only as a way of creating luck for himself.

Finally, I push through the low boughs of the beachside trees and ease my burden down. Afternoon sun throbs off the water, but a chill north wind takes all warmth from it. Little gusts splay in dark patterns across the anchorage; the boat paces on its mooring line; the Sound is racing with whitecaps. I take a good rest, watching a fox sparrow flit among the drift logs and a bunch of crows hassling over some bit of food at the water's edge.

Though I feel utterly satisfied, grateful, and contented, there is much to do and the day will slope away quickly. We are allowed more than one deer, so I will stay on the island for another look around tomorrow. It takes two trips to get everything out to the skiff, then we head up the shore toward the little cabin and secure anchorage at Bear Creek. By the time the boat is unloaded and tied off, the wind has faded and a late afternoon chill sinks down in the pitched, hard shadow of Sarichef.

Half-dry wood hisses and sputters, giving way reluctantly to flames in the rusted stove. It is nearly dusk when I bring the deer inside and set to work on it. Better to do this now than to wait, in case tomorrow is another day of luck. The animal hangs from a low beam, dim-lit by the kerosene lamp. I feel strange in its presence, as if it still watches, still glows with something of its life, still demands that nothing be done or spoken carelessly. A hunter should never let himself be deluded by pride or a false sense of dominance. It is not through our own power that we take life in nature; it is through the power of nature that life is given to us.

The soft hide peels away slowly from shining muscles, and the inner perfection of the deer's body is revealed. Koyukon and Eskimo hunters teach a refined art of taking an animal into its component parts, easing blades through crisp cartilage where bone joins bone, following the body's own design until it is disarticulated. There is no ugliness in it, only hands moving in concert with the beauty of an animal's making. Perhaps we have been too removed from this to understand, and we have lost touch with the process of one life being passed on to another. As my hands work inside the deer, it is as if something has already begun to flow into me.

When the work is finished, I take two large slices from the hind quarter and put them in a pan atop the now-crackling stove. In a separate pot, I boil scraps of meat and fat for Shungnak, who has waited with as much patience as possible for a husky raised in a hunter's team up north. When the meat is finished cooking I sit on a sawed log and eat straight from the pan.

A meal could not be simpler, more satisfying, or more directly a part of the living process. I wish Ethan was here to share it, and I would explain to him again that when we eat the deer its flesh is then our flesh. The deer changes form and becomes us, and we in turn become creatures made of deer. Each time we eat the deer we should remember it and feel gratitude for what it has given us. And each time, we should carry a thought like a prayer inside: "Thanks to the animal and to all that made it—the island and the forest, the air, and the rain . . ." We should remember that in the course of things, we are all generations of deer and of the earth-life that feeds us.

Warm inside my sleeping bag, I let the fire ebb away to coals. The lamp is out. The cabin roof creaks in the growing cold. I drift toward sleep, feeling pleased that there is no moon, so the deer will wait until dawn to feed. On the floor beside me, Shungnak jerks and whimpers in her dog's dreams.

Next morning we are in the woods with the early light. We follow yesterday's tracks, and just beyond the place of the buck, a pair of does drifts at the edge of sight and disappears. For an hour we angle north, then come slowly back somewhat deeper in the woods, moving crosswise to a growing easterly breeze. In two separate places, deer snort and pound away, invisible beyond a shroud of brush. Otherwise there is nothing.

Sometime after noon we come to a narrow muskeg with scattered lodgepole pines and a ragged edge of bushy, low-growing cedar. I squint against the sharp glare of snow. It has that peculiar look of old powder, a bit settled and touched by wind, very lovely but without the airy magic of a fresh fall. I gaze up the muskeg's easy slope, and above the encroaching wall of timber, seamed against the deep blue sky, is the brilliant peak of Sarichef with a great plume of snow streaming off in what must be a shuddering gale. It has a contradictory look of absoluteness and unreality about it, like a Himalayan summit suspended in mid-air over the saddle of a low ridge.

I move very slowly up the muskeg's east side, away from the

breeze and in the sun's full warmth. Deer tracks crisscross the opening, but none of the animals stopped here to feed. Next to the bordering trees, the tracks follow a single, hard-packed trail, showing the deers' preference for cover. Shungnak keeps her nose to the thickly scented snow. We come across a pine sapling that a buck has torn with his antlers, scattering twigs and flakes of bark all around. But his tracks are hardened, frosted, and lack sharpness, so they are at least a day old.

We slip through a narrow point of trees, then follow the open edge again, pausing long moments between each footstep. A mixed tinkle of crossbills and siskins moves through the high timber, and a squirrel rattles from deep in the woods, too far off to be scolding us. Shungnak begins to pick up a strong ribbon of scent, but she hears nothing. I stop for several minutes to study the muskeg's long, raveled fringe, the tangle of shade and thicket, the glaze of mantled boughs.

Then my eye barely catches a fleck of movement up ahead, near the ground and almost hidden behind the trunk of a leaning pine, perhaps a squirrel's tail or a bird. I lift my hand slowly to shade the sun, stand dead still, and wait to see if something is there. Finally it moves again.

At the very edge of the trees, almost out of sight in a little swale, small and furry and bright-tinged, turning one direction and then another, is the funnel of a single ear. Having seen this, I soon make out the other ear and the slope of a doe's forehead. Her neck is behind the leaning pine, but on the other side I can barely see the soft, dark curve of her back above the snow. She is comfortably bedded, gazing placidly into the distance, chewing her cud.

Shungnak has stopped twenty yards behind me in the point of trees and has no idea about the deer. I shake my finger at her until she lays her ears back and sits. Then I watch the doe again. She is fifty yards ahead of me, ten yards beyond the leaning tree, and still looking off at an angle. Her left eye is clearly visible and she refuses to turn her head away, so it might be impossible to get any closer. Perhaps I should just wait here, in case a buck is attending her nearby. But however improbable it might be under these circumstances, a thought is lodged in my mind: I can get near her.

My first step sinks down softly, but the second makes a loud budging sound. She snaps my way, stops chewing, and stares for several minutes. It seems hopeless, especially out here in an open field of crisp snow with only the narrow treetrunk for a screen. But she slowly turns away and starts to chew again. I move just enough so the tree blocks her eye and the rest of her head, but I can still see her ears. Every time she chews they shake just a bit, so I can watch them and step when her hearing is obscured by the sound of her own jaws.

Either this works or the deer has decided to ignore me, because after a short while I am near enough so the noise of my feet has to reach her easily. She should have jumped up and run long ago, but instead she lays there in serene repose. I deliberate on every step, try for the softest snow, wait long minutes before the next move, stalking like a cat toward ambush. I watch beyond her, into the surrounding shadows and across to the muskeg's farther edge, for the shape of a buck deer; but there is nothing. I feel ponderous, clumsy-footed, out-of-place, inimical. I should turn and run away, take fear on the deer's behalf, flee the mirrored image in my mind. But I clutch the cold rifle at my side and creep closer.

The wind refuses to blow and my footsteps seem like thunder in the still sunshine. But the doe only turns once to look my way, without even pointing her ears toward me, then stares off and begins to chew again.

I am ten feet from the leaning tree. My heart pounds so hard, I think those enchanted ears should hear the rush of blood in my temples. Yet a strange certainty has come into me, a quite unmystical confidence. Perhaps she has decided I am another deer, a buck attracted by her musk or a doe feeding gradually toward her. My slow pace and lapses of stillness would not seem human. For myself, I have lost awareness of elapsed time; I have no feeling of patience or impatience. It is as if the deer has moved slowly toward me on a cloud of snow, and I am adrift in the pure motion of experience.

I take the last step to the trunk of the leaning pine. It is bare of branches, scarcely wider than my hand, but perfectly placed to break my odd profile. There is no hope of getting any closer, so I slowly poke my head out to watch. She has an ideal spot: screened from the wind, warmed by the sun, and with a clear view of the muskeg. I can see muscles working beneath the close fur of her jaw, the rise and fall of her side each time she breathes, the shining edge of her ebony eye.

I hold absolutely still, but her body begins to stiffen, she lifts her head higher, and her ears twitch anxiously. Then instead of looking at me she turns her face to the woods, shifting her ears toward a sound I cannot hear. A few seconds later, the unmistakable voice of a buck drifts up, strangely disembodied, as if it comes from an animal somewhere underneath the snow. I huddle as close to the tree as I can, press against the hard, dry bark, and peek out around its edge.

There is a gentle rise behind the doe, scattered with sapling pines and clusters of juniper bushes. A rhythmic crunching of snow comes invisibly from the slope, then a bough shakes . . . and a buck walks easily into the open sunshine.

Focusing his attention completely on the doe, he comes straight toward her and never sees my intrusive shape just beyond. He slips through a patch of small trees, stops a few feet from where she lies, lowers his head and stretches it toward her, then holds this odd pose for a long moment. She reaches her muzzle out to one side, trying to find his scent. When he starts to move up behind her she stands quickly, bends her body into a strange sideways arc, and stares back at him. A moment later she walks off a bit, lifts her tail, and puts droppings in her tracks. The buck moves to the warm ground of her bed and lowers his nose to the place where her female scent is strongest.

Inching like a reptile on a cold rock, I have stepped out from the tree and let my whole menacing profile become visible. The deer are thirty feet away and stand well apart, so they can both see me easily. I am a hunter hovering near his prey and a watcher craving inhuman love, torn between the deepest impulses, hot and shallow-breathed and seething with unreconciled intent, hidden from opened eyes that look into the nimbus of sun and see nothing but the shadow they have chosen for themselves. In this shadow now, the hunter has vanished and only the watcher remains.

Drawn by the honey of the doe's scent, the buck steps quickly toward her. And now the most extraordinary thing happens. The doe turns away from him and walks straight for me. There is no hesitation, only a wild deer coming along the trail of hardened snow where the other deer have passed, the trail in which I stand at this moment. She raises her head, looks at me, and steps without hesitation.

My existence is reduced to a pair of eyes; a rush of unbearable heat flushes through my cheeks; and a sense of absolute certainty fuses in my mind.

The snow blazes so brightly that my head aches. The deer is a dark form growing larger. I look up at the buck, half embarrassed, as if to apologize that she has chosen me over him. He stares at her for a moment, turns to follow, then stops and watches anxiously. I am struck by how gently her narrow hooves touch the trail, how little sound they make as she steps, how thick the fur is on her flank and shoulder, how unfathomable her eyes look. I am consumed with a sense of her perfect elegance in the brilliant light. And then I am lost again in the whirling intensity of experience.

The doe is now ten feet from me. She never pauses or looks away. Her feet punch down mechanically into the snow, coming closer and closer, until they are less than a yard from my own. Then she stops, stretches her neck calmly toward me, and lifts her nose.

There is not the slightest question in my mind, as if this was certain to happen and I have known all along exactly what to do. I slowly raise my hand and reach out . . .

And my fingers touch the soft, dry, gently needling fur on top of the deer's head, and press down to the living warmth of flesh underneath.

She makes no move and shows no fear, but I can feel the flaming strength and tension that flow in her wild body as in no other animal I have ever touched. Time expands and I am suspended in the clear reality of that moment.

Then, by the flawed conditioning of a lifetime among fearless domesticated things, I instinctively drop my hand and let the deer smell it. Her dark nose, wet and shining, touches gently against my skin at the exact instant I realize the absoluteness of my error. And a jolt runs through her entire body as she realizes hers. Her muscles seize and harden; she seems to wrench her eyes away from me but her body remains, rigid and paralyzed. Having been deceived by her other senses, she keeps her nose tight against my hand for one more moment.

Then all the energy inside her triggers in a series of exquisite bounds. She flings out over the hummocks of snow-covered moss, suspended in effortless flight like fog blown over the muskeg in a gale. Her body leaps with such power that the muscles should twang aloud like a bowstring; the earth should shudder and drum; but I hear no sound. In the center of the muskeg she stops to look back, as if to confirm what must seem impossible. The buck follows in more earth-bound undulations; they dance away together, and I am left in the meeting-place alone.

There is a blur of rushing feet behind me. No longer able to restrain herself, Shungnak dashes past, buries her nose in the soft tracks, and then looks back to ask if we can run after them. I had completely forgotten her, sitting near enough to watch the whole encounter, somehow resisting what must have been a prodigious urge to explode in chase. When I reach out to hug her, she smells the hand that touched the deer. And it seems as if it happened long ago.

For the past year I have kept a secret dream, that I would someday come close enough to touch a deer on this island. But since the idea came it seemed harder than ever to get near them. Now, totally unexpected and in a strange way, it has happened. Was the deer caught by some reckless twinge of curiosity? Had she never encountered a human on this wild island? Did she yield to some odd amorous confusion? I really do not care. I would rather accept this as pure experience and not give in to the notion that everything must be explained.

Nor do I care to think that I was chosen to see some manifestation of power, because I have little tolerance for such dreams of self-importance. I have never asked that nature open any doors to reveal the truth of spirit or mystery; I aspire to no shaman's path; I expect no visions, no miracles except the ones that fill every instant of ordinary life.

But there are vital lessons in the experience of moments such as these, if we live them in the light of wisdom taken from the earth and shaped by generations of elders. Two deer came and gave the choices to me. One deer I took and we will now share a single body. The other deer I touched and we will now share that moment. These events could be seen as opposites, but they are in fact identical. Both are founded in the same principles, the same relationship, the same reciprocity.

Move slowly, stay quiet, watch carefully . . . and be ever humble. Never show the slightest arrogance or disrespect. Koyukon elders would explain, in words quite different from my own, that I moved into two moments of grace, or what they would call luck. This is the source of success for a hunter or a watcher, not skill, not cleverness, not guile. Something is only given in nature, never taken.

I have heard the elders say that everything in nature has its own spirit and possesses a power beyond ours. There is no way to prove them right or wrong, though the beauty and interrelatedness of things should be evidence enough. We need not ask for shining visions as proof, or for a message from a golden deer glowing in the sky of our dreams. Above all else, we should assume that power moves in the world around us and act accordingly. If it is a myth, then spirit is within the myth and we should live by it. And if there is a commandment to follow, it is to approach all of earth-life, of which we are a part, with humility and respect.

Well soaked and shivering from a rough trip across the Sound, we pull into the dark waters of the bay. Sunset burns on Twin Peaks and the spindled ridge of Antler Mountain. The little house is warm with lights that shimmer on the calm near shore. I see Nita looking from the window and Ethan dashes out to wait by the tide, pitching rocks at the mooring buoy. He strains to see inside the boat, knowing that a hunter who tells his news aloud may offend the animals by sounding boastful. But when he sees the deer his excited voice seems to roll up and down the mountainside.

He runs for the house with Shungnak, carrying a load of gear, and I know he will burst inside with the news. Ethan, joyous and alive, boy made of deer.

David Abram

The Ecology of Magic

A PERSONAL INTRODUCTION TO THE INQUIRY

Late one evening I stepped out of my little hut in the rice paddies of eastern Bali and found myself falling through space. Over my head the black sky was rippling with stars, densely clustered in some regions, almost blocking out the darkness between them, and more loosely scattered in other areas, pulsing and beckoning to each other. Behind them all streamed the great river of light with its several tributaries. Yet the Milky Way churned beneath me as well, for my hut was set in the middle of a large patchwork of rice paddies, separated from each other by narrow two-foot-high dikes, and these paddies were all filled with water. The surface of these pools, by day, reflected perfectly the blue sky, a reflection broken only by the thin, bright green tips of new rice. But by night the stars themselves glimmered from the surface of the paddies, and the river of light whirled through the darkness underfoot as well as above; there seemed no ground in front of my feet, only the abyss of star-studded space falling away forever.

I was no longer simply beneath the night sky, but also *above* it—the immediate impression was of weightlessness. I might have been able to reorient myself, to regain some sense of ground and gravity, were it not for a fact that confounded my senses entirely: between the constellations below and the constellations above drifted countless fireflies, their lights flickering like the stars, some drifting up to join the clusters of stars overhead, others, like graceful meteors, slipping down from above to join the constellations underfoot, and all these paths of light upward and downward were mirrored, as well, in the still surface of the paddies. I felt myself at times falling through space, at other moments floating and drifting. I simply could not dispel the profound vertigo and giddiness; the paths of the fireflies, and their reflections in the water's surface, held me in a sustained trance. Even after I crawled back to my hut and shut the door on this whirling world, I felt that now the little room in which I lay was itself floating free of the earth.

Magic in its perhaps most primordial sense, is the experience of existing in a world made up of multiple intelligences, the intuition that every form one perceives—from the swallow swooping overhead to the fly on a blade of grass, and indeed the blade of grass itself—is an *experiencing* form, an entity with its own predilections and sensations, albeit sensations that are very different from our own.

To be sure, the shaman's ecological function, his or her role as intermediary between human society and the land, is not always obvious at first blush, even to a sensitive observer. We see the sorcerer being called upon to cure an ailing tribesman of his sleeplessness, or perhaps simply to locate some missing goods; we witness him entering into a trance and sending his awareness into other dimensions in search of insight and aid. Yet we should not be so ready to interpret these dimensions as "supernatural," nor to view them as realms entirely "internal" to the personal psyche of the practitioner. For it is likely that the "inner world" of our Western psychological experience, like the supernatural heaven of Christian belief, originates in the loss of our ancestral reciprocity with the animate earth. When the animate powers that surround us are suddenly construed as having less significance than ourselves, when the generative earth is abruptly defined as a determinate object devoid of its own sensations and feelings, then the sense of a wild and multiplicitous otherness (in relation to which human existence has always oriented itself) must migrate, either into a supersensory heaven beyond the natural world, or else into the human skull itself—the only allowable refuge, in this world, for what is ineffable and unfathomable.

But in genuinely oral, indigenous cultures, the sensuous world itself remains the dwelling place of the gods, of the numinous powers that can either sustain or extinguish human life. It is not by sending his awareness out beyond the natural world that the shaman makes contact with the purveyors of life and health, nor by journeying into his personal psyche; rather, it is by propelling his awareness laterally, outward into the depths of a landscape at once both sensuous and psychological, the living dream that we share with the soaring hawk, the spider, and the stone silently sprouting lichens on its coarse surface.

The magician's intimate relationship with nonhuman nature becomes most evident when we attend to the easily overlooked background of his or her practice—not just to the more visible tasks of curing and ritual aid to which she is called by individual clients, or to the larger ceremonies at which she presides and dances, but to the content of the prayers by which she prepares for such ceremonies, and to the countless ritual gestures that she enacts when alone, the daily propitiations and praise that flow from her toward the land and *its* many voices.

* * *

All this attention to nonhuman nature was, very far from my intended focus when I embarked on my research into the uses of magic and medicine in Indonesia, and it was only gradually that I became aware of this more subtle dimension of the native magician's craft. The first shift in my preconceptions came rather quietly, when I was staying for some days in the home of a young "balian," or magic practitioner, in the interior of Bali. I had been provided with a simple bed in a separate, one-room building in the balian's family compound (most compound homes, in Bali, are comprised of several separate small buildings, for sleeping and for cooking, set on a single enclosed plot of land), and early each morning the balian's wife came to bring me a small but delicious bowl of fruit, which I ate by myself, sitting on the ground outside, leaning against the wall of my hut and watching the sun slowly climb through the rustling palm leaves. I noticed, when she delivered the fruit, that my hostess was also balancing a tray containing many little green plates: actually, they were little boat-shaped platters, each woven simply and neatly from a freshly cut section of palm frond. The platters were two or three inches long, and within each was a little mound of white rice. After handing me my breakfast, the woman and the tray disappeared from view behind the other buildings, and when she came by some minutes later to pick up my empty bowl, the tray in her hands was empty as well.

The second time that I saw the array of tiny rice platters, I asked my hostess what they were for. Patiently, she explained to me that they were offerings for the household spirits. When I inquired about the Balinese term that she used for "spirit," she repeated the same explanation, now in Indonesian, that these were gifts for the spirits of the family compound, and I saw that I had understood her correctly. She handed me a bowl of sliced papaya and mango, and disappeared around the corner. I pondered for a minute, then set down the bowl, stepped to the side of my hut, and peered through the trees. At first unable to see her, I soon caught sight of her crouched low beside the corner of one of the other buildings, carefully setting what I presumed was one of the offerings on the ground at that spot. Then she stood up with the tray, walked to the other visible corner of the same building, and there slowly and carefully set another offering on the ground. I returned to my bowl of fruit and finished my breakfast. That afternoon, when the rest of the household was busy, I walked back behind the building where I had seen her set down the two offerings. There were the little green platters, resting neatly at the two rear corners of the building. But the mounds of rice that had been within them were gone.

The next morning I finished the sliced fruit, waited for my hostess to come by for the empty bowl, then quietly headed back behind the buildings. Two fresh palm-leaf offerings sat at the same spots where the others had been the day before. These were filled with rice. Yet as I gazed at one of these offerings, I abruptly realized, with a start, that one of the rice kernels was actually moving.

Only when I knelt down to look more closely did I notice a line of tiny black ants winding through the dirt to the offering. Peering still closer, I saw that two ants had already climbed onto the offering and were struggling with the uppermost kernel of rice; as I watched, one of them dragged the kernel down and off the leaf, then set off with it back along the line of ants advancing on the offering. The second ant took another kernel and climbed down with it, dragging and pushing, and fell over the edge of the leaf, then a third climbed onto the offering. The line of ants seemed to emerge from a thick clump of grass around a nearby palm tree. I walked over to the other offering and discovered another line of ants dragging away the white kernels. This line emerged from the top of a little mound of dirt, about fifteen feet away from the buildings. There was an offering on the ground by a corner of my building as well, and a nearly identical line of ants. I walked into my room chuckling to myself: the balian and his wife had gone to so much trouble to placate the household spirits with gifts, only to have their offerings stolen by little six-legged thieves. What a waste! But then a strange thought dawned on me: what if the ants were the very "household spirits" to whom the offerings were being made?

The family compound, like most on this tropical island, had been constructed in the vicinity of several ant colonies. Since a great deal of cooking took place in the compound (which housed, along with the balian and his wife and children, various members of their extended family), and also much preparation of elaborate offerings of foodstuffs for various rituals and festivals in the surrounding villages, the grounds and the buildings at the compound were vulnerable to infestations by the sizable ant population. Such invasions could range from rare nuisances to a periodic or even constant siege. It became apparent that the daily palm-frond offerings served to preclude such an attack by the natural forces that surrounded (and underlay) the family's land. The daily gifts of rice kept the ant colonies occupied—and, presumably, satisfied. Placed in regular, repeated locations at the corners of various structures around the compound, the offerings seemed to establish certain boundaries between the human and ant communities; by honoring this boundary with gifts, the humans apparently hoped to persuade the insects to respect the boundary and not enter the buildings.

Yet I remained puzzled by my hostess's assertion that these were gifts "for the spirits." To be sure, there has always been some confusion between our Western notion of "spirit" (which so often is defined in contrast to matter or "flesh"), and the mysterious presences to which tribal and indigenous cultures pay so much respect. I have already alluded to the gross misunderstandings arising from the circumstance that many of the earliest Western students of these other customs were Christian missionaries all too ready to see occult ghosts and immaterial phantoms where the tribespeople were simply offering their respect to the local winds. While the notion of "spirit" has come to have, for us in the West, a primarily anthropomorphic or human association, my encounter with the ants was the first of many experiences suggesting to me that the "spirits" of an indigenous culture are primarily those modes of intelligence or awareness that do *not* possess a human form.

As humans, we are well acquainted with the needs and capacities of the human body—we *live* our own bodies and so know, from within, the possibilities of our form. We cannot know, with the same familiarity and intimacy, the lived experience of a grass snake or a snapping turtle; we cannot readily experience the precise sensations of a hummingbird sipping nectar from a flower or a rubber tree soaking up sunlight. And yet we do know how it feels to sip from a fresh pool of water or to bask and stretch in the sun. Our experience may indeed be a variant of these other modes of sensitivity; nevertheless, we cannot, as humans, precisely experience the living sensations of another form. We do not know, with full clarity, their desires or motivations; we cannot know, or can never be sure that we know, what they know. That the deer does experience sensations, that it carries knowledge of how to orient in the land, of where to find food and how to protect its young, that it knows well how to survive in the forest without the tools upon which we depend, is readily evident to our human senses. That the mango tree has the ability to create fruit, or the yarrow plant the power to reduce a child's fever, is also evident. To humankind, these Others are purveyors of secrets, carriers of intelligence that we ourselves often need: it is these Others who can inform us of unseasonable changes in the weather, or warn us of imminent eruptions and earthquakes, who show us, when foraging, where we may find the ripest berries or the best route to follow back home. By watching them build their nests and shelters, we glean clues regarding how to strengthen our own dwellings, and their deaths teach us of our own. We receive from them countless gifts of food, fuel, shelter, and clothing. Yet still they remain Other to us, inhabiting their own cultures and displaying their own rituals, never wholly fathomable.

Moreover, it is not only those entities acknowledged by Western civilizations as "alive," not only the other animals and the plants that speak, as spirits, to the senses of an oral culture, but also the meandering river from which those animals drink, and the torrential monsoon rains, and the stone that fits neatly into the palm of the hand. The mountain, too, has its thoughts. The forest birds whirring and chattering as the sun slips below the horizon are vocal organs of the rain forest itself.

Bali, of course, is hardly an aboriginal culture; the complexity of its temple architecture, the intricacy of its irrigation systems, the resplendence of its colorful festivals and crafts all bespeak the influence of various civilizations, most notably the Hindu complex of India. In Bali, nevertheless, these influences are thoroughly intertwined with the indigenous animism of the Indonesian archipelago; the Hindu gods and goddesses have been appropriated, as it were, by the more volcanic, eruptive spirits of the local terrain.

Yet the underlying animistic cultures of Indonesia, like those of many islands in the Pacific, are steeped as well in beliefs often referred to by ethnologists as "ancestor worship," and some may argue that the ritual reverence paid to one's long-dead human ancestors (and the assumption of their influence in present life), easily invalidates my assertion that the various "powers" or "spirits" that move through the discourse of indigenous, oral peoples are ultimately tied to nonhuman (but nonetheless sentient) forces in the enveloping landscape.

This objection rests upon certain assumptions implicit in Christian civilization, such as the assumption that the "spirits" of dead persons necessarily retain their human form, and that they reside in a domain outside of the physical world to which our senses give us access. However, most indigenous tribal peoples have no such ready recourse to an immaterial realm outside earthly nature. Our strictly human heavens and hells have only recently been abstracted from the sensuous world that surrounds us, from this more-than-human realm that abounds in its own winged intelligences and cloven-hoofed powers. For almost all oral cultures, the enveloping and sensuous earth remains the dwelling place of both the living *and* the dead. The "body"—whether human or otherwise—is not yet a mechanical object in such cultures, but is a magical entity, the mind's own sensuous aspect, and at death the body's decomposition into soil, worms, and dust can only signify the gradual reintegration of one's ancestors and elders into the living landscape, from which all, too, are born.

Each indigenous culture elaborates this recognition of metamorphosis in its own fashion, taking its clues from the particular terrain in which it is situated. Often the invisible atmosphere that animates the visible world—the subtle presence that circulates both within us and between all things—retains within itself the spirit or breath of the dead person until the time when that breath will enter and animate another visible body—a bird, or a deer, or a field of wild grain. Some cultures may burn, or "cremate," the body in order to more completely return the person, as smoke, to the swirling air, while that which departs as flame is offered to the sun and stars, and that which lingers as ash is fed to the dense earth. Still other cultures may dismember the body, leaving certain parts in precise locations where they will likely be found by condors, or where they will be consumed by mountain lions or by wolves, thus hastening the re-incarnation of that person into a particular animal realm within the landscape. Such examples illustrate simply that death, in tribal cultures, initiates a metamorphosis wherein the person's presence does not "vanish" from the sensible world (where would it go?) but rather remains as an animating force within the vastness of the landscape, whether subtly, in the wind, or more visibly, in animal form, or even as the eruptive, ever to be appeased, wrath of the volcano. "Ancestor worship," in its myriad forms, then, is ultimately another mode of attentiveness to nonhuman nature; it signifies not so much an awe or reverence of human powers, but rather a reverence for those forms that awareness takes when it is *not* in human form, when the familiar human embodiment dies and decays to become part of the encompassing cosmos.

This cycling of the human back into the larger world ensures that the other forms of experience that we encounter—whether ants, or willow trees, or clouds—are never absolutely alien to ourselves. Despite the obvious differences in shape, and ability, and style of being, they remain at least distantly familiar, even familial. It is, paradoxically, this perceived kinship or consanguinity that renders the difference, or otherness, so eerily potent.

* * *

Several months after my arrival in Bali, I left the village in which I was staying to visit one of the pre-Hindu sites on the island. I arrived on my bicycle early in the afternoon, after the bus carrying tourists from the coast had departed. A flight of steps took me down into a lush, emerald valley, lined by cliffs on either side, awash with the speech of the river and the sighing of the wind through high, unharvested grasses. On a small bridge crossing the river I met an old woman carrying a wide basket on her head and holding the hand of a little, shy child; the woman grinned at me with the red, toothless smile of à beetle nut chewer. On the far side of the river I stood in front of a great moss-covered complex of passageways, rooms, and courtyards carved by hand out of the black volcanic rock.

I noticed, at a bend in the canyon downstream, a further series of caves carved into the cliffs. These appeared more isolated and remote, unattended by any footpath I could discern. I set out through the grasses to explore them. This proved much more difficult than I anticipated, but after getting lost in the tall grasses, and fording the river three times, I at last found myself beneath the caves. A short scramble up the rock wall brought me to the mouth of one of them, and I entered on my hands and knees. It was a wide but low opening, perhaps only four feet high, and the interior receded only about five or six feet into the cliff. The floor and walls were covered with mosses, painting the cave with green patterns and softening the harshness of the rock; the place, despite its small size—or perhaps because of it— had an air of great friendliness. I climbed to two other caves, each about the same size, but then felt drawn back to the first one, to sit cross-legged on the cushioning moss and gaze out across the emerald canyon. It was quiet inside, a kind of intimate sanctuary hewn into the stone. I began to explore the rich resonance of the enclosure, first just humming, then intoning a simple chant taught to me by a balian some days before. I was delighted by the overtones that the cave added to my voice, and sat there singing for a long while. I did not notice the change in the wind outside, or the cloud shadows darkening the valley, until the rains broke—suddenly and with great force. The first storm of the monsoon!

I had experienced only slight rains on the island before then, and was startled by the torrential downpour now sending stones tumbling along the cliffs, building puddles and then ponds in the green landscape below, swelling the river. There was no question of returning home—I would be unable to make my way back through the flood to the valley's entrance. And so, thankful for the shelter, I recrossed my legs to wait out the storm. Before long the rivulets falling along the cliff above gathered themselves into streams, and two small waterfalls cascaded across the cave's mouth. Soon I was looking into a solid curtain of water, thin in some places, where the canyon's image flickered unsteadily, and thickly rushing in others. My senses were all but overcome by the wild beauty of the cascade and by the roar of sound, my body trembling inwardly at the weird sense of being sealed into my hiding place.

And then, in the midst of all this tumult, I noticed a small, delicate activity. Just in front of me, and only an inch or two to my side of the torrent, a spider was climbing a thin thread stretched across the mouth of the cave. As I watched, it anchored another thread to the top of the opening, then slipped back along the first thread and joined the two at a point about midway between the roof and the floor. I lost sight of the spider then, and for a while it seemed that it had vanished, thread and all, until my focus rediscovered it. Two more threads now radiated from the center to the floor, and then another; soon the spider began to swing between these as on a circular trellis, trailing an ever-lengthening thread which it affixed to each radiating rung as it moved from one to the next, spiraling outward. The spider seemed wholly undaunted by the tumult of waters spilling past it, although every now and then it broke off its spiral dance and climbed to the roof or the floor to tug on the radii there, assuring the tautness of the threads, then crawled back to where it left off. Whenever I lost the correct focus, I waited to catch sight of the spinning arachnid, and then let its dancing form gradually draw the lineaments of the web back into visibility, tying my focus into each new knot of silk as it moved, weaving my gaze into the everdeepening pattern.

And then, abruptly, my vision snagged on a strange incongruity: another thread slanted across the web, neither radiating nor spiraling from the central juncture, violating the symmetry. As I followed it with my eyes, pondering its purpose in the overall pattern, I began to realize that it was on a different plane from the rest of the web, for the web slipped out of focus whenever this new line became clearer. I soon saw that it led to its own center, about twelve inches to the right of the first, another nexus of forces from which several threads stretched to the floor and the ceiling. And then I saw that there was a *different* spider spinning this web, testing its tautness by dancing around it like the first, now setting the silken cross weaves around the nodal point and winding outward. The two spiders spun independently of each other, but to my eyes they wove a single intersecting pattern. This widening of my gaze soon disclosed yet another spider spiraling in the cave's mouth, and suddenly I realized that there were *many* overlapping webs coming into being, radiating out at different rhythms from myriad centers poised—some higher, some lower, some minutely closer to my eyes and some farther—between the stone above and the stone below.

I sat stunned and mesmerized before this ever-complexifying expanse of living patterns upon patterns, my gaze drawn like a breath into one converging group of lines, then breathed out into open space, then drawn down into another convergence. The curtain of water had become utterly silent—I tried at one point to hear it, but could not. My senses were entranced.

I had the distinct impression that I was watching the universe being born, galaxy upon galaxy. . . .

Night filled the cave with darkness. The rain had not stopped. Yet, strangely, I felt neither cold nor hungry—only remarkably peaceful and at home. Stretching out upon the moist, mossy floor near the back of the cave, I slept.

When I awoke, the sun was staring into the canyon, the grasses below rippling with bright blues and greens. I could see no trace of the webs, nor their weavers. Thinking that they were invisible to my eyes without the curtain of water behind them, I felt carefully with my hands around and through the mouth of the cave. But the webs were gone. I climbed down to the river and washed, then hiked across and out of the canyon to where my cycle was drying in the sun, and headed back to my own valley.

I have never, since that time, been able to encounter a spider without feeling a great strangeness and awe. To be sure, insects and spiders are not the only powers, or even central presences, in the Indonesian universe. But they were *my* introduction to the spirits, to the magic afoot in the land. It was from them that I first learned of the intelligence that lurks in nonhuman nature, the ability that an alien form of sentience has to echo one's own, to instill a reverberation in oneself that temporarily shatters habitual ways of seeing and feeling, leaving one open to a world all alive, awake, and aware. It was from such small beings that my senses first learned of the countless worlds within worlds that spin in the depths of this world that we commonly inhabit, and from them that I learned that my body could, with practice, enter sensorially into these dimensions. The precise and minuscule craft of the spiders had so honed and focused my awareness that the very webwork of the universe, of which my own flesh was a part, seemed to be being spun by their arcane art. I have already spoken of the ants, and of the fireflies, whose sensory likeness to the lights in the night sky had taught me the fickleness of gravity. The long and cyclical trance that we call malaria was also brought to me by insects, in this case mosquitoes, and I lived for three weeks in a feverish state of shivers, sweat, and visions.

I had rarely before paid much attention to the natural world. But my exposure to traditional magicians and seers was shifting my senses; I became increasingly susceptible to the solicitations of non-human things. In the course of struggling to decipher the magicians' odd gestures or to fathom their constant spoken references to powers unseen and unheard, I began to *see* and to *hear* in a manner I never had before. When a magician spoke of a power or "presence" lingering in the corner of his house, I learned to notice the ray of sunlight that was then pouring through a chink in the roof, illuminating a column of drifting dust, and to realize that that column of light was indeed a power, influencing the air currents by its warmth, and indeed influencing the whole mood of the room; although I had not consciously seen it before, it had already been structuring my experience. My ears began to attend, in a new way, to the songs of birds—no longer just a melodic background to human speech, but meaningful speech in its own right, responding to and commenting on events in the surrounding earth. I became a student of subtle differences: the way a breeze may flutter a single leaf on a whole tree, leaving the other leaves silent and unmoved (had not that leaf, then, been brushed by a magic?); or the way the intensity of the sun's heat expresses itself in the precise rhythm of the crickets. Walking along the dirt paths, I learned to slow my pace in order to *feel* the difference between one nearby hill and the next, or to taste the presence of a particular field at a certain time of day when, as I had been told by a local *dukun,* the place had a special power and proffered unique gifts. It was a power communicated to my senses by the way the shadows of the trees fell at that hour, and by smells that only then lingered in the tops of the grasses without being wafted away by the wind, and other elements I could only isolate after many days of stopping and listening.

And gradually, then, other animals began to intercept me in my wanderings, as if some quality in my posture or the rhythm of my breathing had disarmed their wariness; I would find myself face-to-face with monkeys, and with large lizards that did not slither away when I spoke, but leaned forward in apparent curiosity. In rural Java, I often noticed monkeys accompanying me in the branches overhead, and ravens walked toward me on the road, croaking. While at Pangandaran, a nature preserve on a peninsula jutting out from the south coast of Java ("a place of many spirits," I was told by nearby fishermen), I stepped out from a clutch of trees and found myself looking into the face of one of the rare and beautiful bison that exist only on that island. Our eyes locked. When it snorted, I snorted back; when it shifted its shoulders, I shifted my stance; when I tossed my head, it tossed *its* head in reply. I found myself caught in a nonverbal conversation with this Other, a gestural duet with which my conscious awareness had very little to do. It was as if my body in its actions was suddenly being motivated by a wisdom older than my thinking mind, as though it was held and moved by a logos, deeper than words, spoken by the Other's body, the trees, and the stony ground on which we stood.

John Fowles

The Green Man

One of the oldest and most diffused bodies of myth and folklore has accreted round the idea of the man in the trees. In all his manifestations, as dryad, as stag-headed Herne, as outlaw, he possesses the characteristic of elusiveness, a power of 'melting' into the trees, and I am certain the attraction of the myth is so profound and universal because it is constantly 'played' inside every individual consciousness.

This notion of the green man — or green woman, as W. H. Hudson made her — seen as emblem of the close connection between the actuality of present consciousness (not least in its habitual flight into a mental greenwood) and what science has censored in man's attitude to nature — that is, the 'wild' side, the inner feeling as opposed to the outer, fact-bound, conforming face imposed by fashion — helped me question my old pseudo-scientist self. But it also misled me for a time. In the 1950s I grew interested in the Zen theories of 'seeing' and of aesthétics: of learning to look beyond names at things-in-themselves. I stopped bothering to identify species new to me, I concentrated more and more on the familiar, daily nature around me, where I then lived. But living without names is impossible, if not downright idiocy, in a writer; and living without explanation or speculation as to causality, little better — for Western man, at least. I discovered, too, that there was less conflict than I had imagined between nature as external assembly of names and facts and nature as internal feeling; that the two modes of seeing or knowing could in fact marry and take place almost simultaneously, and enrich each other.

Achieving a relationship with nature is both a science and an art, beyond mere knowledge or mere feeling alone; and I now think beyond oriental mysticism, transcendentalism, 'meditation techniques' and the rest — or at least as we in the West have converted them to our use, which seems increasingly in a narcissistic way: to make ourselves feel more positive, more meaningful, more dynamic. I do not believe nature is to be reached that way either, by turning it into a therapy, a free clinic for admirers of their own sensitivity. The subtlest of our alienations from it, the most difficult to comprehend, is our need to use it in some way, to derive some personal yield. We shall never fully understand nature (or ourselves), and certainly never respect it, until we dissociate the wild from the notion of usability—however innocent and harmless the use. For it is the general uselessness of so much of nature that lies at the root of our ancient hostility and indifference to it.

There is a kind of coldness, I would rather say a stillness, an empty space, at the heart of our forced co-existence with all the other species of the planet. Richard Jefferies coined a word for it: the ultra-humanity of all that is not man . . . not with us or against us, but outside and beyond us, truly alien. It may sound paradoxical, but we shall not cease to be alienated—by our knowledge, by our greed, by our vanity—from nature until we grant it its unconscious alienation from us.

I am not one of those supreme optimists who think all the world's ills, and especially this growing divide between man and nature, can be cured by a return to a quasi-agricultural, ecologically 'caring' society. It is not that I doubt it might theoretically be so cured; but the possibility of the return defeats my powers of imagination. The majority of Western man is now urban, and the whole world will soon follow suit. A very significant tilt of balance in human history is expected by the end of the coming decade: over half of all mankind will by then have moved inside towns and cities. Any hope of reversing that trend, short of some universal catastrophe, is as tiny and precarious as the Monarch butterflies I watched, an autumn or two ago, migrating between the Fifth Avenue skyscrapers in central Manhattan. All chance of a close acquaintance with nature, be it through intellect and education, be it in the simplest way of all, by having it near at hand, recedes from the many who already effectively live in a support system in outer space, a creation of science, and without means to escape it, culturally or economically.

But the problem is not, or only minimally, that nature itself is in imminent danger or that we shall lose touch with it simply because we have less access to it. A number of species, environments, unusual ecologies are in danger, there are major pollution problems; but even in our most densely populated countries the ordinary wild remains far from the brink of extinction. We may not exaggerate the future threats and dangers, but we do exaggerate the present and actual state of this global nation—underestimate the degree to which it is still surviving and accessible to those who want to experience it. It is far less nature itself that is yet in true danger than our attitude to it. Already we behave as if we live in a world that holds only a remnant of what there actually is; in a world that may come, but remains a black hypothesis, not a present reality.

I believe the major cause of this more mental than physical rift lies less in the folly or one-sidedness of our societies and educational systems, or in the historical evolution of man into a predominantly urban and industrial creature, a thinking termite, than in the way we have, during these last hundred and fifty years, devalued the kind of experience or knowledge we loosely define as art; and especially in the way we have failed to grasp its deepest difference from science. No art is truly teachable in its essence. All the knowledge in the world of its techniques can provide in itself no more than imitations or replicas of previous art. What is irreplaceable in any object of art is never, in the final analysis, its technique or craft, but the personality of the artist, the expression of his or her unique and individual feeling. All major advances in technique have come about to serve this need. Techniques in themselves are always reducible to sciences, that is, to learnability. Once Joyce has written, Picasso painted, Webern composed, it requires only a minimal gift, besides patience and practice, to copy their techniques exactly; yet we all know why this kind of technique-copy, even when it is so painstakingly done—for instance, in painting—that it deceives museum and auction-house experts, is counted worthless beside the work of the original artist. It is not *of* him or her, it is not art, but imitation.

As it is with the true 'making' arts, so it is with the other aspects of human life of which we say that full knowledge or experience also requires an art—some inwardly creative or purely personal factor beyond the power of external teaching to instil or science to predict. Attempts to impart recipes or set formulae as to practice and enjoyment are always two-edged, since the question is not so much whether they may or may not enrich the normal experience of that abstract thing, the normal man or woman, but the certainty that they must in some way damage that other essential component of the process, the contribution of the artist in this sense—the individual experiencer, the 'green man' hidden in the leaves of his or her unique and once-only being.

Telling people why, how and when they ought to feel this or that—whether it be with regard to the enjoyment of nature, of food, or sex, or anything else—may, undoubtedly sometimes does, have a useful function in dispelling various kinds of socially harmful ignorance. But what this instruction cannot give is the deepest benefit of any art, be it of making, or of knowing, or of experiencing: which is self-expression and self-discovery. The last thing a sex-manual can be is an *ars amoris* — a science of coupling, perhaps, but never an art of love. Exactly the same is true of so many nature-manuals. They may teach you how and what to look for, what to question in external nature; but never in your own nature.

In science greater knowledge is always and indisputably good; it is by no means so throughout all human existence. We know it from art proper, where achievement and great factual knowledge, or taste, or intelligence, are in no way essential companions; if they were, our best artists would also be our most learned academics. We can know it by reducing the matter to the absurd, and imagining that God, or some Protean visitor from outer space, were at one fell swoop to grant us all knowledge. Such omniscience would be worse than the worst natural catastrophe, for our species as a whole; would extinguish its soul, lose it all pleasure and reason for living.

This is not the only area in which, like the rogue computer beloved of science fiction fans, some socially or culturally consecrated proposition — which may be true or good in its social or cultural context — exends itself to the individual; but it is one of the most devitalizing. Most mature artists know that great general knowledge is more a hindrance than a help. It is only innately mechanical, salami-factory novelists who set such great store by research; in nine cases out of ten what natural knowledge and imagination cannot supply is in any case precisely what needs to be left out. The green man in all of us is well aware of this. In practice we spend far more time rejecting knowledge than trying to gain it, and wisely. But it is in the nature of all society, let alone one deeply imbued with a scientific and technological ethos, to bombard us with ever more knowledge — and to make any questioning or rejection of it unpatriotic and immoral.

Art and nature are siblings, branches of the one tree; and nowhere more than in the continuing inexplicability of many of their processes, and above all those of creation and of effect on their respective audiences. Our approach to art, as to nature, has become increasingly scientized (and dreadfully serious) during this last century. It sometimes seems now as if it is principally there not for itself but to provide material for labeling, classifying, analysing — specimens for 'setting,' as I used to set moths and butterflies. This is of course especially true of

— and pernicious in — our schools and universities. I think the first sign that I might one day become a novelist (though I did not then realize it) was the passionate detestation I developed at my own school for all those editions of examination books that began with a long introduction: an anatomy lesson that always reduced the original text to a corpse by the time one got to it, a lifeless demonstration of a pre-established proposition. It took me years to realize that even geniuses, the Shakespeares, the Racines, the Austens, have human faults.

Obscurity, the opportunity a work of art gives for professional explainers to show their skills, has become almost an aesthetic virtue; at another extreme the notion of art as vocation (that is, something to which one is genetically suited) is dismissed as non-scientific and inegalitarian. It is not a gift beyond personal choice, but one that can be acquired, like knowledge of science, by rote, recipe and hard work. Elsewhere we become so patterned and persuaded by the tone of the more serious reviewing of art in our magazines and newspapers that we no longer notice their overwhelmingly scientific tone, or the paradox of this knowing-naming technique being applied to a non-scientific object — one whose production the artist himself cannot fully explain, and one whose effect the vast majority of the non-reviewing audience do not attempt to explain.

The professional critic or academic would no doubt say this is mere ignorance, that both artists and audiences have to be taught to understand themselves and the object that links them, to make the relationship articulate and fully conscious; defoliate the wicked green man, hunt him out of his trees. Of course there is a place for the scientific, or quasi-scientific, analysis of art, as there is (and far greater) for that of nature. But the danger, in both art and nature, is that all emphasis is placed on the created, not the creation.

All artefacts, all bits of scientific knowledge, share one thing in common: that is, they come to us from the past, they are relics of something already observed, deduced, formulated, created, and as such qualify to go through the Linnaean and every other scientific mill. Yet we cannot say that the 'green' or creating process does not happen or has no importance just because it is largely private and beyond lucid description and rational analysis. We might as well argue that the young wheat-plant is irrelevant because it can yield nothing to the miller and his stones. We know that in any sane reality the green blade is as much the ripe grain as the child is father to the man. Nor of course does the simile apply to art alone, since we are all in a way creating our future out of our present, our 'published' outward behaviour out of our inner green being. One main reason we may seldom feel this happening is that society does not want us to. Such random personal creativity is offensive to all machines.

I began this wander through the trees . . . in search of that much looser use of the word 'art' to describe a way of knowing and experiencing and enjoying outside the major modes of science and art proper . . . a way not concerned with scientific discovery and artefacts, a way that is internally rather than externally creative, that leaves very little public trace; and yet which for those very reasons is almost wholly concentrated in its own creative process. It is really only the qualified scientist or artist who can escape from the interiority and constant nowness, the green chaos of this experience, by making some aspect of it exterior and so fixing it in past time, or known knowledge. Thereby they create new, essentially parasitical orders and categories of phenomena that in turn require both a science and an art of experiencing.

But nature is unlike art in terms of its product—what we in general know it by. The difference is that it is not only created, an external object with a history, and so belonging to a past; but also creating in the present, as we experience it. As we watch, it is so to speak rewriting, reformulating, repainting, rephotographing itself. It refuses to stay fixed and fossilized in the past, as both the scientist and the artist feel it somehow ought to; and both will generally try to impose this fossilization on it.

Verbal tenses can be very misleading here: we stick adamantly in speech to the strict protocol of actual time. Of and in the present we speak in the present, of the past in the past. But our psychological tenses can be very different. Perhaps because I am a writer (and nothing is more fictitious than the past in which the first, intensely alive and present, draft of a novel goes down on the page), I long ago noticed this in my naturalist self: that is, a disproportionately backward element in any present experience of nature, a retreat or running-back to past knowledge and experience, whether it was the definite past of personal memory or the indefinite, the imperfect, of stored 'ological' knowledge and proper scientific behaviour. This seemed to me often to cast a mysterious veil of deadness, of having already happened, over the actual and present event or phenomenon.

I had a vivid example of it only a few years ago in France, long after I thought I had grown wise to this self-imposed brainwashing. I came on my first Soldier Orchid, a species I had long wanted to encounter, but hitherto never seen outside a book. I fell on my knees before it in a way that all botanists will know. I identified, to be quite certain, with Professors Clapham, Tutin and Warburg in hand (the standard British *Flora*), I measured, I photographed, I worked out where I was on the map, for future reference. I was excited, very happy, one always remembers one's 'firsts' of the rarer species. Yet five minutes after my wife had finally (other women are not the only form of adultery) torn me away, I suffered a strange feeling. I realized I had not actually *seen* the three plants in the little colony we had found. Despite all the identifying, measuring, photographing, I had managed to set the experience in a kind of present past, a having-looked, even as I was temporally and physically still looking. If I had the courage, and my wife the patience, I would have asked her to turn and drive back, because I knew I had just fallen, in the stupidest possible way, into an ancient trap. It is not necessarily too little knowledge that causes ignorance; possessing too much, or wanting to gain too much, can produce the same result.

There is something in the nature of nature, in its presentness, its seeming transience, its creative ferment and hidden potential, that corresponds very closely with the wild, or green man, in our psyches; and it is a something that disappears as soon as it is relegated to an automatic pastness, a status of merely classifiable *thing*, image taken *then*. 'Thing' and 'then' attract each other. If it is thing, it was then; if it was then, it is thing. We lack trust in the present, this moment, this actual seeing, because our culture tells us to trust only the reported back, the publicly framed, the edited, the thing set in the clearly artistic or the clearly scientific angle of perspective. One of the deepest lessons we have to learn is that nature, of its nature, resists this. It waits to be seen otherwise, in its individual presentness and from our individual presentness.

I come now near the heart of what seems to me to be the single greatest danger in the rich legacy left us by Linnaeus and the other founding fathers of all our sciences and scientific mores and methods—or more fairly, left us by our leaping evolutionary ingenuity in the invention of tools. All tools, from the simplest word to the most advanced space probe, are disturbers and rearrangers of primordial nature and reality—are, in the dictionary definition, 'mechanical implements for working upon something.' What they have done, and I suspect in direct proportion to our ever-increasing dependence on them, is to addict us o purpose: both to looking for purpose in everything external to us and to looking internally for purpose in everything we do — to seek explanation of the outside world by purpose, to justify our seeking by purpose. This addiction to finding a reason, a function, a quantifiable yield, has now infiltrated all aspects of our lives — and become effectively synonymous with pleasure. The modern version of hell is purposelessness.

Nature suffers particularly in this, and our indifference and hostility to it is closely connected with the fact that its only purpose appears to be being and surviving. We may think that this comprehends all animate existence, including our own; and so it must, ultimately; but we have long ceased to be content with so abstract a motive. A scientist would rightly say that all form and behaviour in nature is highly purposive, or strictly designed for the end of survival — specific or genetic, according to theory. But most of this functional purpose is hidden to the non-scientist, indecipherable; and the immense variety of nature appears to hide nothing, nothing but a green chaos at the core — which we brilliantly purposive apes can use and exploit as we please, with a free conscience.

A green chaos. Or a wood.

Gary Nabhan

Enduring Seeds—
The Sacred Lotus and the Common Bean

I

Cupping my two hands together, I can hold a single seed of each plant that grows on the acres of desert lands where I live. Filling a bottlegourd canteen full with one seed from each genetically-distinct cultivated variety native to this continent, I could also carry around samples of all of the domesticated crop strains known to have existed prehistorically in North America.

When pooled together, these microcosms of life called germ plasm contain more information than is contained in the Library of Congress. In a handful of wild seeds taken from any one natural community, there is hidden the distillation of millions of years of coevolution of plants and animals, of their coming together, coexisting, partitioning various resources, competing or becoming dependent upon one another. In a gourdful of crop seeds taken from fields of Native American farmers, we have the living reverberations of how past cultures selected plant characters that reflected their human sense of taste, color, proportion, and fitness in a particular environment. We also have the germ that generates many stories, many ceremonies, and many blessings.

Seeds. One might simply define them as fertilized, matured ovules, the results of sexual reproduction in plants. Usually, we think of seeds as the enclosed germ of flowering plants, but "naked" ovules such as those of conifers and cycads qualify as well. We tend to focus on the seeds of flowering plants—the angiosperms—because they make up more than half the food that humankind ingests every day. They are the pits of fruits, the grains, the nuts, and the beans that have sustained us ever since we emerged as a species 200,000–500,000 years ago. Today, the fate of these angiosperms is in our hands more than ever before.

In one hand, you hold the seedlike fruits of the sacred lotus, in the other, a common bean. Both of these seeds are elliptic in shape and enclosed in hard, glossy coats. Each is weighty enough for its presence to be felt in the palm of your hand, much the same as a small coin or other historic form of monetary currency—certain seashells or precious stones. Yet in contrast to these other forms of currency, the sacred lotus and the common bean are living, and capable of regeneration. The lotus seed, in fact, can outlive you. And if scientists' dreams come true, beans dunked in liquid nitrogen deep freezes may soon outstrip the human lifespan.

Humankind has long associated itself with both of these seeds, but has affected them in different ways. The aquatic lotus retains its wild-type survival mechanisms; the garden bean does not.

The sacred lotus, *Nelumbo nucifera*, falls into the most primitive flowering plant group still surviving, the ranalean complex, which also includes water lilies, magnolias, and tulip trees. It and its New World counterpart, the water chinquapin, *Nelumbo lutea*, are both aquatic plants. They produce sweetly scented, solitary blossoms that project above their umbrellalike leaves, escaping the muddy waters.

Their seed-bearing receptacle is like a pepper shaker, pocked with openings through which ten to thirty marble-sized seeds protrude. If gentle waves vibrate the lotus stalk, its seeds rattle out. If harder winds break the shaker free, it floats upside down, dropping seeds as it drifts along.

The corky, root-like rhizomes of both lotus species are anchored in the muck beneath shallow lakes and ponds. In North America, native gatherers historically harvested and ate both the acrid "roots" and the seeds of *Nelumbo lutea*. Even today in the Orient, the sacred lotus rhizomes demand high prices thanks to their highly digestible starch, artichoke-like flavor, and medicinal use as a tonic.

However, the sacred lotus did not originate in the Far East. It appears to have been taken there soon after Buddhism was introduced into China from India, where the lotus had already been a powerful religious symbol for centuries: the unfolding flower of consciousness. The Hindu creator, Brahma, is often portrayed as emerging from a lotus flower as it floated on the floodwaters that destroyed an earlier world. Brahma then recreated the universe from the lotus, turning its petals into the hills, swales, and valleys inhabited today. Riding the tide of such powerful imagery, the lotus was dispersed by seed from India and Sri Lanka to China, and then to Japan and Korea.

The lotus arrived in Egypt a few centuries before the time of Jesus of Nazareth, and soon entered Occidental literature and art. It was dispersed to Hawaii and the eastern United States more than eighteen centuries later. The Old World lotus now abounds in ponds maintained by the National Park Service—keepers of America's natural heritage—in Washington, D.C.

One of the pond populations in Washington's Kenilworth Botanical Gardens attests to the fact that the lotus has not lost its wild resilience. It was initiated from a single seed germinated in 1951 by Horace Wester—one of a cache of lotus seeds that scientists currently believe to have been deposited on a now-dry lake bottom in Manchuria over 460 years ago. From this naturally-deposited cache, many seeds have been germinated over the last seventy years. One of them is considered the oldest viable seed in the world.

III

A Japanese scientist named Ichiro Ohga first drew world attention to a layer of these seeds found at Pulantien in southeastern Manchuria, for he suspected that they were of incomparable antiquity. They were found in an oxygen-poor peat deposit that indicated the presence of a lake where written and oral history had recorded no such water body for more than a century-and-a-half.

The seeds were worn and discolored when compared to freshly-harvested ones. They were lighter, and shrunken. Still, they were solid enough for Ohga to think of attempting to germinate them. A few days after digging them up, he placed them in water, where he left them for eight months without noticing any visible change. Finally, Ohga filed through the hard seed-coat—actually the shell-like skin of the lotus "fruit"—and within four days of additional soaking, all of the ancient embryos sprouted.

Concerned that other scientists would not believe him, Ohga distributed several of the lotus seeds found in the same deposit, and encouraged independent confirmation of their germinability by well-known physiologists. While Ohga remained alive, his colleagues failed to agree on just how old these lotus seeds might be. Three decades passed between the time of Ohga's 1923 excavation and the first direct dating of the seeds by Nobel Prize winner Willard Libby. Libby assumed that he had refined radiocarbon dating techniques well enough to estimate the age of the seeds. His results suggested that they were 1040 years old, plus or minus 210 years. Later, however, a team of skeptical geochronologists disputed this projection. Their analysis returned a date of one hundred years, plus or minus sixty.

More recently, an age estimate of 440 to 460 years has been derived from both geological studies of the lake bed as well as refined methods used to carbon date other seeds from Ohga's cache. In 1942, an Englishman named Ramsbottom successfully germinated *Nelumbo* seeds taken off a dried herbarium specimen in the British Museum, known to have been collected 237 years earlier. Additional museum specimens of lotus have usually germinated, but only after the nearly impervious seedcoat is sawn through, or softened by sulfuric acid.

How does the lotus ever germinate in the wild if it is that difficult to open in the laboratory? Unless abraded by scouring or scarified by acidic organics slowly accumulating on a lake bed, the tough shell of the lotus seed will remain fairly impermeable. Inside, the oil-rich seed maintains a quiescent metabolism over decades, even centuries. Perhaps lotus populations are propagated largely by rhizomes, and new germination occurs only after catastrophic floods of a magnitude that sends even Brahma hiding.

Is it not fitting that the lotus has become associated with immortality? Millions of charcoal-colored lotus seeds now sit in deposits of peat, still respiring, even after their plant populations wane and ponds fill in with sediment. All the while, their images are passed down to us on the sides of prehistoric pottery, in jewelry, in tapestries, and as statuary. The seeds dropping to the bottom of the ponds at Kenilworth Gardens today will probably outlive you and me. Will they outlive our culture, or even our species?

IV

Now, the common bean is in your other hand. Within the Americas, bean images were part of prehistoric art. In ancient Peru, bean figures were painted with legs upon them. The Inca are believed to have used beans as a kind of communications medium, with runners carrying them long distances down sophisticated roadway systems, transmitting messages from one leader to another. The Inca apparently selected beans of different colors, shapes, and sizes, and gave each type a meaning. A handful of beans transported hundreds of miles from runner to runner could be deciphered by an experienced Inca cryptographer and proclaimed as the "world news" as it was known at that time.

Even though the bean family as a whole is known for its relatively long seed viability, commonly cultivated garden bean seeds die young. A batch of domesticated Navy bean seed cannot normally germinate if it is stored a dozen or more years at room temperature. Over its eight to ten thousand years of being genetically domesticated and cultivated by American Indians, the bean has lost much of its hard-seeded qualities when compared to its wild ancestors growing in Latin America. The seedcoat has become thinner, more easy to break or deteriorate as moisture is imbibed, even as the food reserves within it have increased in volume.

Archaeobotanist Lawrence Kaplan has devoted thirty years to contemplating bean domestication in the New World. Collaborating with archaeologists all over the Americas, Dr. Kaplan has received bean seeds and empty pods excavated from prehistoric dwellings and food caches. He is routinely asked to identify them, measure them, and determine whether they appear to be wild or domesticated. After having amassed hundreds of records of common beans, Kaplan noticed a startling trend. The pattern of American bean domestication conflicts with that found in the Old World. In the Mediterranean region, gradual seed size increase through time occurred as pulses such as peas, lentils, garbanzos, and favas were progressively domesticated. In the Americas, beans appear to have been transformed more quickly than the eye of an archaeologist can see.

Although small wild beans with explosive pods are found in a few Mesoamerican sites, the first clearly domesticated beans in the archaeological record are nearly the size of modern-day bean crop varieties. The transition from small to large seeds that accompanied bean domestication is simply not represented in the American archaeological record. This change, Kaplan argues, must have come early and rapidly in the history of New World agriculture—prior to 8,000–10,000 years ago in South America, and as early as 7,000 years ago in the Mexican highlands of North America. And Kaplan has guessed how such a rapid evolutionary change may have taken place.

Wild beans have seedcoats almost as tough as that of the lotus. Some have cuticles that harbor chemicals to discourage consumption by tiny bruchid beetles. These beetles feed on legumes throughout the Americas, seeking out larger seeds and laying their eggs on the surface of the mature ones. When their eggs hatch, the larvae penetrate the seed. They consume the carbohydrate- and protein-rich food reserves within the seed, and often ravage the embryo, destroying its capacity to germinate.

Other factors being equal, the smaller the seed, the less likely it is for the beetles to select it for egg deposition. Recently, researchers have found lectins and pigments in wild bean seedcoats that function as feeding deterrants for beetles, yet Kaplan believes that small-seededness alone may offer enough protection. In any case, the tiny-seeded ancestors of common beans had a working set of protective mechanisms.

Rather suddenly, when early bean gatherers began to remove beans from the environments where beetles proliferated, the pressures to remain small and tough were released. By bringing gathered seed home to dry by mild heating for storage over the winter, the beans were guarded from the effects of bean beetles. Kaplan suggests that rapid "selection for large seed size could have taken place . . . as a result of simple storage practices by nonagricultural, gathering peoples." Subsequently, with sowing, other colors of beans were selected as "markers," and some did not have or need the pigments that served as feeding deterrents for so long. Over a rather short period of time, beans were allowed to diversify into new shapes, sizes, and colors that had been unknown in the wild during the previous thousands of years.

There was only one hitch. These newly domesticated beans could not thereafter survive on their own in the wild. With a relatively thinner seed-coat, the cultivated beans could more readily take up moisture during hot, humid months, and were easily spoiled. At room temperature in a semiarid or subhumid climate, fifty out of every hundred beans will lose their viability within six years' time. For a bean variety to survive, its seeds must be planted every few years. Its destiny has become inextricably linked with the human cultures that draw upon it as a favored food.

That is the irony—or better, fallacy—of the widespread folklore regarding "prehistoric Indian beans" said to have come from archaeological sites in the American West. Amateurs claim that they were given such beans by friends, who obtained them from other friends, who found them within pots left in caves or cliff shelters. Upon planting them, the ancient seeds supposedly germinated! Hundreds of tall tales of this sort have been heard in the Southwest, sometimes about Jacob's Cattle beans, in other instances about Aztec, Anasazi, Moctezuma, or Gila Cliff beans. Virtually none of the stories record the exact place, sedimentary stratum, or cultural provenience from which the beans were derived.

To my knowledge, none of the "original" germinable caches have been directly radiocarbon-dated. Most often, the beans actually came from contemporary gardens situated near prehistoric ruins, or from historic monuments where modern analogs of pre-Columbian crops are grown for educational purposes. In most cases, well-meaning individuals simply pass on a few seeds and a vague story to other curious folks. However, a few snake-oil peddlers have gotten involved. In Silver City, New Mexico, such beans are portrayed as mementos of the Old Southwest, and sold for one dollar a bean or one hundred dollars a pound. It seems that people *want to believe* that the very crops so dependent upon man for survival from year to year can somehow last millennia without human intervention.

The only way that the diversity of cultivated beans will persist on this earth is if human cultures care wisely for them. Where Indian farming has persisted in North America, families frequently grow four or five different kinds of beans every year. Even today, it is possible to find villages that harbor ten to eighteen "land races" or locally-adapted bean variants, most of which have been passed generation to generation for no less than a century.

Still, such bean-growing areas seldom surface in statistical reviews of legume production in North America. The tonnages of beans that reach the supermarkets across the continent are from a very few highly uniform microregions, where one, at most three, bean cultivars dominate the fields. Under the present circumstances, the U.S. National Research Council has predicted that an epidemic could easily devastate the entire Western dry bean industry. Diseases or pestilence could also have catastrophic consequences if they ever hit the Eastern green bean production areas at the wrong time, for they too are supported by a stringbean-thin genetic base.

The thinning-out of bean diversity has happened in a matter of a few generations, at least in places such as New York state. As late as 1908, the Iroquois nations of upstate New York were growing no less than sixty varieties of beans, including Cornstalk, Wild Goose, Marrowfat, Hummingbird, Wampum, plus Kidneys and Cranberries of several colors. Their seasonal festivals included a Green Bean Ceremony; with maize and squashes, beans were one of the "Three Sisters," also called *diohe'ko*, meaning "these which sustain us." One Iroquois legend, "The Weeping of Corn, and Bean, and Squash People," tells of an elderly woman who hears the crying of crop plants that had not received proper care. As she begins to weep as well, other villagers come to the fields. When they hear the cause of her sorrow, they join in the wailing. Stephen Lewandowski interprets this story as reminding people today that crop failures of the Three Sisters were caused by the community neglecting their duties.

Today, the Green Bean Ceremony is but a memory, and most of the sixty Iroquois beans are gone. Gone too are most of the 260 other kinds of common beans found on the thousands of small farms which once dotted New York. They have been replaced by just two introduced varieties on over three quarters of the state's dry bean acreage, and by a handful or so of stream-lined, college-bred green beans in the gardens and truck farms else-where in the state.

Once the last farmer decides not to plant or harvest a variety again, the remaining seed might be harvested and eaten until none remain. If there are plants drying in the field when the market changes, they may simply be plowed under, seeds and all. The beans left in the soil cannot persist the way the lotus can that is buried in organic muck, or wedged into a peat layer. The bean will not have the wild-type resilience or a low-oxygen environ-ment in which to take refuge.

The only factors that have stood between some old-fashioned beans and their extinction are the kindness and curiosity found among exceptional individuals, or encoded within the values of entire cultural communities. How else do you explain the 900 or so heirloom bean samples that John Withee grew out "as a hobby" in New England over the past few decades? Is there any other way to account for "the Bean King of Michigan," Ralph Stevenson, who told a journalist that he planted two hundred and fifty kinds of beans in his garden each year because "I just like to see them grow"? Except for his plots near Tekonsha, an old bean-producing center in south-ern Michigan, "there isn't hardly a bean raised around here" anymore.

The same tenacity was found in the late Burt Berrier's thirty-year quest for beans across the West, conducted while he worked his way through small towns as a John Deere farm machinery demonstrator. He collected the beans that Brigham Young reputedly carried with him from the Mid-west to Utah. Berrier also guarded a native Southwestern bean given to him by a Navajo woman. She had been able to grow it only by hauling pots of water for irrigation across miles of desert lands.

V

The lotus and the common bean. The lotus might persist regardless of whether humans were ever again to paddle into an Oriental lake. Common beans, on the other hand, are entirely dependent upon the planters, thresh-ers, and storage shelves of humankind. Our destinies are intimately inter-twined. If beans persist another four hundred and sixty years, it will surely be because of the curiosity and care—and perhaps the sense of commu-nity—of folks like you and me.

Annie Dillard

Total Eclipse

1

It had been like dying, that sliding down the mountain pass; it had been like the death of someone, irrational, that sliding down the mountain pass and into the region of dread. It was like slipping into fever, or falling down that hole in sleep from which you wake yourself whimpering. We had crossed the mountains that day, and now we were in a strange place—a hotel in central Washington, in a town near Yakima.

I lay in bed. My husband, Gary, was reading beside me. I lay in bed and looked at the painting on the hotel-room wall. It was a print of a detailed and lifelike painting of a smiling clown's head, made out of vegetables. It was a painting of the sort which you do not intend to look at, and which, alas, you never forget. Some tasteless fate presses it upon you; it becomes part of the complex interior junk you carry with you wherever you go. Two years have passed since the total eclipse of which I write. During those years I have forgotten, I assume, a great many things I wanted to remember—but I have not forgotten that clown painting or its lunatic setting in the old hotel.

The clown was bald. Actually, he wore a clown's tight rubber wig, painted white; this stretched over the top of his skull, which was a cabbage. His hair was bunches of baby carrots. Inset in his white clown makeup, and in his cabbage skull, were his small and laughing human eyes. The clown's glance was like the glance of Rembrandt in some of the self-portraits: lively, knowing, deep, and loving. The crinkled shadows around his eyes were string beans. His eyebrows were parsley. Each of his ears was a broad bean. His thin, joyful lips were red chili peppers; between his lips were wet rows of human teeth and a suggestion of a real tongue. The clown print was framed in gilt and glassed.

To put ourselves in the path of a total eclipse, that day we had driven five hours inland from the Washington coast where we lived. When we tried to cross the Cascades range, an avalanche had blocked the pass.

A slope's worth of snow blocked the road; traffic backed up. Had the avalanche buried any cars that morning? We could not learn. This highway was the only winter road over the mountains. We waited as highway crews bulldozed a passage through the avalanche. With two-by-fours and walls of plyboard, they erected a one-way, roofed tunnel through the avalanche. We drove through the avalanche tunnel, crossed the pass, and descended several thousand feet into Central Washington and the broad Yakima Valley, about which we knew only that it was orchard country. As we lost altitude, the snows disappeared; our ears popped; the trees changed, and in the trees were strange birds. I watched the landscape innocently, like a fool, like a diver in the rapture of the deep who plays on the bottom while his air runs out.

The hotel lobby was a dark, derelict room, narrow as a corridor, and seemingly without air. We waited on a couch while the manager vanished upstairs to do something unknown to our room. Beside us on an overstuffed chair, absolutely motionless, was a platinum-blond woman in her forties wearing a black silk dress and a strand of pearls. Her long legs were crossed; she supported her head on her fist. At the dim far end of the room, their backs towards us, sat six bald old men in their shirtsleeves, around a loud television. Two of them seemed asleep. They were drunks. "Number six!" cried the man on television. "Number six!"

On the broad lobby desk, lighted and bubbling, was a ten-gallon aquarium containing one large fish; the fish tilted up and down in its water. Against the long opposite wall sang a live canary in its cage. Beneath the cage, among spilled millet seeds on the carpet, were a decorated child's sand bucket and matching sand shovel.

Now the alarm was set for six. "When I was at home," said _____, "I was in a better place." I lay awake remembering an article I had read downstairs in the lobby, in an engineering magazine. The article was about gold mining.

In South Africa, in India, and in South Dakota, the gold mines extend so deeply into the earth's crust that they are hot. The rock walls burn the miners' hands. The companies have to air-condition the mines; if the air-conditioners break, the miners die. The elevators in the mine shafts run very slowly, down and up, so the miners' ears do not pop in their skulls. When the miners return to the surface, their faces are white.

Early the next morning we checked out. It was February 26, 1979, a Monday morning. We would drive out of town, find a hilltop, watch the eclipse, and then drive back over the mountains and home to the coast. How familiar things are here; how adept we are; how smoothly and professionally we check out! I had forgotten the clown's smiling head and the hotel lobby as if they had never existed. Gary put the car in gear and off we went, as off we have gone to a hundred other adventures.

It was before dawn when we found a highway out of town and drove into the unfamiliar countryside. By the growing light we could see a band of cirro-stratus clouds in the sky. Later the rising sun would clear these clouds before the eclipse began. We drove at random until we came to a range of unfenced hills. We pulled off the highway, bundled up, and climbed one of these hills.

2

The hill was five hundred feet high. Long winter-killed grass covered it, as high as our knees. We climbed and rested, sweating in the cold; we passed clumps of bundled people on the hillside who were setting up telescopes and fiddling with cameras. The top of the hill stuck up in the middle of the sky. We tightened our scarves and looked around.

East of us rose another hill like ours. Between the hills, far below, was the highway which threaded south into the valley. This was the Yakima Valley; I had never seen it before. It is justly famous for its beauty, like every planted valley. It extended south into the horizon, a distant dream of a valley, a Shangri-La. All its hundreds of low, golden slopes bore orchards. Among the orchards were towns, and roads, and plowed and fallow fields. Through the valley wandered a thin, shining river; from the river extended fine, frozen irrigation ditches. Distance blurred and blued the sight, so that the whole valley looked like a thickening or sediment at the bottom of the sky. Directly behind us was more sky, and empty lowlands blued by distance, and Mount Adams.

Mount Adams was an enormous, snow-covered volcanic cone rising flat, like so much scenery.

Now the sun was up. We could not see it; but the sky behind the band of clouds was yellow, and, far down the valley, some hillside orchards had lighted up. More people were parking near the highway and climbing the hills. It was the West. All of us rugged individualists were wearing knit caps and blue nylon parkas. People were climbing the nearby hills and setting up shop in clumps among the dead grasses. It looked as though we had all gathered on hilltops to pray for the world on its last day. It looked as though we had all crawled out of spaceships and were preparing to assault the valley below. It looked as though we were scattered on hilltops at dawn to sacrifice virgins, make rain, set stone stelae in a ring. There was no place out of the wind. The straw grasses banged our legs.

Up in the sky where we stood the air was lusterless yellow. To the west the sky was blue. Now the sun cleared the clouds. We cast rough shadows on the blowing grass; freezing, we waved our arms. Near the sun, the sky was bright and colorless. There was nothing to see.

It began with no ado. It was odd that such a well-advertised public event should have no starting gun, no overture, no introductory speaker. I should have known right then that I was out of my depth. Without pause or preamble, silent as orbits, a piece of the sun went away. We looked at it through welders' goggles. A piece of the sun was missing; in its place we saw empty sky.

I had seen a partial eclipse in 1970. A partial eclipse is very interesting. It bears almost no relation to a total eclipse. Seeing a partial eclipse bears the same relation to seeing a total eclipse as kissing a man does to marrying him, or as flying in an airplane does to falling out of an airplane. Although the one experience precedes the other, it in no way prepares you for it. During a partial eclipse the sky does not darken—not even when 94% of the sun is hidden. Nor does the sun, seen colorless through protective devices, seem terribly strange. We have all seen a sliver of light in the sky; we have all seen the crescent moon by day. However, during a partial eclipse the air does indeed get cold, precisely as if someone were standing between you and the fire. And blackbirds do fly back to their roosts. I had seen a partial eclipse before, and here was another.

What you see in an eclipse is entirely different from what you know. (It is especially different for those of us whose grasp of astronomy is so frail that, given a flashlight, a grapefruit, two oranges, and fifteen years, we still could not figure out which way to set the clocks for Daylight Saving Time.) Usually it is a bit of a trick to keep your knowledge from blinding you. But during an eclipse it is easy. What you see is much more convincing than any wild-eyed theory you may know.

You may read that the moon has something to do with eclipses. I have never seen the moon yet. You do not see the moon. So near the sun, it is as completely invisible as the stars are by day. What you see before your eyes is the sun going through phases. It gets narrower and narrower, as the waning moon does, and, like the ordinary moon, it travels alone in the simple sky. The sky is of course background. It does not appear to eat the sun; it is far behind the sun. The sun simply shaves away; gradually, you see less sun and more sky.

The sky's blue was deepening, but there was no darkness. The sun was a wide crescent, like a segment of tangerine. The wind freshened and blew steadily over the hill. The eastern hill across the highway grew dusky and sharp. The towns and orchards in the valley to the south were dissolving into the blue light. Only the thin river held a trickle of sun.

Now the sky to the west deepened to indigo, a color never seen. A dark sky usually loses color. This was a saturated deep indigo, up in the air. Stuck up into that unworldly sky was the cone of Mount Adams, and the *alpenglow* was upon it. The *alpenglow* is that red light of sunset which holds out on snowy mountaintops long after the valleys and tablelands are dimmed. "Look at Mount Adams," I said, and that was the last sane moment I remember.

I turned back to the sun. It was going. The sun was going, and the world was wrong. The grasses were wrong; they were platinum. Their every detail of stem, head, and blade shone lightless and artificially distinct as an art photographer's platinum print. This color has never been seen on earth. The hues were metallic; their finish was matte. The hillside was a nineteenth-century tinted photograph from which the tints had faded. All of the people you see in the photograph, distinct and detailed as their faces look, are now dead. The sky was navy blue.

My hands were silver. All the distant hills' grasses were fine-spun metal which the wind lay down. I was watching a faded color print of a movie filmed in the Middle Ages; I was standing in it, by some mistake. I was standing in a movie of hillside grasses filmed in the Middle Ages. I missed my own century, the people I knew, and the real light of day.

I looked at Gary. He was in the film. Everything was lost. He was a platinum print, a dead artist's version of life. I saw on his skull the darkness of night mixed with the colors of day. My mind was going out; my eyes were receding the way galaxies recede to the rim of space. Gary was lightyears away, gesturing inside a circle of darkness, down the wrong end of a telescope. He smiled as if he saw me; the stringy wrinkles around his eyes moved. The sight of him, familiar and wrong, was something I was remembering from centuries hence, from the other side of death; yes, *that* is the way he used to look, when we were living. When it was our generation's turn to be alive. I could not hear him; the wind was too loud. Behind him the sun was going. We had all started down a chute of time. At first it was pleasant; now there was no stopping it. Gary was chuting away across space, moving and talking and catching my eye, chuting down the long corridor of separation. The skin on his face moved like thin bronze plating that would peel.

The grass at our feet was wild barley. It was the wild einkorn wheat which grew on the hilly flanks of the Zagros Mountains, above the Euphrates Valley, above the valley of the river we called *River*. We harvested the grass with stone sickles, I remember. We found the grasses on the hillsides; we built our shelter beside them and cut them down. That is how he used to look then, that one, moving and living and catching my eye, with the sky so dark behind him, and the wind blowing. God save our life.

From all the hills came screams. A piece of sky beside the crescent sun was detaching. It was a loosened circle of evening sky, suddenly lighted from the back. It was an abrupt black body out of nowhere; it was a flat disc; it was almost over the sun. That is when there were screams. At once this disc of sky slid over the sun like a lid. The sky snapped over the sun like a lens cover. The hatch in the brain slammed. Abruptly it was dark night, on the land and in the sky. In the night sky was a tiny ring of light. The hole where the sun belongs is very small. A thin ring of light marked its place. There was no sound. The eyes dried, the arteries drained, the lungs hushed. There was no world. We were the world's dead people rotating and orbiting around and around, embedded in the planet's crust, while the earth rolled down. Our minds were lightyears distant, forgetful of almost everything. Only an extraordinary act of will could recall to us our former, living selves and our contexts in matter and time. We had, it seems, loved the planet and loved our lives, but could no longer remember the way of them. We got the light wrong. In the sky was something that should not be there. In the black sky was a ring of light. It was a thin ring, an old, thin silver wedding band in the sky, or a morsel of bone. There were stars. It was all over.

3

It is now that the temptation is strongest to leave those regions. We have seen enough; let's go. Why burn our hands any more than we have to? But two years have passed; the price of gold has risen. I return to the same buried alluvial beds and pick through the strata again.

I saw, early in the morning, the sun diminish against a backdrop of sky. I saw a circular piece of that sky appear, suddenly detached, blackened, and back-lighted; from nowhere it came and overlapped the sun. It did not look like the moon. It was enormous and black. If I had not read that it was the moon, I could have seen the sight a hundred times and never thought of the moon once. (If, however, I had not read that it was the moon — if, like most of the world's people throughout time I had simply glanced up and seen this thing — then I doubtless would not have speculated much, but would simply have, like Emperor Louis of Bavaria in 840, died of fright on the spot). It did not look like a dragon, although it looked more like a dragon than the moon. It looked like a lens cover, or the lid of a pot. It materialized out of thin air — black, and flat, and sliding, outlined in flame.

Seeing this black body was like seeing a mushroom cloud. The heart screeched. The meaning of the sight overwhelmed its fascination. It obliterated meaning itself. If you were to glance out one day and see a row of mushroom clouds rising on the horizon, you would know at once that what you were seeing, remarkable as it was, was intrinsically not worth remarking. No use running to tell anyone. Significant as it was, it did not matter a whit. For what is significance? It is significance for people. No people, no significance. This is all I have to tell you.

In the deeps are the violence and terror of which psychology has warned us. But if you ride these monsters deeper down, if you drop with them farther over the world's rim, you find what our sciences cannot locate or name, the substrata, the ocean or matrix or ether which buoys the rest, which gives goodness its power for good, and evil its power for evil, the unified field: our complex and inexplicable caring for each other, and for our life together here. This is given. It is not learned.

The world which lay under darkness and stillness following the closing of the lid was not the world we know. The event was over. Its devastation lay round about us. The clamoring mind and heart stilled, almost indifferent, certainly disembodied, frail, and exhausted. The hills were hushed, obliterated. Up in the sky, like a crater from some distant cataclysm, was a hollow ring. The ring was as small as one goose in a flock of migrating geese—if you happened to notice a flock of migrating geese. It was one 360th part of the visible sky. The sun we see is less than half the diameter of a dime held at arm's length.

The sight had nothing to do with anything. The sun was too small, and too cold, and too far away, to keep the world alive. The white ring was not enough. It was feeble and worthless. It was as useless as a memory; it was as off-kilter and hollow and wretched as a memory.

When you try your hardest to recall someone's face, or the look of a place, you see in your mind's eye some vague and terrible sight such as this. It is dark; it is insubstantial; it is all wrong.

The white ring and the saturated darkness made the earth and the sky look as they must look in the memories of the careless dead. What I saw, what I seemed to be standing in, was all the wrecked light that the memories of the dead could shed upon the living world. We had all died in our boots on the hilltops of Yakima, and were alone in eternity. Empty space stoppered our eyes and mouths; we cared for nothing. We remembered our living days wrong. With great effort we had remembered some sort of circular light in the sky—but only the outline. Oh, and then the orchard trees withered, the ground froze, the glaciers slid down the valleys and overlapped the towns. If there had ever been people on earth, nobody knew it. The dead had forgotten those they had loved. The dead were parted one from the other and could no longer remember the faces and lands they had loved in the light. They seemed to stand on darkened hilltops, looking down.

4

We teach our children one thing only, as we were taught: to wake up. We teach our children to look alive there, to join by words and activities the life of human culture on the planet's crust. As adults we are almost all adept at waking up. We have so mastered the transition we have forgotten we ever learned it. Yet it is a transition we make a hundred times a day, as, like so many will-less dolphins, we plunge and surface, lapse and emerge. We live half our waking lives and all of our sleeping lives in some private, useless, and insensible waters we never mention or recall. Useless, I say. Valueless, I might add—until someone hauls their wealth up to the surface and into the wide-awake city, in a form that people can use.

I do not know how we got to the restaurant. Like Roethke, "I take my waking slow." Gradually I seemed more or less alive, and already forgetful. It was now almost nine in the morning. It was the day of a solar eclipse in central Washington, and a fine adventure for everyone. The sky was clear; there was a fresh breeze out of the north.

The restaurant was a roadside place with tables and booths. The other eclipse-watchers were there. From our booth we could see their cars' California license plates, their University of Washington parking stickers. Inside the restaurant we were all eating eggs or waffles; people were fairly shouting and exchanging enthusiasms, like fans after a World Series game. Did you see—? Did you see—? Then somebody said something which knocked me for a loop.

A college student, a boy in a blue parka who carried a Hasselblad, said to us, "Did you see that little white ring? It looked like a Life-saver. It looked like a Life-saver up in the sky."

And so it did. The boy spoke well. He was a walking alarm clock. I myself had at that time no access to such a word. He could write a sentence, and I could not. I grabbed that Life-saver and rode it to the surface. And I had to laugh. I had been dumbstruck on the Euphrates River, I had been dead and gone and grieving, all over the sight of something which, if you could claw your way up to that level, you would grant looked very much like a Life-saver. It was good to be back among people so clever; it was good to have all the world's words at the mind's disposal, so the mind could begin its task. All those things for which we have no words are lost. The mind—the culture—has two little tools, grammar and lexicon: a decorated sand bucket and a matching shovel. With these we bluster about the continents and do all the world's work. With these we try to save our very lives.

There are a few more things to tell from this level, the level of the restaurant. One is the old joke about breakfast. "It can never be satisfied, the mind, never." Wallace Stevens wrote that, and in the long run he was right. The mind wants to live forever, or to learn a very good reason why not. The mind wants the world to return its love, or its awareness; the mind wants to know all the world, and all eternity, and God. The mind's sidekick, however, will settle for two eggs over easy.

The dear, stupid body is as easily satisfied as a spaniel. And, incredibly, the simple spaniel can lure the brawling mind to its dish. It is everlastingly funny that the proud, metaphysically ambitious, clamoring mind will hush if you give it an egg. Each self is multiple, a mob.

Further: while the mind reels in deep space, while the mind grieves or fears or exults, the workaday senses, in ignorance or idiocy, like so many computer terminals printing out market prices while the world blows up, still transcribe their little data and transmit them to the warehouse in the skull. Later, under the tranquilizing influence of fried eggs, the mind can sort through this data. The restaurant was a halfway house, a decompression chamber. There I remembered a few things more.

The deepest, and most terrifying, was this. I have said that I heard screams. (I have since read that screaming, with hysteria, is a common reaction even to expected total eclipses.) People on all the hillsides, including, I think, myself, screamed when the black body of the moon detached from the sky and rolled over the sun. But something else was happening at that same instant, and it was this, I believe, which made us scream.

The second before the sun went out we saw a wall of dark shadow come speeding at us. We no sooner saw it than it was upon us, like thunder. It roared up the valley. It slammed our hill and knocked us out. It was the monstrous swift shadow-cone of the moon. I have since read that this wave of shadow moves 1800 miles an hour. Language can give no sense of this sort of speed—1800 miles an hour. It was 195 miles wide. No end was in sight—you saw only the edge. It rolled at you across the land at 1800 miles an hour, hauling darkness like plague behind it. Seeing it, and knowing it was coming straight for you, was like feeling a slug of anesthetic shoot up your arm. If you think very fast, you may have time to think, "Soon it will hit my brain." You can feel the deadness race up your arm; you can feel the appalling, inhuman speed of your own blood. We saw the wall of shadow coming, and screamed before it hit.

This was the universe about which we have read so much and never before felt: the universe as a clockwork of loose spheres flung at stupefying, unauthorized speeds. How could anything moving so fast not crash, not veer from its orbit amok like a car out of control on a turn?

Less than two minutes later when the sum emerged, the trailing edge of the shadow-cone sped away. It coursed down our hill and raced eastward over the plain, faster than the eye could believe; it swept over the plain and dropped over the planet's rim in a twinkling. It had clobbered us, and now it roared away. We blinked in the light. It was as though an enormous, loping god in the sky had reached down and slapped the earth's face.

Something else, something more ordinary, came back to me along about the third cup of coffee. During the moments of totality, it was so dark that drivers on the highway below turned on their cars' headlights. We could see the highway's route as a strand of lights. It was bumper-to-bumper down there. It was 8:15 in the morning, Monday morning, and people were driving into Yakima to work. That it was as dark as night, and eerie as hell, an hour after dawn, apparently meant that, in order to *see* to drive to work, people had to use their headlights. Four or five cars pulled off the road. The rest, in a line at least five miles long, drove to town. The highway ran between hills; the people could not have seen any of the eclipsed sun at all. Yakima will have another total eclipse in _____. Perhaps in _____, businesses will give their employees an hour off.

From the restaurant we drove back to the coast. The highway crossing the Cascades range was open. We drove over the mountain like old pros. We joined our places on the planet's thin crust; it held. For the time being, we were home free.

Early that morning at six when we had checked out, the six bald men were sitting on folding chairs in the dim hotel lobby. The television was on. Most of them were awake. You might drown in your own spittle, God knows, at any time; you might wake up dead in a small hotel, a cabbage-head watching TV while snows pile up in the passes, watching TV while the chili peppers smile and the mountain blows up and the moon passes over the sun and nothing changes and nothing is learned because you have lost your bucket and shovel and no longer care. What if you regain the surface and open your sack and find, instead of treasure, a beast which jumps at you? Or, you may not come back at all. The winches may jam, the scaffolding buckle, the air-conditioning collapse. You may glance up one day and see by your headlamp the canary keeled over in its cage. You may reach into a cranny for pearls and touch a moray eel. You yank on your rope; it is too late.

Apparently people share a sense of these hazards, for when the total eclipse ended, an odd thing happened.

When the sun appeared as a blinding bead on the ring's side, the eclipse was over. The black lens cover appeared again, back-lighted, and slid away. At once the yellow light made the sky blue again; the black lid dissolved and vanished. The real world began there. I remember now: we all hurried away. We were born and bored at a stroke. We rushed down the hill. We found our car; we saw the other people streaming down the hillsides; we joined the highway traffic and drove away.

We never looked back. It was a general vamoose, and an odd one, for when we left the hill, the sun was still partially eclipsed—a sight rare enough, and one which, in itself, we would probably have driven five hours to see. But enough is enough. One turns at last even from glory itself with a sigh of relief. From the depths of mystery, and even from the heights of splendor, we bounce back and hurry for the latitudes of home.

Gretel Ehrlich

Spring

We have a nine-acre lake on our ranch and a warm spring that feeds it all winter. By mid-March the lake ice begins to melt where the spring feeds in, and every year the same pair of mallards come ahead of the others and wait. Though there is very little open water they seem content. They glide back and forth through a thin estuary, brushing watercress with their elegant, folded wings, then tip end-up to eat and after, clamber onto the lip of ice that retreats, hardens forward, and retreats again.

Mornings, a transparent pane of ice lies over the meltwater. I peer through and see some kind of waterbug—perhaps a leech—paddling like a sea turtle between green ladders of lakeweed. Cattails and sweetgrass from the previous summer are bone-dry, marked with black mold spots, and bend like elbows into the ice. They are swords which cut away the hard tenancy of winter. At the wide end a mat of dead waterplants has rolled back into a thick, impregnable breakwater. Near it, bubbles trapped under the ice are lenses focused straight up to catch the coming season.

It's spring again and I wasn't finished with winter. That's what I said at the end of summer too. I stood on the twenty-foot-high haystack and yelled, "No!" as the first snow fell. We had been up since four in the morning picking the last bales of hay from the oatfield by hand, slipping under the weight of them in the mud, and by the time we finished the stack, six inches of snow had fallen.

It's spring but I was still cataloguing the different kinds of snow: snow that falls dry but is rained on; snow that melts down into hard crusts; wind-driven snow that looks blue; powder snow on hardpack on powder—a Linzertorte of snow. I look up. The troposphere is the seven-to-ten-mile-wide sleeve of air out of which all our weather shakes. A bank of clouds drives in from the south. Where in it, I wonder, does a snowflake take on its thumbprint uniqueness? Inside the cloud where schools of flakes are flung this way and that like schools of fish? What gives the snowflake its needle, plate, column, branching shapes—the battering wind or the dust particles around which water vapor clings?

Near town the river ice breaks up and lies stacked in industrial-sized hunks—big as railway cars—on the banks, and is flecked black by wheeling hurricanes of newly plowed topsoil. That's how I feel when winter breaks up inside me: heavy, onerous, up-ended, inert against the flow of water. I had thought about ice during the cold months too. How it is movement betrayed, water seized in the moment of falling. In November, ice thickened over the lake like a cataract, and from the air looked like a Cyclops, one bad eye. Under its milky spans over irrigation ditches, the sound of water running south was muffled. One solitary spire of ice hung noiselessly against dark rock at the Falls as if mocking or mirroring the broom-tail comet on the horizon. Then, in February, I tried for words not about ice, but words hacked from it—the ice at the end of the mind, so to speak— and failed.

Those were winter things and now it is spring, though one name can't describe what, in Wyoming, is a three-part affair: false spring, the vernal equinox, and the spring when flowers come and the grass grows.

Spring means restlessness. The physicist I've been talking to all winter says if I look more widely, deeply, and microscopically all at once I might see how springlike the whole cosmos is. What I see as order and stillness—the robust, time-bound determinacy of my life— is really a mirage suspended above chaos. "There's a lot of random jiggling going on all the time, everywhere," he tells me. Winter's tight sky hovers. Under it, the hayfields are green, then white, then green growing under white. The confinement I've felt since November resembles the confinement of subatomic particles, I'm told. A natural velocity finally shows itself. The particle moves; it becomes a wave.

The sap rises in trees and in me and the hard knot of perseverance I cultivated to meet winter dissipates; I walk away from the obsidian of bitter nights. Now, when snow comes, it is wet and heavy, but the air it traverses feels light. I sleep less and dream not of human entanglements, but of animals I've never seen: a caterpillar fat as a man's thumb, made of linked silver tubes, has two heads—one human, one a butterfly's.

Last spring at this time I was coming out of a bout with pneumonia. I went to bed on January first and didn't get up until the end of February. Winter was a cocoon in which my gagging, basso cough shook the dark figures at the end of my bed. Had I read too much Hemingway? Or was I dying? I'd lie on my stomach and look out. Nothing close up interested me. All engagements of mind—the circumlocutions of love-interests and internal gossip—appeared false. Only my body was true. And my body was trying to close down, go out the window without me.

I saw things out there. Our ranch faces south down a long treeless valley whose vanishing point is two gray hills, folded one in front of the other like two hands, and after that—space, cerulean air, clouds like pleated skirts, and red mesas standing up like breeching whales in a valley three thousand feet below. Afternoons, our young horses played, rearing up on back legs and pawing oh so carefully at each other, reaching around, ears flat back, nipping manes and withers. One of those times their falsetto squeals looped across the pasture and hung on frozen currents of air. But when I tried to ingest their sounds of delight, I found my lungs had no air.

It was thirty-five below zero that night. Our plumbing froze and because I was very weak my husband had to bundle me up and help me to the outhouse. Nothing close at hand seemed to register with me: neither the cold nor the semi-coziness of an uninsulated house. But the stars were lurid. For a while I thought I saw the horses, dead now, and eating each other, and spinning round and round in the ice of the air.

My scientist friends talk with relish about how insignificant we humans are when placed against the time-scale of geology and the cosmos. I had heard it a hundred times, but never felt it truly. As I lay in bed, the black room was a screen through which some part of my body traveled, leaving the rest behind. I thought I was a sun flying over a barge whose iron holds soaked me up until I became rust, floating on a bright river.

A ferocious loneliness took hold of me. I felt spring-inspired desire, a sense of trajectory, but no interception was in sight. In fact, I wanted none. My body was a parenthetical dash laid against a landscape so spacious it defied space as we know it—space as a membrane—and curved out of time. That night a luscious, creamy fog rolled in, like a roll of fat, hugging me, but it was snow.

Recuperation is like spring: dormancy and vitality collide. In any year I'm like a bear, a partial hibernator. During January thaws I stick my nose out and peruse the frozen desolation as if reading a book whose language I don't know. In March I'm ramshackle, weak in the knees, giddy, dazzled by broken-backed clouds, the passing of Halley's comet, the on-and-off strobe of sun. Like a sheepherder I "X" out each calendar day as if time were a forest through which I could clearcut a way to the future. My physicist friend straightens me out on this point too. The notion of "time passing," like a train through a landscape, is an illusion, he says. I hold the Big Ben clock taken from a dead sheepherder's wagon and look at it. The clock measures intervals of time, not the speed of time, and the calendar is a scaffolding we hang as if time were rushing water we could harness. Time-bound I hinge myself to a linear bias — cause and effect all laid out in a neat row — and in this we learn two things: blame and shame.

Julius Caesar had a sense of humor about time. The Roman calendar with its Kalends, Nones, and Ides — counting days — changed according to who was in power. Caesar serendipitously added days, changed the names of certain months, and when he was through, the calendar was so skewed that January fell in autumn.

Einsteinian time is too big for even Julius Caesar to touch. It stretches and shrinks and dilates. In fact, it is the antithesis of the mechanistic concept we've imposed on it. Time, indecipherable from space, is not one thing, but an infinity of spacetimes, overlapping, interfering, wavelike. There is no future that is not now, no past that is not now. Time includes every moment.

It's the Ides of March today.

I've walked to a hill a mile from the house. It's not really a hill but a mountain slope that heaves up, turns sideways, and comes down again, straight down to a foot-wide creek. Everything I can see from here used to be a flatland covered with shallow water. "Used to be" means several hundred million years ago, and the land itself was not really "here" at all, but part of a continent floating near Bermuda. On top is a fin of rock, a marine deposition created during Jurassic times by small waves moving in and out slapping the shore.

I've come here for peace and quiet and to see what's going on in this secluded valley, away from ranch work and sorting corrals, but what I get is a slap on the ass by a prehistoric wave, gains and losses in altitude and aridity, outcrops of mud composed of rotting volcanic ash which fell continuously for ten thousand years a hundred million years ago. The soils are a geologic flag — red, white, green, and gray. On one side of the hill, mountain mahogany gives off a scent like orange blossoms, on the other, colonies of sagebrush root wide in ground the color of Spanish roof tiles. And it still looks like the ocean to me. "How much truth can a man stand, sitting by the ocean, all that perpetual motion," Mose Allison, the jazz singer, sings.

The wind picks up and blusters. Its fat underbelly scrapes the uneven ground, twisting like taffy towards me, slips up over the mountain and showers out across the Great Plains. The sea smell it carried all the way from Seattle has long since been absorbed by pink grus — the rotting granite that spills down the slopes of the Rockies. Somewhere over the Midwest the wind slows, tangling in the hair of hardwood forests, and finally drops into the corridors of the cities, past Manhattan's World Trade Center, ripping free again as it crosses the Atlantic's green swell.

Spring jitterbugs inside me. Spring *is* wind, symphonic and billowing. A dark cloud pops like a blood blister over me, letting hail down. It comes on a piece of wind that seems to have widened the sky, comes so the birds have something to fly on.

A message reports to my brain but I can't believe my eyes. The sheet of wind had a hole in it: an eagle just fell out of the sky. It fell as if down the chute of a troubled airplane. Landed, falling to one side as if a leg were broken. I was standing on the hill overlooking the narrow valley that had been a seashore 170,000,000 years ago, whose sides had lifted like a medic's litter to catch up this eagle now.

She hops and flaps seven feet of wing and closes them down and sways. She had come down (on purpose?) near a dead fawn whose carcass had recently been feasted upon. When I walked closer, all I could see of the animal was a ribcage rubbed red with fine tissue and the decapitated head lying peacefully against sagebrush, eyes closed.

At twenty yards the eagle opened her wings halfway and rose up, her whole back lengthening and growing stiff. At forty feet she looked as big as a small person. She craned her neck, first to one side, then the other, and stared hard. She's giving me "the eagle eye," I thought.

Friends who have investigated eagles' nests have literally feared for their lives. It's not that they were in danger of being pecked to death but, rather, grabbed. An eagle's talons are a powerful jaw. Their grip is so strong the talons can slice down through flesh to bone in one motion.

But I had come close only to see what was wrong, to see what I could do. An eagle with a bum leg will starve to death. Was it broken, bruised, or sprained? How could I get close enough to know? I approached again. She hopped up in the air dashing the critical distance between us with her great wings. Best to leave her alone, I decided. My husband dragged a road-killed deer up the mountain slope so she could eat, and I brought a bucket of water. Then we turned towards home.

A golden eagle is not golden but black with yellow spots on the neck and wings. Looking at her, I had wondered how feathers came to be, how their construction—the rachis, vane, and quill—is unlike anything else in nature.

Birds are glorified flying lizards. The remarkable feathers which, positioned together, are like hundreds of smaller wings, evolved from reptilian scales. Ancestral birds had thirteen pairs of cone-shaped teeth that grew in separate sockets like a snake's, rounded ribs, and bony tails. Archaeopteryx was half bird, half dinosaur who glided instead of flying; Ichthyornis was a fish-bird, a relative of the pelican; Diatryma was a giant, seven feet tall with a huge beak and wings so absurdly small they must have been useless, though later the wingbone sprouted from them. *Aquila chrysaëtos*, the modern golden eagle, has seven thousand contour feathers, no teeth, and weighs about eight pounds.

I think about the eagle. How big she was, how each time she spread her wings it was like a thought stretching between two seasons.

Back at the house I relax with a beer. At 5:03 the vernal equinox occurs. I go outside and stand in the middle of a hayfield with my eyes closed. The universe is restless but I want to feel celestial equipoise: twelve hours of daylight, twelve of dark, and the earth ramrod straight on its axis. In celebration I straighten my posture in an effort to resist the magnetic tilt back into dormancy, spiritual and emotional reticence. Far to the south I imagine the equatorial sash, now nose to nose with the sun, sizzling like a piece of bacon, then the earth slowly tilting again.

In the morning I walk up to the valley again. I glass both hillsides, back and forth through the sagebrush, but the eagle isn't there. The hindquarters of the road-killed deer have been eaten. Coyote tracks circle the carcass. Did they have eagle for dinner too?

Afternoon. I return. Far up on the opposite hill I see her, flapping and hopping to the top. When I stop, she stops and turns her head. Her neck is the plumbline on which earth revolves. Even at two hundred yards, I can feel her binocular vision zeroing in; I can feel the heat of her stare.

Later, I look through my binoculars at all sorts of things. I'm seeing the world with an eagle eye. I glass the crescent moon. How jaded I've become, taking the moon at face value only, forgetting the charcoal, shaded backside, as if it weren't there at all.

That night I dream about two moons. One is pink and spins fast; the other is an eagle's head, farther away and spinning in the opposite direction. Slowly, both moons descend and then it is day.

At first light I clamber up the hill. Now the dead deer my husband brought is only a hoop of ribs, two forelegs, and hair. The eagle is not here or along the creek or on either hill. I go to the hill and sit. After a long time an eagle careens out from the narrow slit of the red-walled canyon whose creek drains into this valley. Surely it's the same bird. She flies by. I can hear the bone-creak and whoosh of air under her wings. She cocks her head and looks at me. I smile. What is a smile to her? Now she is not so much flying as lifting above the planet, far from me.

Late March. The emerald of the hayfields brightens. A flock of gray-capped rosy finches who overwintered here swarms a leafless apple tree, then falls from the smooth boughs like cut grass. The tree was planted by the Texan who homesteaded this ranch. As I walk past, one of the boughs, shaped like an undulating dragon, splits off from the trunk and falls.

Space is an arena in which the rowdy particles that are the building blocks of life perform their antics. All spring, things fall; the general law of increasing disorder is on the take. I try to think of what it is to be a cause without an effect, an effect without a cause. To abandon time-bound thinking, the use of tenses, the temporally related emotions of impatience, expectation, hope, and fear. But I can't. I go to the edge of the lake and watch the ducks. Like them, my thinking rises and falls on the same water.

Another day. Sometimes when I'm feeling small-minded I take a plane ride over Wyoming. As we take off I feel the plane's resistance to accepting air under its wings. Is this how an eagle feels? Ernst Mach's principle tells me that an object's resistance against being accelerated is not the intrinsic property of matter, but a measure of its interaction with the universe; that matter only has inertia because it exists in relation to other matter.

Airborne, then, I'm not aloof but in relation to everything — like Wallace Stevens's floating eagle for whom the whole, intricate Alps is a nest. We fly southeast from Heart Mountain across the Big Horn River, over the long red wall where Butch Cassidy trailed stolen horses, across the high plains to Laramie. Coming home the next day, we hit clouds. Turbulence, like many forms of trouble, cannot always be seen. We bounce so hard my arms sail helplessly above my head. In evolution, wingbones became arms and hands; perhaps I'm de-evolving.

From ten thousand feet I can see that spring is only half here: the southern part of the state is white, the northern half is green. Land is also time. The greening of time is a clock whose hands are blades of grass moving vertically, up through the fringe of numbers, spreading across the middle of the face, sinking again as the sun moves from one horizon to the other. Time doesn't go anywhere; the shadow of the plane, my shadow, moves across it.

To sit on a plane is to sit on the edge of sleep where the mind's forge brightens into incongruities. Down there I see disparate whole-nesses strung together and the string dissolving. Mountains run like rivers; I fly through waves and waves of chiaroscuro light. The land looks bare but is articulate. The body of the plane is my body, pressing into spring, pressing matter into relation with matter. Is it even necessary to say the obvious? That spring brings on surges of desire? From this disinterested height I say out loud what Saint Augustine wrote: "My love is my weight. Because of it I move."

Directly below us now is the fine old Wyoming ranch where Joel, Mart, Dave, Hughy, and I have moved thousands of head of cattle. Joel's father, Smokey, was one of two brothers who put the outfit together. They worked hard, lived frugally, and even after Fred died, Smokey did not marry until his late fifties. As testimony to a long bachelorhood, there is no kitchen in the main house. The cookhouse stands separate from all the other buildings. In back is a bedroom and bath which has housed a list of itinerant cooks ten pages long.

Over the years I've helped during roundup and branding. We'd rise at four. Smokey, now in his eighties, cooked flapjacks and boiled coffee on the wood cookstove. There was a long table. Joel and Smokey always sat at one end. They were look-alikes, both skin-and-bones tall with tipped-up dark eyes set in narrow faces. Stern and vigilant, Smokey once threw a young hired hand out of the cookhouse because he hadn't grained his saddle horse after a long day's ride. "On this outfit we take care of our animals first," he said. "Then if there's time, we eat."

Even in his early twenties, Joel had his father's dignity and razor-sharp wit. They both wore white Stetsons identically shaped. Only their hands were different: Joel had eight fingers and one thumb—the other he lost while roping.

Eight summers ago my parents visited their ranch. We ate a hearty meal of homemade whiskey left over from Prohibition days, steaks cut from an Angus bull, four kinds of vegetables, watermelon, ice cream, and pie. Despite a thirteen-year difference in our ages, Smokey wanted Joel and me to marry. As we rose from the meal, he shook my father's hand. "I guess you'll be my son's father-in-law," he said. That was news to all of us. Joel's face turned crimson. My father threw me an astonished look, cleared his throat, and thanked his host for the fine meal.

One night Joel did come to my house and asked me if I would take him into my bed. It was a gentlemanly proposition—doffed hat, moist eyes, a smile almost grimacing with loneliness. "You're an older woman. Think of all you could teach me," he said jauntily, but with a blush. He stood ramrod straight waiting for an answer. My silence turned him away like a rolling wave and he drove to the home ranch, spread out across the Emblem Bench thirty-five miles away.

The night Joel died I was staying at a writer's farm in Missouri. I had fallen asleep early, then awakened suddenly, feeling claustrophobic. I jumped out of bed and stood in the dark. I wanted to get out of there, drive home to Wyoming and I didn't know why. Finally, at seven in the morning, I was able to sleep. I dreamed about a bird landing, then lifting out of a tree along a river bank. That was the night Joel's pickup rolled. He was found five hours after the accident occurred—just about daylight—and died on the way to the hospital.

Now I'm sitting on a fin of Gypsum Springs rock looking west. The sun is setting. What I see are three gray cloud towers letting rain down at the horizon. The sky behind these massifs is gilded gold, and long fingers of land—benches where the Hunt Oil Company's Charolais cattle graze—are pink. Somewhere over Joel's grave the sky is bright. The road where he died shines like a dash in a Paul Klee painting. Over my head, it is still winter: snow so dry it feels like styrofoam when squeezed together, tumbles into my lap. I think about flying and falling. The place in the sky where the eagle fell is dark, as if its shadow had burned into the backdrop of rock—Hiroshima style. Why does a wounded eagle get well and fly away; why do the head wounds of a young man cut him down? Useless questions.

Sex and death are the riddles thrown into the hopper, thrown down on the planet like hailstones. Where one hits the earth, it makes a crater and melts, perhaps a seed germinates, perhaps not. If I dice life down into atoms, the trajectories I find are so wild, so random, anything could happen: life or nonlife. But once we have a body, who can give it up easily? Our own or others'? We check our clocks and build our beautiful narratives, under which indeterminacy seethes.

Sometimes, lying in bed, I feel like a flounder with its two eyes on one side pointing upward into nothingness. The casings of thought rattle. Then I realize there are no casings at all. Is it possible that the mind, like space, is finite, but has no boundaries, no center or edge? I sit cross-legged on old blankets. My bare feet strain against the crotch of my knees. Time is between my toes, it seems. Just as morning comes and the indigo lifts, the leaflessness of the old apple tree looks ornate. Nothing in this world is plain.

"Every atom in your body was once inside a star," another physicist says, but he's only trying to humor me. Not all atoms in all kinds of matter are shared. But who wouldn't find that idea appealing? Outside, shadows trade places with a sliver of sun which trades places with shadow. Finally the lake ice goes and the water — pale and slate blue — wears its coat of diamonds all day. The mallards number twenty-six pairs now. They nest on two tiny islands and squabble amicably among themselves. A Pacific storm blows in from the south like a jibsail reaching far out, backhanding me with a gust of something tropical. It snows into my mouth, between my breasts, against my shins. Spring teaches me what space and time teach me: that I am a random multiple; that the many fit together like waves; that my swell is a collisions of particles. Spring is a kind of music, a seething minor, a twelve-tone scale. Even the odd harmonies amassed only lift up to dissolve.

Spring passes harder and harder and is feral. The first thunder cracks the sky into a larger domain. Sap rises in obdurateness. For the first time in seven months, rain slants down in a slow pavanne — sharp but soft — like desire, like the laying on of hands. I drive the highway that crosses the wild-horse range. Near Emblem I watch a black studhorse trot across the range all alone. He travels north, then turns in my direction as if trotting to me. Now, when I dream of Joel, he is riding that horse and he knows he is dead. One night he rides to my house, all smiles and shyness. I let him in.

Edward O. Wilson

Storm Over the Amazon

The Amazonian forest of Brazil whipsaws the imagination. After two or three days there I grow familiar with the earthy smell and vegetation as though in a Massachusetts woodlot, so that what was recently new and wonderful starts to fade from my senses. Then some small event occurs to shift my conceptual framework, and the mystery comes back in its original force. One night I walked into the forest north of Manaus with a headlamp to study the ground surface and everywhere I saw — diamonds! At regular intervals of several yards, intense pinpoints of white light flashed on and off with each turning of the lamp. They were reflections from the eyes of wolf spiders on the prowl. When the spiders were spotlighted they froze into stillness, allowing me to peer at them from inches away. I could distinguish a wide variety of species by size, color, and hairiness. Where did they all come from? What was their prey, and how could so many kinds exist there in these numbers? By morning they would retreat into the leaf litter and soil, yielding the microterrain to a new set of predators. Because I had come for other purposes, I abandoned their study to the arachnologists who would surely follow.

Each evening after dinner I carried a folding chair to a clearing to escape the noise and stink of the camp I shared with Brazilian field hands. The forest around us was in the process of being clearcut northward along an east-west line, mostly to create short-lived pastures. Even so, what remained was and is one of the few great wildernesses of the world, stretching almost unbroken from where I sat across five hundred miles to the Venezuelan savannas.

Just knowing I was on the edge of that immensity deepened the sense of my own purpose. I stared straight into the dark for hours at a time, thinking in spurts about the ecological research that had attracted me there, dreaming pleasantly about the forest as a reservoir of the unknown, so complicated that its measure will not be taken in my lifetime. I was a would-be conquistador of sorts, searching not for Amazonian gold but for great discoveries to be made in the interior. I fantasized about new phenomena and unborn insights. I confess this without embarrassment, because science is built on fantasies that can be proved true. For me the rain forest is the greatest of fantasy lands, a place of hope still unchained by exact knowledge.

And I strained to catch any trace of sound or light. The rain forest at night is an experience in sensory deprivation, black and silent as a tomb. Life is moving out there all right, but the organisms communicate chiefly by faint chemical trails laid over the surface, puffs of odor released into the air, and body scents detected downwind. Most animals are geniuses in this chemical channel where we are idiots. On the other hand, we are masters of the audiovisual channel, matched in that category only by a few odd groups like birds and lizards. At the risk of oversimplification, I can say that this is why we wait for the dawn while they wait for the fall of darkness.

So I welcomed every meteorite's streak and distant mating flash from luminescent beetles. Even the passage of a jetliner five miles up was exciting, having been transformed from the familiar urban irritant to a rare sign of the continuance of my own species.

Then one August night in the dry season, with the moon down and starlight etching the tops of the trees, everything changed with wrenching suddenness. A great storm came up from the west and moved quickly toward where I sat. It began as a flickering of light on the horizon and a faint roll of thunder. In the course of an hour the lightning grew like a menacing organism into flashes that spread across the sky and illuminated the thunderhead section by section. The sound expanded into focused claps to my left, front, and right. Now the rain came walking through the forest with a hiss made oddly soothing by its evenness of pitch. At this moment the clouds rose straight up and even seemed to tilt a little toward me, like a gigantic cliff about to topple over. The brilliance of the flashes was intimidating. Here, I knew, was the greatest havoc that inanimate nature can inflict in a short span of time: 10,000 volts dropping down an ionizing path at 500 miles an hour and a countersurge in excess of 30,000 amperes back up the path at ten times that speed, then additional back-and-forth surges faster than the eye can follow, all perceived as a single flash and crack of sound.

In the midst of the clamor something distracted my attention off to the side. The lightning bolts were acting like photoflashes to illuminate the wall of the rain forest. In glimpses I studied its superb triple-tiered structure: top canopy a hundred feet off the ground, middle tree layer below that, and a scattering of lowest trees and shrubs. At least 800 kinds of trees had been found along a short transect eastward from the camp, more than occur natively in all of North America. A hundred thousand or more species of insects and other small animals were thought to live in the same area, many of which lack scientific names and are otherwise wholly unstudied. The symmetry was complete: the Amazonian rain forest is the most that life has been able to accomplish within the constraints of this stormy planet.

Large splashing drops turned into sheets of water driven by gusts of wind. I retreated into the camp and waited with my *mateiros* friends under the dripping canvas roof. In a short time leptodactylid frogs began to honk their territorial calls in the forest nearby. To me they seemed to be saying rejoice! rejoice! The powers of nature are within our compass.

For that is the way it is in the nonhuman world. The greatest powers of the physical environment slam into the resilient forces of life and nothing much happens. The next morning the forest is still there, and although a few old trees have fallen to create clearings and the way to new plant growth, the profile stays the same. For a very long time, approximately 150 million years, the species of the rain forest evolved to absorb precisely this form and magnitude of violence. They even coded its frequent occurrence into their genes. Organisms use heavy rain and floods to time their mating and other episodes of the life cycle.

Awe is what I am talking about here. It is the most peculiar human response, an overwhelming feeling of reverence or fear produced by that which is sublime or extremely powerful, sometimes changing perception in a basic way. I had experienced it by seeing a living system in a dramatic and newly symbolic fashion. Far larger storms occur on Venus and Jupiter, but they disclose no life underneath. Nothing like the forest wall exists anywhere else we will ever visit. To drop onto another planet would be a journey into death.

A few days later the grinding of gears announced the approach of the truck sent to return me and two workers to Manaus. We watched it coming across the pastureland, a terrain strewn with fire-blackened stumps and logs, the battlefield the rain forest finally lost. On the ride back I tried not to look at it. No awe there, only defeat and decay. I think that the ultimate irony of organic evolution is that in the instant of achieving self-understanding through the mind of man, it doomed its most beautiful creations.

William Langewiesche

The Physics of Blown Sand

I stayed on in El Oued and in the early hours walked south along a crumbling paved road under assault from the sand sea. The morning was bright and hot, and the dunes carved crisp lines against the sky. I passed a turbaned man on a donkey carrying empty gas cans into town. There was no other traffic. The road led eventually to a village, or what was left of it. It was a village that had been mostly buried in drifting sand. The corners and roofs of stone structures still showed, but only three houses remained inhabitable, and from the evidence of digging around them, they, too, were threatened.

I drank at a well with a rope and bucket. There was no farming here. The only sign of industry was a freestanding stone oven, a baker's oven, against which palm wood had been stacked. The wind blew sand, but otherwise nothing stirred. Two men sat in the shadow of a wall by a fire on which they had placed a blackened pot. They motioned me over and offered me tea in a dirty glass. The men were older than I, bearded and thin, and had no work. We spent a few hours together. They pointed to where the school lay buried, and to where most of the village stood beneath the sands. I asked them the details of its burial.

They said the sands are fickle. Dunes may drift for decades in one direction, or not drift at all, then suddenly turn and consume you. Consumption by the sand is like other forms of terminal illness: it starts so gently that at first you don't worry. One day the grains begin to accumulate against your walls. You've seen the grains before, and naturally assume that a change in the wind will carry them away. But this time the wind does not change, and the illness persists. Over weeks or longer, the sand grows. You fight back with a shovel, and manage to keep your walls clear. Fighting back feels good and gives you something to do. But the grains never let up, and one morning while shoveling you realize that the dunes have moved closer. You enlist your sons and brothers. But eventually the land around your house swells with sand, and you begin standing on sand to shovel sand. Finally no amount of digging will clear your walls. The dunes tower above you, and send sand sheets cascading down their advancing slip faces. You have to gather your belongings and flee.

But your house is your heritage, and you would like somehow to preserve it. As the dunes bear down on it they will collapse the walls. The defense is again the Saharan acceptance of destiny: having lost the fight against the sand, you must now invite it in. Sleeping on the sand, covering your floors with it for all these years, helped prepare you mentally. But shoveling in the sand is not enough. Your last act is to break out the windows, take off the doors, and knock holes in the roof. You allow the wind to work for you. If it succeeds, and fills your house, the walls will stand. Then in a hundred years, when the wind requires it, the dunes will drift on and uncover the village. Your descendants will bless God and his Prophet. They will not care that you were thin and poor and had no work. They will remember you as a man at peace with his world. The desert takes away but also delivers.

I left the men to their contemplation, and climbed out over the dune that had engulfed their village. From its crest I discovered a valley two hundred feet below, where the desert floor was exposed and a stretch of blacktop emerged from the sand. The road was not on the map. It lay beyond the village and ran south toward the empty center of the Eastern Erg. I thought it might lead to an old settlement, perhaps one that had been uncovered by the wind, and I set off to follow it.

I should have been more careful. I was traveling too lightly, with neither a hat nor water nor any enduring sense of direction. The road kept turning, diving into sand, reemerging. Eventually it ran under a mountainous dune and disappeared entirely. I climbed that dune, and a string of the highest ones beyond it, and knew even as I proceeded that I had gone too far. The dunes were like giant starfish, covered by ripples, linking curved tentacles to form lines. In all directions, the erg stretched to the horizons in a confusion of sand.

This was the landscape that inspired the British officer Ralph A. Bagnold, history's closest observer of Saharan sands. Bagnold was an English gentleman of the old school. He fought in the trenches of Flanders during World War I, then earned an honors degree in engineering from Cambridge, and later reenlisted in the British Army for overseas assignment. While stationed in Egypt and India between 1929 and 1934, he led expeditions in modified Fords to explore the sand seas of Libya. These were big places in need of understanding. One *erg* alone was the size of all France.

Bagnold had a strong and inquiring mind. He marveled at the desert's patterns, saw magic in the dunes, and wanted it all explained. To his surprise, he found that scientific knowledge was as yet merely descriptive: dune shapes had been catalogued, but little was understood about the processes involved in their formation. Bagnold set out to understand for himself. In 1935 he went back to England, retired from the army, hammered together a personal wind tunnel, and began a series of meticulous experiments with blown sand. He considered himself to be a dabbler, a tinkerer, an amateur scientist. But his research resulted in the publication, in 1941, of a small masterpiece of scientific exploration: *The Physics of Blown Sand and Desert Dunes*. It was a treatment so rigorous, and so pleasantly written, that it remains the standard today. Throughout it, Bagnold never lost his wonder. He wrote:

> Here, instead of finding chaos and disorder, the observer never fails to be amazed at a simplicity of form, an exactitude of repetition and a geometric order unknown in nature on a scale larger than that of crystalline structure. In places vast accumulations of sand weighing millions of tons move inexorably, in regular formation, over the surface of the country, growing, retaining their shape, even breeding, in a manner which, by its grotesque imitation of life, is vaguely disturbing to the imaginative mind.

Bagnold's genius was his ability to think grain by grain. He defined sand as a rock particle small enough to be moved by the wind, yet not so small that, like dust, it can float indefinitely in suspension—and he proceeded from there, exploring the movement of each grain. He did his best work on that level, in a laboratory far from the desert. But he was never a tedious man. He understood the power of multiplication. And when he returned to the Sahara, and stood as I did on the crests of the great ergs, he found in these accumulations his truest companions. Just before his death, in May 1990, he wrote a short memoir—an unintentionally sad remembrance of a strong life. He wrote about two world wars, about great men he had known, and about his beloved family. But again he wrote best about the sand. Bagnold's health was declining. It is a measure of the man that when he described the dunes' ability to heal themselves, his writing remained free of longing.

I gave up on finding the road. For all I knew it ended where I stood, in a lost village hundreds of feet below. The sand was a brilliant shade of tan that reflected the sun and filled the air with its heat. Bare rock can produce the same effect. As a result, the Sahara is one of the most reflective places on earth: in heat and light, it fends off 90 percent of the solar energy that assaults its surface. For burrowing creatures like scorpions, this has an essential side effect—it means that just inches underground life feels cool. For creatures above the surface, however, all that redirected energy poses problems. This is something that Bagnold hardly bothered to mention: by early afternoon, when you walk across the sands, the sun burns you from below.

Though I happened to carry a small thermometer, I did not measure the temperature on the Eastern Erg. It was autumn, a gentle season, and I had already been through the greater heat of Saharan summers. Still my hands trembled, and I suffered from the dryness of mouth and tightening of the throat that marks the onset of deep thirst. Retracing my path across the sandy swells, I thought wishfully about more genuine seas.

Imagining water is a normal human reaction to the Sahara. For that reason, and because of the superficial resemblance of the ergs to stormy seas, comparisons to the ocean are inevitable. Still, they have been overdone. Camels are not ships, and nomads do not sail across the sand. *Erg* is Arabic not literally for a sea but for a vein or belt. Dunes do undulate, but they never form genuine waves. Bagnold wrote:

> The resemblance [to a wave] is in appearance only. For the essence of a true wave is the propagation of energy, either through the body of a material as in the case of sound, or along its surface as with a surface water wave. In a sand ripple or wave there is no such propagation of energy. A sand ripple is merely a crumpling or heaping up of the surface, brought about by wind action, and cannot be regarded as a true wave in a strict dynamical sense. The similarity lies only in the regular repetition of surface form.

On the subject of sand, Bagnold was disciplined. He distinguished sternly between drifts, which form below windbreaks, and "true dunes," which achieve their greatest perfection on flat, featureless ground. True dunes breed incestuously, and live in immense look-alike families, sometimes extending across hundreds of miles. Their features depend on the wealth of the sand supply, and on the force and direction of the prevailing winds. In detail they seem infinitely variable. However, it is possible to distinguish between a few basic types.

The barchan is the elemental one—a migratory, crescent-shaped formation with a gentle windward slope up which grains slowly creep, and a steep leeward slip face down which those same grains eventually cascade. Barchans advance by avalanche, sending shallow horns ahead on each side.

They are solitary by nature, and careful conservationists: born of unidirectional winds and limited resources, they retain their shape and bulk by constantly turning over their supply of sand.

Where sand supplies are abundant, the barchans multiply in ever-denser colonies, until eventually they link horns to form scalloped chains perpendicular to the wind.

As the sand thickens, the chains become high ridges across which smaller secondary barchans may begin to migrate. Such compound crescent-shaped dunes are common to the northeast corner of the Eastern Erg, and to other parts of the Sahara where the wind blows from a single direction.

Where the wind is fickle, the sand assumes an entirely different form. Bidirectional winds herd the grains by pushing them first from one angle, then shifting and pushing them from a slightly different angle, finally organizing them into elongated formations that stream downwind in parallel ranks.

Bagnold described these dunes with the word *sief,* which is Arabic for "sword." But they are more like serpents in the way they hump and crawl across the desert floor.

Where the winds blow energetically from around the compass, typically in a pattern of regular seasonal shifts, the sand crawls around less, but builds upward into high-peaked imitations of starfish.

Star dunes embrace El Oued with their tentacles. When one of them stretches, whole villages may disappear.

The forms that dunes take in real sand seas are rarely as simple as their idealized models. Even the concept of sorting—by which the dune types are meant to keep mostly to themselves—is more useful as a theoretical tool than as a practical guide to the field. Bagnold's first achievement, without an airplane and in a time before satellite mapping, was to visualize the geometry. Star dunes sprout on the crests of crescents, which bleed into barchan-crossing barchans. Bagnold's "simplicity of form," his "exactitude of repetition," and his "geometric order," tangle together with the symmetry of a maze.

I blundered into that maze now. Having left my earlier tracks to skirt the highest peaks, I climbed a ridge to reconnoiter, and instead of spotting the old road where I had expected it, found only sand. I could have doubled back to my earlier tracks, but I felt sure the road lay nearby—over the next ridge, or the one beyond. My thirst urged me ahead. I had a few hours still, because the season was not summer, so I was not immediately afraid. But I knew enough about the Sahara to want to keep moving. I ignored the romance of the erg and the mechanics of its dunes. I remembered the stories.

I walked, grew thirsty, and imagined cool water. And where I thought I would find the abandoned road or the half-buried village, I found instead a farmer with a camel, tending his palms behind a palm-front fence. He was dressed in pants and a shirt, and wore a loose turban. He seemed unsurprised that I had strolled out of the dunes.

"Banger, monsieur," he said, in accented French. "You have enjoyed your walk?"

I said I had.

He offered me water, and I drank deeply. He watched this with interest. Saharans sip.

IV

AMERICAN DIRECTIVES

Robert Hass

The Apple Trees at Olema

They are walking in the woods along the coast
and in a grassy meadow, wasting, they come upon
two old neglected apple trees. Moss thickened
every bough and the wood of the limbs looked rotten
but the trees were wild with blossom and a green fire
of small new leaves flickered even on the deadest branches.
Blue-eyes, crane's-bills, little Dutchmen
flecked the meadow, and an intricate, leopard-spotted
leaf-green flower whose name they didn't know.
Trout lily, he said; she said, adder's-tongue.
She is shaken by the raw, white, backlit flaring
of the apple blossoms. He is exultant,
as if some thing he felt were verified,
and looks to her to mirror his response.
If it is afternoon, a thin moon of my own dismay
fades like a scar in the sky to the east of them.
He could be knocking wildly at a closed door
in a dream. She thinks, meanwhile, that moss
resembles seaweed drying lightly on a dock.
Torn flesh, it was the repetitive torn flesh
of appetite in the cold white blossoms
that had startled her. Now they seem tender
and where she was repelled she takes the measure
of the trees and lets them in. But he no longer
has the apple trees. This is as sad or happy
as the tide, going out or coming in, at sunset.
The light catching in the spray that spumes up
on the reef is the color of the lesser finch
they notice now flashing dull gold in the light
above the field. They admire the bird together,
it draws them closer, and they start to walk again.
A small boy wanders corridors of a hotel that way.

Behind one door, a maid. Behind another one, a man
in striped pajamas shaving. He holds the number
of his room close to the center of his mind
gravely and delicately, as if it were the key,
and then he wanders among strangers all he wants.

Gary Snyder

The Rediscovery of Turtle Island

For John Wesley Powell, watershed visionary,
and for Wallace Stegner

I

We human beings of the developed societies have once more been expelled from a garden—the formal garden of Euro-American humanism and its assumptions of human superiority, priority, uniqueness, and dominance. We have been thrown back into that other garden with all the other animals and fungi and insects, where we can no longer be sure we are so privileged. The walls between "nature" and "culture" begin to crumble as we enter a posthuman era. Darwinian insights force occidental people, often unwillingly, to acknowledge their literal kinship with critters.

Ecological science investigates the interconnections of organisms and their constant transactions with energy and matter. Human societies come into being along with the rest of nature. There is no name yet for a humanistic scholarship that embraces the nonhuman. I suggest (in a spirit of pagan play) we call it "panhumanism."

Environmental activists, ecological scientists, and panhumanists are still in the process of reevaluating how to think about, how to create policy with, nature. The professional resource managers of the Forest Service and the Bureau of Land Management have been driven (partly by people of conscience within their own ranks) into rethinking their old utilitarian view of the vast lands in their charge. This is a time of lively confluence, as scientists, self-taught ecosystem experts from the communities, land management agency experts, and a new breed of ecologically aware loggers and ranchers (a few, but growing) are beginning to get together.

In the more rarefied world of ecological and social theory, the confluence is rockier. Nature writing, environmental history, and ecological philosophy have become subjects of study in the humanities. There are, however, still a few otherwise humane historians and philosophers who unreflectingly assume that the natural world is primarily a building-supply yard for human projects. That is what the Occident has said and thought for a couple thousand years.

Right now there are two sets of ideas circling about each other. One group, which we could call the "Savers," places value on extensive preservation of wilderness areas and argues for the importance of the original condition of nature. This view has been tied to the idea that the mature condition of an ecosystem is a stable and diverse state technically called "climax." The other position holds that nature is constantly changing, that human agency has altered things to the point that there is no "natural condition" left, that there is no reason to value climax (or "fitness") over any other succession phase, and that human beings are not only part of nature but that they are also dominant over nature and should keep on using and changing it. They can be called the "Users." The Savers' view is attributed to the Sierra Club and other leading national organizations, to various "radical environmentalists," and to many environmental thinkers and writers. The Users' view, which has a few supporters in the biological sciences, has already become a favorite of the World Bank and those developers who are vexed by the problems associated with legislation that requires protection for creatures whose time and space are running out. It has been quickly seized on by the industry-sponsored pseudopopulist-flavored "Wise Use" movement.

Different as they are, both groups reflect the instrumentalist view of nature that has long been a mainstay of occidental thought. The Savers' idea of freezing some parts of nature into an icon of "pristine, uninhabited wilderness" is also to treat nature like a commodity, kept in a golden cage. Some preservationists have been insensitive to the plight of indigenous peoples whose home grounds were turned into protected wildlife preserves or parks, or to the plight of local workers and farmers who lose jobs as logging and grazing policies change.

The Users, in turn, are both pseudopopulist and multi-national. On the local level they claim to speak for communities and workers (whose dilemma is real enough), but a little probing discloses industry funding. On the global scale their backers line up with huge forces of governments and corporations, with NAFTA and GATT, and raise the specter of further destruction of local communities. Their organizations are staffed by the sort of professionals whom Wendell Berry calls "hired itinerant vandals."

Postmodern theoreticians and critics have recently ventured into nature politics. Many of them have sided with the Users—they like to argue that nature is part of history, that human beings are part of nature, that there is little in the natural world that has not already been altered by human agency, that in any case our idea of "nature" is a projection of our social condition and that there is no sense in trying to preserve a theoretical wild. However, to say that the natural world is subject to continual change, that nature is shaped by history, or that our idea of reality is a self-serving illusion is not new. These positions still fail to come to grips with the question of how to deal with the pain and distress of real beings, plants and animals, as real as suffering humanity; and how to preserve natural variety. The need to protect worldwide biodiversity may be economically difficult and socially controversial, but there are strong scientific and practical arguments in support of it, and it is for many of us a profound ethical issue.

Hominids have obviously had some effect on the natural world, going back for half a million or more years. So we can totally drop the use of the word *pristine* in regard to nature as meaning "untouched by human agency." "Pristine" should now be understood as meaning "virtually" pristine. Almost any apparently untouched natural environment has in fact experienced some tiny degree of human impact. Historically there were huge preagricultural environments where the human impact, rather like deer or cougar activities, was normally almost invisible to any but a tracker's eye. The greatest single preagricultural human effect on wild nature, yet to be fully grasped, was the deliberate use of fire. In some cases human-caused fire seemed to mimic natural process, as with deliberate use of fire by native Californians. Alvar Núñez "Cabeza de Vaca," in his early-sixteenth-century walk across what is now Texas and the Southwest, found well-worn trails everywhere. But the fact still remains that there were great numbers of species, vast grasslands, fertile wetlands, and extensive forests in mosaics of all different stages in the preindustrial world. Barry Commoner has said that the greatest destruction of the world environment—by far—has taken place since 1950.

Furthermore, there is no "original condition" that once altered can never be redeemed. Original nature can be understood in terms of the myth of the "pool of Artemis"—the pool hidden in the forest that Artemis, goddess of wild things, visits to renew her virginity. The wild has—nay, *is*—a kind of hip, renewable virginity.

We are still laying the groundwork for a "culture of nature." The critique of the Judeo-Christian-Cartesian view of nature (by which complex of views all developed nations excuse themselves for their drastically destructive treatment of the landscape) is well under way. Some of us would hope to resume, reevaluate, re-create, and bring into line with complex science that old view that holds the whole phenomenal world to be our own being: multicentered, "alive" in its own manner, and effortlessly self-organizing in its own chaotic way. Elements of this view are found in a wide range of ancient vernacular philosophies, and it turns up in a variety of more sophisticated but still tentative forms in recent thought. It offers a third way, not caught up in the dualisms of body and mind, spirit and matter, or culture and nature. It is a noninstrumentalist view that extends intrinsic value to the nonhuman natural world.

Scouting parties are now following a skein of old tracks, aiming to cross and explore beyond the occidental (and post-modern) divide. I am going to lay out the case history of one of these probes. It's a potentially new story for the North American identity. It has already been in the making for more than thirty years. I call it "the rediscovery of Turtle Island."

II

In January 1969 I attended a gathering of Native American activists in southern California. Hundreds of people had come from all over the West. After sundown we went out to a gravelly wash that came down from the desert mountains. Drums were set up, a fire started, and for most of the night we sang the pantribal songs called "forty-nines." The night conversations circled around the idea of a native-inspired cultural and ecological renaissance for all of North America. I first heard this continent called "Turtle Island" there by a man who said his work was to be a messenger. He had his dark brown long hair tied in a Navajo men's knot, and he wore dusty khakis. He said that Turtle Island was the term that the people were coming to, a new name to help us build the future of North America. I asked him whom or where it came from. He said, "There are many creation myths with Turtle, East Coast and West Coast. But also you can just hear it."

I had recently returned to the West Coast from a ten-year residence in Japan. It was instantly illuminating to hear this continent renamed "Turtle Island." The realignments that conversation suggested were rich and complex. I was reminded that the indigenous people here have a long history of subtle and effective ways of working with their home grounds. They have had an exuberant variety of cultures and economies and some distinctive social forms (such as communal households) that were found throughout the hemisphere. They sometimes fought with each other, but usually with a deep sense of mutual respect. Within each of their various forms of religious life lay a powerful spiritual teaching on the matter of human and natural relationships, and for some individuals a practice of self-realization that came with trying to see through nonhuman eyes. The landscape was intimately known, and the very idea of community and kinship embraced and included the huge populations of wild beings. Much of the truth of Native American history and culture has been obscured by the self-serving histories that were written on behalf of the conquerors, the present dominant society.

This gathering took place one year before the first Earth Day. As I reentered American life during the spring of 1969, I saw the use of the term "Turtle Island" spread through the fugitive Native American newsletters and other communications. I became aware that there was a notable groundswell of white people, too, who were seeing their life in the Western Hemisphere in a new way. Many whites figured that the best they could do on behalf of Turtle Island was to work for the environment, reinhabit the urban or rural margins, learn the landscape, and give support to Native Americans when asked. By 1970 I had moved with my family to the Sierra Nevada and was developing a forest homestead north of the South Yuba River. Many others entered the mountains and hills of the Pacific slope with virtually identical intentions, from the San Diego backcountry north into British Columbia. They had begun the reinhabitory move.

Through the early seventies I worked with my local forest community, but made regular trips to the cities, and was out on long swings around the country reading poems or leading workshops—many in urban areas. Our new sense of the Western Hemisphere permeated everything we did. So I called the book of poems I wrote from that period *Turtle Island* (New York: New Directions, 1974). The introduction says:

> Turtle Island—the old-new name for the continent, based on many creation myths of the people who have been living here for millennia, and reapplied by some of them to "North America" in recent years. Also, an idea found worldwide, of the earth, or cosmos even, sustained by a great turtle or serpent-of-eternity.
>
> A name: that we may see ourselves more accurately on this continent of watersheds and life communities—plant zones, physiographic provinces, culture areas, following natural boundaries. The "U.S.A." and its states and counties are arbitrary and inaccurate impositions on what is really here.
>
> The poems speak of place, and the energy pathways that sustain life. Each living being is a swirl in the flow, a formal turbulence, a "song." The land, the planet itself, is also a living being—at another pace. Anglos, black people, Chicanos, and others beached up on these shores all share such views at the deepest levels of their old cultural

traditions—African, Asian, or European. Hark again to those roots, to see our ancient solidarity, and then to the work of being together on Turtle Island.

Following the publication of these poems, I began to hear back from a lot of people—many in Canada—who were remaking a North American life. Many other writers got into this sort of work each on his or her own—a brilliant and cranky bunch that included Jerry Rothenberg and his translation of Native American song and story into powerful little poem events; Peter Blue Cloud with his evocation of Coyote in a contemporary context; Dennis Tedlock, who offered a storyteller's representation of Zuni oral narrative in English; Ed Abbey, calling for a passionate commitment to the wild; Leslie Silko in her shivery novel *Ceremony;* Simon Ortiz in his early poems and stories—and many more.

A lot of this followed on the heels of the back-to-the-land movement and the diaspora of longhairs and dropout graduate students to rural places in the early seventies. There are thousands of people from those days still making a culture: being teachers, plumbers, chair and cabinet makers, contractors and carpenters, poets in the schools, auto mechanics, geographic information computer consultants, registered foresters, professional storytellers, wildlife workers, river guides, mountain guides, architects, or organic gardeners. Many have simultaneously mastered grass-roots politics and the intricacies of public lands policies. Such people can be found tucked away in the cities, too.

The first wave of writers mentioned left some strong legacies: Rothenberg, Tedlock, and Dell Hymes gave us the field of ethnopoetics (the basis for truly appreciating multicultural literature); Leslie Silko and Simon Ortiz opened the way for a distinguished and diverse body of new American Indian writing; Ed Abbey's eco-warrior spirit led toward the emergence of the radical environmental group Earth First!, which (in splitting) later generated the Wild Lands Project. Some of my own writings contributed to the inclusion of Buddhist ethics and lumber industry work life in the mix, and writers as different as Wes Jackson, Wendell Berry, and Gary Paul Nabhan opened the way for a serious discussion of place, nature in place, and community. The Native American movement has become a serious player in the national debate, and the environmental movement has become (in some cases) big and controversial politics. Although the counterculture has faded and blended in, its fundamental concerns remain a serious part of the dialogue.

A key question is that of our ethical obligations to the nonhuman world. The very notion rattles the foundations of occidental thought. Native American religious beliefs, although not identical coast to coast, are overwhelmingly in support of a full and sensitive acknowledgment of the subjecthood—the intrinsic value—of nature. This in no way backs off from an unflinching awareness of the painful side of wild nature, of acknowledging how everything is being eaten alive. The twentieth-century syncretism of the "Turtle Island view" gathers ideas from Buddhism and Taoism and from the lively details of worldwide animism and paganism. There is no imposition of ideas of progress or order on the natural world—Buddhism teaches impermanence, suffering, compassion, and wisdom. Buddhist teachings go on to say that the true source of compassion and ethical behavior is paradoxically none other than one's own realization of the insubstantial and ephemeral nature of everything. Much of animism and paganism celebrates the actual, with its inevitable pain and death, and affirms the beauty of the process. Add contemporary ecosystem theory and environmental history to this, and you get a sense of what's at work.

Conservation biology, deep ecology, and other new disciplines are given a community constituency and real grounding by the bioregional movement. Bioregionalism calls for commitment to this continent *place by place*, in terms of biogeographical regions and watersheds. It calls us to see our country in terms of its landforms, plant life, weather patterns, and seasonal changes—its whole natural history before the net of political jurisdictions was cast over it. People are challenged to become "reinhabitory"—that is, to become people who are learning to live and think "as if" they were totally engaged with their place for the long future. This doesn't mean some return to a primitive lifestyle or utopian provincialism; it simply implies an engagement with community and a search for the sustainable sophisticated mix of economic practices that would enable people to live regionally and yet learn from and contribute to a planetary society. (Some of the best bioregional work is being done in cities, as people try to restore both human and ecological neighborhoods.) Such people are, regardless of national or ethnic backgrounds, in the process of becoming something deeper than "American (or Mexican or Canadian) citizens"—they are becoming natives of Turtle Island.

Now in the nineties the term "Turtle Island" continues, modestly, to extend its sway. There is a Turtle Island Office that moves around the country with its newsletter; it acts as a national information center for the many bioregional groups that every other year hold a "Turtle Island Congress." Participants come from Canada and Mexico as well as the United States. The use of the term is now standard in a number of Native American periodicals and circles. There is even a "Turtle Island String Quartet" based in San Francisco. In the winter of 1992 I practically convinced the director of the Centro de Estudios Norteamericanos at the Universidad de Alcalá in Madrid to change his department's name to "Estudios de la Isla de Tortuga." He much enjoyed the idea of the shift. We agreed: speak of the United States, and you are talking two centuries of basically English-speaking affairs; speak of "America" and you invoke five centuries of Euro-American schemes in the Western Hemisphere; speak of "Turtle Island" and a vast past, an open future, and all the life communities of plants, humans, and critters come into focus.

III

The Nisenan and Maidu, indigenous people who live on the east side of the Sacramento Valley and into the northern Sierra foothills, tell a creation story that goes something like this:

> Coyote and Earthmaker were blowing around in the swirl of things. Coyote finally had enough of this aimlessness and said, "Earthmaker, find us a world!"
>
> Earthmaker tried to get out of it, tried to excuse himself, because he knew that a world can only mean trouble. But Coyote nagged him into trying. So leaning over the surface of the vast waters, Earthmaker called up Turtle. After a long time Turtle surfaced, and Earthmaker said, "Turtle, can you get me a bit of mud? Coyote wants a world."
>
> "A world," said Turtle. "Why bother? Oh, well." And down she dived. She went down and down and down, to the bottom of the sea. She took a great gob of mud, and started swimming toward the surface. As she spiraled and paddled upward, the streaming water washed the mud from the sides of her mouth, from the back of her mouth—and by the time she reached the surface (the trip took six years), nothing was left but one grain of dirt between the tips of her beak.
>
> "That'll be enough!" said Earthmaker, taking it in his hands and giving it a pat like a tortilla. Suddenly Coyote and Earthmaker were standing on a piece of ground as big as a tarp. Then Earthmaker stamped his feet, and they were standing on a flat wide plain of mud. The ocean was gone. They stood on the land.

And then Coyote began to want trees and plants, and scenery, and the story goes on to tell how Coyote imagined landscapes that then came forth, and how he started naming the animals and plants as they appeared. "I'll call you skunk because you look like skunk." And the landscapes Coyote imagined are there today.

My children grew up with this as their first creation story. When they later heard the Bible story, they said, "That's a lot like Coyote and Earthmaker." But the Nisenan story gave them their own immediate landscape, complete with details, and the characters were animals from their own world.

Mythopoetic play can be part of what jump-starts long-range social change. But what about the short term? There are some immediate outcomes worth mentioning: a new era of community interaction with public lands has begun. In California a new set of ecosystem-based government/community joint-management discussions are beginning to take place. Some of the most vital environmental politics is being done by watershed or ecosystem-based groups. "Ecosystem management" by definition includes private landowners in the mix. In my corner of the northern Sierra, we are practicing being a "human-inhabited wildlife corridor"—an area that functions as a biological connector—and are coming to certain agreed-on practices that will enhance wildlife survival even as dozens of households continue to live here. Such neighborhood agreements would be one key to preserving wildlife diversity in most Third World countries.

Ultimately we can all lay claim to the term *native* and the songs and dances, the beads and feathers, and the profound responsibilities that go with it. We are all indigenous to this planet, this mosaic of wild gardens we are being called by nature and history to reinhabit in good spirit. Part of that responsibility is to choose a place. To restore the land one must live and work in a place. To work in a place is to work with others. People who work together in a place become a community, and a community, in time, grows a culture. To work on behalf of the wild is to restore culture.

[The University of California Humanities Research Institute sponsored a yearlong study called "Reinventing Nature" in 1992–93. Four conferences were held at four different campuses. It was an odd exercise: the occulted agenda seemed to ask that a critique of naive and sentimental environmentalism be done by postmodernist humanists and critics. The good-hearted humanists in fact had nothing against the environmentalists, and the conservation biology and bioregional enthusiasts (like me) told the narratives they knew best—our own goofy breakaway revision of nature based on backpacking, zazen, Taoist parables, Coyote tales, half-understood cutting-edge science, Mahayana sutras, and field biology handbooks. This essay is based on a talk given at "Reinventing Nature/Recovering the Wild," the last conference in the series, held at the University of California at Davis, October 1993.]

Edward Abbey

The Moon-Eyed Horse

When we reached Salt Creek we stopped to water the horses. I needed a drink myself but the water here would make a man sick. We'd find good water farther up the canyon at Cigarette Spring.

While Mackie indulged himself in a smoke I looked at the scenery, staring out from under the shelter of my hat brim. The glare was hard on the eyes and for relief I looked down, past the mane and ears of my drinking horse, to something near at hand. There was the clear shallow stream, the green wiregrass standing stiff as bristles out of the alkali-encrusted mud, the usual deerflies and gnats swarming above the cattle tracks and dung.

I noticed something I thought a little odd. Cutting directly across the cattle paths were the hoofprints of an unshod horse. They led straight to the water and back again, following a vague little trail that led into the nearest side canyon, winding around blackbrush and cactus, shortcutting the meanders of the wash.

I studied the evidence for a while, trying to figure everything out for myself before mentioning it to Mackie, who knew this country far better than I ever would. He was a local man, a Moabite, temporarily filling in for Viviano Jacquez, who'd had another quarrel with old Roy Scobie and disappeared for a few days.

"There's a horse living up that canyon," I announced; "a wild horse. And a big one—feet like frying pans."

Slowly Mackie turned his head and looked where I pointed. "Wrong again," he said, after a moment's consideration.

"What do you mean, wrong again? If it's not a horse it must be a unicorn. Or a centaur? Look at those tracks—unshod. And from the wear and tear on that trail it's been living out here for a long time. Who runs horses out here?" We were about twenty miles from the nearest ranch.

"Nobody," Mackie agreed.

"You agree it's a horse."

"Of course it's a horse."

"Of course it's a horse. Well thank you very much. And no shoes, living out here in the middle of nothing, it must be a *wild* horse."

"Sorry," Mackie said. "Wrong again."

"Then what the hell is it?"

"Old Moon-Eye is what you might call an independent horse. He don't belong to anybody. But he ain't wild. He's a gelding and he's got Roy Scobie's brand on his hide."

I stared up the side canyon to where the tracks went out of sight around the first bend. "And this Moon-Eye lives up there all by himself?"

"That's right. He's been up in that canyon for ten years."

"Have you seen him?"

"No. Moon-Eye is very shy. But I heard about him."

Our mounts had raised their heads from the water and shifting rest-lessly under our weight, they seemed anxious to move on. Mackie turned his horse up the main trail along the stream and I followed, thinking.

"I want that horse," I said.

"What for?"

"I don't know."

"You can have him."

We rode steadily up the canyon, now and then splashing through the water, passing under the high red walls, the hanging gardens of poison ivy and panicgrass, the flowing sky. Where the trail widened I jogged my horse beside Mackie's and after a while, with a little prodding, extracted from him the story of the independent horse.

First of all, Moon-Eye had suffered. He had problems. His name de-rived from an inflamed condition of one of his eyes called moonblindness, which affected him periodically and inflamed his temper. The gelding op-eration had not improved his disposition. On top of that he'd been dude-spoiled, for old Roy had used him for many years—since he made a poor cow horse—in his string of horses for hire. The horse Moon-Eye seemed safe and well-behaved but his actual feelings were revealed one day on a sight-seeing tour through the Arches when all his angers came to a boil and he bucked off a middle-aged lady from Salt Lake City. Viviano Jacquez, leading the ride, lost his temper and gave the horse a savage beating. Moon-Eye broke away and ran off into the canyons with a good saddle on his back. He didn't come back that night. Didn't come back the next day. Never came back at all. For two weeks Viviano and Roy tracked that horse not because they wanted the horse but because Roy wanted his saddle back. When they found the saddle, caught on the stub of a limb, the cinch straps broken, they gave up the search for the horse. The bridle they never recovered. Later on a few boys from town came out to try to catch the horse and almost got him boxed up in Salt Creek Canyon. But he got away, clattering over the slickrock wall at an angle of 45 degrees, and was seldom seen afterward. After that he stayed out of box canyons and came down to the creek only when he needed a drink. That was the story of Moon-Eye.

We came at noon to the spring, dismounted, unsaddled the horses and let them graze on the tough brown grass near the cottonwoods. We dipped our cupped hands in the water and drank, leaned back against a log in the cool of the shade and ate some lunch. Mackie lit a cigarette. I stared out past the horses at the sweet green of the willows and cottonwoods under the hot red canyon wall. Far above, a strip of blue sky, cloudless. In the silence I heard quite clearly the buzzing of individual flies down by the creek, the shake and whisper of the dry cottonwood leaves, the bright tinkling song of a canyon wren. The horses shuffled slowly through the dead leaves, ripping up the grass with their powerful, hungry jaws—a solid and pleasing sound. The canyon filled with heat and stillness.

"Look, Mackie," I said, "what do you suppose that horse does up in there?"

"What horse?"

"Moon-Eye. You say he's been up that dry canyon by himself for ten years."

"Right."

"What does he *do* up in there?"

"That is a ridiculous question."

"All right it's a ridiculous question. Try and answer it."

"How the hell should I know? Who cares? What difference does it make?"

"Answer the question."

"He eats. He sleeps. He walks down to the creek once a day for a drink. He turns around and walks back. He eats again. He sleeps again."

"The horse is a gregarious beast," I said, "a herd animal, like the cow, like the human. It's not natural for a horse to live alone."

"Moon-Eye is not a natural horse."

"He's supernatural?"

"He's crazy. How should I know? Go ask the horse."

"Okay, I'll do that."

"Only not today," Mackie said. "Let's get on up and out of here."

We'd laid around long enough. Mackie threw away the butt of his cigarette; I tanked up on more water. We mounted again, rode on to the head of the canyon where a forty-foot overhang barred the way, turned and rode back the way we'd come, clearing out the cattle from the brush and tamarisk thickets, driving them before us in a growing herd as we proceeded. By the time we reached the mouth of the canyon we had a troop of twenty head plodding before us through the dust and heat, half of them little white-faced calves who'd never seen a man or a horse before. We drove them into the catchpen and shut them up. Tomorrow the calves would be branded, castrated, earmarked, dehorned, inoculated against blackleg, and the whole herd trucked to the mountains for the summer. But that would be a job for Mackie and Roy, not for me; for me tomorrow meant a return to sentry duty at the entrance of the Monument, the juniper guard and the cloud-formation survey.

As we loaded the horses into the truck for the return to the ranch I asked Mackie how he liked this kind of work. He looked at me. His shirt and the rag around his neck were dark with sweat, his face coated with dust; there was a stripe of dried blood across his cheek where a willow branch had struck him when he plunged through the brush after some ignorant cow.

"Look at yourself," he said.

I looked; I was in the same condition. "I do this only for fun," I explained. "If I did it for pay I might not like it. Anyway you haven't answered my question. How do *you* like this kind of work?"

"I'd rather be rich."

"What would you do if you were rich?"

He grinned through the dust. "Buy some cows of my own."

I hadn't forgotten the moon-eyed horse. A month later I was back at the spot by Salt Creek where I'd first seen the tracks, this time alone, though again on horseback. We were deep into the desert summer now and the stream had shrunk to a dribble of slimy water oozing along between sun-baked flats of mud.

As before I let my pony drink what he wanted from the stream while I pondered the view from beneath the meager shelter of my hat. The alkali, white as lime, dazzled the eyes; the wiregrass looked sere and shriveled and even the hosts of flies and gnats had disappeared, hiding from the sun.

There was no sound but the noise of my drinking mount, no sight anywhere of animate life. In the still air the pinkish plumes of the tamarisk, light and delicate as lace, drooped from the tips of their branches without a tremor. Nothing moved, nothing stirred, except the shimmer of heat waves rising before the red canyon walls.

I could hardly have picked a more hostile day for a venture into the canyons. If anyone had asked I'd have said that not even a mad horse would endure a summer in such a place. Yet there were the tracks as before, coming down the pathway out of the side canyon and leading back again. Moon-Eye was still around. Or at any rate his tracks were still here, fresh prints in the dust that looked as if they might have been made only minutes before my arrival.

Out of the heat and stillness came an inaudible whisper, a sort of telepathic intimation that perhaps the horse did not exist at all—only his tracks. You ought to get out of this heat, I told myself, taking a drink from the canteen. My saddle horse raised his dripping muzzle from the water and waited. He turned his head to look at me with one drowsy eye; strings of algae hung from the corner of his mouth.

"No," I said, "we're not going home yet." I prodded the animal with my heels; slowly we moved up into the side canyon following the narrow trail. As we advanced I reviewed my strategy: since Moon-Eye had learned to fear and distrust men on horseback I would approach him on foot; I would carry nothing in my hands but a hackamore and a short lead rope. Better yet, I would hide these inside my shirt and go up to Moon-Eye with empty hands. Others had attempted the violent method of pursuit and capture and had failed. I was going to use nothing but sympathy and understanding, in direct violation of common sense and all precedent, to bring Moon-Eye home again.

I rounded the first bend in the canyon and stopped. Ahead was the typical scene of dry wash, saltbush and prickly pear, talus slopes at the foot of vertical canyon walls. No hint of animal life. Nothing but the silence, the stark suspension of all sound. I rode on. I was sure that Moon-Eye would not go far from water in this weather.

At the next turn in the canyon, a mile farther, I found a pile of fresh droppings on the path. I slid from the saddle and led my pony to the east side of the nearest boulder and tied him. Late in the afternoon he'd get a little shade. It was the best I could do for him; nothing else was available.

I pulled off the saddle and sat down on the ground to open a can of tomatoes. One o'clock by the sun and not a cloud in the sky: hot. I squatted under the belly of the horse and ate my lunch.

When I was finished I got up, reluctantly, stuffed hackamore and rope inside my shirt, hung the canteen over my shoulder and started off. The pony watched me go, head hanging, the familiar look of dull misery in his eyes. I know how you feel, I thought, but by God you're just going to have to stand there and suffer. If I can take it you can. The midday heat figured in my plan: I believed that in such heat the moon-eyed outlaw would be docile as a plow horse, amenable to reason. I thought I could amble close, slip the hackamore over his head and lead him home like a pet dog on a leash.

A mile farther and I had to take refuge beneath a slight overhang in the canyon wall. I took off my hat to let the evaporation of my sweaty brow cool my brains. Tilted the canteen to my mouth. Already I was having visions of iced drinks, waterfalls, shade trees, clear deep emerald pools.

Forward. I shuffled through the sand, over the rocks, around the prickly pear and the spiny hedgehog cactus. I found a yellowish pebble the size of a crab apple and put it in my mouth. Kept going, pushing through the heat.

If you were really clever, I thought, you'd go back to Moon-Eye's watering place on Salt Creek, wait for him there, catch him by starlight. But you're not clever, you're stupid, I reminded myself: stick to the plan. I stopped to swab the sweat from my face. The silence locked around me again like a sphere of glass. Even the noise I made unscrewing the cap from the canteen seemed harsh and exaggerated, a gross intrusion.

I listened:

Something breathing nearby—I was in the presence of a tree. On the slope above stood a giant old juniper with massive, twisted trunk, its boughs sprinkled with the pale-blue inedible berries. Hanging from one of the limbs was what looked at first glance like a pair of trousers that reached to the ground. Blinking the sweat out of my eyes I looked harder and saw the trousers transform themselves into the legs of a large animal, focused my attention and distinguished through the obscurity of the branches and foliage the outline of a tall horse. A very tall horse.

Gently I lowered my canteen to the ground.

I touched the rope and hackamore bunched up inside my shirt. Still there. I took the pebble from my mouth, held it in my palm, and slowly and carefully and quietly stepped toward the tree. Out of the tree a gleaming eyeball watched me coming.

I said, "That you, Moon-Eye?"

Who else? The eyeball rolled, I saw the flash of white. The eye in the tree.

I stepped closer. "What are you doing out here, you old fool?"

The horse stood not under the tree—the juniper was not big enough for that—but within it, among its branches. There'd be an awful smashing and crashing of dry wood if he tried to drive out of there.

"Eh? What do you think you're up to anyway? Damned old idiot. . . ." I showed him the yellowish stone in my hand, round as a little apple. "Why don't you answer me, Moon-Eye? Forgotten how to talk?"

Moving closer. The horse remained rigid, ears up. I could see both eyes now, the good one and the bad one—moonstruck, like a bloodshot cueball.

"I've come to take you home, old horse. What do you think of that?"

He was a giant about seventeen hands high, with a buckskin hide as faded as an old rug and a big ugly coffin-shaped head.

"You've been out here in the wilderness long enough, old man. It's time to go home."

He looked old, all right, he looked his years. He looked more than old—he looked like a spectre. Apocalyptic, a creature out of a bad dream.

"You hear me, Moon-Eye? I'm coming closer. . . ."

His nineteen ribs jutted out like the rack of a skeleton and his neck, like a camel's, seemed far too gaunt and long to carry that oversize head off the ground.

"You old brute," I murmured, "you hideous old gargoyle. You goddamned nightmare of a horse. . . . Moon-Eye, look at this. Look at this in my hand, Moon-Eye."

He watched me, watched my eyes. I was within twenty feet of him and except for the eyes he had yet to reveal a twitch of nerve or muscle; he might have been petrified. Mesmerized by sun and loneliness. He hadn't seen a man for—how many years?

"Moon-Eye," I said, approaching slowly, one short step, a pause, another step, "how long since you've stuck that ugly face of yours into a bucket of barley and bran? Remember what alfalfa tastes like, old pardner? How about grass, Moon-Eye? Green sweet fresh succulent grass, Moon-Eye, what do you think of that, eh?"

We were ten feet apart. Only the branches of the juniper tree separated us. Standing there watching the horse I could smell the odor of cedarwood, the fragrance of the tree.

Another step. "Moon-Eye. . . ."

I hesitated; to get any closer I'd have to push through the branches or stoop underneath them. "Come on, Moon-Eye, I want to take you home. It's time to go home, oldtimer."

We stared at each other, unmoving. If that animal was breathing I couldn't hear it—the silence seemed absolute. Not a fly, not a single fly crawled over his arid skin or whined around his rheumy eyeballs. If it hadn't been for the light of something like consciousness in his good eye I might have imagined I was talking to a scarecrow, a dried stuffed completely mummified horse. He didn't even smell like a horse, didn't seem to have any smell about him at all. Perhaps if I reached out and touched him he would crumble to a cloud of dust, vanish like a shadow.

My head ached from the heat and glare and for a moment I wondered if this horselike shape in front of me was anything more than hallucination.

"Moon-Eye. . . . ?" Keep talking.

I couldn't stand there all afternoon. I took another step forward, pressing against a branch. Got to keep talking.

"Moon-Eye. . . ."

He lowered his head a couple of inches, the ears flattened back. Watch out. He was still alive after all. For the first time I felt a little fear. He was a big horse and that moon-glazed eye was not comforting. We watched each other intently through the branches of the tree. If I could only wait, only be patient, I might yet sweet-talk him into surrender. But it was too hot.

"Look here, old horse, have a sniff of this." I offered him the pebble with one hand and with the other unbuttoned a button of my shirt, preparing to ease out the rope when the chance came. "Go on, have a look. . . ."

I was within six feet of the monster.

"Now you just relax, Moon-Eye old boy. I'm coming in where you are now." I started to push through the boughs of the juniper. "Easy boy, easy now. . . ."

He backed violently, jarring the whole tree. Loose twigs and berries rained around us. The good eye glared at me, the bad one shone like a boiled egg—monocular vision.

"Take it easy, old buddy." Speaking softly. I had one hand on the rope. I stepped forward again, pushing under the branches. Softly—"Easy, easy, don't be scared—"

Moon-Eye tried to back again but his retreat was blocked. Snorting like a truck he came forward, right at me, bursting through the branches. Dry wood snapped and popped, dust filled the air, and as I dove for the ground I had a glimpse of a lunatic horse expanding suddenly, growing bigger than all the world and soaring over me on wings that flapped like a bat's and nearly tore the tree out of the earth.

When I opened my eyes a second later I was still alive and Moon-Eye was down in the wash fifty feet away, motionless as a statue, waiting. He stood with his ragged broomtail and his right angled pelvic bones toward me but had that long neck and coffin head cranked around, watching me with the good eye, waiting to see what I would do next. He didn't intend to exert himself unless he was forced to.

The shade of the tree was pleasant and I made no hurry to get up. I sat against the trunk and checked for broken bones. Everything seemed all right except my hat a few feet away, crushed into the dirt by a mighty hoof. I was thirsty though and looked around for the canteen before remembering where I'd left it; I could see it down in the wash, near the horse.

Moon-Eye didn't move. He stood rigid as stone, conserving every drop of moisture in his body. But he was in the sun now and I was in the shade. Perhaps if I waited long enough he'd be forced to come back to the tree. I made myself comfortable and waited. The silence settled in again.

But that horse wouldn't come, though I waited a full hour by the sun. The horse moved only once in all that time, lowering his head for a sniff at a bush near his foreleg.

The red cliffs rippled behind the veil of heat, radiant as hot iron. Thirst was getting to me. I stirred myself, got up painfully, and stepped out of the wreckage of the juniper. The horse made no move.

"Moon-Eye," I said—he listened carefully—"let's get out of here. What do you say? Let's go home, you miserable old bucket of guts. Okay?"

I picked up my flattened hat, reformed it, put it on.

"Well, what do you say?"

I started down the slope. He raised his head, twitched one ear, watching me. "Are you crazy, old horse, standing out here in the heat? Don't you have any sense at all?"

I did not approach him directly this time but moved obliquely across the slope, hoping to head him down the canyon toward the creek and the trail to the corral. Moon-Eye saw my purpose and started up the canyon. I hurried; the horse moved faster. I slowed to a walk; he did the same. I stopped and he stopped.

"Moon-Eye, let me tell you something. I can outrun you if I have to. These Utah cowboys would laugh themselves sick if I ever mentioned it out loud but it's a fact and you ought to know it. Over the long haul, say twenty or thirty miles, it's a known fact that a healthy man can outrun a horse."

Moon-Eye listened.

"But my God, in this heat, Moon-Eye, do you think we should? Be sensible. Let's not make fools of ourselves."

He waited. I squatted on my heels and passed my forefinger, like a windshield wiper, across my forehead, brushing off the streams of sweat. My head felt hot, damp, feverish.

"What's the matter with you, Moon-Eye?"

The horse kept his good eye on me.

"Are you crazy, maybe? You don't want to die out here, do you, all alone like a hermit? In this awful place. . . ." He watched me and listened. "The Turkey buzzards will get you, Moon-Eye. They'll smell you dying, they'll come flapping down on you like foul and dirty kites and roost on your neck and drink your eyeballs while you're still alive. Yes, they do that. And just before that good eye is punctured you'll see those black wings shutting off the sky, shutting out the sun, you'll see a crooked yellow beak and a red neck crawling with lice and a pair of insane eyes looking into yours. You won't like that, old horse. . . ."

I paused. Moon-Eye was listening, he seemed attentive, but I sensed that he wasn't really much interested in what I was saying. Perhaps it was all an old story to him. Maybe he didn't care.

I continued with the sermon. "And when the buzzards are through with you, Moon-Eye—and you'll be glad when *that's* over—why then a quiet little coyote will come loping down the canyon in the middle of the night under the moon, Moon-Eye, nosing out your soul. He'll come to within fifty yards of you, old comrade, and sit for a few hours, thinking, and then he'll circle around you a few times trying to smell out the hand of man. Pretty soon his belly will get the best of his caution—maybe he hasn't eaten for two weeks and hasn't had a chance at a dead horse for two years—and so he'll come nosing close to you, tongue out and eyes bright with happiness, and all at once when you're hardly expecting it he'll pounce and hook his fangs into your scrawny old haunch and tear off a steak. Are you listening to me, Moon-Eye? And when he's gorged himself sick he'll retire for a few hours of peaceful digestion. In the meantime the ants and beetles and blowflies will go to work, excavating tunnels through your lungs, kidneys, stomach, windpipe, brains and entrails and whatever else the buzzards and the coyote leave."

Moon-Eye watched me as I spoke; I watched him. "And in a couple of weeks you won't even stink anymore and after a couple of months there'll be nothing left but your mangled hide and your separated bones and—get this, Moon-Eye get the picture—way out in eternity somewhere, on the far side of the sun, they'll hang up a brass plaque with the image of your moon-eyed soul stamped on it. That's about all. Years later some tired and dirty cowboy looking for a lost horse, some weary prospector looking for potash or beryllium will stumble up this way and come across your clean white rib cage, your immaculate skull, a few other bones. . . ."

I stopped talking. I was tired. Would that sun never go down beyond the canyon wall? Wasn't there a cloud in the whole state of Utah?

The horse stood motionless as a rock. He looked like part of that burnt-out landscape. He looked like the steed of Don Quixote carved out of wood by Giacometti. I could see the blue of the sky between his ribs, through the eyesockets of his skull. Dry, odorless, still and silent, he looked like the idea—without the substance—of a horse.

My brain and eyes ached, my limbs felt hollow, I had to breathe deliberately, making a conscious effort. The thought of the long walk back to my saddle pony, the long ride back to the pickup truck, made my heart sink. I didn't want to move. So I'd wait, too, wait for sundown before starting the march home, the *anabasis* in retreat. I glanced toward the sun. About four o'clock. Another hour before that sun would reach the rim of the canyon. I crawled back to the spotted shade of the juniper and waited.

We waited then, the horse and I, enduring the endless afternoon, the heartbreaking heat, and passed the time as best we could in one-sided conversation. I'd speak a sentence and wait about ten minutes for the next thought and speak again. Moon-Eye watched me all the time and made no move.

At last the sun touched the skyline, merged with it for a moment in a final explosive blaze of light and heat and sank out of sight. The shadow of the canyon wall advanced across the canyon floor, included the horse, touched the rocks and brush on the far side. A wave of cooling relief like a breeze, like an actual movement of air, washed through the canyon. A rock wren sang, a few flies came out of hiding and droned around the juniper tree. I could almost see the leaves of the saltbush and blackbush relax a little, uncurling in the evening air.

I stood up and emerged from the shelter of the broken tree. Old Moon-Eye took a few steps away from me, stopped. Still watching. We faced each other across some fifty feet of sand and rock. No doubt for the last time. I tried to think of something suitable to say but my mouth was so dry, my tongue so stiff, my lips so dried-out and cracked, I could barely utter a word.

"You damned stupid harrr. . . ." I croaked, and gave it up.

Moon-Eye blinked his good eye once, twitched his hide and kept watching me as all around us, along the wash and on the canyon walls and in the air the desert birds and desert bugs resumed their inexplicable careers. A whiptail lizard scurried past my feet. A primrose opened its petals a few inches above the still-hot sand. Knees shaking, I stepped toward the horse, pulled the ropy hackamore out of my shirt—to Moon-Eye it must have looked as if I were pulling out my intestines—and threw the thing with all the strength I had left straight at him. It slithered over his back like a hairy snake, scaring him into a few quick steps. Again he stopped, the eye on me.

Enough. I turned my back on the horse and went to the canteen, picked it up. The water was almost too hot to drink but I drank it. Drank it all, except a few drops which I poured on my fingers and dabbed on my aching forehead. Refusing to look again at the spectre horse, I slung the canteen over my shoulder and started homeward, trudging over the clashing stones and through the sand down-canyon toward my pony and Salt Creek.

Once, twice, I thought I heard footsteps following me but when I looked back I saw nothing.

Barry Lopez

The Stone Horse

1

The deserts of southern California, the high, relatively cooler and wetter Mojave and the hotter, dryer Colorado to the south of it, carry the signatures of many cultures. Prehistoric rock drawings in the Mojave's Coso Range, representing the greatest concentration of petroglyphs in North America, are probably 3,000 years old. Big-game-hunting cultures that flourished there six or seven thousand years before that are known from broken spear tips, choppers, and burins left scattered along the shores of great Pleistocene lakes, long since evaporated. A burial site in the Yuha Basin in the Colorado Desert may be 20,000 years old; and worked stone from a quarry in the Calico Mountains is, many argue, evidence that human beings were here more than 200,000 years ago.

Because of the long-term stability of such arid environments, many of these prehistoric stone artifacts still lie exposed on the ground, accessible to anyone who passes by — the studious, the acquisitive, the indifferent, the merely curious. Archaeologists do not agree on the cultural sequence beyond about 10,000 years ago, but it is clear that these broken bits of chalcedony, chert, and obsidian, like the animal drawings and geometric designs etched on walls of basalt throughout the desert, anchor the earliest threads of human history, the first record of human endeavor here.

Western man did not journey into the California desert until the end of the eighteenth century, 250 years after Coronado brought his soldiers into the Zuni pueblos in a bewildered search for the cities of Cibola. The earliest appraisals of the land were cursory, hurried. People traveled *through* it, en route to Santa Fe or the California coastal settlements. Only miners tarried. In 1823 what had been Spain's became Mexico's and in 1848 what had been Mexico's became America's; but the bare, jagged mountains and dry lake beds, the vast and uniform plains of creosote bush and yucca plants, remained as obscure as the northern Sudan until the end of the nineteenth century.

Before 1940 the tangible evidence of twentieth-century man's passage here consisted of very little—the hard tracery of his travel corridors; the widely scattered, relatively insignificant evidence of his mining operations; and the fair expanse of his irrigated fields at the desert's periphery. In the space of a hundred years or so the wagon roads were paved, railroads were laid down, and canals and high-tension lines were built to bring water and electricity across the desert to Los Angeles from the Colorado River. The dark mouths of gold, talc, and tin mines yawned from the bony flanks of desert ranges. Dust-encrusted chemical plants stood at work on the lonely edges of dry lake beds. And crops of grapes, lettuce, dates, alfalfa, and cotton covered the Coachella and Imperial valleys, north and south of the Salton Sea, and the Palo Verde Valley along the Colorado.

These developments proceeded with little or no awareness of earlier human occupations by the cultures that preceded those of the historic Indians—the Mohave, the Chemehuevi, the Quechan, and others. (Extensive irrigation began to actually change the climate of the Colorado Desert, and human settlements, the railroads, and farming introduced many new, successful plants and animals into the region.)

During World War II, the American military moved into the desert in great force, to train troops and to test equipment. They found the dry air, isolation, and clear weather conducive to year-round flying very attractive. After the war, the complex of training grounds, storage facilities, and gunnery and test ranges was permanently settled on more than three million acres of military reservations. Few perceived the extent or significance of the destruction of aboriginal sites that took place during tank maneuvers and bombing runs or in the laying out of highways, railroads, mining districts, and irrigated fields. The few who intuited that something like an American Dordogne Valley lay exposed here were (only) amateur archaeologists; even they reasoned that the desert was too vast for any of this to matter.

After World War II, people began moving out of the crowded Los Angeles basin into homes in Lucerne, Apple, and Antelope valleys in the western Mojave. They emigrated as well to a stretch of resort land at the foot of the San Jacinto Mountains that included Palm Springs, and farther out to old railroad and military towns like Needles and Barstow. People also began exploring the desert, at first in military-surplus jeeps and then with a variety of all-terrain and off-road vehicles that became available in the 1960s. By the mid-1970s, the number of people using such vehicles for desert recreation had increased exponentially. Most came and went in innocent curiosity; the few who didn't wreaked a unique havoc all out of proportion to their numbers. The disturbance of previously isolated archaeological sites increased substantially. Many of these early-man sites as well as prehistoric rock drawings were vandalized before archaeologists, themselves late to the desert, had any firm grasp of the bounds of human history in the desert. It was as though an Aztec library had been found intact and at the same moment numerous lacunae had appeared.

The vandalism was of three sorts: the general disturbance usually caused by souvenir hunters and by the curious and the oblivious; the wholesale stripping of a place by professional thieves for black-market sale and trade; and outright destruction, in which vehicles were actually used to ram and trench an area. By 1980, the Bureau of Land Management estimated that probably 35 percent of the archaeological sites in the desert had been vandalized. The destruction at some places by rifles and shotguns, or by power winches mounted on vehicles, were, if one cared for history, demoralizing to behold.

In spite of public education, land closures, and stricter law enforcement in recent years, the BLM estimates that, annually, about 1 percent of the archaeological record in the desert continues to be destroyed or stolen.

2

A BLM archaeologist told me, with understandable reluctance, where to find the intaglio. I spread my Automobile Club of Southern California map of Imperial County out on his desk, and he traced the route with a pink, felt-tip pen. The line crossed Interstate 8 and then turned west along the Mexican border.

"You can't drive any farther than about here," he said, marking a small X. "There's boulders in the wash. You walk up past them."

On a separate piece of paper he drew a route in a smaller scale that would take me up the arroyo to a certain point where I was to cross back east, to another arroyo. At its head, on higher ground just to the north, I would find the horse.

"It's tough to spot unless you know it's there. Once you pick it up . . ." He shook his head slowly, in a gesture of wonder at its existence.

I waited until I held his eye. I assured him I would not tell anyone else how to get there. He looked at me with stoical despair, like a man who had been robbed twice, whose belief in human beings was offered without conviction.

I did not go until the following day because I wanted to see it at dawn. I ate breakfast at 4 a.m. in El Centro and then drove south. The route was easy to follow, though the last section of road proved difficult, broken and drifted over with sand in some spots. I came to the barricade of boulders and parked. It was light enough by then to find my way over the ground with little trouble. The contours of the landscape were stark, without any masking vegetation. I worried only about rattlesnakes.

I traversed the stone plain as directed, but, in spite of the frankness of the land, I came on the horse unawares. In the first moment of recognition I was without feeling. I recalled later being startled, and that I held my breath. It was laid out on the ground with its head to the east, three times life size. As I took in its outline I felt a growing concentration of all my senses, as though my attentiveness to the pale rose color of the morning sky and other peripheral images had now ceased to be important. I was aware that I was straining for sound in the windless air and I felt the uneven pressure of the earth hard against my feet. The horse, outlined in a standing profile on the dark ground, was as vivid before me as a bed of tulips.

I've come upon animals suddenly before, and felt a similar tension, a precipitate heightening of the senses. And I have felt the inexplicable but sharply boosted intensity of a wild moment in the bush, where it is not until some minutes later that you discover the source of electricity — the warm remains of a grizzly bear kill, or the still moist tracks of a wolverine.

But this was slightly different. I felt I had stepped into an unoccupied corridor. I had no familiar sense of history, the temporal structure in which to think: This horse was made by Quechan people three hundred years ago. I felt instead a headlong rush of images: people hunting wild horses with spears on the Pleistocene veld of southern California; Cortés riding across the causeway into Montezuma's Tenochtitlán; a short-legged Comanche, astride his horse like some sort of ferret, slashing through cavalry lines of young men who rode like farmers. A hoof exploding past my face one morning in a corral in Wyoming. These images had the weight and silence of stone.

When I released my breath, the images softened. My initial feeling, of facing a wild animal in a remote region, was replaced with a calm sense of antiquity. It was then that I became conscious, like an ordinary tourist, of what was before me, and thought: This horse was probably laid out by Quechan people. But when, I wondered? The first horses they saw, I knew, might have been those that came north from Mexico in 1692 with Father Eusebio Kino. But Cocopa people, I recalled, also came this far north on occasion, to fight with their neighbors, the Quechan. And *they* could have seen horses with Melchior Díaz, at the mouth of the Colorado River in the fall of 1540. So, it could be four hundred years old. (No one in fact knows.)

I still had not moved. I took my eyes off the horse for a moment to look south over the desert plain into Mexico, to look east past its head at the brightening sunrise, to situate myself. Then, finally, I brought my trailing foot slowly forward and stood erect. Sunlight was running like a thin sheet of water over the stony ground and it threw the horse into relief. It looked as though no hand had ever disturbed the stones that gave it its form.

The horse had been brought to life on ground called desert pavement, a tight, flat matrix of small cobbles blasted smooth by sand-laden winds. The uniform, monochromatic blackness of the stones, a patina of iron and magnesium oxides called desert varnish, is caused by long-term exposure to the sun. To make this type of low-relief ground glyph, or intaglio, the artist either selectively turns individual stones over to their lighter side or removes areas of stone to expose the lighter soil underneath, creating a negative image. This horse, about eighteen feet from brow to rump and eight feet from withers to hoof, had been made in the latter way, and its outline was bermed at certain points with low ridges of stone a few inches high to enhance its three-dimensional qualities. (The left side of the horse was in full profile; each leg was extended at 90 degrees to the body and fully visible, as though seen in three-quarter profile.)

I was not eager to move. The moment I did I would be back in the flow of time, the horse no longer quivering in the same way before me. I did not want to feel again the sequence of quotidian events—to be drawn off into deliberation and analysis. A human being, a four-footed animal, the open land. That was all that was present—and a "thoughtless" understanding of the very old desires bearing on this particular animal: to hunt it, to render it, to fathom it, to subjugate it, to honor it, to take it as a companion.

What finally made me move was the light. The sun now filled the shallow basin of the horse's body. The weighted line of the stone berm created the illusion of a mane and the distinctive roundness of an equine belly. The change in definition impelled me. I moved to the left, circling past its rump, to see how the light might flesh the horse out from various points of view. I circled it completely before squatting on my haunches. Ten or fifteen minutes later I chose another view. The third time I moved, to a point near the rear hooves, I spotted a stone tool at my feet. I stared at it a long while, more in awe than disbelief, before reaching out to pick it up. I turned it over in my left palm and took it between my fingers to feel its cutting edge. It is always difficult, especially with something so portable, to rechannel the desire to steal.

I spent several hours with the horse. As I changed positions and as the angle of the light continued to change I noticed a number of things. The angle at which the pastern carried the hoof away from the ankle was perfect. Also, stones had been placed within the image to suggest at precisely the right spot the left shoulder above the foreleg. The line that joined thigh and hock was similarly accurate. The muzzle alone seemed distorted — but perhaps these stones had been moved by a later hand. It was an admirably accurate representation, but not what a breeder would call perfect conformation. There was the suggestion of a bowed neck and an undershot jaw, and the tail, as full as a winter coyote's, did not appear to be precisely to scale.

The more I thought about it, the more I felt I was looking at an individual horse, a unique combination of generic and specific detail. It was easy to imagine one of Kino's horses as a model, or a horse that ran off from one of Coronado's columns. What kind of horses would these have been, I wondered? In the sixteenth century the most sought-after horses in Europe were Spanish, the offspring of Arabian stock and Barbary horses that the Moors brought to Iberia and bred to the older, eastern European strains brought in by the Romans. The model for this horse, I speculated, could easily have been a palomino, or a descendant of horses trained for lion-hunting in North Africa.

A few generations ago, cowboys, cavalry quartermasters, and draymen would have taken this horse before me under consideration and not let up their scrutiny until they had its heritage fixed to their satisfaction. Today, the distinction between draft and harness horses is arcane knowledge, and no image may come to mind for a blue roan or a claybank horse. The loss of such refinement in everyday conversation leaves me unsettled. People praise the Eskimo's ability to distinguish among forty types of snow but forget the skill of others who routinely differentiate between overo and tobiano pintos. Such distinctions are made for the same reason. You have to do it to be able to talk clearly about the world.

For parts of two years I worked as a horse wrangler and packer in Wyoming. It is dim knowledge now; I would have to think to remember if a buckskin was a kind of dun horse. And I couldn't throw a double-diamond hitch over a set of panniers — the packer's basic tie-down — without guidance. As I squatted there in the desert, however, these more personal memories seemed tenuous in comparison with the sweep of this animal in human time. My memories had no depth. I thought of the Hittite cavalry riding against the Syrians 3,500 years ago. And the first of the Chinese emperors, Ch'in Shih Huang, buried in Shensi Province in 210 B.C. with thousands of life-size horses and soldiers, a terra-cotta guardian army. What could I know of what was in the mind of whoever made this horse? Was there some racial memory of it as an animal that had once fed the artist's ancestors and then disappeared from North America? And then returned in this strange alliance with another race of men?

Certainly, whoever it was, the artist had observed the animal very closely. Certainly the animal's speed had impressed him. Among the first things the Quechan would have learned from an encounter with Kino's horses was that their own long-distance runners — men who could run down mule deer — were no match for this animal.

From where I squatted I could look far out over the Mexican plain. Juan Bautista de Anza passed this way in 1774, extending El Camino Real into Alta California from Sinaloa. He was followed by others, all of them astride the magical horse; *gente de razón*, the people of reason, coming into the country of *los primitivos*. The horse, like the stone animals of Egypt, urged these memories upon me. And as I drew them up from some forgotten corner of my mind — huge horses carved in the white chalk downs of southern England by an Iron Age people; Spanish horses rearing and wheeling in fear before alligators in Florida — the images seemed tethered before me. With this sense of proportion, a memory of my own — the morning I almost lost my face to a horse's hoof — now had somewhere to fit.

I rose up and began to walk slowly around the horse again. I had taken the first long measure of it and was looking now for a way to depart, a new angle of light, a fading of the image itself before the rising sun, that would break its hold on me. As I circled, feeling both heady and serene at the encounter, I realized again how strangely vivid it was. It had been created on a barren bajada between two arroyos, as nondescript a place as one could imagine. The only plant life here was a few wands of ocotillo cactus. The ground beneath my shoes was so hard it wouldn't take the print of a heavy animal even after a rain. The only sounds I had heard here were the voices of quail.

The archaeologist had been correct. For all its forcefulness, the horse is inconspicuous. If you don't care to see it you can walk right past it. That pleases him, I think. Unmarked on this bleak shoulder of the plain, the site signals to no one; so he wants no protective fences here, no informative plaque, to act as beacons. He would rather take a chance that no motorcyclist, no aimless wanderer with a flair for violence and a depth of ignorance, will ever find his way here.

The archaeologist had given me something before I left his office that now seemed peculiar—an aerial photograph of the horse. It is widely believed that an aerial view of an intaglio provides a fair and accurate depiction. It does not. In the photograph the horse looks somewhat crudely constructed; from the ground it appears far more deftly rendered. The photograph is of a single moment, and in that split second the horse seems vaguely impotent. I watched light pool in the intaglio at dawn; I imagine you could watch it withdraw at dusk and sense the same animation I did. In those prolonged moments its shape and so, too, its general character changed—noticeably. The living quality of the image, its immediacy to the eye, was brought out by the light-in-time, not, at least here, in the camera's frozen instant.

Intaglios, I thought, were never meant to be seen by gods in the sky above. They were meant to be seen by people on the ground, over a long period of shifting light. This could even be true of the huge figures on the Plain of Nazca in Peru, where people could walk for the length of a day beside them. It is our own impatience that leads us to think otherwise.

This process of abstraction, almost unintentional, drew me gradually away from the horse. I came to a position of attention at the edge of the sphere of its influence. With a slight bow I paid my respects to the horse, its maker, and the history of us all, and departed.

3

A short distance away I stopped the car in the middle of the road to make a few notes. I could not write down what I was thinking when I was with the horse. It would have seemed disrespectful, and it would have required another kind of attention. So now I patiently drained my memory of the details it had fastened itself upon. The road I'd stopped on was adjacent to the All American Canal, the major source of water for the Imperial and Coachella valleys. The water flowed west placidly. A disjointed flock of coots, small, dark birds with white bills, was paddling against the current, foraging in the rushes.

I was peripherally aware of the birds as I wrote, the only movement in the desert; and of a series of sounds from a village a half-mile away. The first sounds from this collection of ramshackle houses in a grove of cottonwoods were the distracted dawn voices of dogs. I heard them intermingled with the cries of a rooster. Later, the high-pitched voices of children calling out to each other came disembodied through the dry desert air. Now, a little after seven, I could hear someone practicing on the trumpet, the same rough phrases played over and over. I suddenly remembered how as children we had tried to get the rhythm of a galloping horse with hands against our thighs, or by fluttering our tongues against the roofs of our mouths.

After the trumpet, the impatient calls of adults, summoning children. Sunday morning. Wood smoke hung like a lens in the trees. The first car starts—a cold eight-cylinder engine, of Chrysler extraction perhaps, goosed to life, then throttled back to murmur through dual mufflers, the obbligato music of a shade-tree mechanic. The rote bark of mongrel dogs at dawn, the jagged outcries of men and women, an engine coming to life. Like a thousand villages from West Virginia to Guadalajara.

I finished my notes—where was I going to find a description of the horses that came north with the conquistadors? Did their manes come forward prominently over the brow, like this one's, like the forelocks of Blackfeet and Assiniboine men in nineteenth-century paintings? I set the notes on the seat beside me.

The road followed the canal for a while and then arced north, toward Interstate 8. It was slow driving and I fell to thinking how the desert had changed since Anza had come through. New plants and animals—the MacDougall cottonwood, the English house sparrow, the chukar from China—have about them now the air of the native-born.

Of the native species, some—no one knows how many—are extinct. The populations of many others, especially the animals, have been sharply reduced. The idea of a desert impoverished by agricultural poisons and varmint hunters, by off-road vehicles and military operations, did not seem as disturbing to me, however, as this other horror, now that I had been those hours with the horse. The vandals, the few who crowbar rock art off the desert's walls, who dig up graves, who punish the ground that holds intaglios, are people who devour history. Their self-centered scorn, their disrespect for ideas and images beyond their ken, create the awful atmosphere of loose ends in which totalitarianism thrives, in which the past is merely curious or wrong.

I thought about the horse sitting out there on the unprotected plain. I enumerated its qualities in my mind until a sense of its vulnerability receded and it became an anchor for something else. I remembered that history, a history like this one, which ran deeper than Mexico, deeper than the Spanish, was a kind of medicine. It permitted the great breadth of human expression to reverberate, and it did not urge you to locate its apotheosis in the present.

Each of us, individuals and civilizations, has been held upside down like Achilles in the River Styx. The artist mixing his colors in the dim light of Altamira; an Egyptian ruler lying still now, wrapped in his byssus, stored against time in a pyramid; the faded Dorset culture of the Arctic; the Hmong and Samburu and Walbiri of historic time; the modern nations. This great, imperfect stretch of human expression is the clarification and encouragement, the urging and the reminder, we call history. And it is inscribed everywhere in the face of the land, from the mountain passes of the Himalayas to a nameless bajada in the California desert.

Small birds rose up in the road ahead, startled, and flew off. I prayed no infidel would ever find that horse.

Jim Harrison

Passacaglia on Getting Lost

The most immediate sensation when totally and unfathomably lost is that you might die. I live in a world where I still very much regret the deaths of Romeo and Juliet; even the fate of Petrouchka moistens my single eye — the blind left eye weeps only underwater, or when I'm asleep and the dreams are harrowing. The first time I got lost in the winter I think I was about fourteen. I worked my way inside an enormous hollow white pine stump, the remnant of an 1897 forest fire in an area of northern Michigan. It was quite comfortable in there and it saddened me to start the stump on fire in order to be found.

It is particularly stupid to get lost in the winter because, barring a blizzard, you can retrace your steps. But I hate this in life the same as I do in poems and novels. It is a little painful to keep saying hello. The baked bean and onion sandwich was partially frozen in my coat pocket. The sun was covered with a dense cloud mass. The fire burned orange and balsamic, pitchy, melting the snow in a circle around the stump. I was a little goofy from hypothermia and thought of Cyd Charisse, and what all three of the McGuire sisters would look like bare naked. To retrace your steps: it is not in my nature to want to repeat a single day of my life. Maybe a portion of a day that involved lovemaking or a meal — a sauté of truffles and foie gras at Faugeron's in Paris ruined by jet lag, or a girl that disappeared into heaven in a Chevrolet after a single, brief encounter. I would repeat an hour with the cotton, lilac skirt; the white sleeveless blouse, the grass stain on her elbow. I could breathe through the back of her knee.

I am not going to talk about the well-equipped Republican clones you see marching like Hitler youth up and down the spine of the Rockies, or in any of the national parks, national forests, wilderness areas in America. On the tops of mountains I've seen their cocaine wrappers and fluorescent shoestrings. At five thousand feet in the Smokies there were tiny red piss-ants crowding around a discarded Dalkon shield.

Hikers, like Midwestern drivers, are bent on telling you how "far" they've hiked. "I did twenty-three miles carrying fifty-one pounds." I usually advise more lateral or circular movement. A trail, other than an animal trail, is an insult to the perceptions. It is the hike as an extension of the encounter group. Over in the Rainy River area a big Cree once portaged eighteen miles carrying five hundred pounds in a single day. His sister carried three hundred twenty.

There is clearly not enough wilderness left for the rising number of people who say they desire it. It's not wilderness anyway if it only exists by our permission and stewardship. The famous Thoreau quote said "wildness" not wilderness. We have become Europe and each, with a sense of privacy and tact, must secure our own wildness.

It strikes me that Peter Matthiessen has the best public understanding of the natural world; I say "public" because there might be someone out there who can still walk on water. It is the generalists who have the grace that translates; the specialist, like those tiny novels that emerge from the academy, wants to be correct above all else. The specialist is part of a doubtless useful collective enterprise. We are fortunate to have generalists who make leaps for those of us who are too clumsy or lazy, or who have adjusted to the fact that we can't do everything: Hoagland, Abbey, Nabhan, Lopez, Schulteis, Peacock and his grizzlies, among others, but these come to mind.

Getting lost is to sense the "animus" of nature. James Hillman said that animals we see in dreams are often "soul doctors." When you first sense you are lost there is a goofy, tingling sensation. The mouth tends to dry up, the flesh becomes spongy. This can occur when you disbelieve your compass. Made in Germany, indeed! Post-Nazi terrorists dooming the poet to a night in the woods. But then the compass was only wrong on one occasion — a cheapish Taiwanese compass.

When we are lost we lose our peripheries. Our thoughts zoom outward and infect the landscape. Years later you can revisit an area and find these thoughts still diseasing the same landscape. It requires a particular kind of behavior to heal the location.

Gullies, hummocks in swamps, swales in the middle of large fields, the small alluvial fan created by feeder creeks, undercut river banks, miniature springs, dense thickets on the tops of hills: like Bachelard's attics, seashells, drawers, cellars, these places are a balm to me. Magic (as opposed to the hocus-pocus of miracles) is equated to the quality of

attentiveness. Perhaps magic "is" the quality of attentiveness, the ultimate attentiveness. D. H. Lawrence said that the only aristocracy is
that of consciousness. Certain locations seem to demand consciousness. Once I sat still so long I was lucky enough to have a warbler sit on
my elbow. Certain of the dead also made brief visits.

Perhaps getting lost temporarily destroys the acquisitive sense.
We tend to look at earth as an elaborate system out of which we may
draw useful information. We "profit" from nature — that is the taught
system. The natural world exists so that we may draw conclusions
about it. This is the kind of soul-destroying bullshit that drove young
people to lysergic acid in the sixties.

One night last summer I was lucky enough to see "time" herself —
the moon shooting across the sky, the constellations adjusting wobbily,
the sun rising and setting in seconds. I jumped in the river at daylight
to come to my senses. Checked a calendar to make sure. No one really
wants to be Hölderlin out in the garden with a foot of snow gathered on
top of his head.

It is interesting to see the Nature Establishment and the Nature Anti-
Establishment suffocating in the same avalanche of tedium and bit-
terness. There is insufficient street experience to see how bad the bad
guys are. They forget it was greed that discovered the country, greed
that propelled the Westward movement, greed that shipped the blacks,
greed that murdered the Indians, greed that daily shits on the heads of
those who love nature. Why are we shit upon, they wonder.

I prefer places valued by no one else. The Upper Peninsula has
many of these places that lack the drama and differentiation favored by
the garden variety nature buff. I have a personal stump back in a forest
clearing. Someone, probably a deerhunter, has left a beer bottle beside
the stump. I leave the beer bottle there to conceal the value of the
stump.

It took me twenty years to see a timber wolf in the wild. I could
have foreshortened this time period by going to Isle Royale or Canada
but I wanted to see the wolf as part of a day rather than as a novelty.
We startled each other. From this single incident I dreamt I found the
wolf with her back broken on a logging road. I knelt down and she went
inside me, becoming part of my body and skeleton.

The shock of being lost as a metaphor is the discovery that you've
never been "found" in any meaningful sense. When you're lost you

know who you are. You're the only one out there. One day I was dressed in camouflage and stalking a small group of sandhill cranes which were feeding on frogs in the pine barrens not far from my cabin. I got within a few yards of them after an hour of crawling. I said "good morning," a phrase they were unfamiliar with; in fact, they were enraged and threatening. I made a little coyote yodel and they flapped skyward, the wind of their immense wings whooshing around my head. I ordered this camouflage outfit from Texas, not a bad place if you ignore the inhabitants and their peculiar urge to mythologize themselves against the evidence. One of the great empty and lovely drives left in the U.S. is from El Paso to San Antonio. Someday I will move to Nebraska for the same reason.

Of course getting lost is not ordinarily a threatening occasion. Two snowmobilers died a few years ago not all that far from my cabin but it was poignantly unnecessary. They could have piled deadfall wood around their machines and dropped matches into the remnants of the gas in the tanks, creating an enormous pyre for the search planes. Euphemisms for getting lost range from "I got a little turned around for a few hours" to "I wasn't lost, I just couldn't find my car until morning." The enemies are the occasional snowflakes in July, the cold and rain, the blackflies and mosquitoes, drinking swamp or creek water when a spring can always be found. Of course the greatest enemy is panic. The greatest panic I've ever felt was at an Umbanda rite in Brazil when I sensed that the others present weren't actually people. I became ill when a man leapfrogged through a garden on his back, and an old woman rubbed her left eyeball against my own and told me pointedly about my life in northern Michigan.

An old Chippewa I know carries a folded-up garbage bag in his pocket. He claims it is his portable home, keeping him warm and dry if he gets lost or tired. He finds coyote dens by scent, and whittles the heads of canes into renditions of his "dream birds." His favorite drink is a double martini. He asked me to check for a phone number of a "love" he had lost in 1931. He was somewhat disturbed, he told me, when it occurred to him that people didn't know that every single tree was different from every other tree. He is making me a cane to repel bears and to attract wolves and women. I will hang this cane on the cabin wall, being genetically too Calvinist to have any interest in sorcery.

It seems I will never be reviewed by Edmund Wilson or Randall Jarrell or Kenneth Burke, something I aspired to at nineteen in the jungle of Grove Street. For years I've wanted to take a walk with E. M.

Cioran. I've rid myself of the usual fantasies about money, actresses, models, food, fishing, hunting, travel, by enacting them, though the money evaporated at startling speed through what accountants refer to as "spending habits." Cioran's mind is unique, the modernist temperament at an antipode not reached by novelists. I would get us mildly lost on the walk, which might amuse him. The name of Wittgenstein will not be mentioned. I want to ask Cioran to what degree the perception of reality is consensual. The answer will help me account for all of my bad reviews! Many of us apparently live in different worlds. Do we see the same sky as Crazy Horse? Think of Anne Frank's comprehension of the closet.

I know a pyramidical hill at least fifteen miles from the nearest dwelling. On this hill three small river systems have their beginnings, each of them a hundred or so miles long. I'm not giving out any directions to this place. The first two times I tried to go there I got turned around, succeeding on the third trip. My yellow Labrador was frightened on this hill, which in turn served to disturb me. The dog, however, is frightened of bears, coyotes, thunder, northern lights, the moon. I only stayed a few minutes.

Rilke said something on the order of "With all of its eyes the creature world beholds the open . . ." (Everyone should buy the astonishing new translation of Sonnets to Orpheus by Stephen Mitchell.) Unfavorable comparisons to animals are contraindicated. I confess I've talked at length to ravens, porcupines, crows, coyotes, infant porpoises, and particularly beautiful heads of garlic, but then others talk back at the television. It is natural for a child to imagine what a bird sees. "How do we know but that every bird that cuts the airy way is an immense world of delight closed to our senses five?" We don't. We should encourage ourselves to be a whale, a woman, a plant or planet, a lake, the night sky. There was a Cheyenne warrior named One Who Sees As A Bird: the tops of trees are ovoids bending away from the wind.

I'm a poor naturalist. A bird evokes the other times I've seen the bird, a delicious continuity, not a wish to run to my collection of bird books. I'm not against the idea of my work being forgotten if I can be an old geezer in a cabin smelling of wood smoke, kerosene, a Bordeaux stain on my T-shirt, cooking a not so simple "salmi" of woodcock. It has only lately occurred to me that many of my concerns are anachronistic. Walking in the forest at night can be a cocaine substitute in addition to simply walking in the forest at night. Kokopele owned the best of all spirits for an artist. He led Picasso to do a gavotte at the age of eighty. He made Henry Miller a ping-pong champion.

Last August when I was turned around in a swamp I sat on a hummock and had a vision of death as a suck-hole in the universe, an interior plug, out of which we all go with a gurgle. I gurgled in the swamp. Frogs and birds answered. This is the sensuality of death, not the less beautiful for being terminal.

John Haines

*Shadows and Vistas**

There are shadows over the land. They come out of the ground, from the dust and the tumbled bones of the earth. Tree shadows that haunt the woodlands of childhood, holding fear in their branches. Stone shadows on the desert, cloud shadows on the sea and over the summer hills, bringing water. Shapes of shadow in pools and wells, vague forms in the sandlight.

Out of the past come these wind-figures, the flapping sails of primitive birds with terrible beaks and claws. Shadows of things that walked once and went away. Lickers of blood that fasten by night to the veins of standing cattle, to the foot of a sleeping man. In the Far North, the heavy, stalled bodies of mastodons chilled in a black ooze, and their fur-clad bones still come out of the ground. Triceratops was feeding in the marshlands by the verge of the coal-making forest.

Shadows in doorways, and under the eaves of ancient buildings, where the fallen creatures of stone grimace in sleep. Domestic, wind-tugged shadows cast by icy branches upon a bedroom window: they tap on the glass and wake us. They speak to the shadows within us, old ghosts that will not die. Like trapped, primordial birds they break from an ice-pool in the heart's well and fly into walls built long ago.

Stand still where you are—at the end of pavement, in a sunbreak of the forest, on the open, cloud-peopled terrace of the plains. Look deeply into the wind-furrows of the grass, into the leaf-stilled water of pools. Think back through the silence, of the life that was and is not here now, of the strong pastness of things—shadows of the end and the beginning.

It is autumn. Leaves are flying, a storm of them over the land. They are brown and yellow, parched and pale—Shelley's

*Keynote address, Alaska Environmental Assembly, Anchorage, May 22, 1982.

"pestilence-stricken multitudes." Out of an evening darkness they fly in our faces and scare us; like resigned spirits they whirl away and spill into hollows, to lie still, one on the other, waiting for snow.

I begin with "Shadows," a piece I wrote some years ago, as a way of speaking. Laurens van der Post, in *The Lost World of the Kalahari*, acknowledges that he believes in ghosts, in the spirits of a life that the land once held but which cannot be found any longer. Van der Post was looking for the Bushman, who for him signified a lost Africa, one that he had been told about as a boy; but all that he could find of it was the changed land itself and a few sites where decades before the Bushmen had camped and hunted. According to an old African of his household, from whom he learned much, the Bushman disappeared because *he would not be tamed.*

It is difficult to describe here as fully as I would like how deeply this view of things affects us — not only those of us who live in Alaska, but throughout North America generally. I can refer to an incident in my own life. I remember clearly a long-ago afternoon in early October when I stood on the edge of that high overlook near Maclaren Summit on the Denali Highway, gazing down onto the wide sweep of the Maclaren River basin. The cold, late-afternoon sun came through broken clouds, and the tundra below me was patched with sunlight. The river, a thin, silvery-blue thread, twisted through the fall-subdued coloration of the land, stretching far up into the Alaska Range, into the dark and gloomy hills on which the first light snow had fallen.

I was entirely alone at that moment; no traffic disturbed the gravel road a few yards behind me. The land before me seemed incredibly vast and empty. But it was not empty. Far below me a few scattered caribou were feeding in the meadows of the river basin, their brown, white-maned forms dispersed among the bogs and ponds, moving slowly upriver toward the mountains. They were the first individuals of a herd that would appear later.

I felt as if I were looking down on a landscape elementary to our being, and that nothing had occurred to change it since the last of the continental ice had melted from the earth, and the first grasses and shrubs began to grow, and very slowly the animals moved north into the newly restored land, finding their way, feeding on the fresh, undisturbed forage for the first time.

That image has remained with me as one sure glimpse into our past. Even the road that crossed the river on a tiny bridge in the distance did not break the continuity of the feeling I had then. It was all part of an essential vista, a sheer sense of the land in its original presence. On that afternoon, when the guns of hunters along the road were silent and no cars passed, I easily slipped back a thousand years into a twilight approaching winter; a dusk in which I and a few others, following the game herds upriver, would find meat, fire and shelter.

That was many years ago, when the tundra life along the Denali road was still fairly abundant. I have looked over that same view a number of times since, but I have not seen the caribou feeding as they were then. And yet I know that their ghosts are there, that the land contains them and refuses in some mysterious way to give them up, though to the surface view the land appears empty.

It is not simply nostalgia, I think, that compels me to believe that this vista, its possibility, needs to be kept. We need it as a kind of model of life, whose images we are bound in some way to resurrect and imitate, even though the original may be destroyed. It is not a matter of saving a species, a particular herd and its habitat, but of saving something essential of life and ourselves. And not only our immediate selves, you and I, but those others who were here before us and will come after us, and whose land and nature we have so easily confiscated and misused to our long-standing peril.

It is foolish to believe that we erase life by killing it off, by driving into extinction the remaining game, by paving over the grazing grounds, cutting the forests, and pretending to ourselves that it did not matter after all. Too bad, we say, but let's get on with the business of things. Vanquished in one place, life springs back in another, as at the present time, in spite of all sophistication of transport and communication, coyotes are barking in the Los Angeles suburbs, and as all the killed and vanished life, animal and people, continues in one way or another to haunt us and question our wasting passage through the world.

As a friend of mine said to me a while ago when in the course of conversation we both remarked on the great physical presence of Kluane Lake in Yukon: "That place," she exclaimed, "*really* has spirit!" It does indeed.

And what does this mean? That places, lands, regions, watersheds all have a life, a felt quality of their own, which we can call *spirit*, and we cannot kill that spirit without destroying something in ourselves. A degraded land inevitably produces degraded people. It is, in fact, ourselves we are destroying (and sometimes saving), a possibility of life that once gone will be a long time returning. I say "a long time," and not that it will never come back, because I do not hold with the view that *we* have the power to destroy life on earth forever. That notion is part of our problem, a part of our arrogance and self-bemusement. We have got it backwards: life has power to destroy *us*, and do so with our own connivance, using our own misaligned purposes. A few degrees of climate change, a few more inches of topsoil lost, and our descendants can read the record for themselves.

Is it destined to be a law with us, an iron and withering rule, that anything that cannot be tamed, domesticated, and put to work, to *use*, shall die? A river, a wolf, a small tribe of hunting people? All the while we preserve a few wretched specimens of this or that in a zoo, a controlled park or reservation or as a collection of images on film, part of an ever-growing catalogue of fossil life?

You can kill off the original inhabitants, and most of the world's wildlife, and still live on the land. But I doubt that we can live fully on that land accompanied only by increasing crowds of consumers like ourselves and a few hybrid domesticated animals turned into producing machines. A sure poverty will follow us, an inner desolation to match the devastation without. And having rid the earth of wilderness and of wild things in general, we will look into space, to other planets, to find their replacements there.

We are all familiar with a continuing effort today to save some part of a wild heritage, to rethink our lives in relation to the land on which we drive and park and from which we mainly draw what certainty we have. And we know the forces assembled in opposition to this effort—there is no need to name or rank them, they all flock under the flag of an ever more questionable progress and enterprise, whose hidden name is poverty. T. S. Eliot wrote, on the occasion of a visit to New England in the 1930s:

> My local feelings were stirred very sadly by my first view of New England, on arriving from Montreal, and journeying all one day through the beautiful desolate country of Vermont. Those hills had once, I suppose, been covered with primeval forest; the forest was razed to make sheep pastures for the English settlers; now the sheep are gone, and most of the descendants of the settlers; and a new forest appeared blazing with the melancholy glory of October

maple and beech and birch scattered among the evergreens; and after this process of scarlet and gold and purple wilderness you descend to the sordor of the half-dead milltowns of southern New Hampshire and Massachusetts. It is not necessarily those lands which are most fertile or most favored in climate that seem to me the happiest, but those in which a long struggle of adaptation between man and his environment has brought out the best qualities of both; in which the landscape has been moulded by numerous generations of one race, and in which the landscape has in turn modified the race to its own character. And those New England mountains seemed to me to give evidence of a human success so meager and transitory as to be more desperate than the desert. (T. S. Eliot, *After Strange Gods*, 1934)

Certainly Eliot's description and the feeling it evokes could with a little effort be transferred to many an urban Alaska landscape, be it Mountain View, North Pole, or one of those lost highway settlements in which it seems as if all the unwanted debris and waste of American life had somehow blown there to settle into an impervious drift composed of tarpaper, crushed plastic, ripped shingles, and foundered hopes. I suppose there are few more unreal and depressing aspects than some of the housing sites in Anchorage. And what is unreal will sooner or later disappear — the transitory inspiration of a people come to plunder and leave. Van der Post, in another of his books, remarks on the physical fact of Africa as being by far the most exciting thing about that continent. And for him a definite sadness lay in the fact that it had not yet produced the people and the towns worthy of it. By comparison with its physical self, everything else was drab and commonplace.

We who have learned to call the North country home are perhaps only at the beginning of a struggle of adaptation between ourselves and the land, and if the evidence so far seems pretty meager, there's a long road yet to travel. The prospect of an Alaska in which a million or so people are on the prowl with guns, snowmachines, airboats, and three-wheelers is not only terrifying, it is finally unacceptable. An environmental ethic, believed in, practiced, and enforced, is not just an alternative, it is the only one, though another name for it is self-restraint. And it is sometimes possible to sense, behind all the noise and confrontation, a genuine urge toward a real satisfaction, a sane kind of plenitude, a fullness of spirit and being.

It can be asked what these remarks of mine have to do with immediate politics and practical tasks. And I have no immediate answer, no claim that poetic imagery — the personal mythologies of which a writer is sometimes the master — can solve anything. And yet without this dimension of imagination, the instilled power to think and to visualize that poetry, for example, nourishes in us, the solutions, the resolved difficulties seem bound to lose a necessary human element.

So it is a matter of language, also, of words common and uncommon, that with something of their original freshness and power have the ability to restore a much-needed sense of reality and reveal a few essential things with clarity and concreteness.

Not long ago I saw a marsh hawk, a harrier, hunting the Tanana River islands below Richardson, Alaska, the first arrival of its kind. And that bird was, in a vivid way, rather like a ghost with its gray and white plumage slanting in the spring sunlight as it hovered and sailed over the winter-brown willows and frost-seared grasses. A real spirit, if you like, come back to claim its territory, as it or its ancestors have returned to those flats and adjacent meadows for far longer than our race has existed or can easily imagine. A small but definite image to end on, and returning me halfway to that glimpse into the Maclaren River I described earlier, haunted as I am by its persistent contours, and by what seems sometimes destined to become a vanished hope on earth.

And to think from this diminished perspective in time, from this long vista of empty light and deepening shade, that so small and refined a creature could fill an uncertain niche in the world; and that its absence would leave, not just a momentary gap in nature, but a lack in one's own existence, one less possibility of being.

As if we were to look out on a cherished landscape, hoping to see on the distant, wrinkled plain, among the cloud-shadows passing over its face, groups of animals feeding and resting; and in the air above them a compact flock of waterfowl swiftly winging its way to a farther pond; and higher still, a watchful hawk on the wind. To look, straining one's eyesight, noting each detail of lake, meadow and bog; and to find nothing, nothing alive and moving. Only the wind and the distance, the silence of a vast, creatureless earth.

Joyce Carol Oates

Against Nature

> *We soon get through with Nature. She excites an expectation*
> *which she cannot satisfy.*
>
> —THOREAU, Journal, *1854*

> *Sir, if a man has experienced the inexpressible, he is under no*
> *obligation to attempt to express it.*
>
> — SAMUEL JOHNSON

The writer's resistance to Nature.

It has no sense of humor: in its beauty, as in its ugliness, or its neutrality, there is no laughter.

It lacks a moral purpose.

It lacks a satiric dimension, registers no irony.

Its pleasures lack resonance, being accidental; its horrors, even when premeditated, are equally perfunctory, "red in tooth and claw" et cetera.

It lacks a symbolic subtext—excepting that provided by man.

It has no (verbal) language.

It has no interest in ours.

It inspires a painfully limited set of responses in "nature-writers" — REVERENCE, AWE, PIETY, MYSTICAL ONENESS.

It eludes us even as it prepares to swallow us up, books and all.

* * *

I was lying on my back in the dirt-gravel of the towpath beside the Delaware-Raritan Canal, Titusville, New Jersey, staring up at the sky and trying, with no success, to overcome a sudden attack of tachycardia that had come upon me out of nowhere—such attacks are always "out of nowhere," that's their charm—and all around me Nature thrummed with life, the air smelling of moisture and sunlight, the canal reflecting the sky, red-winged blackbirds testing their spring calls — the usual. I'd become the jar in Tennessee, a fictitious center, or parenthesis, aware beyond my erratic heartbeat of the numberless heartbeats of the earth, its pulsing pumping life, sheer life, incalculable. Struck down in the midst of motion — I'd been jogging a minute before — I was "out of time" like a fallen, stunned boxer, privileged (in an abstract manner of speaking) to be an involuntary witness to the random, wayward, nameless motion on all sides of me.

Paroxysmal tachycardia is rarely fatal, but if the heartbeat accelerates to 250–270 beats a minute you're in trouble. The average attack is about 100–150 beats and mine seemed so far to be about average; the trick now was to prevent it from getting worse. Brainy people try brainy strategies, such as thinking calming thoughts, pseudo-mystic thoughts, *If I die now it's a good death*, that sort of thing, *if I die this is a good place and a good time*, the idea is to deceive the frenzied heartbeat that, really, you don't care: you hadn't any other plans for the afternoon. The important thing with tachycardia is to prevent panic! you must prevent panic! otherwise you'll have to be taken by ambulance to the closest emergency room, which is not so very nice a way to spend the afternoon, really. So I contemplated the blue sky overhead. The earth beneath my head. Nature surrounding me on all sides, I couldn't quite see it but I could hear it, smell it, sense it — there is something *there*, no mistake about it. Completely oblivious to the predicament of the individual but that's only "natural" after all, one hardly expects otherwise.

When you discover yourself lying on the ground, limp and unresisting, head in the dirt, and helpless, the earth seems to shift forward as a presence; hard, emphatic, not mere surface but a genuine force — there is no other word for it but *presence*. To keep in motion is to keep in time and to be stopped, stilled, is to be abruptly out of time, in another time-dimension perhaps, an alien one, where human language has no resonance. Nothing to be said about it expresses it, nothing touches it, it's an absolute against which nothing human can be measured. . . . Moving through space and time by way of your own volition you inhabit an interior consciousness, a hallucinatory consciousness, it might be said, so long as breath, heartbeat, the body's autonomy hold; when motion is stopped you are jarred out of it. The interior is invaded by the exterior. The outside wants to come in, and only the self's fragile membrane prevents it.

The fly buzzing at Emily's death.

Still, the earth *is* your place. A tidy grave-site measured to your size. Or, from another angle of vision, one vast democratic grave.

Let's contemplate the sky. Forget the crazy hammering heartbeat, don't listen to it, don't start counting, remember that there is a clever way of breathing that conserves oxygen as if you're lying below the surface of a body of water breathing through a very thin straw but you *can* breathe through it if you're careful, if you don't panic, one breath and then another and then another, isn't that the story of all lives? careers? Just a matter of breathing. Of course it is. But contemplate the sky, it's there to be contemplated. A mild shock to see it so blank, blue, a thin airy ghostly blue, no clouds to disguise its emptiness. You are beginning to feel not only weightless but near-bodiless, lying on the earth like a scrap of paper about to be blown off. Two dimensions and you'd imagined you were three! And there's the sky rolling away forever, into infinity — if "infinity" can be "rolled into" — and the forlorn truth is, that's where you're going too. And the lovely blue isn't even blue, is it? isn't even there, is it? a mere optical illusion, isn't it? no matter what art has urged you to believe.

* * *

Early Nature memories. Which it's best not to suppress.

. . . Wading, as a small child, in Tonawanda Creek near our house, and afterward trying to tear off, in a frenzy of terror and revulsion, the sticky fat black bloodsuckers that had attached themselves to my feet, particularly between my toes.

. . . Coming upon a friend's dog in a drainage ditch, dead for several days, evidently the poor creature had been shot by a hunter and left to die, bleeding to death, and we're stupefied with grief and horror but can't resist sliding down to where he's lying on his belly, and we can't resist squatting over him, turning the body over . . .

. . . The raccoon, mad with rabies, frothing at the mouth and tearing at his own belly with his teeth, so that his intestines spilled out onto the ground . . . a sight I seem to remember though in fact I did not see. I've been told I did not see.

* * *

Consequently, my chronic uneasiness with Nature-mysticism; Nature-adoration; Nature-as-(moral)-instruction-for-mankind. My doubt that one can, with philosophical validity, address "Nature" as a single coherent noun, anything other than a Platonic, hence discredited, is-ness. My resistance to "Nature-writing" as a genre, except when it is brilliantly fictionalized in the service of a writer's individual vision — Thoreau's books and *Journal*, of course — but also, less known in this country, the miniaturist prose-poems of Colette (*Flowers and Fruit*) and Ponge (*Taking the Side of Things*) — in which case it becomes yet another, and ingenious, form of storytelling. The subject is *there* only by the grace of the author's language.

Nature has no instructions for mankind except that our poor beleaguered humanist-democratic way of life, our fantasies of the individual's high worth, our sense that the weak, no less than the strong, have a right to survive, are absurd.

In any case, where *is* Nature? one might (skeptically) inquire. Who has looked upon her/its face and survived?

* * *

But isn't this all exaggeration, in the spirit of rhetorical contentiousness? Surely Nature is, for you, as for most reasonably intelligent people, a "perennial" source of beauty, comfort, peace, escape from the delirium of civilized life; a respite from the ego's ever-frantic strategies of self-promotion, as a way of insuring (at least in fantasy) some small measure of immortality? Surely Nature, as it is understood in the usual slapdash way, as human, if not dilettante, *experience* (hiking in a national park, jogging on the beach at dawn, even tending, with the usual comical frustrations, a suburban garden), is wonderfully consoling; a place where, when you go there, it has to take you in? — a palimpsest of sorts you choose to read, layer by layer, always with care, always cautiously, in proportion to your psychological strength?

Nature: as in Thoreau's upbeat Transcendentalist mode ("The indescribable innocence and beneficence of Nature, — such health, such cheer, they afford forever! and such sympathy have they ever with our race, that all Nature would be affected . . . if any man should ever for a just cause grieve"), and not in Thoreau's grim mode ("Nature is hard to be overcome but she must be overcome").

Another way of saying, not *Nature-in-itself* but *Nature-as-experience*.

The former, Nature-in-itself, is, to allude slantwise to Melville, a blankness ten times blank; the latter is what we commonly, or perhaps always, mean when we speak of Nature as a noun, a single entity — something of *ours*. Most of the time it's just an activity, a sort of hobby, a weekend, a few days, perhaps a few hours, staring out the window at the mind-dazzling autumn foliage of, say, Northern Michigan, being rendered speechless—temporarily—at the sight of Mt. Shasta, the Grand Canyon, Ansel Adams's West. Or Nature writ small, contained in the back yard. Nature filtered through our optical nerves, our "senses," our fiercely romantic expectations. Nature that pleases us because it mirrors our souls, or gives the comforting illusion of doing so. As in our first mother's awakening to the self's fatal beauty—

> I thither went
> With unexperienc't thought, and laid me down
> On the green bank, to look into the clear
> Smooth Lake, that to me seem'd another Sky.
> As I bent down to look, just opposite,
> A Shape within the watr'y gleam appear'd
> Bending to look on me, I started back,
> It started back, but pleas'd I soon return'd,
> Pleas'd it return'd as soon with answering looks
> Of sympathy and love; there I had fixt
> Mine eyes till now, and pin'd with vain desire.

—in these surpassingly beautiful lines from Book IV of Milton's *Paradise Lost*.

Nature as the self's (flattering) mirror, but not ever, no, never, Nature-in-itself.

* * *

Nature is mouths, or maybe a single mouth. Why glamorize it, romanticize it, well yes but we must, we're writers, poets, mystics (of a sort) aren't we, precisely what else are we to do but glamorize and romanticize and generally exaggerate the significance of anything we focus the white heat of our "creativity" upon . . . ? And why not Nature, since it's there, common property, mute, can't talk back, allows us the possibility of transcending the human condition for a while, writing prettily of mountain ranges, white-tailed deer, the purple crocuses outside this very window, the thrumming dazzling "life-force" we imagine we all support. Why not.

Nature *is* more than a mouth—it's a dazzling variety of mouths. And it pleases the senses, in any case, as the physicists' chill universe of numbers certainly does not.

* * *

Oscar Wilde, on our subject: "Nature is no great mother who has borne us. She is our creation. It is in our brain that she quickens to life. Things are because we see them, and what we see, and how we see it, depends on the Arts that have influenced us. To look at a thing is very different from seeing a thing. . . . At present, people see fogs, not because there are fogs, but because poets and painters have taught them the mysterious loveliness of such effects. There may have been fogs for centuries in London. I dare say there were. But no one saw them. They did not exist until Art had invented them. . . . Yesterday evening Mrs. Arundel insisted on my going to the window and looking at the glorious sky, as she called it. And so I had to look at it. . . . And what was it? It was simply a very second-rate Turner, a Turner of a bad period, with all the painter's worst faults exaggerated and over-emphasized."

(If we were to put it to Oscar Wilde that he exaggerates, his reply might well be: "Exaggeration? I don't know the meaning of the word.")

* * *

Walden, that most artfully composed of prose fictions, concludes, in the rhapsodic chapter "Spring," with Henry David Thoreau's contemplation of death, decay, and regeneration as it is suggested to him, or to his protagonist, by the spectacle of vultures feeding off carrion. There is a dead horse close by his cabin and the stench of its decomposition, in certain winds, is daunting. Yet: ". . . the assurance it gave me of the strong appetite and inviolable health of Nature was my compensation. I love to see that Nature is so rife with life that myriads can be afforded to be sacrificed and suffered to prey upon one another; that tender organizations can be so serenely squashed out of existence like pulp, — tadpoles which herons gobble up, and tortoises and toads run over in the road; and that sometimes it has rained flesh and blood! . . . The impression made on a wise man is that of universal innocence."

Come off it, Henry David. You've grieved these many years for your elder brother John, who died a ghastly death of lockjaw; you've never wholly recovered from the experience of watching him die. And you know, or must know, that you're fated too to die young of consumption. . . . But this doctrinaire Transcendentalist passage ends *Walden* on just the right note. It's as impersonal, as coolly detached, as the Oversoul itself: a "wise man" filters his emotions through his brain.

Or through his prose.

* * *

Nietzsche: "We all pretend to ourselves that we are more simple-minded than we are: that is how we get a rest from our fellow men."

* * *

> Once out of nature I shall never take
> My bodily form from any natural thing,
> But such a form as Grecian goldsmiths make
> Of hammered gold and gold enamelling
> To keep a drowsy Emperor awake;
> Or set upon a golden bough to sing
> To lords and ladies of Byzantium
> Of what is past, or passing, or to come.

> — William Butler Yeats, "Sailing to
> Byzantium"

Yet even the golden bird is a "bodily form taken from (a) natural thing." No, it's impossible to escape!

* * *

The writer's resistance to Nature.
     Wallace Stevens: "In the presence of extraordinary actuality, consciousness takes the place of imagination."

* * *

Once, years ago, in 1972 to be precise, when I seemed to have been another person, related to the person I am now as one is related, tangentially, sometimes embarrassingly, to cousins not seen for decades, — once, when we were living in London, and I was very sick, I had a mystical vision. That is, I "had" a "mystical vision" — the heart sinks: such pretension — or something resembling one. A fever-dream, let's call it. It impressed me enormously and impresses me still, though I've long since lost the capacity to see it with my mind's eye, or even, I suppose, to believe in it. There is a statute of limitations on "mystical visions" as on romantic love.
     I was very sick, and I imagined my life as a thread, a thread of breath, or heartbeat, or pulse, or light, yes it was light, radiant light, I was burning with fever and I ascended to that plane of serenity that might be mistaken for (or *is*, in fact) Nirvana, where I had a waking dream of uncanny lucidity —

My body is a tall column of light and heat.

My body is not "I" but "it."

My body is not one but many.

My body, which "I" inhabit, is inhabited as well by other creatures, unknown to me, imperceptible — the smallest of them mere sparks of light.

My body, which I perceive as substance, is in fact an organization of infinitely complex, overlapping, imbricated structures, radiant light their manifestation, the "body" a tall column of light and blood-heat, a temporary agreement among atoms, like a high-rise building with numberless rooms, corridors, corners, elevator shafts, windows. . . . In this fantastical structure the "I" is deluded as to its sovereignty, let alone its autonomy in the (outside) world; the most astonishing secret is that the "I" doesn't exist! — but it behaves as if it does, as if it were one and not many.

In any case, without the "I" the tall column of light and heat would die, and the microscopic life-particles would die with it . . . will die with it. The "I," which doesn't exist, is everything.

But Dr. Johnson is right, the inexpressible need not be expressed. And what resistance, finally? There is none.

* * *

This morning, an invasion of tiny black ants. One by one they appear, out of nowhere — that's their charm too! — moving single file across the white Parsons table where I am sitting, trying without much success to write a poem. A poem of only three or four lines is what I want, something short, tight, mean, I want it to hurt like a white-hot wire up the nostrils, small and compact and turned in upon itself with the density of a hunk of rock from the planet Jupiter. . . .

But here come the black ants: harbingers, you might say, of spring. One by one by one they appear on the dazzling white table and one by one I kill them with a forefinger, my deft right forefinger, mashing each against the surface of the table and then dropping it into a wastebasket at my side. Idle labor, mesmerizing, effortless, and I'm curious as to how long I can do it, sit here in the brilliant March sunshine killing ants with my right forefinger, how long I, and the ants, can keep it up.

After a while I realize that I can do it a long time. And that I've written my poem.

V

CREATURES

Ted Hughes

Hawk Roosting

I sit in the top of the wood, my eyes closed.
Inaction, no falsifying dream
Between my hooked head and hooked feet:
Or in sleep rehearse perfect kills and eat.

The convenience of the high trees!
The air's buoyancy and the sun's ray
Are of advantage to me;
And the earth's face upward for my inspection.

My feet are locked upon the rough bark.
It took the whole of Creation
To produce my foot, my each feather:
Now I hold Creation in my foot

Or fly up, and revolve it all slowly—
I kill where I please because it is all mine.
There is no sophistry in my body:
My manners are tearing off heads—

The allotment of death.
For the one path of my flight is direct
Through the bones of the living.
No arguments assert my right:

The sun is behind me.
Nothing has changed since I began.
My eye has permitted no change.
I am going to keep things like this.

Peter Matthiessen

The Cranes of Hokkaido

On a cold winter morning of northwest wind, the snow cone of Mount Fuji lights the sky in an aerial view never beheld by the immortal Hokusai, who painted Fuji-san from many vantage points on land and sea. On previous journeys to Japan, in spring and summer, I lived in its foothills for a week in a Zen monastery and climbed to the treeline, but never before have I had such a clear prospect of Fuji (literally, "Deathless"—the eternal mountain). The old volcano rules the southerly horizon, and the prospect seems an auspicious omen for a journey to see the red-crowned crane, or *tancho*, dance in its winter snows, one of the ultimate pilgrimages for ornithologists.

The silver plane with a *tancho* emblazoned on its tail banks wide and turns northeast, entering clouds. When the clouds part, the plane is over the snow country of northern Honshu, the main island of Japan. In former days, the red-crowned crane was resident in these river marshes, and perhaps as far south as Kamakura, where in the 11th century, at the Hachi-man Shinto temple, "the shogun Yoshiye at the ocean gate set free a multitude of cranes with silver and gold prayer strips attached to their legs . . . and a wind of awe rose at the spectacle of the great white birds, trailing the streamers down the Pacific sky." But in Japan today, this largest of the world's great cranes is confined to Hokkaido, the northern-most island of an archipelago that extends for some 1,800 miles north and south in a great arc off the coast of Asia, in the same latitudes as the Atlantic coast from Maine to Florida.

Peering out the window in the seat behind me is my old friend Victor Emanuel, with whom I have gone craning since 1976, when together we observed wintering whooping cranes and sandhill cranes along the coast of Texas. Since then, together and separately, we have observed most of the crane species around the world.

The trip to Hokkaido is the final leg of an often arduous journey to crane wintering grounds that began a month ago in western India, where we encountered the sarus and Eurasian cranes, the demoiselle and the rare

Siberian. In the past few weeks, enjoying good luck and good weather, we have seen seven of the eight species of Asian cranes. The sightings of hooded and white-naped cranes in southeastern China were the first for Victor and the sarus and Siberian were firsts for me, while the uncommon black-necked cranes seen in Bhutan were a first for us both. All but the sarus are considered to be rare and threatened species; yet all are considerably more numerous than the eighth species, the Japanese, or red-crowned, crane, which next to the whooping crane of North America is the rarest member of this splendid family.

In the old days, in the more southerly islands, the magnificent *tancho* was reserved for the nobility, which hunted it with falcons. Not until after the Meiji Restoration, in 1867, were peasants permitted to kill and eat— and salt and market—any *tancho* that foraged in their fields. As recently as a century ago a few still wandered as far south as Tokyo, but very soon the last birds on Honshu were killed. By World War II only the small population in southeastern Hokkaido still survived, and this flock was being steadily reduced by loss of habitat due to the draining of wetlands for agriculture.

In a bad freeze in 1950, the remnant band of 25 that hunched, half-starved, around a hot spring had to be rescued by farmers, who put out grain for them. Since then, several winter feeding stations and a ban on killing cranes have restored the Hokkaido flock to about 600 birds—roughly half the size of the Manchurian population, which breeds in the Amur River drainage of Siberia and northeast China.

Hokkaido now supports as many cranes as its limited marsh habitat can handle, and quite possibly more, judging from the fact that the size of the large breeding territory normally maintained by each pair of cranes has been steadily shrinking since their numbers rose after the 1950s.

Until recent years it was assumed that the *tancho* was an offshoot of the Manchurian population, and that most of the Japanese cranes crossed to the mainland in breeding season, since only a few local nests had been reported. Then, in the spring of 1972, an American crane student, George Archibald, noticed that juvenile birds were coming to the feeding stations in numbers greater than could be accounted for by those few nests. With the endorsement and support of the New York Zoological Society and a local airplane company, Archibald conducted an air survey of Hokkaido's southeast marshes. He located 53 active nests in just three hours, confirming his guess that the whole Japanese population of *Grus japonensis* was non-migratory. Dr. Archibald, now a world authority on the evolution of these cranes and director of the International Crane Foundation, based in Wisconsin, is presently convinced that the birds on Hokkaido have no connection with the mainland population, from which they have probably been separated for thousands of years.

Two years ago in Siberia, Archibald told me that when he first visited Hokkaido, in the winter of 1972, he was familiar with eight species of crane but had never laid eyes on *Grus japonensis* in the wild. "And when I saw it raise its wings and arch its back during its dancing, I realized that this species had gone far beyond the others in its pair-bonding behavior. Later I learned that the Siberian crane did something very similar, and that in this respect, these two species are quite different from the others. . . . But of all crane species, the red-crowned may be the most exciting."

The clouds gather again, for the weather is unsettled in Japan's far north, with severe earthquakes in recent days. The next glimpse is of the jade-green, choppy sea of the Tsugaru Strait, and then the volcanoes and snow-scapes of Hokkaido, or "North Sea Island," which lies off the coast of southeastern Siberia.

At the paper-mill and fishing town of Kushiro, on the Pacific coast, Victor and I are met at the small airport by Yulia Satsuki Momose. On Archibald's first visit to Kushiro, he lived with the family of Shoichiro Satsuki, and though Dr. Satsuki died some years ago, his kind family looks after Archibald and his friends to this day. Both of the Satsuki daughters have studied in the United States and speak good English. Yulia and her ornithologist husband, Kunikazu Momose, will serve as our expert guides in the Kushiro region.

Yulia Momose takes us straightaway to the haunts of *tancho*. In winter these haunts are largely confined to the region of the great Kushiro Marsh, which surrounds small rivers flowing down to the Pacific from the wooded Akan Mountains. The 104-square-mile marsh is the heart of the whole crane conservation effort, supporting about 35 of the estimated 161 nesting pairs on Hokkaido; another large group breeds in the region of Nemuro, to the east. Like wetlands all around the earth, the Kushiro Marsh is under great pressure from development (the developers like to call it reclamation), and it is shrinking. But in 1987 a part of it was set aside as a national park—the largest wetland still relatively undamaged on the four main islands of Japan.

Yulia Momose's first stop is Tsurumidai ("Crane Lookout"), a feeding station on the farm of Mr. and Mrs. Yoshiaki Watanabe, where observers are engaged in the annual crane census. The countryside is frozen deep beneath heavy snow—Hokkaido receives more snow than any other location at this latitude on earth—but the day is bright, without much wind, and it is pleasant out of doors if one stamps hard enough.

The eighth and rarest of the Asian cranes is also the least difficult to see, being nonmigratory on its range in Japan and therefore quite accessible to its well-wishers. To the minds of most people who know one crane from another, *Grus japonensis* is the most striking of the world's 15 species, with its snow-white body accented by a bright-red crown and, when the bird is alighted, by a fine bustle of velvety black plumes that are not tail feathers but the long secondary feathers of its folded wings.

The magnificent *tancho* most resembles its close relative the whooping crane, which is also a striking black-white-and-red. However, in *Grus americana* the red crown and black lores form a pointed mask, and the bustle is white, since the black of the wing is not in the secondary feathers but in the outer primaries. These long black feathers are usually hidden when the wings are folded, so that the whooper, from any distance, is almost pure white in appearance, like the Siberian. There are only about 140 whoopers in the wild, as opposed to an estimated 1,800 in the combined populations of the red-crowned, and perhaps twice that number for the Siberian. (Why the three white cranes should be the least numerous of the 15 species is not known, but large size and high visibility on the breeding grounds cannot have helped.)

At the feeding station a group of whooper swans with jet-black legs and golden bills is basking in the snow light, with assorted tits and woodpeckers flittering around a bird feeder and a large golden thrush (White's thrush) loitering nearby. One nervous *tancho* stalks restlessly across the snow, but finding no food, it flies off almost before Victor, still in shock from the bitter cold, can bundle up warmly enough to go get a look. At the next feeding station (a former farm sold by Yoshitaka Ito to the Wild Bird Society of Japan) there are no cranes at all. Not that Victor cares much, since, like me, he was looking forward to a first impression of *Grus japonensis* in wilder surroundings.

Near the Akan River, where most of the cranes roost every night all winter, is the main feeding area, Akan-cho Tancho. (The first *cho* is "town," and the second is "peak." *Tan* is a Chinese word for "red"—*akai* in Japanese. Thus "red peak" is "red-crowned," a more fitting name than "Japanese crane" for a bird that also breeds in mainland Asia.) At Akan-cho Tancho, which is supervised by the former owner, Teisaku Yamazaki, we finally catch up with Yulia's husband, Kuni Momose, the ornithologist overseeing the crane census at this main feeding station. Here 23 wary cranes await the daily offering of *ugui*, a coarse fish of the carp family that is netted in the mountain lakes and delivered live to the crane station each week.

The cranes stalk about and preen and dance, without much fervor—they are here to feed. As Mr. Yamazaki flings the flopping fish onto the snow, the cranes draw closer, and more fly in from the Akan River, but the elegant big birds take their time, making no effort to compete with the gang of crows or the black kites or four white-tailed eagles that circle overhead. Then they swoop down and up again in a graceful arc, having seized a flopping, red-finned *ugui* off the snow. The spectacle attracts visitors, and so there is a small building with a food counter, tea, souvenirs, and even an observatory on the second floor—little used except for warmth, since the feeding birds are but a fish throw from the wood barricade outside.

Beyond the meadow where the cranes dance and feed is a line of spruce trees along the Akan River; beyond the river rise low, wooded hills of bare brown trees. In pairs and family groups of three or (rarely) four, the great white birds swing in through the conifers, alighting so daintily on long black legs that the toes seem to strain to touch the snow and even to lift a little at the final second, as if flinching from the frozen surface.

A red fox (a warmer red, and lacking the black points—ears, paws, and tail—of its new-world cousin) comes trotting from the spruce, staying low to the ground as it slips among the cranes. Biting at the still-flopping fish, it struggles to manage two or three at once, running to drop them in a little cache at some distance from the birds, then trotting back for more. No doubt the bold fox is watched keenly by the beady black eyes of the vixen and their kits back in the spruce. In spring the fox preys on the crane nests, taking eggs as well as chicks, though it probably scavenges less than the ever-alert crows. Occasionally a white-tailed eagle makes off with a chick, and Mr. Watanabe at Crane Lookout has seen a fox attack and kill an unwary adult crane that it caught probing in a ditch, permitting the fox to leap onto its neck from the bank above.

Like Mr. and Mrs. Watanabe and Mr. Ito, who are elderly people, now retired, Mr. Yamazaki's father began feeding the cranes many years ago, in the freezing year of 1950, when it was clear that without help the dwindling cranes of Hokkaido might not survive. Mrs. Tome Watanabe sent local schoolchildren out to feed the cranes in 1952, and Mr. Ito joined the cause a little later. In 1957 a Crane Club was founded at Akan Junior High School that remained active for many years, but not until 1965 did the town of Akan and nearby Tsurui village help the farmers pay for the grain they were dispensing and hire Mr. Ito and Mr. Yamazaki as watchmen-caretakers.

In the evening, Yulia Momose's sister, Rori Satsuki, a musician, and their lively mother, Mrs. Yoshie Satsuki, escort us to Kushiro's most ancient restaurant, called Yatsunami, for a wonderful fresh-seafood supper. The name means "Eight Waves"—that is, eight generations. Eight is a lucky number, Rori tells us. As for Kushiro, its name derives from the Ainu word *kusuri*, sometimes translated as "place where people gather." Perhaps there were Ainu settlements on this coast even in A.D. 794, when Japan's first shogun, or "general for subduing the barbarians," was sent out to deal with invasions of "a wild blue-eyed people called Emishi [the Ainu] from the northern island of Hokkaido, who 'gathered together like ants but dispersed like birds.' "

Though there were still a few old Ainu to be found during Rori's childhood, their descendants are almost entirely assimilated—only recently has there been a movement to document some of the traditional Ainu culture. Today Kushiro is a fisheries, coal, and papermill town ("Newsprint and cardboard," says Rori. "It's the cardboard plant that smells"); having used up all the local forest, Kushiro now imports its rough wood from abroad. Though nobody kills the cranes anymore, according to Rori, many local farmers still resent them—they consume the maize needed for livestock and may damage the new green shoots of the spring crops.

Despite its long history in Japanese culture, the *tancho* has been the national bird only since 1952, when that notion was borrowed from the Americans. As Rori remarks tartly in a discussion of the great film director Akiro Kurosawa, who went unappreciated in his own land for many years, "We Japanese tend to appreciate certain things about our country only after other countries admire them first."

At 6 A.M. the next morning we set off from Kushiro with the Momoses, going first to the road that follows the Shitakara River upstream toward the Akan foothills. Deciduous woods climb to the spruce ridge, and behind the ridge rises the cone of the snow-peaked volcano known as Akan-Fuji. The day is clear and very cold—it is −20 degrees centigrade, or −4 degrees Fahrenheit—and our boots squeak on the snowy road that leads along the frosted trees by the Shitakara (sometimes translated as "Place of Elms" in the language of the Ainu; but the elms were displaced long ago, and the Ainu too). Smiling in honest delight, Mr. Yamazaki has already located 18 or 20 cranes that are still roosted a little way upriver, and we stoop to peer at them from between the icy branches.

Beyond the stream bend, the huge white birds hunch in the mist.

Where soft, plump snow descends to the very edges of the ice, the cranes, one-legged, have formed a line of motionless black-and-white shapes, strung like a snow fence all the way across the stream. Already one or two are waking, and one preens a little, but they seem to await the first cold rays of sun before starting to move about in a small riffle, the only stretch of water not frozen. In an ancient defense against mammal predators, now all but gone (wolves are extinct here, and the bears hibernate), the cranes of Kushiro roost in streams—the largest group roosts in the Akan River—and few if any are caught by the ice, though they sometimes fly up with long legs ringed with ice anklets.

Most are preening, moving a little, the black-and-white patterns shifting mysteriously in the ice mist. Suddenly two elevate their necks, point their bills skyward, and utter together the loud, wild call that I last heard on the breeding grounds in Siberia. The unison call, as this bonding cry is known, rings across the brittle cold of the dawn valley.

Though we are 200 yards away, well screened by bushes, these exceptionally alert and sharp-eyed birds are quite aware of us. But they do not fly, and they remain calm when we walk quietly away. Though wary, the *tancho* in Japan seem to know that man is no longer their enemy. Perhaps one day they will regain the confiding behavior that is so stirring in wild creatures of remote places that man reached very late, such as the Galápagos, or of places where man has long honored a prohibition against killing, as in certain Buddhist regions of the Himalayas.

In connection with their crane census, the Momoses take us on a survey of the Onbetsu River drainage to the west, where last year they located cranes that rarely come in to the Kushiro stations. Last month's earthquake damage—landslides and big cracks in the roads—is much more apparent west of Kushiro, and in places the road over the foothills to the town of Onbetsu has fallen away into the valleys. Farther on, a herd of pretty sika deer, white-tailed, in gray winter pelage, waits large-eyed at the wood edge, peering out as if seeking to determine whether this road might still be safe to cross.

From Onbetsu, a road follows the river north into the mountains, and here there are work crews, for the lower Onbetsu has been blocked and diverted by the landslides. Though the upper river is still clear, there are no cranes, only a white-tailed eagle, broad-backed in a tree, and a lone dog in the river meadows, running to somewhere across the shining snow.

Eventually a side road leads up the Muri tributary ("Foggy Village," though the town is long since gone), where a few old farms lie well scattered in the valley. Soon a pair of cranes appear on a river bend, then three more back downstream a little ways, then two more that join the first pair, feeding along on small insects and larvae under the stream rocks as they must have done before the feeding stations were established, all the time moving unhurriedly away from their would-be admirers.

Soon the four climb up onto a snowbank, in a sun-bright composition of black-white birds inlaid in the white-black of snow and water. Traditionally, *tancho* is perceived as an emblem of the yin-yang of existence—the "dark-light"—with the blood-red crown as the essence or source of All That Is. In this brilliant moment one might believe that the red crowns are the crimson heart of being, and the dark evergreens the great mystery looming behind.

Victor wonders why these red-crowned cranes, which apparently endure the coldest temperatures of any crane species, have longer bills and necks and legs than the black-necked cranes in the mountains of Bhutan, which are bulkier birds whose shorter necks and legs are adaptations to a cold climate. (The black-necked crane's altitudinal migration rarely takes it below 10,000 feet even in winter, and it nests at 16,000 feet or more on the Tibetan Plateau, so that it lives in a cold climate all year round.) I, in turn, wonder if the red-crowneds, which enjoy temperate summers, are intrinsically the hardiest or only circumstantially so, since all known *Grus japonensis* of the mainland population also migrate, and presumably these Hokkaido birds once flew south to the island of Honshu in winter. Only in the last century, having been extirpated on Honshu (where not only were they hunted hard but where the last large wetlands have been despoiled or destroyed), has the species been reduced to this nonmigrant population on the northern island.

Kuni Momose, intrigued by the question, is undecided. He speculates, in the absence of much evidence, that even in the old days some of the Hokkaido population migrated and some didn't.

These hills, clear-cut years ago to feed the sawmills, are healed over with a small second-growth forest of oak and birch and larch and spruce. Elsewhere they have been replanted with conifers. Reforestation, Yulia says, has become "a passion" in Japan. The valley farms are well spread out and appear prosperous, and many more small birds are to be seen than in the Kushiro Valley. A lovely fawn-and-blue Eurasian jay is common here—six together peck seeds from a manure heap in a cattle yard—and we also note four dusky thrushes, great and marsh tits, a spotted woodpecker, and a brown-eared bulbul in fresh country colors that looks nothing like the soiled street specimens in Tokyo.

Farther upriver, three red-black-and-white heads on long white necks come up over a snowbank on a bend. The heads turn, catching the bright light, against a dark background of steep, wooded hillside already overtaken by afternoon shadow. We are able to get closer, though not close. The sight of these sun-silvered silhouettes, stalking away unhurriedly and yet so swiftly in the snow and black-diamond shimmer of the Muri River, is a crane spectacle almost too elegant to be imagined.

The Muri Valley birds seem wilder than those that come so blithely to the Kushiro stations, or so I happily suggest as we turn back downriver. The Momoses agree, but we also agree that perhaps this is illusion, wishful thinking. A few years ago, the local government down near the confluence with the Onbetsu established a crane-feeding program like those at Akan and Tsurui villages, administered by an old gentleman, Ichiro Sato, who feeds the cranes in a pasture outside his small farmhouse. The cranes, Mr. Sato assures us, will appear about 3:30 P.M.—late afternoon at this time of the year, not long before dusk, when they go to roost—and each will peck up 50 grains of maize before resting awhile, perhaps eating a little snow to wash them down.

Whether or not they draw the line at 50 grains, Mr. Sato's cranes are certainly not greedy—the reticence of all crane species in the presence of food is one of their numerous attractive traits. They stand around awhile after sailing down the valley at the time appointed, swinging up into the freezing wind until it fills their broad, cupped wings, and stepping lightly down out of the air. They may preen a little, dance a little, even stand upon one leg, lifting the other foot into their breast feathers to warm it, after delicately shaking off any ice or snow. Like the Kushiro cranes, these birds are becoming dependent upon humans, but they are still nervous and more quickly wary. Here in an honest farmyard that makes no concessions to visitors, they seem somehow less demeaned than the birds in the *ugui* show at Akan-cho Tan-cho.

When the cranes have fed (I forget to count the grains), they move away a little, and some begin to bow and dance, using the cold twilight wind to lift themselves straight up, legs dangling, four or five feet into the air. Even the immatures join in, to get some practice. Still steeped in winter, most of the *tancho* remain silent after the low, rolling greeting call made in flight as they sail in; but sometimes newcomers are challenged with a loud unison call by a pair already present. Soon 23 birds have arrived, with a pair of twins among the five immature birds born last spring. These young birds are brown-headed, with brown feathers in their bustles as well as a light-brown spackle on the mantle. Late this spring, though not yet mated, they will attain full adult size and will be driven off by the breeding parents.

As the sun descends behind the wooded ridge and faint stars appear in the fading blue above, the cranes dance forward and lift off the snow into the north wind. They bank away toward the Muri River, which they will follow down along a ridge to their roost in an open stretch of the Onbetsu. There they will form their line in the black water and feathershift and preen and hunch and place their heads under their wings and settle for the night.

Soon all that may be seen in the near dusk are the last pairs of white wings flicking upward, the black plumes of the trailing edge like ancient Oriental symbols, even to the sharp black arrow in the middle of the wing that points straight forward like a black compass needle. At first that mark appears to spoil the black-white *symmetry* of the great wings, but in truth it intensifies their beauty, like the twisted pine on a high ridge that redeems the dull perfection of the moon.

David Quammen

Rattlesnake Passion

The world is a changeful place and Texas, despite what some folks might think, is part of the world. It was 17 years since I'd set foot inside the snake farm at New Braunfels.

All I remembered was a turnstile and rows of cages, a pit full of diamondback rattlesnakes, a fellow named John Deck, and the shriveled carcass of a two-headed monkey. Probably the two-headed monkey was a figment, I'd begun to suspect, invented by my own brain in the course of telling and retelling a good story. It was too mythic. It was too precisely the sort of detail that a person would concoct for some ludicrous, gothic piece of fiction. This two-headed monkey in my mind's eye, this pitiful thing, was dried like a piece of jerky. And oh yes, there was also a vegetable scale—a tin pan beneath a spring gauge—hung up above the pit. I couldn't have told you whether the vegetable scale was an artifact of imagination or of memory. Memory, imagination, whichever, as I drove back into New Braunfels last spring I had no expectation of finding it. I had no expectation of seeing a two-headed monkey. Probably, I thought, the snake farm itself would be gone.

I envisioned it: long since foreclosed upon or lost in the pot of a poker game, fallen derelict, a sad nightmare of broken windows and ragged chickenwire and fading signs; haunted by dozens of snakes that had suffered terminal neglect in their cages, left to starve so slowly that even they didn't notice the exact moment of death, dried by the Texas heat into pretzel shapes more pitifully macabre than even a two-headed monkey; the whole enterprise gone defunct, a casualty to shifting values and new fashions in entertainment. Once, I reminded myself, there had indeed been a snake farm beside the highway at New Braunfels, Texas. But most likely it was bulldozed away to clear the lot. Most likely it had transmogrified into a Mini Mart or a video store. The world is a changeful place. What's that scale for? I had asked John Deck back in springtime of 1973.

Weighing rattlesnakes, he had told me. We buy them by the pound.

John Deck was a young man with a particular attitude toward snakes. In Texas, where venomous serpents still outnumber humans and cows and

Japanese automobiles, you find quite a sampling of particular attitudes toward snakes. Some folks just plain hate them. With purblind passion they detest the poor animals from the depths of their tiny sour hearts. The diamondback rattlesnake, *Crotalus atrox*, being common and large and modestly dangerous, is the bête noire of these people. Snake-haters kill diamondbacks for fun. They kill diamondbacks with a righteous zeal that they'd like to believe is somehow religious or patriotic or, at very least, neighborly. They kill diamondbacks from habit. These people gather together annually in great civic festivals of cartoonish abuse, and slaughter, and ecstatic adolescent loathing, that go by the label of rattlesnake roundups. Often as not, for such an event, the local Jaycees serve as sponsor. Diamondback rattlesnakes are bought by the pound. A cash prize for the longest snake; a prize for the most rattles; and a prize for the weightiest total delivery of snake flesh. Admission is charged, crowds gather, Coke and Dr Pepper and gobbets of fried diamondback are available at concession stands. Of course it's all high-minded and innocent, on the surface. It's a way to raise money for the hospital or the fire truck. Deeper down it's a pageant of hatred, wonderfully medieval, reflecting the same dire élan you might have found in a Bavarian village during the early days of the Black Death. March is the favored month for such doings, notwithstanding the notion that April is the cruelest. In March, the snakes are still groggy from winter and loafing in underground dens, from which they can be conveniently flushed with infusions of gasoline. By April, they've likely dispersed. Or they might defend themselves.

Other people, a smaller minority of contrasting disposition, are what you might call snake fanciers. Snake fanciers buy and sell, they trade and collect. They view snakes as precious and transcendent commodities—same way another person, hardly more sane, might dote upon canceled stamps or antique Packards or the Pete Rose rookie baseball card. Snake fanciers know the blue-book value of any species at any given moment. The Mexican milk snake, *Lampropeltis triangulum annulata*, is smallish and non-venomous but beautifully banded in red and yellow and black, a close mimic of the coral snake, and therefore it's highly prized. The Western coachwhip is a big matinee-idol of a snake, but too common to interest a fancier. The California kingsnake, not native to Texas, might go for $50 as a hatchling. And among fanciers, as amid roundups: Diamondback rattlesnakes are wholesaled by the pound. It's a matter of supply and demand.

John Deck was a snake fancier. He had only been rattler-bit a few times. At an early age he'd had his own pit full of diamondbacks, a plywood affair out near the garage. Cocky lad, he used to knock the climbers back down off those plywood walls with his own quick right hand, delivering a light tap to the back of a snake's head, until one day he caught a palmload of fangs. John had come back from Vietnam with a bag full of cobras, which he'd collected while walking patrol, using the butt of his M-16 for a pinning stick. When I met him, he was a full-time professional attendant at the New Braunfels snake farm—like a boy's dream of the perfect job, yes?— and still snake-hunting on his own time to fill out his private collection. I was fascinated. Sure, he told me, come along if you want. We'll go on down there to Terrell County.

Terrell County was not chosen at random. This was the place to go, this was the scene, if you were a serious fancier of the Texas herpetofauna. Diamondbacks could be had anywhere, but down in the rolling hills and gullies of Terrell County you might find a mottled rock rattler, or a Mojave rattler, or a trans-Pecos copperhead, or that exceptionally prized rarity, a Blair's kingsnake. So we drove in John's pickup, all through a hot afternoon and a warm evening, to reach this Elysian desert on the far side of the Pecos River, just northwest of a border town called Langtry. We provisioned ourselves with sardines and Vienna sausages from the Langtry store. We cruised up and down the dirt roads by night, scanning the shoulders with high beams, on the lookout for nocturnal snakes, and then, after a few hours sleep, by daylight we climbed through the gullies.

At some point we shanghaied a tarantula, which John locked away in a brown paper bag and which cost me sleep in the back of the pickup (we shared the truck bed, that spider and I, while John slept on the ground among scorpions) with its sedulous scratching for freedom. In the privacy of the cab, as we cruised, John chattered with other snake-hunters over the CB. He talked guardedly to me about Vietnam, a delightful country if you happened to like deadly snakes. He told me some rattlesnake stories—the one about getting bit on the palm, the more elaborately comical one about getting bit on the ass, the one about the excitable emergency-room nurse who ran and tripped and broke her arm when he mentioned the word "rattlesnake," though that particular bite turned out to be empty of venom. At another moment John mashed the brakes and dove out to grab a yellowbelly racer, *Coluber constrictor flaviventris*, a nonvenomous species and probably one of the more common in Texas. Notwithstanding the rarity theory of value, this yellowbelly was big and pretty and he wanted it; too eager to use a pinning stick, he nearly got chewed on before subduing it clumsily by covering its head with his hat. John Deck had an unheedful passion for snakes, almost any snakes, that an ecology-minded person just couldn't sanction and a generous-minded person just couldn't hate.

He didn't kill them. He didn't fry them. He didn't abuse them before crowds to prove the octane of his testosterone. He kidnapped them out of their habitat, yes. Sometimes he sold them or traded them, yes. Mainly he just fancied them.

In his company I enjoyed two days of vivid lunacy. And our quest for herpetological jewels was rewarded. We caught a nice little specimen of mottled rock rattler. We caught a trans-Pecos copperhead, elegant with its russet and tan bands. In those days this foolishness was legal. It even seemed like a good idea. The Blair's kingsnake, happy to say, eluded us.

A month later I left Texas. Too dry and too hot, I decided, with not nearly enough trout. I never saw John Deck again. But who could forget him?

Some of the things you can witness at a rattlesnake roundup in Texas or Oklahoma:

You can see thousands of pounds of diamondback rattlesnakes being measured and weighed. "We had 5,000 pounds of snakes turned in before noon the first morning," a snake-weigher at the Sweetwater Rattlesnake Roundup told a reporter from *Time* after the 1988 event. "They're brought in U-Hauls so they don't freeze. We don't buy dead snakes." The total at Sweetwater that year was 11,709 pounds, and Sweetwater is just one roundup among dozens. Although dead snakes aren't bought, dying snakes are, and if you looked closely you might see that many are not in the pink of health. Some have suffered broken necks from rough handling with tongs. Some are starved and dehydrated, having been captured months earlier and stockpiled in anticipation of roundup day. One Texas herpetologist reckons that 95 percent of the rattlesnakes turned in at a given roundup have not been collected that weekend or in that vicinity. So much for the traditional notion of roundups, as festive occasions for de-snaking the local countryside.

You can see an arts-and-crafts show. Among the items on sale, you're liable to find snakeskin belts, snakeskin gimme hats, plastic paperweights containing diamondback heads, earrings made from rattles, and perhaps the ultimate, a toilet seat in the clear plastic of which are embedded baby diamondbacks. Whether the toilet seat (retail, around $75) qualifies in these towns as a piece of art or merely of craft, is a question I'm not in position to answer.

You might see children, whole families, being photographed holding live diamondbacks—squeamish but grinning folks, secure in the knowledge that these particular animals have had their mouths sewn shut. You might see parents paying $5 to buy a child the privilege of decapitating a rattlesnake with a hatchet. You can certainly see a sacking competition, wherein contestants race against a stopwatch to stuff ten diamondbacks into a sack, with a five-second penalty added each time the sacker gets bitten. The world rattlesnake-sacking record has been intermittently held by a Texan named Cotton Dillard, according to Mr. Dillard anyway; he posted a time of 18.6 seconds at the town of Taylor in 1984. In a more recent year, Mr. Dillard slipped to 34 seconds, after a penalty.

You can see the Heart of Texas Snake Handlers, based in Waco but on the road during roundup season, performing vainglorious antics in their matching T-shirts. You can see them do the Kung Fu Walk of Death, strutting barefoot down a gauntlet of diamondbacks and kicking the snakes aside. You can see them stack coiled diamondbacks on their heads. You can see them lie still in sleeping bags filled with rattlesnakes, purportedly to make an educational point about safe camping. Some guys have motorcycles; some guys have golf; some guys get drunk and beat people up with cue sticks on Friday night; the Heart of Texas Handlers have snakes. You can see that these boys possess, in their own right, a very particular attitude.

Confession: I've never gone to a roundup, though often over the years I've threatened myself with the notion. Much of my information comes from A. J. Seippel, a mild-mannered computer executive and amateur herpetologist, who's got an attitude of his own. "If this were rabbits, or any other animal, it would have been stopped a long time ago," Seippel says. He and others are working to stop it now.

Sign-carrying and leaflet-distributing protestors, including Jim Seippel, have laid siege to the roundups. Conservationists, animal-rights groups, Earth First!ers, Humane Society chapters, reputable herpetological clubs—more than two dozen organizations have united to raise the long-overdue cry that rattlesnake roundups are retrograde and indecent. Jim Seippel is a persuasive spokesman. In dry tones tinged only slightly with outrage and sarcasm, he tells me about the stockpiling, the Kung Fu Walk of Death, the sewing-shut of mouths, the decapitation-for-fun ("What they're teaching kids is that wildlife can be abused"), and the lucrative harvest of gall bladders, which get pickled in whiskey and shipped to the Orient as aphrodisiacs. "Most of these people are really not interested in snakes," he says damningly. "They're interested in a profit from them."

Seippel wears a blue pinstripe suit. He is stealing moments from work in order to meet with me, a generous act, since his group at IBM is debuting a new family of products this week. We're seated over spinach salads at a yuppie restaurant in Austin. Times have changed.

Jim Seippel was the focus of my visit but of course I have to go back to New Braunfels. For company I recruit my sweet and respectable older sister, who has raised two toddlers to college age and begun a computer career herself since the last time I made this drive. Lo, the snake farm is still there. EXCITING EDUCATIONAL ENTERTAINING, says the sign. Open for business, though it turns out that we are the only customers. We pay, and pass by the counter where the dried snake-heads and scorpion paperweights and snakeskin wallets are on sale. My sister browses the cages, while I struggle to steady myself in the space-time continuum.

"John Deck still work here, by any chance?"

No. The current attendant doesn't know John Deck. This attendant is an amiable, heavyset old boy in jeans and a white T-shirt. I admit to him that, long ago, Deck and I made an expedition to Terrell County.

"You still hunt?" he asks me.

"Uh. No. Not anymore."

I mention that we had been on the lookout for a Blair's kingsnake. Then again, I say, probably anyone who goes down to Terrell County is on the lookout for a Blair's. He informs me that the Blair's kingsnake no longer bears that name: "gray-banded kingsnake" is what the field guides now say. And here in one of the glass cages is a specimen, a gorgeous little snake banded with black and orange and white and gray, hiding shyly behind its water dish. "Those gray-bands, they're up to 300 dollars now," says the attendant. "Me, I just can't get into the same ballpark as that myself." In central Texas, as anywhere, inflation is pricing the working stiff out of the market.

"What'd you catch, down there in Terrell?" he asks. "You and old Deck." Oh, we got a trans-Pecos copperhead, I say, and a little bitty rock rattler. I don't bother to wonder why I should remember such tiny details, after 17 years. Memory is memory and, like love, it knows no logic.

"Now, both of those snakes," he says. "They're just out of sight now. Very highly prized."

Leaving my sister to carry the conversation, I wander off. I look for the big rattlesnake pit but find no sign of it. Maybe I imagined that part. No sign of a vegetable scale either.

Turning down the back row of cages, I admire this world-class collection of unpopular beasts. There is an Ottoman viper, an emperor scorpion, an orange-kneed tarantula, a blue krait. There is a hefty arthropod identified only as a "bird-eating spider," presumably from some South American forest. There is an albino monocled cobra. A trans-Pecos rat snake, a Mexican kingsnake, a blacktail rattler. A speckled rattler, a Panamint rattler. A Sonoran sidewinder, which is also of course a rattlesnake. I find it hard to fathom how anyone could loathe and abuse such lovely creatures. Surely that kind of twisted passion went out with the Black Death. Suddenly I raise my eyes to a dusty bell jar resting before me on a shelf.

Inside is the carcass of a two-headed monkey, dry as jerky. When things change, it's always surprising. And when they remain unchanged, it's astonishing.

Guy de la Valdéne

Quail Farm

I live on the outskirts of Tallahassee, Florida, on a farm in Gadsden
County, eleven miles west of Coon Bottom and thirteen miles south of
Booger Bay, Georgia. The region is referred to as the red hills of Florida
for its abundance of clay and the rolling nature of its topography. All in all,
a fine place to live, particularly if one has the means to travel every so often
to a place where people speak the King's English and where chewing tobacco is thought of in the same vein as messing one's pants. A small price
to pay, I might add, for an otherwise wild and as yet untainted piece of geography.

Shade-tobacco farming in Gadsden County (specifically, cultivation of
the broad outer leaf used to wrap Cuban cigars) had enriched the local
economy since the turn of the century. Until 1960 or so, the sweet fragrance
of tobacco was carried on every breeze, coins jingled in men's pockets, and
life in the county was sweet and full of promise. However, as with most un-
dertakings that rely on the poverty of one class for the benefit of another,
there are always tiers of hungrier people with lower expectations who will
work for less. This is how Gadsden County lost its hold on the tobacco market to the field hands of Central America.

A handful of long, rectangular barns, fashioned out of the hearts of
tall slash pines, once swollen with stringers of curing tobacco leaves and the
smoke from carefully tended charcoal fires, stand as silent witnesses. Resin
lingers in the darkness of the few remaining barns, but outside the wood
shingles are weather-warped and the roofs dull. They endure, unused except as occasional hideouts for children and as shelters for the mice and swallows that come and go through the wind tears of summer storms.

The country's sudden loss of wealth (Gadsden was, for a moment in
history, the richest county in the state) left a huge workforce wanting and
unemployed, an undertow of penurious souls that never recovered economically. Thirty years later, at the end of every month, mothers send their
children to public school on empty stomachs. Food swells the grocery shelves,
but in many households the money has run out. I live in the poorest county
in Florida.

My land lies between the sandy coastal soil south of Tallahassee and the flat piney forests of Georgia. The barrel-like clay hills, hardwood bottoms, and deep chasms that cut into the earth exist, I am told, because this is where the southern grade of the Appalachian mountain range falls to the sea, a romantic theory that explains some of the tortured gullies in which my turkeys strut.

This earth is not as rich as the tenderloin of grade-one soil that runs north and south between Thomasville, Georgia, and Tallahassee, Florida, but then, neither am I, so my aim is to improve what I have as best I can within certain financial boundaries.

The farm was once part of a much larger plantation and, throughout its existence, has produced cotton and the slaves to pick it, cattle, shade tobacco, peanuts, corn, and a large, rambunctious Southern family. In 1990 I bought eight hundred acres of what remained of the homestead, changed its name and status to Dogwood Farm, and to the utter delight of my hunting dogs—Robin, the English springer spaniel who looks like a Stubbs painting; Mabel, the doltish lemon-and-white English pointer; and Carnac, the roan-colored French Brittany puppy who resembles a suckling pig—proceeded to grow birds: wild eastern bobwhite quail (*Colinus virginianus* for those interested in the specifics of what things are and where they come from).

The woods, which comprise 50 percent of the property, are composed of second-growth loblollies, slash, a handful of long-leaf pine trees, thousands of white, red, and water oaks, gum trees, hickories, dogwoods, ironwoods, chinaberries, pecans, poplars, willows, sassafras, magnolias, and crab apples. A number of eighty-year-old live oaks round out the selection. Uniformity bores me senseless, and while some of the finest plantations north and east of me grow beautiful, manicured rows of plum-perfect pinewoods, no matter how straight and how old those trees may be (and I can attest that they are), a few hours under their homogeneous canopy make me long for the garish play of light that glances over the boughs of my hardwoods.

Our most eccentric tree, the live oak *(Quercus virginiana)*, also named after the state of Virginia, spends its life draped in Spanish moss, a rootless epiphyte that the Southeast Indian women fashioned into skirts and which African slaves later used to stuff their mattresses. These are hugely reassuring trees, trees that define insouciance, poets among trees, and I feel a kinship to them, as I would feel a kinship to baobabs if I lived in Senegal. As luck would have it, bobwhite quail relish the bittersweet taste of acorns, and in plentiful years—about one out of every three—they march down to the bottoms, to where the hardwoods grow thick, where the deer and the turkey live, and where food falls from the sky.

The other half of the farm is given over to half a dozen fields and abandoned pastures. One such cornfield was so large—two hundred acres—that I didn't know how to manage it until it was brought to my attention that quail, like most gallinaceous birds, are stalkers of edges. Because small openings yield more edges than larger ones, I broke this monotonous expanse into ten or twelve long, narrow fields with trees, food plots, and cover. The pastures yield Pensacola Bahia grass and to a lesser degree Bermuda grass, thick, mat types, savored by cows and by bobwhites during their nesting season, grasses that once established are difficult to get rid of. Two small wet-weather ponds stain both ends of the two-hundred-acre field, and a thirty-acre lake, teeming with brim and black bass, fills an old hardwood bottom. On the edge of this lake I built a cabin, officially a writing studio, but in reality the quarters I escape to as early as possible each day and inside of which I spy through high-powered binoculars on wood ducks and ospreys, martins, bluebirds, the quail and doves that visit my feeder, otters, snakes, and whatever other creatures nature pushes across my lenses.

* * *

In the South, a bird means a quail; a mess of birds, a bunch of quail; and a bird dog, a quail dog. To confuse the issue slightly, in some regions, while black bass are thought of as trout, bobwhites are referred to as partridge. However, regardless of colloquial designation, the history of the bobwhite quail is also the history of the men and women who shaped this continent, a broad spectrum of social, historical, and economic personalities, from the Creek Indians who snared quail to the market hunters who netted them, the sharecroppers who ground-sluiced them, the farmers, doctors, and schoolteachers who hunted up and down miles of multiflora fence rows, flushed bobwhites across bean fields, and killed them on the edge of the broom sedge, to the Yankees who, to this day, wear fancy clothes and chase after quail sitting high in the saddle of expensive gaited horses.

A covey of quail is a coterie, an assembly of coquettes and dandies. Eight to ten inches tall, ovate in shape, balanced on overly long toes, scaly legs, and fat thighs, they assume an impeccably upright posture, particularly when perched on logs and fence posts. These are birds that display a vocabulary of fall colors with lively black eyes and strong, horny beaks designed to deal with stubborn seeds. But in hand they feel like soft-boiled eggs, brown, buff, ash, black, and chestnut-colored eggs whose barred and crescent patterns remind one of swollen leaves on the bottom of a pond. Bobwhite quail are plump and malleable like cotton candy. Tender birds without the musculature of distant travelers or even roamers, quail gravitate to where the food is plentiful and within walking distance; they enjoy both grit and chatter and are loath to fly for any reason. The male bird wears a white mask over his cheeks and chin and black eye stripes down to his beak. The female's coloring matches her mate's—a similarity of plumage usually indicates an inclination to sharing of parental duties—except that the hen's mask is ochre yellow in coloring. The entire covey faces its destiny with poised terror.

* * *

The fact that I devote a certain effort to the well-being of bobwhites during these times of political perjury, fast food, and baboonlike talk shows falls on understanding ears in this part of the country; ears that have been conditioned to the hubristic sounds of spring whistling, the startled scatterings of roadside coveys, the resonance of autumn guns, and the invigorating cracklings of fried quail and okra. So when I am asked what kind of a farm I own I say, "A bird farm," readily admitting to being, by modern criteria, a bum. However, instead of being questioned about my motives or the rationale behind them, I am queried on the condition of the land, the dogs, and that year's crop of quail. The questions entertain well-hidden remembrances, reminders of gentler days when slow dancing, drive-in movies, spandex girdles, and Golden Hawk Studebakers were fashionable.

When I am asked the same question up north, I reply, "A big farm."

"Oh! You mean an everything farm?" he or she asks, backpedaling for all it's worth in an effort to forestall any thought I may have regarding honking on about rural life, mud holes, and chiggers.

"Yeah," I answer, looking the asker in the eye. And much to everyone's relief, that's usually the end of it.

* * *

For reasons of life, death, and changing interests, the farm had not been managed for quail for fifteen years prior to my arrival. Deer were culled from tree stands and doves were shot in the cornfields, but for a long time there was only one serious quail hunter: a fine old Southern gentleman whose family name is that of a famous American shotgun, a friend of the family who ran his pointers three or four times a season as much for the exercise it offered his dogs as for the memories; treasured memories of the quick, full, busy years of youth when turning over twenty coveys of quail in a day's hunting meant little more than a comfortable number of birds to drink to at sundown.

To the best of my knowledge there were but seven coveys of quail living on the farm when I bought it; a year later there were fifteen; the following winter twenty-one; and now, as I write, I have counted and marked twenty-five coveys on the map. My original plan was to raise the number of bobwhite quail to saturation point, partly as an exercise in management, partly because it stimulates my dogs' raison d'être, and partly because I was cocksure that by increasing the population I would be doing the birds a favor. Now that I have settled on the land and lived through a progression of seasons, I better understand the pace and guidelines nature has set for herself on this particular piece of dirt, guidelines that encourage certain endeavors and discourage others. I can improve the habitat by removing or adding to what is already here, but there is nothing that I, or for that matter any man, can do, to impress nature. By saturating the farm with bobwhite quail what I really had in mind was impressing myself and my friends.

On the other hand, I am going to shape this small corner of nature into a vision of what I believe will best glorify its inherent qualities, a sculpturing of the land—heresy to some who would leave nature to her own devices—gardening on a large scale, subjective landscaping for beauty's sake. And, as I like to see as far as my eyes allow, I remove what is diseased, repetitious, or ugly: catfaced, topless, rachitic, stunted, and otherwise suppressed trees that compete with specimens that would otherwise grow strong and relatively straight. To offset this inclination to prune, I plant five times as many trees as I remove, so that one day, unless I go broke in the process, no matter where I stand I will see only what pleases me. When I want ugly I'll drive into town.

In conjunction with this bit of gardening insanity, I do everything short of killing hawks, bobcats, and coyotes (I do set live traps for the nest destroyers such as opossums, raccoons, and skunks) to provide *Colinus virginianus*, visiting turkeys, and the local deer herd with a comfortable place to live. I realize that the culling of predators is subjective, but culling is an everyday aspect of farm life. In every other respect I do my best to offer free bed and board to those animals or birds that migrate to or take up residence on this land.

In the fall and winter I kill a small percentage of my tenants and eat them. Those I don't eat I give to others who do. Nothing is wasted except the money and time it takes to run the operation, and it might be argued that neither is wasted. In my life I have polluted and abused nature and thousands of her residents, and despite this questionable behavior nature has granted me a life of pleasure and unqualified beauty. Now that I have the wherewithal to manage and tend to this farm and the species that live on it, it would be a moral insult not to do so. The more food and cover I plant the more game and nongame species will thrive, the more water holes, the more fish, the more wildlife, the more predators. Small as it may be, I will make this sequestered world of mine revolve with the assurance of time.

Francis Thompson, an English poet, wrote that one could not pick a flower without troubling a star. To be protective of things because they happen to live here is a new experience, one that I am trying to sort out. So far, owning land has made me aware of nature's ingrained patience, of weather and its reign over every action and conversation, of the feel of steel disks cutting new ground, of the stretching noises of growing corn on a warm summer night, of the weight that monotony bears on those who work the earth, of how the simplicity of rural life is unnecessarily complicated to give it weight and importance, and of how grateful I am to have such a canvas on which to create whatever pleases me; a cocoon inside which I live and love and fight my demons. I keep my contact with the outside world to a minimum and my address book thin; my wife, meanwhile, has joined the contemplative order of the Carmelites. Should I wonder why?

Jennifer Ackerman

Five Fathoms

Crabs again. Real crabs this time, *Ocypode quadrata*, the swift-footed ghost crab, abundant from Cape Henlopen to Brazil and hunter of night beaches. I've come down to the cape at sunset on an early summer day. The only sounds are those of crickets buzzing in the beach grass and the regular slap of waves. The sun, a ball of fire, sinks and is swallowed by a bank of clouds long before it reaches the horizon. The light warms and reddens. A flock of gulls lets me come very close before they send up an explosion of white wings. They circle about and a few seconds later, settle again behind me, a quarrelsome knot of dim shadows picking through the sea scraps. A squadron of cormorants passes low against the reflected afterlight. The waters darken. For a brief moment Venus shines alone, then stars fill the night.

I flip on my light and startle a ghost crab. It's a good size, two and a half inches of furious activity against the pale sand. I've watched smaller members of its tribe, sidling from dune to sea, halting to dig for mole crabs, then dashing madly back, their camouflage so effective they look like bits of wind-shifted sand or detritus. Their exquisite protective disguise arises from pigmented cells called chromatophores. The pigment migrates in response to light and temperature, causing color changes that help the crab mimic its surroundings.

This one scuttles sideways on the tips of eight legs. When I press in, it raises the last pair of legs off the ground and accelerates, disappearing down a hole at the toe of the foredunes. I flash my light in the opening, but to no avail. The burrow may shoot or spiral down to depths of five or six feet. One morning I saw an adult crab emerge popeyed from a burrow beneath the awning of a horseshoe crab shell, cradling a load of sand in its legs. It paused for a moment, then flung its load down and flashed back into the hole. It was some time later before it reemerged with another load.

Ghost crabs breathe air through narrow, slitlike openings between their third and fourth legs and can live for long periods out of water, but their gills must be kept moist in order to function. At intervals they visit the swash zone to replenish the moisture. Theirs is an evolutionary drama, says Rachel Carson, the coming to land of a sea creature. The larvae begin life as part of the plankton drifting in the open ocean. They become amphibious as they grow, at some point following an urge to pop through the water membrane into the throttling air. They come ashore a rolled-up, fistlike ball of legs and torso, protected from the bruising surf by a tough cuticle. Small immature crabs burrow near the water, just above high-tide line. As they mature, the crabs become more and more independent of the sea, foraging as much as a quarter of a mile inland. Still, they must return to the wash of broken surf to wet their gills and release their eggs.

In their bondage to the sea, ghost crabs resemble their sometime prey, a tiny creature only a half inch in length that leaps about the light of my lamp when I set it on the sand. Beach fleas explode into the air with an agile flexing of legs. Not fleas at all, but crustaceans with flealike powers of jumping, they hop distances of more than fifty times their own length using three pairs of short, stiff rear legs. The fleas also bear three abdominal legs modified for swimming. They, too, hover between land and sea, still possessing gills, though much reduced in size from those of their marine ancestors.

A beach flea lives close to the wrack line, burrowing in the moist sand beneath drift seaweed in the heat of day to avoid desiccating its gills and body and emerging only at night to browse on bits of decaying plant and animal matter. Using the moon and other celestial cues to guide it, the flea moves up and down the beach with the tides, staying within a narrow ribbon of damp sand. It shares with the ghost crab a fear of the full tide. Both crab and flea will drown if kept under water for any period of time, as we ourselves might drown.

I switch off my lamp. A pale moon has risen, spreading its diffuse light across the water's surface. Small waves shower light foam on the shore. Otherwise the night is black. It was 350 million years ago that the first pioneer of land life heaved itself out of the sea: an arthropod, one of the great phyla that later gave rise to crabs and insects, a stumbling, adventurous refugee that lived the strange half-aquatic, half-terrestrial life of the ghost crab and beach flea. The small scuttlings at my feet presage the future, pointing out that life is not fixed like a butterfly pinned on a board, but still brewing, groping on in countless directions.

* * *

One hot morning in late June, I set off in a Boston whaler with friends to look for pelagic birds. I sit in the front of the boat where the jolts are hard, bouncing along toward the open blue, the sea disappearing as we mount a rise, then reappearing as we smack down hard. The coast recedes to a thin featureless crust, then disappears altogether. It takes most of the morning to reach Five Fathoms, a fishing spot forty miles out to sea. Alone with our boat, we cut the motor and drift, binoculars trained on the horizon. Not a pelagic bird in sight. A gull swaying gently overhead cocks its head as if to ask what we are doing way out here in such a duckling of a boat.

Our whaler carries some sophisticated electronic navigation equipment, but I can't help wondering what would happen if it failed, along with our motor, and the weather turned bad. Sea nomads in the archipelagoes of Southeast Asia can look up at the sun and clouds, look down at the sea, and accurately read both time and their whereabouts. But for most of us, the open ocean seems mute and lonely when you're out there in the middle of it. A report I read in *The Journal of Navigation* suggested that humans have an innate sense of direction. Laboratory experiments showed that people's ability to pinpoint North gradually improved after multiple challenges. "Orientation in humans is a latent sense," said the researchers, though in most of us it seems to have disappeared from lack of use.

I don't know how long we sit. The sun beats down, and the water calms to a sheet of thick, undulating metal. Suddenly, twenty yards from our tiny craft, a great slick-backed blue mass lifts in a rising swell and rolls forward, flashing a sharp hook of fin and a bright turquoise patch. It disappears, then rises again, slow, cloudlike, and blows a jet of white vapor ten feet high, like an upside-down pyramid.

It is a finback whale, the second largest baleen whale after the blue, and Earth's only asymmetrically colored mammal. The left side of its head and jaw is dark, the right side light. The purpose of this asymmetrical pigmentation remains a mystery, although it may be an adaptation for the capture of small schooling fish such as herring. The whale swims around the fish to the right in smaller and smaller circles, showing only its translucent, invisible white side so as not to startle its prey. As the herring clump together, the whale turns into the pack, mouth open, and gobbles them up, its pleated throat bulging, expanding bellowlike to take in the liquid meal. Then it presses the water out of the baleen plates that grow down from its upper gums and swallows what's left behind.

Our boat bobs about in the waves above Five Fathoms. We each face a different direction to cover the scope of ocean, but the giant beast has disappeared. Finbacks can swim underwater for forty minutes without drawing breath. Like other whales, their ancestors were four-legged land animals that hunted in the tidal shallows around river deltas and the edges of the warm, shallow seas. Sometime around fifty or sixty million years ago, they abandoned land life for the ocean, perhaps following their prey farther and farther out to sea. Paleontologists digging in Pakistan recently unearthed the remains of an ancient whale with legs and long feet like a seal, a missing link in the evolutionary chain. The scientists called the animal *Ambulocetus natans,* "the walking whale that swam."

Over the course of millions of years, these creatures slipped protean through many shapes, losing their legs and pelvises and developing a horizontal fluked tail to propel them through the seas. Their bodies eventually assumed a smooth, hairless form perfectly suited to swimming and swept back for speed. Their forelimbs grew into organs for steering and balancing in a liquid environment. Sound became their light and hearing their vision. Deep within the fifty-ton body of a finback is born a pure, radiant booming an octave deeper than the lowest note on a piano. Such sound waves can travel enormous distances in the sea. Trapped in the deep sound channel, a layer of water where sound waves bend back on themselves and retain their energy, whale sounds can carry several hundred miles.

Both whales and dolphins bear traces of their kinship to land creatures. Their flippers have bones similar to those in a human arm and hand, though much reshaped. Whales often retain tiny leg bones. Dolphins catch the same diseases as pigs and cattle. In a throwback to a dim past, dolphins along the coast of the Carolinas briefly revisit the world of their ancestors, having learned once again to feed at low tide on the edge of the land, herding schools of fish toward the mud flats, riding the waves in, and plucking the fish from the shore.

Once, on a visit to a whaling ship, biologist Victor Scheffer acquired a whale fetus only four inches long. "I took the little creature, packed in ice cubes, to the mainland," he wrote. "At my hotel I bought a pint of vodka and a bottle of shaving lotion. I mixed these in a washbasin, slit the belly and chest of the fetus with a razor blade, and embalmed it overnight in the fragrant solution. Later I dissected it in my laboratory. . . . In profile, the little head could . . . have belonged to an infant pig, with eyes shut, lower jaw protruding beyond the snout, and nostrils at the front. . . . The penis protruded; the rudimentary nipples were evident; even the ears were there—tiny ridges of skin, most unfitting for a whale. There were actually traces of whiskers, casting a long shadow from an ancestor dead now forty million years."

In the course of development, embryonic whales grow rudimentary legs, nostrils, and surface genitals. Then the hindlimbs disappear, the nostrils slide backward to become blowholes, the genitals vanish inside a slit. In the fetus of a finback whale, tooth germs appear in the gums, but by the time the fetus has reached a length of thirteen feet, they have vanished.

I once saw a jar containing a pickled human embryo in the National

Museum of Natural History. It had a bulging reptilian head, a tail, and arches like gills just beneath the head. Our own living organs, eyes, backbones, hands, and feet originated in far places and different eras of time. Four hundred million years ago our piscine forebears wiggled over muddy flats, throwing their bodies in an S-curve. As a consequence, our arms swing in opposition to the swing of our legs. Our reflected past and some shadow of the future is paradoxically written in our bodies. We, too, are changelings, made of millions of bits of information strung together from an odd little alphabet and brought into being by an astronomical number of chance events over the long course of evolution. But for this we might be hovering just above the warm mud. As Stephen Jay Gould has written, those stubby, sluggish fins that became weight-bearing limbs—the necessary prerequisite to terrestrial life—evolved in an uncommon group of fishes off the main line. They were a fluke.

In some way all creatures bear traces of their past: ghost crabs their gills, whales their vestigial limbs, humans our liquid cells, the salt water running in our veins, our feeling for the sea. "Why upon your first voyage as a passenger," wrote Melville, "did you yourself feel such a mystical vibration when first told that you and your ship were out of sight of land?"

John McPhee

Under the Snow

When my third daughter was an infant, I could place her against my shoulder and she would stick there like velvet. Only her eyes jumped from place to place. In a breeze, her bright-red hair might stir, but she would not. Even then, there was profundity in her repose.

When my fourth daughter was an infant, I wondered if her veins were full of ants. Placing her against a shoulder was a risk both to her and to the shoulder. Impulsively, constantly, everything about her moved. Her head seemed about to revolve as it followed the bestirring world.

These memories became very much alive some months ago when—one after another—I had bear cubs under my vest. Weighing three, four, 5.6 pounds, they were wild bears, and for an hour or so had been taken from their dens in Pennsylvania. They were about two months old, with fine short brown hair. When they were made to stand alone, to be photographed in the mouth of a den, they shivered. Instinctively, a person would be moved to hold them. Picked up by the scruff of the neck, they splayed their paws like kittens and screamed like baby bears. The cry of a baby bear is muted, like a human infant's heard from her crib down the hall. The first cub I placed on my shoulder stayed there like a piece of velvet. The shivering stopped. Her bright-blue eyes looked about, not seeing much of anything. My hand, cupped against her back, all but encompassed her rib cage, which was warm and calm. I covered her to the shoulders with a flap of down vest and zipped up my parka to hold her in place.

I was there by invitation, an indirect result of work I had been doing nearby. Would I be busy on March 14th? If there had been a conflict—if, say, I had been invited to lunch on that day with the Queen of Scotland and the King of Spain—I would have gone to the cubs. The first den was a rock cavity in a lichen-covered sandstone outcrop near the top of a slope, a couple of hundred yards from a road in Hawley. It was on posted property of the Scrub Oak Hunting Club—dry hardwood forest underlain by laurel and patches of snow—in the northern Pocono woods. Up in the sky was Buck Alt. Not long ago, he was a dairy farmer, and now he was working for the Keystone State, with directional antennae on his wing struts angled in the direction of bears. Many bears in Pennsylvania have radios around their necks as a result of the summer trapping work of Alt's son Gary, who is a wildlife biologist. In winter, Buck Alt flies the country listening to the radio, crissing and crossing until the bears come on. They come on stronger the closer to them he flies. The transmitters are not omnidirectional. Suddenly, the sound cuts out. Buck looks down, chooses a landmark, approaches it again, on another vector. Gradually, he works his way in, until he is flying in ever tighter circles above the bear. He marks a map. He is accurate within two acres. The plane he flies is a Super Cub.

The den could have served as a set for a Passion play. It was a small chamber, open on one side, with a rock across its entrance. Between the free-standing rock and the back of the cave was room for one large bear, and she was curled in a corner on a bed of leaves, her broad head plainly visible from the outside, her cubs invisible between the rock and a soft place, chuckling, suckling, in the wintertime tropics of their own mammalian heaven. Invisible they were, yes, but by no means inaudible. What biologists call chuckling sounded like starlings in a tree.

People walking in woods sometimes come close enough to a den to cause the mother to get up and run off, unmindful of her reputation as a fearless defender of cubs. The cubs stop chuckling and begin to cry: possibly three, four cubs—a ward of mewling bears. The people hear the crying. They find the den and see the cubs. Sometimes they pick them up and carry them away, reporting to the state that they have saved the lives of bear cubs abandoned by their mother. Wherever and whenever this occurs, Gary Alt collects the cubs. After ten years of bear trapping and biological study, Alt has equipped so many sows with radios that he has been able to conduct a foster-mother program with an amazingly high rate of success. A mother in hibernation will readily accept a foster cub. If the need to place an orphan arises somewhat later, when mothers and their cubs are out and around, a sow will kill an alien cub as soon as she smells it. Alt has overcome this problem by stuffing sows' noses with Vicks VapoRub. One way or another, he has found new families for forty-seven orphaned cubs. Forty-six have survived. The other, which had become accustomed over three weeks to feedings and caresses by human hands, was not content in a foster den, crawled outside, and died in the snow.

With a hypodermic jab stick, Alt now drugged the mother, putting her to sleep for the duration of the visit. From deeps of shining fur, he fished out cubs. One. Two. A third. A fourth. Five! The fifth was a foster daughter brought earlier in the winter from two hundred miles away. Three of the four others were male—a ratio consistent with the heavy preponderance of males that Alt's studies have shown through the years. To various onlookers he handed the cubs for safekeeping while he and several assistants carried the mother into the open and weighed her with block and tackle. To protect her eyes, Alt had blindfolded her with a red bandanna. They carried her upside down, being extremely careful lest they scrape and damage her nipples. She weighed two hundred and nineteen pounds. Alt had caught her and weighed her some months before. In the den, she had lost ninety pounds. When she was four years old, she had had four cubs; two years later, four more cubs; and now, after two more years, four cubs. He knew all that about her, he had caught her so many times. He referred to her as Daisy. Daisy was as nothing compared with Vanessa, who was sleeping off the winter somewhere else. In ten seasons, Vanessa had given birth to twenty-three cubs and had lost none. The growth and reproductive rates of black bears are greater in Pennsylvania than anywhere else. Black bears in Pennsylvania grow more rapidly than grizzlies in Montana. Eastern black bears are generally much larger than Western ones. A seven-hundred-pound bear is unusual but not rare in Pennsylvania. Alt once caught a big bear like that who had a thirty-seven-inch neck and was a hair under seven feet long.

This bear, nose to tail, measured five feet five. Alt said, "That's a nice long sow." For weighing the cubs, he had a small nylon stuff sack. He stuffed it with bear and hung it on a scale. Two months before, when the cubs were born, each would have weighed approximately half a pound—less than a newborn porcupine. Now the cubs weighed 3.4, 4.1, 4.4, 4.6, 5.6—cute little numbers with soft tan noses and erectile pyramid ears. Bears have sex in June and July, but the mother's system holds the fertilized egg away from the uterus until November, when implantation occurs. Fetal development lasts scarcely six weeks. Therefore, the creatures who live upon the hibernating mother are so small that everyone survives.

The orphan, less winsome than the others, looked like a chocolate-covered possum. I kept her under my vest. She seemed content there and scarcely moved. In time, I exchanged her for 5.6—the big boy in the litter. Lifted by the scruff and held in the air, he bawled, flashed his claws, and curled his lips like a woofing bear. I stuffed him under the vest, where he shut up and nuzzled. His claws were already more than half an inch long. Alt said that the family would come out of the den in a few weeks but that much of the spring would go by before the cubs gained weight. The difference would be that they were no longer malleable and ductile. They would become pugnacious and scratchy, not to say vicious, and would chew up the hand that caressed them. He said, "If you have an enemy, give him a bear cub."

Six men carried the mother back to the den, the red bandanna still tied around her eyes. Alt repacked her into the rock. "We like to return her to the den as close as possible to the way we found her," he said. Someone remarked that one biologist can work a coon, while an army is needed to deal with a bear. An army seemed to be present. Twelve people had followed Alt to the den. Some days, the group around him is four times as large. Alt, who is in his thirties, was wearing a visored khaki cap with a blue-and-gold keystone on the forehead, and a khaki cardigan under a khaki jumpsuit. A lithe and light-bodied man with tinted glasses and a blond mustache, he looked like a lieutenant in the Ardennes Forest. Included in the retinue were two reporters and a news photographer. Alt encourages media attention, the better to soften the image of the bears. He says, "People fear bears more than they need to, and respect them not enough." Over the next twenty days, he had scheduled four hundred visitors—state senators, representatives, commissioners, television reporters, word processors, biologists, friends— to go along on his rounds of dens. Days before, he and the denned bears had been hosts to the BBC. The Brits wanted snow. God was having none of it. The BBC brought in the snow.

In the course of the day, we made a brief tour of dens that for the time being stood vacant. Most were rock cavities. They had been used before, and in all likelihood would be used again. Bears in winter in the Pocono Plateau are like chocolate chips in a cookie. The bears seldom go back to the same den two years running, and they often change dens in the course of a winter. In a forty-five-hundred-acre housing development called Hemlock Farms are twenty-three dens known to be in current use and countless others awaiting new tenants. Alt showed one that was within fifteen feet of the intersection of East Spur Court and Pommel Drive. He said that when a sow with two cubs was in there he had seen deer browsing by the outcrop and ignorant dogs stopping off to lift a leg. Hemlock Farms is expensive, and full of cantilevered cypress and unencumbered glass. Houses perch on high flat rock. Now and again, there are bears in the rock—in, say, a floor-through cavity just under the porch. The owners are from New York. Alt does not always tell them that their property is zoned for bears. Once, when he did so, a "FOR SALE" sign went up within two weeks.

Not far away is Interstate 84. Flying over it one day, Buck Alt heard an oddly intermittent signal. Instead of breaking off once and cleanly, it broke off many times. Crossing back over, he heard it again. Soon he was in a tight turn, now hearing something, now nothing, in a pattern that did not suggest anything he had heard before. It did, however, suggest the interstate. Where a big green sign says, "MILFORD 11, PORT JERVIS 20," Gary hunted around and found the bear. He took us now to see the den. We went down a steep slope at the side of the highway and, crouching, peered into a culvert. It was about fifty yards long. There was a disk of daylight at the opposite end. Thirty inches in diameter, it was a perfect place to stash a body, and that is what the bear thought, too. On Gary's first visit, the disk of daylight had not been visible. The bear had denned under the eastbound lanes. She had given birth to three cubs. Soon after he found her, heavy rains were predicted. He hauled the family out and off to a vacant den. The cubs weighed less than a pound. Two days later, water a foot deep was racing through the culvert.

Under High Knob, in remote undeveloped forest about six hundred metres above sea level, a slope falling away in an easterly direction contained a classic excavated den: a small entrance leading into an intimate ovate cavern, with a depression in the center for a bed—in all, about twenty-four cubic feet, the size of a refrigerator-freezer. The den had not been occupied in several seasons, but Rob Buss, a district game protector who works regularly with Gary Alt, had been around to check it three days before and had shined his flashlight into a darkness stuffed with fur. Meanwhile, six inches of fresh snow had fallen on High Knob, and now Alt and his team, making preparations a short distance from the den, scooped up snow in their arms and filled a big sack. They had nets of nylon mesh. There was a fifty-fifty likelihood of yearling bears in the den. Mothers keep cubs until their second spring. When a biologist comes along and provokes the occupants to emerge, there is no way to predict how many will appear. Sometimes they keep coming and coming, like clowns from a compact car. As a bear emerges, it walks into the nylon mesh. A drawstring closes. At the same time, the den entrance is stuffed with a bag of snow. That stops the others. After the first bear has been dealt with, Alt removes the sack of snow. Out comes another bear. A yearling weighs about eighty pounds, and may move so fast that it runs over someone on the biological team and stands on top of him sniffing at his ears. Or her ears. Janice Gruttadauria, a research assistant, is a part of the team. Bear after bear, the procedure is repeated until the bag of snow is pulled away and nothing comes out. That is when Alt asks Rob Buss to go inside and see if anything is there.

Now, moving close to the entrance, Alt spread a tarp on the snow, lay down on it, turned on a five-cell flashlight, and put his head inside the den. The beam played over thick black fur and came to rest on a tiny foot. The sack of snow would not be needed. After drugging the mother with a jab stick, he joined her in the den. The entrance was so narrow he had to shrug his shoulders to get in. He shoved the sleeping mother, head first, out of the darkness and into the light.

While she was away, I shrugged my own shoulders and had a look inside. The den smelled of earth but not of bear. The walls were dripping with roots. The water and protein metabolism of hibernating black bears has been explored by the Mayo Clinic as a research model for, among other things, human endurance on long flights through space and medical situations closer to home, such as the maintenance of anephric human beings who are awaiting kidney transplants.

Outside, each in turn, the cubs were put in the stuff sack—a male and a female. The female weighed four pounds. Greedily, I reached for her when Alt took her out of the bag. I planted her on my shoulder while I wrote down facts about her mother: weight, a hundred and ninety-two pounds; length, fifty-eight inches; some toes missing; severe frostbite from a bygone winter evidenced along the edges of the ears.

Eventually, with all weighing and tagging complete, it was time to go. Alt went into the den. Soon he called out that he was ready for the mother. It would be a tight fit. Feet first, she was shoved in, like a safe-deposit box. Inside, Alt tugged at her in close embrace, and the two of them gradually revolved until she was at the back and their positions had reversed. He shaped her like a doughnut—her accustomed den position. The cubs go in the center. The male was handed in to him. Now he was asking for the female. For a moment, I glanced around as if looking to see who had her. The thought crossed my mind that if I bolted and ran far enough and fast enough I could flag a passing car and keep her. Then I pulled her from under the flap of my vest and handed her away.

Alt and others covered the entrance with laurel boughs, and covered the boughs with snow. They camouflaged the den, but that was not the purpose. Practicing wildlife management to a fare-thee-well, Alt wanted the den to be even darker than it had been before; this would cause the family to stay longer inside and improve the cubs' chances when at last they faced the world.

In the evening, I drove down off the Pocono Plateau and over the folded mountains and across the Great Valley and up the New Jersey Highlands and down into the basin and home. No amount of intervening terrain, though—and no amount of distance—could remove from my mind the picture of the covered entrance in the Pennsylvania hillside, or the thought of what was up there under the snow.

Terry Tempest Williams

To Be Taken

"The revolutionary question is: What about the Other? . . . It is not enough to rail against the descending darkness of barbarity . . . One can refuse to play the game. A holding action can be fought. Alternatives must be kept alive. While learning the slow art of revolutionary patience."

—BREYTEN BREYTENBACH
"Tortoise Steps"

Tortoise steps.
Slow steps.
Four steps like a tank with a tail dragging in the sand.
Tortoise steps—land-based, land-locked, dusty like the desert
tortoise himself, fenced in, a prisoner on his own reservation
teaching us the slow art of revolutionary patience.

It is Christmas. We gather in our grandparents home: aunts, uncles, cousins, babies—four generations wipe their feet at the holiday mat. One by one, we open the front door, "Hello," "We're here," glass panes iced are beginning to melt from the heat of bodies together. Our grandfather Jack, now ninety, presides. His sons, John and Richard walk in dressed in tweed sport coats and Levi's, their polished boots could kill spiders in corners. My aunt Ruth enters with her arms full of gifts. Jack's sister, Norinne, in her eighties, sits in the living room with her hands folded tightly, greeting each one of us with a formality we have come to expect.

Tradition.

On this night, we know a buffet is prepared: filet mignon, marinated carrots, asparagus, and cauliflower, a cranberry salad, warbread (a recipe our great-grandmother Mamie Comstock Tempest improvised during the Depression when provisions were scarce and raisins plentiful), and the same silver serving piece is obscene with chocolates.

The Christmas tree stands in the center of the room, "the grandchildren's tree," and we remember our grandmother, Mimi, the matriarch of this family whose last Christmas was in 1988. We remember her. We remember all of our dead.

Candles burn. I walk into the dining room, pick up a plate and circle the table.

"What's new, Terrence?" my uncle asks ribbing me.

"Not a thing, Rich." I respond. We both look up from the buffet smiling.

I take some meat with my fingers. He spears vegetables. We return to the living room and find a seat. The rest of the family gathers. Jack sits in the wing-backed chair, his hands on both arm rests. My father sits across the room from his brother.

"So how did the meeting go last week?"

"Terrible," Rich says.

"What did they decide?"

"Simple," my uncle says, "Tortoises are more important than people."

Heads turn, attention fixes on matters of the Tempest Company, the family construction business that began with our Great-grandfather in the early part of the century, a company my brothers all work for, cousins, too.

"What are you talking about?" I ask.

"Where have you been?" my father asks incredulously. "We've been shut down eighteen months because of that—(he stops himself in deference to his aunt) that *stupid* Endangered Species Act."

I look at my brother Steve who nods his head who looks at our cousin Bob who looks at his sister Lynne who shakes her head as she turns to my husband Brooke.

"I attended the public meeting where they discussed the Habitat Management Plan." Rich says to us.

"And?" Lynne asks as she walks over to her father and offers him a piece of warbread.

"They ruled in favor of the tortoise."

"Which job is this, John?" asks Brooke, who at the time was working for the governor's office of budget and planning as the liaison between environmental groups and the state.

"It's the last leg of the Information Highway," Dad says. "Seven miles of fiber optic cable running from the town of Hurricane to St. George linking rural Utah to the Wasatch Front."

"We're held up in permits," Rich explains. "A construction permit won't be issued until U.S. West complies with federal agencies."

"The government's gone too far," my great aunt interjects.

"Too far?" My father says his voice rising like water ready to boil. "Too far? We've had to hire a full time biologist at $60.00 an hour who does nothing but look for these imaginary animals. Everyday he circles the crew singing the same song, "Nope, haven't seen one yet."

"The guy's from BYU and sits in the cab of his truck most of the day reading scriptures." adds Steve, who is the superintendent.

"Thou shall not kill a turtle," someone mutters under their breath.

"Sixty bucks an hour," Dad reiterates. "That's twice as much as our foremen make! It would be cheaper to buy a poolside condominium for each mating pair of tortoises than to adhere to the costs of this ridiculous Act."

"The government's gone too far," my aunt restates like a delayed echo.

"And on top of that we have to conduct a 'turtle training course—' "

"Tortoise, John." his granddaughter Callie interrupts. I wink at my niece.

"A turtle training course for our men, so they can learn to identify one and then remember to check under the tires and skids for tortoises looking for shade before turning on the backhoes after lunch."

Rich stands up to get some more food.

"$100,000.00 if we run over one," he says, making himself a sandwich.

"What's St. George now, the fourth fastest growing community in the country?" Brooke asks.

"What do you kids want?" Rich says. "To stop progress? You and your environmentalist friends have lost all credibility. One local told us, a bunch of radicals actually planted a tortoise in the parking lot of the Walmart Distribution Center just to shut it down."

"How do you know it didn't walk onto the asphalt by itself?" I ask.

"They had its stomach pumped and it was full of lettuce," Rich replies. We all roll our eyes.

Steve asks his cousin Matt who is a first year medical student, "Have you performed an autopsy on a desert tortoise yet?"

"Not yet," Matt responds. "Just human beings."

"Can I get anyone anything?" Ruth asks, holding her granddaughter Hannah on her hip. She looks around. No response. "Just checking."

"And you wonder why people are upset," my father says, turning to me. "It's easy for you to sit here and tell us what animals we should protect while you write poems about them as a hobby—It's not your pocketbook that's hurting."

"And is yours?" I ask, fearing I have now gone as far as my father has.

I was not aware of the background music until now, Nat King Cole singing, "Have a Merry, Merry Christmas. . . ."

"I don't know," Jack says clearing his throat and pulling himself out of his chair. "Why don't you boys tell them the story?"

John and Richard look puzzled.

"What story?" Rich asks.

"Hardpan." Jack says.

"Never mind." my father says grinning. "Just keep that quiet."

Richard starts giggling like a little boy.

"Tell!" We beg our grandfather.

He placed his hands on the back of the lounge. "We had twenty-two crews during the war, put all the piping in the airbases at Tooele, Salt Lake, Hill, and Ogden. I never went to bed for five years: 1941, 42, 43, 44, 45, just dropped dead on this lounge from exhaustion every night. We even had work in Las Vegas putting in a big waterline to the north. I was away for weeks, missing Kathryn and the boys. Then one day, I was walking along the trench when I spotted what I thought was a helmet. I bent down. It moved. I realized it was a tortoise. I picked it up, its head and feet shot back into its shell. I put him in the back of my truck and brought him home for the boys. We named him, "Hardpan."

He looks at his sons, smiles and walks out of the room.

"Everybody else had a dog—" my father says. "German shepherds, Doberman pinchers, black labs. We drilled a hole in his shell and tied a long cord to it and walked him around the block."

We all look at each other.

"No kidding," Rich says. "Everyday we walked him."

"Hardpan?" I ask.

"You know, the desert without rain—hardpan, no give to the sand." Dad's voice is tender.

"He was reliable, old hardpan, you have to say that about him," Rich adds.

"Until he disappeared—" Jack says, returning to his chair.

Gopherus agassizii. Desert tortoise. Land turtle. An elder among us. Even among my family. For some of us he represents "land-locked" like the wildlands before us. Designate wilderness and development is locked out. Find a tortoise and another invisible fence is erected. The tortoise's presence compromises our own. He is an obstruction. For others, the tortoise is "land-based," a sovereign on Earth, an extension of family—human and non-human alike—living in arid country. His presence enhances our own. The tension the tortoise inspires calls for wisdom.

These animals may live beyond one hundred years. They walk for miles, largely unnoticed, carrying a stillness with them. Fifteen acres may be home range and they know it well. When they feel in their bodies that it is about to rain, they travel to where water pools. They wait. Clouds gather. Skies darken. It rains. They drink. It may be days, weeks, months before their beaks touch water again.

If native mythologies are true and turtles carry the world on their backs, the carapace of the desert tortoise is designed to bear the weight. It is a landscape with its own aesthetic. Three scutes or plates run down the vertebrae, hexagons, with two larger scutes on top and bottom. Four plates line either side of center. The shell is bordered by twenty four smaller ones that seem to hold the animal in place. The plastron or bottom of the shell fits together like a twelve-tiled floor. The desert tortoise lives inside his own creation like a philosopher who is most at home in his mind.

In winter, the desert tortoise hibernates but not in the manner of bears. Hibernation for reptiles is "brumation," a time of dormancy where cold-blooded creatures retire, rock-still, with physiological changes occurring independent of their body temperatures. Much remains mysterious about this time of seasonal retreat but brumation among turtles suggests it is sparked by conditions of temperature, moisture, photoperiod, and food supply. They stir in their stone-ledged dens when temperatures rise, dens they inhabit year after year, one, two, maybe five individuals together. They leave. They forage. They mate. The females lay eggs in supple sands, two dozen eggs may be dropped in a nest. Buried. Incubated. Hatched. And then the quiet plodding of another generation of desert tortoises meets the sands.

It is a genealogy of evolutionary adaptation until *Gopherus agassizii* suddenly begins bumping into real estate developers after having the desert to himself for millennia.

1996: a lone desert tortoise stands before a bulldozer in the Mojave.

My father and the Endangered Species Act. My father as an endangered species. The Marlboro Man without his cigarette is home on the range—I will list him as threatened by his own vulnerable nature. I will list him as threatened by my emotional nature. Who dares to write the recovery plan that regulates our own constructions? He will resist me. I will resist him. He is my father. I am his daughter. He holds my birth story. I will mourn his death. We face each other.

Hand over our hearts, in the American West united states do not exist even within our own families. "Don't Tread On Me." The snake coils. The tortoise retreats. When the dust devil clears, who remains?

My father, myself, threatened species.

I recall a statement made to me by another elder, a Mormon General Authority who feared I had chosen not to have children. Call it "Ode to the Gene Pool," a manipulation of theology, personalized, tailorized to move me toward motherhood, another bulge in the population.

"A female bird" he wrote to me, "has no options as to whether she will lay eggs or not. She must. God insists. Because if she does not a precious combination will be lost forever. One of your deepest concerns rests with endangered species. If a species dies out its gene pool will be lost forever and we are all the lesser because of the loss. . . . The eggs you possess over which your husband presides [are] precious genes . . . You are an endangered family."

I resist. Who will follow? Must someone follow?

Clouds gather. It rains. The desert tortoise drinks where water has pooled.

Who holds the wisdom? My grandfather, the tortoise, calls for the story, then disappears.

Tortoise steps.

Tortoise tracks.

Tracks in time.

One can refuse to play the game.

* * *

Across from where I sit is a redrock ledge. We are only a stone's toss away from the city of St. George. I am hiking with my father. He has gone on ahead.

Today is the spring equinox, equal light, equal dark—a day of truce.

I have followed tortoise tracks to this place, a den. It is cold, the air stings my face, I did not dress warmly enough. Once again, the desert deceives as wind snaps over the ridge and rides down the valley.

The tortoise is inside. I wish to speak to him, to her, to them about my family, my tribe of people who lose money and make money without recognizing their own threatened status, my tribe of people who keep tortoises, turtles, as pets and wonder why they walk away.

I pull a clipping from the local paper out of my pocket, unfold it and read aloud:

If you're a desert tortoise living in Washington County, take this advice: Start crawling your way toward the hills north of St. George, Utah.

Come March 15, any tortoise living outside a specially designated "desert tortoise reserve" could become subject to "taking"—a biological term for the death of an animal or the destruction of its habitat.

State and federal officials on Friday signed an interlocal agreement that will set aside 61,000 acres of prime tortoise habitat as a reserve that wildlife biologists believe will secure the reptile's recovery.

On the flip side, the agreement also provides permission and means by which developers and others may "take" some 1200 tortoises and develop more than 12,000 acres of tortoise habitat outside the reserve without violating the Endangered Species Act, under which the tortoise is listed as a "threatened species."

Friday's signing ends six years of battles over the slow-moving animal, whose presence around St. George has created headaches for land developers and local governments.

"We feel confident that we're going to be able to work together and have a permit that provides for the recovery and protection of the tortoise," said Bob Williams, assistant supervisor for the Fish and Wildlife Service.

... Between 1980 and 1990, Washington County's population increased 86% from 26,125 to 48,560. It is projected to have between 101,000 and 139,000 people by 2010.

Implementation of the Habitat Conservation Plan is scheduled to last 20 years and cost $11.5 million.

There is no movement inside the den.

"Tortoise, I have two questions for you from Neruda:
'Quien da los nombres y los numeros al inocente innumerable?'
Who assigns names and numbers to the innumerable innocent?
'Como le digo a la tortuga que yo le gano en lentitude?'
How do I tell the turtle that I am slower than he?"

The desert tortoise is still.

I suspect he hears my voice simply for what it is, human.
The news and questions I deliver are returned to me and
somehow dissipate in the silence.

It is enough
   to breathe, here, together.

Our shadows lengthen
   while the white-petaled heart of Datura
opens and closes.

We have forgotten the option of restraint.

It is no longer the survival of the fittest but the survival of
compassion.

Inside the redrock ledge, the emotional endurance of the tortoise stares
back at me. I blink. To take. To be taken. To die. The desert tortoise presses
me on the sand, down on all fours. The shell I now find myself inhabiting
is a keratinous room where my spine is attached to its ceiling. Head, hands,
feet, and tail push through six doors and search for a way home.

Tortoise steps.
Land-based.   Land-locked.
Land-based.   Land-locked.
Learning the slow art of revolutionary patience, I listen to my family.

VI

FICTION

Elizabeth Bishop

The Map

Land lies in water; it is shadowed green.
Shadows, or are they shallows, at its edges
showing the line of long sea-weeded ledges
where weeds hang to the simple blue from green.
Or does the land lean down to lift the sea from under,
drawing it unperturbed around itself?
Along the fine tan sandy shelf
is the land tugging at the sea from under?

The shadow of Newfoundland lies flat and still.
Labrador's yellow, where the moony Eskimo
has oiled it. We can stroke these lovely bays,
under a glass as if they were expected to blossom,
or as if to provide a clean cage for invisible fish.
The names of seashore towns run out to sea,
the names of cities cross the neighboring mountains
—the printer here experiencing the same excitement
as when emotion too far exceeds its cause.
These peninsulas take the water between thumb and finger
like women feeling for the smoothness of yard-goods.

Mapped waters are more quiet than the land is,
lending the land their waves' own conformation:
and Norway's hare runs south in agitation,
profiles investigate the sea, where land is.
Are they assigned, or can the countries pick their colors?
—What suits the character or the native waters best.
Topography displays no favorites; North's as near as West.
More delicate than the historians' are the map-makers' colors.

Bruce Chatwin

The Drought

Many years later, chained hand and foot in the King of Dahomey's prison, Francisco Manoel would remember the year of the drought.

That summer—he was seven at the time—the clouds banked up as usual and burst. For five days rain drenched the earth, seedlings sprouted and there were clouds of yellow butterflies everywhere. Then the clouds went away. The sun quivered in a blue metal sky. The mud cracked.

One sunset, mother and son watched the formations of duck flying south. She hugged him and said, 'The ducks are flying to the river.'

Hot winds blew, hiding the horizon in dust and blowing pellets of goat dung across the yard. When the tank dried up, the cattle stood around the patch of green slime, groaning, with their muzzles full of spines.

In a cabin behind the house lived an old Cariri Indian called Felix, who looked after the widow's few animals in return for food and a roof. One evening, he collapsed in the kitchen and, in a hoarse and hopeless voice, said, 'All of them are dying.' He had cut lengths of cactus, stripped them of spines, and set them out for fodder; but the cattle had gone on dying.

Blood flowed from their flanks from the little pink lumps that were ticks. They slashed themselves trying to reach a single unwithered leaf and, when they did die, the hides were so tough that carrion birds could not break through to the guts.

Fires tore through the country with a resinous crackling, leaving velvety stumps where once there had been trees. The flames caught Felix as he was hacking out a firebreak, and they found him, charred and sheeny, with a grimace of white teeth and green mucus running out of his nose. The woman dug a grave, but a dog unearthed the body and chewed it apart.

Rats ran down the boy's hammock strings and bit him as he slept. Rattlesnakes came into the yard, attracted by anything that still had life. When a column of driver-ants swept through the house, the woman had only the energy to save a saucepan of manioc flour and some strips of wind-dried beef.

Finally, when she had lost hope, Manuelzinho rode out of the thornscrub, where he had lived on the half-roasted bodies of rodents. He dug deeper down the well-shaft and came back with a dribble of foul ferruginous liquid. But within a week all three water jars were empty.

The boy's mouth cracked and ulcerated. His eyelids blazed. His legs went stiff. They gave him mashed palmroots to eat but they swelled in his stomach and the cramps forced him to lie down. All the moisture seemed to have drained from his body. There was no question of being able to cry—even as his mother entered her death agony.

They woke that morning to find her left leg hanging limply over the lip of her hammock. Manuelzinho lifted the cloth that covered her face from the flies. Unspeaking, and with the terrible tenderness of people pushed to the limit, she pleaded for the son whom she had starved herself to save.

Her oases were not of this world: she died in the night without a groan.

The boy watched Manuelzinho bury her. They started south for the river. They passed knots of migrants too tired to go on. Black birds sat waiting on the branches.

The horse died on the second day, but men are tougher than horses.

They reached the river at the ferry station of Santa Maria da Boavista, where Manuelzinho left the orphan with the priest and rode away.

The boy remembered nothing of the journey, yet for years he would keep back a lump of meat and sleep with it under his pillow.

Paul Bowles

The New Day

When she opened her eyes she knew immediately where she was. The moon was low in the sky. She pulled her coat around her legs and shivered slightly, thinking of nothing. There was a part of her mind that ached, that needed rest. It was good merely to lie there, to exist and ask no questions. She was sure that if she wanted to, she could begin remembering all that had happened. It required only a small effort. But she was comfortable there as she was, with that opaque curtain falling between. She would not be the one to lift it, to gaze down into the abyss of yesterday and suffer again its grief and remorse. At present, what had gone before was indistinct, unidentifiable. Resolutely she turned her mind away, refusing to examine it, bending all her efforts to putting a sure barrier between herself and it. Like an insect spinning its cocoon thicker and more resistant, her mind would go on strengthening the thin partition, the danger spot of her being.

She lay quietly, her feet drawn up under her. The sand was soft, but its coldness penetrated her garments. When she felt she could no longer bear to go on shivering, she crawled out from under her protecting tree and set to striding back and forth in front of it in the hope of warming herself. The air was dead; not a breath stirred, and the cold grew by the minute. She began to walk farther afield, munching bread as she went. Each time she returned to the tamarisk tree she was tempted to slide back down under its branches and sleep. However, by the time the first light of dawn appeared, she was wide awake and warm.

The desert landscape is always at its best in the half-light of dawn or dusk. The sense of distance lacks: a ridge nearby can be a far-off mountain range, each small detail can take on the importance of a major variant on the countryside's repetitious theme. The coming of day promises a change; it is only when the day has fully arrived that the watcher suspects it is the same day returned once again—the same day he has been living for a long time, over and over, still blindingly bright and untarnished by time. Kit breathed deeply, looked around at the soft line of the little dunes, at the vast pure light rising up from behind the hammada's mineral rim, at the forest of palms behind her still immersed in night, and knew that it was not the same day. Even when it grew entirely light, even when the huge sun shot up, and the sand, trees and sky gradually resumed their familiar daytime aspect, she had no doubts whatever about its being a new and wholly separate day.

David Malouf

An Imaginary Life

How can I give you any notion—you who know only landscapes that have been shaped for centuries to the idea we all carry in our souls of that ideal scene against which our lives should be played out—of what earth was in its original bleakness, before we brought to it the order of industry, the terraces, fields, orchards, pastures, the irrigated gardens of the world we are making in our own image.

Do you think of Italy—or whatever land it is you now inhabit—as a place given you by the gods, ready-made in all its placid beauty? It is not. It is a created place. If the gods are with you there, glowing out of a tree in some pasture or shaking their spirit over the pebbles of a brook in clear sunlight, in wells, in springs, in a stone that marks the edge of your legal right over a hillside; if the gods are there, it is because you have discovered them there, drawn them up out of your soul's need for them and dreamed them into the landscape to make it shine. They are with you, sure enough. Embrace the tree trunk and feel the spirit flow back into you, feel the warmth of the stone enter your body, lower yourself into the spring as into some liquid place of your body's other life in sleep. But the spirits have to be recognized to become real. They are not outside us, nor even entirely within, but flow back and forth between us and the objects we have made, the landscape we have shaped and move in. We have dreamed all these things in our deepest lives and they are ourselves. It is our self we are making out there, and when the landscape is complete we shall have become the gods who are intended to fill it.

It is as if each creature had the power to dream itself out of one existence into a new one, a step higher on the ladder of things. Having conceived in our sleep the idea of a further being, our bodies find, slowly, painfully, the physical process that will allow them to break their own bonds and leap up to it. So that the stone sleeping in the sun has once been molten fire and became stone when the fire was able to say, in its liquid form: "I would be solid, I would be stone"; and the stone dreams now that the veins of ore in its nature might become liquid again and move, but within its shape as stone, so that slowly, through long centuries of aching for such a condition, for softness, for a pulse, it feels one day that the transformation has begun to occur; the veins loosen and flow, the clay relaxes, the stone, through long ages of imagining some further life, discovers eyes, a mouth, legs to leap with, and is toad. And the toad in turn conceives the possibility, now that it can move over the earth, of taking to the air, and slowly, without ever ceasing to be toad, dreams itself aloft on wings. Our bodies are not final. We are moving, all of us, in our common humankind, through the forms we love so deeply in one another, to what our hands have already touched in lovemaking and our bodies strain towards in each other's darkness. Slowly, and with pain, over centuries, we each move an infinitesimal space towards it. We are creating the lineaments of some final man, for whose delight we have prepared a landscape, and who can only be god.

I have seen the end of all this, clearly, in imagination: the earth transfigured and the gods walking upon it in their bodies' light. And I have seen the earth, as you have reader, already prepared for it, since our minds can conceive, our hands fashion, what we are not yet ready to enter: cornfields a fathom high, stacked in the sunlight, swaying under the moon; olive groves blowing from green to silver in a breeze, as if some god spoke the word *silver,* and his breath in passing over the scene transformed it with the turning of the leaves. You know all this. It is the earth as we have made it, clearing, grafting, transplanting, carrying seeds from one place to another, following no plan that we could enunciate, but allowing our bellies to lead us, and some other, deeper hunger, till the landscape we have made reveals to us the creatures we long for and must become.

I know how far we have come because I have been back to the beginnings. I have seen the unmade earth. It is flat and featureless, swamp in summer, a frozen waste in winter, without a tree or a flower or a made field, and only the wildest seeds growing together in their stunted clumps or blowing about at random on the breeze. It is a place of utter desolation, the beginning. I know it like the inside of my head. You can have no idea how far we have come, or how far back I have been to see all this; how rudimentary our life is in its beginnings.

And yet even here there are stirrings of new life. The first seeds are there to be separated and nurtured, and led on their long path to perfection.

Out walking today in my old sandals and cloak, with a straw hat to keep off the sun, stumbling about talking to myself in the muddy waste towards the river, I was stopped in my tracks by a little puff of scarlet amongst the wild corn.

Scarlet!

It is the first color I have seen in months. Or so it seems. Scarlet. A little wild poppy, of a red so sudden it made my blood stop. I kept saying the word over and over to myself, scarlet, as if the word, like the color, had escaped me till now, and just saying it would keep the little windblown flower in sight. Poppy. The magic of saying the word made my skin prickle, the saying almost a greater miracle than the seeing. I was drunk with joy. I danced. I shouted. Imagine the astonishment of my friends at Rome to see our cynical metropolitan poet, who barely knows a flower or a tree, dancing about in broken sandals on the earth, which is baked hard and cracked in some places, and in others puddled with foul-smelling mud—to see him dancing and singing to himself in celebration of this bloom. Poppy, scarlet poppy, flower of my far-off childhood and the cornfields round our farm at Sulmo, I have brought you into being again, I have raised you out of my earliest memories, out of my blood, to set you blowing in the wind. Scarlet. Magic word on the tongue to flash again on the eye. Scarlet. And with it all the other colors come flooding back, as magic syllables, and the earth explodes with them, they flash about me. I am making the spring. With yellow of the ox-eyed daisy of our weedy olive groves, with blue of cornflower, orange of marigold, purple of foxglove, even the pinks and cyclamens of my mother's garden that I have forgotten all these years. They come back . . . though there was, in fact, just a single poppy, a few blown petals of a tissue fineness and brightness, round the crown of seeds.

Cormac McCarthy

The Mountain

I

East of Knoxville Tennessee the mountains start, small ridges and spines of the folded Appalachians that contort the outgoing roads to their liking. The first of these is Red Mountain; from the crest on a clear day you can see the cool blue line of the watershed like a distant promise.

In late summer the mountain bakes under a sky of pitiless blue. The red dust of the orchard road is like powder from a brick kiln. You can't hold a scoop of it in your hand. Hot winds come up the slope from the valley like a rancid breath, redolent of milkweed, hoglots, rotting vegetation. The red clay banks along the road are crested with withered honeysuckle, peavines dried and sheathed in dust. By late July the corn patches stand parched and sere, stalks askew in defeat. All greens pale and dry. Clay cracks and splits in endless microcataclysm and the limestone lies about the eroded land like schools of sunning dolphin, gray channeled backs humped at the infernal sky.

In the relative cool of the timber stands, possum grapes and muscadine flourish with a cynical fecundity, and the floor of the forest—littered with old mossbacked logs, peopled with toadstools strange and solemn among the ferns and creepers and leaning to show their delicate livercolored gills—has about it a primordial quality, some steamy carboniferous swamp where ancient saurians lurk in feigned sleep.

On the mountain the limestone shelves and climbs in ragged escarpments among the clutching roots of hickories, oaks and tulip poplars which even here brace themselves against the precarious declination allotted them by the chance drop of a seed.

II

At the foot of the mountain the old man found himself in a broad glade grown thick with rushes, a small stream looping placidly over shallow sands stippled with dace shadows, the six-pointed stars of skating waterspiders drifting like bright frail medusas. He squatted and dipped a palmful of water to his lips, watched the dace drift and shimmer. Scout waded past him, elbow-deep into the stream, lapped at it noisily. Strings of red dirt receded from his balding hocks, marbling in the water like blood. The dace skittered into the channel and a watersnake uncurled from a rock at the far bank and glided down the slight current, no more demonstrative of effort or motion than a flute note.

The old man drank and then leaned back against the sledge. The glade hummed softly. A woodhen called from the timber on the mountain and to that sound of all summer days of seclusion and peace the old man slept.

Gabriel García Márquez

To the Sea

José Arcadio Buendía was completely ignorant of the geography of the region. He knew that to the east there lay an impenetrable mountain chain and that on the other side of the mountains there was the ancient city of Riohacha, where in times past—according to what he had been told by the first Aureliano Buendía, his grandfather—Sir Francis Drake had gone crocodile hunting with cannons and that he repaired them and stuffed them with straw to bring to Queen Elizabeth. In his youth, José Arcadio Buendía and his men, with wives and children, animals and all kinds of domestic implements, had crossed the mountains in search of an outlet to the sea, and after twenty-six months they gave up the expedition and founded Macondo, so they would not have to go back. It was, therefore, a route that did not interest him, for it could lead only to the past. To the south lay the swamps, covered with an eternal vegetable scum, and the whole vast universe of the great swamp, which, according to what the gypsies said, had no limits. The great swamp in the west mingled with a boundless extension of water where there were soft-skinned cetaceans that had the head and torso of a woman, causing the ruination of sailors with the charm of their extraordinary breasts. The gypsies sailed along that route for six months before they reached the strip of land over which the mules that carried the mail passed. According to José Arcadio Buendía's calculations, the only possibility of contact with civilization lay along the northern route. So he handed out clearing tools and hunting weapons to the same men who had been with him during the founding of Macondo. He threw his directional instruments and his maps into a knapsack, and he undertook the reckless adventure.

During the first days they did not come across any appreciable obstacle. They went down along the stony bank of the river to the place where years before they had found the soldier's armor, and from there they went into the woods along a path between wild orange trees. At the end of the first week they killed and roasted a deer, but they agreed to eat only half of it and salt the rest for the days that lay ahead. With that precaution they tried to postpone the necessity of having to eat macaws, whose blue flesh had a harsh and musky taste. Then, for more than ten days, they did not see the sun again. The ground became soft and damp, like volcanic ash, and the vegetation was thicker and thicker, and the cries of the birds and the uproar of the monkeys became more and more remote, and the world became eternally sad. The men on the expedition felt overwhelmed by their most ancient memories in that paradise of dampness and silence, going back to before original sin, as their boots sank into pools of steaming oil and their machetes destroyed bloody lilies and golden salamanders. For a week, almost without speaking, they went ahead like sleepwalkers through a universe of grief, lighted only by the tenuous reflection of luminous insects, and their lungs were overwhelmed by a suffocating smell of blood. They could not return because the strip that they were opening as they went along would soon close up with a new vegetation that almost seemed to grow before their eyes. "It's all right," José Arcadio Buendía would say. "The main thing is not to lose our bearings." Always following his compass, he kept on guiding his men toward the invisible north so that they would be able to get out of that enchanted region. It was a thick night, starless, but the darkness was becoming impregnated with a fresh and clear air. Exhausted by the long crossing, they hung up their hammocks and slept deeply for the first time in two weeks. When they woke up, with the sun already high in the sky, they were speechless with fascination. Before them, surrounded by ferns and palm trees, white and powdery in the silent morning light, was an enormous Spanish galleon. Tilted slightly to the starboard, it had hanging from its intact masts the dirty rags of its sails in the midst of its rigging, which was adorned with orchids. The hull, covered with an armor of petrified barnacles and soft moss, was firmly fastened into a surface of stones. The whole structure seemed to occupy its own space, one of solitude and oblivion, protected from the vices of time and the habits of the birds. Inside, where the expeditionaries explored with careful intent, there was nothing but a thick forest of flowers.

The discovery of the galleon, an indication of the proximity of the sea, broke José Arcadio Buendía's drive. He considered it a trick of his whimsical fate to have searched for the sea without finding it, at the cost of countless sacrifices and suffering, and to have found it all of a sudden without looking for it, as if it lay across his path like an insurmountable object.

Richard Ford

Hunters

We walked then for a while without talking. I looked back once to see the Nash far and small in the flat distance. I couldn't see my mother, and I thought that she must've turned on the radio and gone to sleep, which she always did, letting it play all night in her bedroom. Behind the car the sun was nearing the rounded mountains southwest of us, and I knew that when the sun was gone it would be cold. I wished my mother had decided to come along with us, and I thought for a moment of how little I really knew her at all.

Glen walked with me another quarter-mile, crossed another barbed wire fence where sage was growing, then went a hundred yards through wheatgrass and spurge until the ground went up and formed a kind of long hillock bunker built by a farmer against the wind. And I realized the lake was just beyond us. I could hear the sound of a car horn blowing and a dog barking all the way down in the town, then the wind seemed to move and all I could hear then and after then were geese. So many geese, from the sound of them, though I still could not see even one. I stood and listened to the high-pitched shouting sound, a sound I had never heard so close, a sound with size to it—though it was not loud. A sound that meant great numbers and that made your chest rise and your shoulders tighten with ex-pectancy. It was a sound to make you feel separate from it and everything else, as if you were of no importance in the grand scheme of things.

"Do you hear them singing," Glen asked. He held his hand up to make me stand still. And we both listened. "How many do you think, Les, just hearing?"

"A hundred," I said. "More than a hundred."

"Five thousand," Glen said. "More than you can believe when you see them. Go see."

I put down my gun and on my hands and knees crawled up the earth-work through the wheatgrass and thistle, until I could see down to the lake and see the geese. And they were there, like a white bandage laid on the water, wide and long and continuous, a white expanse of snow geese, sev-enty yards from me, on the bank, but stretching far onto the lake, which was large itself—a half-mile across, with thick tules on the far side and wild plums farther and the blue mountain behind them.

"Do you see the big raft?" Glen said from below me, in a whisper.

"I see it," I said, still looking. It was such a thing to see, a view I had never seen and have not since.

"Are any on the land?" he said.

"Some are in the wheatgrass," I said, "but most are swimming."

"Good," Glen said. "They'll have to fly. But we can't wait for that now."

And I crawled backwards down the heel of land to where Glen was, and my gun. We were losing our light, and the air was purplish and cooling. I looked toward the car but couldn't see it, and I was no longer sure where it was below the lighted sky.

"Where do they fly to?" I said in a whisper, since I did not want anything to be ruined because of what I did or said. It was important to Glen to shoot the geese, and it was important to me.

"To the wheat," he said. "Or else they leave for good. I wish your mother had come, Les. Now she'll be sorry."

I could hear the geese quarreling and shouting on the lake surface. And I wondered if they knew we were here now. "She might be," I said with my heart pounding, but I didn't think she would be much.

It was a simple plan he had. I would stay behind the bunker, and he would crawl on his belly with his gun through the wheatgrass as near to the geese as he could. Then he would simply stand up and shoot all the ones he could close up, both in the air and on the ground. And when all the others flew up, with luck some would turn toward me as they came into the wind, and then I could shoot them and turn them back to him, and he would shoot them again. He could kill ten, he said, if he was lucky, and I might kill four. It didn't seem hard.

"Don't show them your face," Glen said. "Wait till you think you can touch them, then stand up and shoot. To hesitate is lost in this."

Then he took off his VFW jacket and put it on the ground, climbed up the side of the bunker, cradling his shotgun in his arms, and slid on his belly into the dry stalks of yellow grass out of my sight.

Then, for the first time in that entire day, I was alone. And I didn't mind it. I sat squat down in the grass, loaded my double gun and took my other two shells out of my pocket to hold. I pushed the safety off and on to see that it was right. The wind rose a little, scuffed the grass and made me shiver.

It was not the warm chinook now, but a wind out of the north, the one geese flew away from if they could.

And then I heard the geese again, their voices in unison, louder and shouting, as if the wind had changed again and put all new sounds in the cold air. And then a *boom*. And I knew Glen was in among them and had stood up to shoot. The noise of geese rose and grew worse, and my fingers burned where I held my gun too tight to the metal, and I put it down and opened my fist to make the burning stop so I could feel the trigger when the moment came. *Boom*, Glen shot again, and I heard him shuck a shell, and all the sounds out beyond the bunker seemed to be rising—the geese, the shots, the air itself going up. *Boom*, Glen shot another time, and I knew he was taking his careful time to make his shots good. And I held my gun and started to crawl up the bunker so as not to be surprised when the geese came over me and I could shoot.

By now the whole raft was in the air, all of it moving in a slow swirl above me and the lake and everywhere, finding the wind and heading out south in long wavering lines that caught the last sun and turned to silver as they gained a distance. It was a thing to see, I will tell you now. Five thousand white geese all in the air around you, making a noise like you have never heard before. And I thought to myself then: this is something I will never see again. I will never forget this. And I was right.

Glen Baxter shot twice more. One he missed, but with the other he hit a goose flying away from him, and knocked it half falling and flying into the empty lake not far from shore, where it began to swim as though it was fine and make its noise.

Glen stood in the stubby grass, looking out at the goose, his gun lowered. "I didn't need to shoot that one, did I, Les?"

"I don't know," I said, sitting on the little knoll of land, looking at the goose swimming in the water.

"I don't know why I shoot 'em. They're so beautiful." He looked at me.

"I don't know either," I said.

"Maybe there's nothing else to do with them." Glen stared at the goose again and shook his head. "Maybe this is exactly what they're put on earth for."

John Berger

Goats

The goat ambled lightly along the path beside her in the forest. As Hélène walked her boots made a scuffing noise in the leaves, which in places were covered with frost like grey salt. She led the goat with a short rope, and in her other hand she carried a stick. After half an hour, she stopped under an oak tree and filled the large pocket of her apron with acorns.

"Jésus Marie!" she said to the goat. "Aren't you ashamed? An old woman collecting acorns for you."

The goat looked at her through the black oblong centres of its eyes. A few specks of snow, no larger than sawdust, fell between the trees.

"The great whiteness will soon cover us," she said and tugged the rope.

"Sometimes I try to pray, but things come into my head and distract me. It's my nature. My poor father told me the same thing. You're always wanting to be in the oven and the flour mill at the same time, he said, and so you can't keep your mind on anything. I'll tell you what you are like, he said, you are like the man whose friend says to him, 'I'll give you my horse if you can say the Lord's Prayer without thinking about anything else.' And the man says, 'Done.' And he begins, 'Our Father which art . . .' "

The old woman and the goat could hear the roar of the stream ahead. The stream was so full that its water frothed like milk.

". . . and when the man gets half-way through the Lord's Prayer he stops and says, 'Can you give me the bridle for the horse too?' "

Everything was grey except for the rushing water and the white flecks of snow on the goat's neck. The path left the forest and climbed between fields. The goat started walking faster, pulling the old woman along. She was the stronger of the two, but instead of checking the goat, she trotted behind. In one place the path was entirely covered with ice.

Cows place their feet with a certain delicacy as if wearing high-heeled shoes; goats, however, are like skaters. The goat danced on the ice and Hélène, letting go of the rope, gingerly felt her way round the edge, holding on to the grass bank. When she was on the other side of the ice, the goat refused to come towards her. She threatened and raised her stick. "It's snowing," she muttered, "it's nearly night. As if all my losses aren't enough, shit, shit, shit, you are playing me up."

On some occasions anger made her cunning. When she let out her chickens and they began to pull up the flowers in her garden, she pretended she had grain in her hand for feeding them, and she clucked sweetly to attract them, until she could lay her hands on one: then she would shake it with both hands and its feathers would fall out and she would hurl it above her head as high as she could against the sky. And the chickens were so stupid they came one by one to get their punishment.

The goat, who was not stupid, stared at her as she waved her stick. "You good-for-nothing carcass of a goat!"

After a while the goat stepped off the ice and the pair of them continued on their way. The very desolation of the scene made them look like accomplices. The rockface rose up above them, sheer as a wall for three hundred and fifty metres. The massive pine trees at the top were just visible in the falling dusk, as small as sprigs of herbs.

Hélène led the goat towards the wall, at the same time calling. Her call was not unlike the noise she made to attract the chickens when she fed them. But it was a shriller and shorter call, punctuated with silence.

After several calls there was an answering one which no voice could have imitated. Perhaps an instrument like a bagpipe would come nearest to reproducing it. The lament of breath issuing from a skin bag. The Greeks called the cry of the he-goat *tragos,* from which they derived the word tragedy.

He was darker than the surrounding dusk and his four horns were entwined with each other, as can sometimes happen with the branches of a tree when the trunk has divided into two. His gait was unhurried.

Hélène hid her left hand in her right armpit to keep it warm. With her right hand she held the rope. The goat stood there waiting. The specks of snow were turning into large flakes. Since she was a child she had done the same thing when the first real flakes fell. She stuck out her tongue. The first snowflake prickled like sherbet on her seventy-five-year-old tongue.

The goat lifted her tail and began to wag it. It made a circular movement like a spoon stirring quickly. The he-goat licked beneath it. Then he straightened his neck and the corners of his lips curled back baring his mouth to the taste. His thin, red-tipped penis emerged from its tuft of hair. He stood as motionless as a boulder. And after a moment his penis retracted. Perhaps the occasion was too inauspicious even for him.

"Jésus, Marie and Joseph!" muttered Hélène. "Hurry, will you! My hands are getting frozen. It's night."

He sniffed and let the goat's tail brush between his eyebrows.

If the snow fell all night, she would be unable to bring the goat again, and she would have one or two kids fewer to sell in the spring.

The he-goat stood there as if waiting for something to pass. In her impatience Hélène squatted down on her heels, the snow settling on her shawl, to look under his body to see whether all hope had gone. There was still a tip of red.

"If I turned my anger into power," she muttered, "it would blow up that wall of rock. Hurry! Will you?"

The he-goat tapped the flank of the goat with one of his forelegs. Several times. Then he tapped her with his other leg on the other side. When she was in position, he mounted and entered her.

Nothing else anywhere under the wall of rockface was visibly moving except the snowflakes and his haunches. His movements were as rapid as the falling flakes were slow. After thirty thrusts, his entire body shook. Then his forelegs slid off her back.

Hélène pressed with all her weight on the centre of the goat's back. This was to encourage the retention of the sperm. The pair set off down towards the village. They took a longer but wider path down, past the house where Archaud lived.

Lloyse, Arthaud's wife, was killed by a boulder which fell from the top of the rockface. They were both asleep in their bed. Where the boulder first hit the earth, it made a hole big enough to bury a horse in. Nevertheless the boulder continued to roll down the slope. Slowly. When it reached the house, it didn't crash right through it. It just broke through one wall and crushed half the bed. Lloyse was killed outright and Arthaud woke up, unhurt, beside the boulder. This was twenty years ago. The boulder was too heavy to move. So, clearing the wood and rubble away, Arthaud built another room on the other side of the house and in this room he now slept.

When Hélène and the goat passed, there was a light in the window of this room and one side of the boulder was already glistening with snow.

Hélène placed her hand, whose joints were swollen so that she could never fully straighten her fingers, on the animal's back. "Goat," she said, "lazy good-for-nothing carcass of a goat, don't lose it!"

The spermatozoa who had survived the beginning of their long journey were swimming inwards in anti-clockwise spirals.

The wind was blowing the snow in whorls and she walked holding the goat's collar in case she slipped.

Jim Crace

The Prospect from the Silver Hill

The company agent—friendless, single, far from home—passed most days alone in a cabin at Ibela-hoy, the Hill Without a Hat. His work was simple. Equipped with a rudimentary knowledge of mineralogy, neat, laborious handwriting, and a skill with ledgers, he had been posted to the high lands to identify the precious metals, the stones, the ores, that (everybody said) were buried there.

This was his life: awake at dawn, awake all day, awake all night. Phrenetic Insomnia was the term. But there were no friends or doctors to make the diagnosis. The agent simply—like a swift, a shark—dared not sleep. He kept moving. He did not close his eyes. At night, at dawn, in the tall heat of the day, he looked out over the land and, watching the shades and colours of the hill and its valley accelerate and reel, he constructed for himself a family and a life less solitary than the one that he was forced to live. He took pills. He drank what little spirit arrived each month with his provisions. He exhausted himself with long, aimless walks amongst the boulders and dry beds. Sometimes he fell forward at work, his nose flattened amongst the gravels on the table, his papers dampened by saliva, his tongue slack. But he did not sleep or close his eyes, though he was still troubled by chimeras, daydreams, which broke his concentration and (because he was conscious) seemed more substantial and coherent than sleeping dreams. As the men had already remarked amongst themselves when they saw the sacs of tiredness spreading across his upper cheeks and listened to his conversation, the company agent either had a fever or the devil had swapped sawdust for his brain.

Several times a week one of the survey gangs arrived in a company mobile to deposit drill cores of augered rock and sand, pumice and shale, and provide the company agent with a profile of the world twenty metres below his feet. He sorted clays as milky as nutsap and eggstones as worn and weathered as a saint's bead into sample bags. Each rock, each smudge of soil, was condemned. Nothing. Nothing. Nothing. A trace of tin. Nothing.

Once, when he had been at Ibela-hoy for a few weeks only, one of the survey gangs offered to take him down to the lumber station where the woodsmen had established a good still and an understanding with some local women. He sat in the cab of the mobile drilling rig and talked nonstop. That's the loneliest place, he told them, as the mobile descended from the cabin. There aren't even ghosts. He spoke, too, about the wife and children, the companionable life, which he had concocted in his daydreams. How he wished he had a camera at home, he told the men. Then he could have shown them photographs of his family, of his garden in the city, his car, his wedding day.

The men indulged him. He was still a stranger, they reasoned, and starved of company, missing home. He would quieten down once he had a glass in his hand. But they had been wrong. He became louder with every sip. He spoke in a voice which sent the women back into their homes, which sent the men early to bed. The voice said, My sadness is stronger than your drink. Nothing can relieve it. Nothing. A trace of tin. Nothing.

He daydreamed: a lifetime of finding nothing. He dreamed of prospecting the night sky and locating a planet of diamonds or an old, cooled sun of solid gold. But then the company had no need for diamonds or gold. Find us sand, they instructed. Find us brown mud. Send us a palmful of pebbles. He dreamed again, and produced a twist of earth and stone which contained new colours, a seam of creamy nougat in a funnel of tar. His dream delivered the funnel to his company offices. Soon secretaries typed Ibela-hoy for the first time—and a name was coined for the new mineral which he had unearthed. Then his dream transported friends and family to Ibela-hoy. They walked behind him as he set out to map the creamy seam. Together they charted an area the shape of a toadstool. A toadstool of the newest mineral in the world. His daydream provided a telephone and a line of poles. He telephoned the company with the good news. They referred him to the Agency and then to the Ministry. His calls were bounced and routed between switchboards and operators and his story retold a dozen times—but nobody was found with sufficient authority to accept such momentous information or to order his return to home, to sleep.

Send me a dream, he said aloud, in which my wife and my children are brought to the cabin. When I wake, they are there. When I sleep, they are there. We sit at the same table. The two boys tumble on the bed. The baby stands on my thighs with crescent legs and tugs at my nose and hair. My wife and I sit together slicing vegetables at the table. But when he had finished speaking there was no reply from amongst the rocks, no promises. He spoke again, in whispers. Have pity, he said.

Sometimes he wrapped his arms round boulders, warmed by the sun, and embraced them. My wife, he said. He kissed boulders.

Now the men kept their distance. They were polite but no longer generous. There were no more invitations to visit the lumber station—and they became watchful on those occasions when they brought drill cores to the cabin. Does this man know his business, they asked amongst themselves. Can he be trusted to know marl from marble? They waited awkwardly at his door or stood at his window as their plugs of earth were spread and sorted on his bench, the soils washed and sieved, the stones stunned and cracked, the unusual flakes of rocks matched with the specimens in the mineral trays. His fatigue—the second stage—had hardened his concentration. He was engrossed. He lowered his head and smelled the soil. He sucked the roundest pebbles. He rubbed stones on the thighs of his trousers and held them to the light. No, nothing, he told them. But when they sat in their camps and looked up from the valley late at night, a light still burned in the agent's cabin and they could see him holding their stones to his oil flame and talking to their earth in his skinned and weary voice.

At first the sorted, worthless plugs were dumped each day in a rough pile at the side of the cabin. The clays of the valley consorted with the volcanic earths of Ibela-hoy. Flints jostled sandstones, topsoils ran loose amongst clods, the rounded pebbles of the river bed bubbled in the wasteland shales. He was struck how—held and turned in the daylight—each stone was a landscape. Here was a planet, a globe, with the continents grey and peninsular, the seas cold and smooth to the touch. And here a coastline, one face the beach, four faces cliff, and a rivulet of green where the children and donkeys could make their descent. And here, twisted and smoothed by the survey drill, were the muddied banks of rivers and the barks of trees modelled and reduced in deep, toffee earth. But in the dump, their shapes and colours clashed and were indecent. He remembered how, when he was a child, they had buried his father. The grave was open when the body came. There were clays and flints piled on the yellow grass. The bottom of his father's trench had filled with water. The digger's spade had severed stones. They said that, in ancient times when humankind went naked and twigged for termites and ate raw meat, the dead were left where they fell. What the animals did not eat became topsoil, loam. The company agent had wished for that, had dreamed of his father free of his grave and spread out on the unbroken ground as calm and breathless as frost. But he could not look at that open grave, those wounded flints, without tears. He could not look at road works, either. Or a ploughed field. Or a broken wall, And whenever he had stared at that squinting corner of his room where the ceiling plaster had fallen and the broken roof laths stuck through, his chest (what was the phrase?) shivered like a parched pea and he dare not sleep. The ceiling doesn't leak, his mother said. It's you that leaks, not it.

Now he wept when he passed the waste pile, when he was drawn at night to stand before it with a lamp or summoned to salvage one lonely stone for his pocket or his table. Sometimes it seemed that the pile was an open wound or an abattoir of stones. But the longer he stood the more it seemed that a piece of the world had been misplaced and abandoned at his cabin side.

Then he took a spade and dug a pit behind the waste pile. First he gathered the chipped yellow stones which lay on the surface and placed them together in a bucket. And then he removed the thin soil crust and piled it neatly on to a tarpaulin. Each individual layer was dug out and piled separately, until the pit was shoulder deep. The continents and planets, the landscapes and coastlines of the waste dump were shovelled into the pit and one by one, in order, the layers of Ibela-hoy were put back in place. Then he scattered the chipped yellow stones on to the bulging ground.

When the gangs delivered drill cores they noticed that the waste had gone. I buried it, he said. I put it back. He showed them where the swollen ground was settling. Well, they said, that's very neat and tidy. Or, Is that what you're paid to do, fool about with spades? His replies made no sense to them. They continued to talk with him roughly or to humour him with banter. What should we do for him, they asked amongst themselves, to bring him back to earth? Should we write, they wondered, to his wife and children or to the boss? Should we let him be and let the illness pass? Some of the kinder, older men went to talk with him, to offer help, to exchange a word or two about the samples on his bench. Yet he seemed indifferent to them and those funnels of earth and stone which could earn them all a fortune. Was that the yellow of bauxite or the rose of cinnabar or the fire-blue of opal? The company agent did not seem to share their excitement or their interest. But when at last they left him in peace he turned to the samples on his bench and sorted through them with unbroken attention. A stone of apple-green he removed and walked with it into the valley where in a cave there were lichens of the same colour. A fistful of grit he scattered in the grass so that it fell amongst the leaf joints like sleet. A round stone he placed on the river bed with other round stones. A grey landscape in an inch of granite he stood in the shadow of the greyest rock. A chip of pitchblende was reunited with black soil.

Once a month when his provisions were delivered together with letters from home, the company agent presented his report and sent back to the city any minerals or gemstones which were worthy of note. Once he had found a fragment of platinum in a sample from the plateau beyond the hill. He and the gang waited a month for the company's response. Low quality platinum, they said. No use to us. And once he had identified graphite amongst the native carbons. But, again, the company was unimpressed. Now he wrapped a piece of damp clay and placed it in a sample bag. Its colours were the colours of pomegranate skins. Its odour was potatoes. He sealed the bag and sent it to the company. Urgent, he wrote on the label. Smell this! And, in the second month, he sent them a cube of sandstone and wrote: See the landscape, the beach, the pathway through the rocks. And later they received the palmful of pebbles that they had requested in his dream.

Alarms rang. Secretaries delivered the agent's file to the company bosses. They searched the certificates and testimonials for any criminal past. Was he a radical? Had he been ill? What should they make of clay, sandstone, pebbles? They called his mother to the offices and questioned her. She showed them her son's monthly letters and pointed to those parts where he spoke of insomnia, an abattoir of stones and a family that never was. He misses home, she said. Why would he send worthless soil and cryptic notes in sample bags? She could not say, except that he had always been a good man, quick to tears. If he had only married, found a girl to love, had children perhaps . . . then who can guess what might have been? But worthless soil? Still she could not say.

The bosses sent their man to Ibela-hoy in their air-conditioned jeep to bring the agent home and to discover what went on. The brick and tarmac of the town and villages lasted for a day. The bosses' man passed the night at the Rest House where the valley greens rose to the implacable evening monochromes of the hills. In the morning, early, he drove on to the bouldered track along the valley side. The Hill Without a Hat swung across his windscreen in the distance. On the summit of the ridge the track widened and cairns marked the route down into the valley of Lekadeeb and then up again towards Ibela-hoy. He stood with his binoculars and sought out the company agent's cabin in the hollow of the hill. He saw the company mobile parked at the door and the antics of men who seemed intoxicated with drink or horseplay. A survey team had returned from the far valley bluffs some days ahead of schedule and hurried to the agent's cabin. The men were wild. They had found silver. They had recognised small fragments in their drill cores and had excavated in the area for larger quantities. They placed a half-dozen jagged specimens on the company agent's bench. Tell us it isn't silver, they challenged him. He looked at one piece of silver shaped like a stem of ginger but metallic grey in colour with puddles of milky-white quartz. What he saw was a bare summit of rock in sunshine. But snow in its crevices was too cold to melt. I'll do some tests, he said.

The men sat outside in their drilling mobile and waited for his confirmation that at last their work had produced minerals of great value. There were bonuses to be claimed, fortunes to be made, celebrations, hugging, turbulent reunions with wives and children to anticipate. The company agent turned the snowy summit in his hand and divined its future. And its past. Once the word Silver was spoken in the company offices, Ibela-hoy could count on chaos; there would be mining engineers, labour camps, a village, roads, bars, drink, soldiers. Bulldozers would push back the soil and roots of silver would be grubbed like truffles from the earth. Dynamite, spoil heaps, scars. And he, the company agent, the man who spilled the beans, would have no time to reconcile the stones, the dreams, the family, the fatigue, the sleeplessness which now had reached its final stage. The turmoil had begun already. He heard the smooth engine of the company jeep as it laboured over the final rise before the cabin. He saw the bosses' man climb out with his folder and his suit and pause to talk with the men who waited inside the mobile's cab. Arms were waved and fingers pointed towards the bluffs where silver lay in wait.

I'll put it back, he said.

By the time the bosses' man had walked into the cabin with a string of false and reassuring greetings on his lips, the company agent had pocketed the half-dozen pieces of silver and had slipped away into the rocks behind the cabin. He climbed as high as was possible without breaking cover and crouched in a gulley. He toyed with the stones on the ground, turning them in his palms, and waited for night. He watched as the bosses' man ran from the cabin and the survey gang jumped from their mobile and searched the landscape for the agent. He watched as they showed the bosses' man where he had buried the waste heap, the world misplaced. He watched as the gang brought picks and shovels, and (insensitive to topsoils and chipped yellow stones) dug into the abattoir. He watched the bosses' man crouch and shake his head as he sorted through the debris for the gold, the agate, the topaz which the men promised had been buried, hidden, there. It was, they said, a matter for the madhouse or the militia. They'd watched the agent for a month or two. He had hugged boulders. He had hidden gemstones, their gemstones, company gemstones, throughout the valley. They'd seen him walking, crouching, placing gemstones in the shade of rocks, in the mouth of caves, under leaves.

A bare summit of rock in sunshine was the location of his dream. There were crevices of unbroken snow and pats of spongy moss. He was naked. There were no clothes. He squatted on his haunches and chipped at flints. Someone had caught a hare—but nobody yet knew how to make fire, so its meat was ripped apart and eaten raw. They washed it down with snow. The carcass was left where it fell. The two boys played with twigs. The baby stood on crescent legs and tugged at grass. He and the woman delved in the softer earth for roots to eat and found silver, a plaything for the boys. He conjured in his dream a world where the rocks were hot and moving, where quakes and volcanoes turned shales to schists, granite to gneiss, limestone to marble, sandstone to quartz, where continents sank and rose like kelp on the tide.

When it was light, he unwrapped himself from the embrace of the boulder where he had passed the night and began to traverse the valley towards the high ground and the rocks where snow survived the sun. His aimless walks had made his legs strong and his mind was soaring with a fever of sleeplessness. He walked and talked, his tongue guiding his feet over the rocks, naming what passed beneath. Molten silicates, he said, as his feet cast bouncing shadows over salt and pepper rocks. Pumice, he said to the hollows. Grass.

In two hours the company agent had reached the ridge where the winds seemed to dip and dive and hug the earth. He turned to the south and, looking down into the valley, he saw the men and the trucks at his cabin and the twist of smoke as breakfast was prepared. Bring my wife and children, he said. And one man, standing at the hut with a hot drink resting on the bonnet of the air-conditioned jeep, saw him calling there and waved his arms. Come down, he said. Come back.

But the company agent walked on until he found that the earth had become slippery with ice and the air white like paper. He looked now for grey rocks, metallic grey, and found them at the summit of his walk, his rendezvous. There was no easy path; the boulders there were shoulder height and he was forced to squeeze and climb. But his hands were taking hold of crevices fossilised with snow and soon, at last, he stood upon the landscape that he had sought, glistening, winking grey with puddles of milky-white quartz. He took the six jagged specimens from his pocket. I am standing here, he said, pointing at an ounce of silver. He took the pieces and placed them in a streak of snow where their colours matched the rock and where, two paces distant, they disappeared for good.

In the afternoon he watched the first helicopter as it beat about the hills, its body bulbous-ended like a floating bone. And then, close by, he heard the grinding motors of the jeep as it found a route between the rocks and stalled. He heard voices and then someone calling him by his first name. Was it his son? He walked to the edge of his grey platform and looked down on the heads of the bosses' man, a soldier and two of the survey gang. Climb down, they said. We're going to take you home. A holiday. I have my job to do, he said. Yes, they said, we all have jobs to do. We understand. But it's cold up here and you must be tired and hungry. Climb down and we'll drive you back to the city. No problems. No awkward questions. Your mother's waiting. Just show us what is hidden and you can be with your family.

Bring my family here, he said. Bring my wife and children here. The men looked at each other and then one of the survey gang spoke. You have no wife and children, he said. You lied. The company agent picked up the largest stone and flung it at the men. It landed on the bonnet of the jeep and its echo was as metallic, as full of silver, as the grey hill.

Leave him there, they said. Let hunger bring him down.

It was cold that night above Ibela-hoy. But there was warmth in numbers. The company agent and his wife encircled their children, their breath directed inwards, their backs turned against the moon. And in the morning when the sun came up and the colours of the hill and its valley accelerated from grey and brown, to red and green, to white, the company agent gathered stones for his family and they breakfasted on snow.

VII

NATURAL HISTORY

AN ANNOTATED BOOKLIST

W. S. Merwin

The Last One

Well they'd made up their minds to be everywhere because why not.
Everywhere was theirs because they thought so.
They with two leaves they whom the birds despise.
In the middle of stones they made up their minds.
They started to cut.

Well they cut everything because why not.
Everything was theirs because they thought so.
It fell into its shadows and they took both away.
Some to have some for burning.

Well cutting everything they came to the water.
They came to the end of the day there was one left standing.
They would cut it tomorrow they went away.
The night gathered in the last branches.
The shadow of the night gathered in the shadow on the water.
The night and the shadow put on the same head.
And it said Now.

Well in the morning they cut the last one.
Like the others the last one fell into its shadow.
It fell into its shadow on the water.
They took it away its shadow stayed on the water.

Well they shrugged they started trying to get the shadow away.
They cut right to the ground the shadow stayed whole.
They laid boards on it the shadow came out on top.
They shone lights on it the shadow got blacker and clearer.
They exploded the water the shadow rocked.
They built a huge fire on the roots.

They sent up black smoke between the shadow and the sun.
The new shadow flowed without changing the old one.
They shrugged they went away to get stones.

They came back the shadow was growing.
They started setting up stones it was growing.
They looked the other way it went on growing.
They decided they would make a stone out of it.
They took stones to the water they poured them into the shadow.
They poured them in they poured them in the stones vanished.
The shadow was not filled it went on growing.
That was one day.

The next day was just the same it went on growing.
They did all the same things it was just the same.
They decided to take its water from under it.
They took away water they took it away the water went down.
The shadow stayed where it was before.
It went on growing it grew onto the land.
They started to scrape the shadow with machines.
When it touched the machines it stayed on them.
They started to beat the shadow with sticks.
Where it touched the sticks it stayed on them.
They started to beat the shadow with hands.
Where it touched the hands it stayed on them.
That was another day.

Well the next day started about the same it went on growing.
They pushed lights into the shadow.
Where the shadow got onto them they went out.
They began to stomp on the edge it got their feet.
And when it got their feet they fell down.
It got into eyes the eyes went blind.
The ones that fell down it grew over and they vanished.
The ones that went blind and walked into it vanished.
The ones that could see and stood still
It swallowed their shadows.
Then it swallowed them too and they vanished.
Well the others ran.

The ones that were left went away to live if it would let them.
They went as far as they could.
The lucky ones with their shadows.

Compiled by the Advisory Editors

Natural History: An Annotated Booklist

ANNIE DILLARD

SOME CLASSICS

Richard K. Nelson, *The Island Within*. This is the writer the nature writers all read: Richard K. Nelson.

Susanna Moodie, *Roughing It in the Bush*. Canadian classic, a stunning pioneer story.

Claude Levi-Strauss, *Tristes Tropiques*.

Joseph Conrad, *The Mirror of the Sea*.

Ivan Turgenev, *Sportsman's Sketches*.

Thomas Hardy, *Return of the Native, Tess of the d'Urbervilles*.

Herman Melville, "The Encantadas."

Willa Cather, *Death Comes for the Archbishop, O Pioneers, My Antonia*.

Izak Dinesen, *Out of Africa*.

Langston Hughes, *The Big Sea*.

Jack Kerouac, *The Dharma Bums*.

Mary Austin, *Land of Little Rain*.

Edwin Muir, *Autobiography*.

Pliny, *Natural History*. (I like the Philemon Holland translation.) Pliny the Elder compiled these bizarre legends posing as observations in the fifth decade B.C., when science and poetry blurred. He wrote energetically; any selection is fascinating.

Izaak Walton, *The Compleat Angler*. The 1653 English pacific philosophy of fishing, mostly in streams.

William Bartram, *Travels*. The American South, mostly, in the eighteenth century, by a lively botanist.

Gilbert White, *The Natural History and Antiquities of Selborne*. Close observation and high literary style by the English country curate.

Charles Darwin, *The Voyage of the Beagle*. This travel account demonstrates the tedium inherent in the journal form. Nevertheless, the breadth of the young scientist's information and the vigor of his curiosity are admirable.

Richard Henry Dana, *Two Years Before the Mast*. The dandy adventure at sea. Young Dana rounds Cape Horn and camps on the southern California coast when it was mostly rattlesnakes.

Ralph Waldo Emerson, "Nature," "The American Scholar," etc.; *Essays*. The essay "Nature" bade John Muir forge for himself a new vocation that never before existed: wandering loose, and writing about the country. Emerson's wild metaphysic still underlies American nature writing and still caps American thinking about nature.

Henry David Thoreau, *Walden; The Maine Woods; Cape Cod; A Week on the Concord and Merrimack Rivers; Journals*. It is absurdly fashionable to promote the journals over *Walden*, artlessness over art. Writing the book, Thoreau compressed the events of two years into one and turned half the landscape into metaphor.

Herman Melville, *Moby-Dick*. The best book ever written about nature.

Henry Walter Bates, *The Naturalist on the River Amazon*. Bates was one of the first naturalists to explore the virgin territory of the Amazon when it was opened in the nineteenth century.

Alfred Russel Wallace, *A Narrative of Travels on the Amazon and Rio Negro*. This remains the best and liveliest book on the South American forest.

J. Henri Fabre, *Souvenirs entomologiques*, or, more likely, *The Insect World of J. Henri Fabre*, edited by Edwin Way Teale. This is beautiful, knowledgeable prose.

W. H. Hudson. *The Purple Land; A Naturalist in La Plata; Far Away and Long Ago; The Book of a Naturalist*. The London writer tells wonderful stories of the Argentina of his boyhood.

John Muir, *My First Summer in the Sierra; Travels in Alaska*. Muir's vivid prose rich in tropes, and his pluck and piety, make him the best writer of the "sublime" school.

Sir Arthur Stanley Eddington, *The Nature of the Physical World*. The Gifford Lectures of 1927 by the English Astronomer Royal. Although it lacks fifty years of newer physics, Eddington's book does postdate not only Einstein's work but also early quantum theory, both of which it vivifies with British sangfroid: "Let us then take a leap over a precipice so that we may contemplate Nature undisturbed."

Sir James Jeans, *The Mysterious Universe*. Eddington's successor as Astronomer Royal writes a philosophical treatment of quantum mechanics. Eddington and Jeans carried on work in a genre to which Einstein also contributed, and in which the general reader may still delight: physicists explain what's up.

TWO OUTSTANDING SECONDARY SOURCES

John Bakeless, *The Eyes of Discovery*. A lively account of the land that would become the United States, seen through the eyes of its earliest explorers and travelers.

Joseph Kastner, *A Species of Eternity*. America's first naturalists describe the new world.

SOME TWENTIETH-CENTURY WORKS OUT OF THE MAINSTREAM

Antoine de Saint-Exupéry, *Wind, Sand, and Stars*. Delivering the mail over North Africa in the early days of aviation. Its landscapes and cloudscapes, its storms, mountains, and starry nights, and the men who live up in the air, make this one of the best books on any subject.

Ernest Hemingway, *Green Hills of Africa*. Hunting a kudu.

Gavin Maxwell, *Ring of Bright Water*. The writer lives in the Scottish Highlands with two otters.

Edward Abbey, *Desert Solitaire*. The Southwest American desert.

TRAVEL

Rockwell Kent, *N by E*. The west coast of Greenland.

Berton Roueche, *The River World and Other Explorations*. Essays by the *New Yorker* writer.

Larry Millman, *Our Like Will Not Be There Again*. The west coast of Ireland.

Katharine Scherman, *Spring on an Arctic Island*.

Wilfred Thesiger, *Arabian Sands*.

Charlton Ogburn, Jr., *The Winter Beach*. The Atlantic coast of North America in winter.

Robert Gibbings, *Over the Reefs*. The best on French Polynesia.

POPULAR ANTHROPOLOGY

Elizabeth Marshall Thomas, *The Harmless People*. This winsome account of the Bushmen and their land is beautifully written, unsentimental.

Peter Freuchen, *The Book of the Eskimo*. Greenland Eskimos in the old days.

Colin Turnbull, *The Forest People.* Pygmies.

Ronald Blythe, *Akenfield.* Oral history of English tenant farmers who worked the land the old way, knocking clods from turnips with hoes.

OTHER TWENTIETH-CENTURY FAVORITES, UNANNOTATED

William de Buys, *River of Traps.*

James Galvin, *The Meadow.*

Annick Smith, *Homestead.*

William Kittredge, *Owning it All.*

Terry Tempest Williams, *Refuge.*

James Kilgo, *Deep Enough for Ivorybills.*

Harry Crews, *A Childhood.*

Joan Colebrook, *A House of Trees.*

Jill Ker Conway, *The Road from Courain.*

Deborah Digges, *Fugitive Spring.*

Howard Ensign Evans, *Life on a Little-Known Planet.*

John Hanson Mitchell, *Living at the End of Time.*

Edward O. Wilson, *Naturalist.*

Peter Matthiessen, anything.

James Trefil, anything.

Gary Nabhan, anything.

Steven Graham, *The Gentle Art of Tramping*.

Stewart Edward White, *The Mountains; The Pass*.

Marjorie Kinnan Rawlings, *Cross Creek*.

Rachel Carson, the trilogy: *The Sea Around Us; The Edge of the Sea; Under the Sea Wind*.

Robert Finch, *The Primal Place; Common Ground*.

Richard Selzer, *Mortal Lessons: Notes on the Art of Surgery; Letters to a Young Doctor; Confessions of a Knife*.

Lewis Thomas, *The Lives of a Cell; The Medusa and the Snail; Late Night Thoughts on Listening to Mahler's Ninth Symphony*.

Paul Horgan, *Great River: The Rio Grande in North American History*.

Edward Hoagland, *Red Wolves and Black Bears; Walking the Dead Diamond River*.

David Quammen, *Natural Acts* or anything.

Gretel Ehrlich, *The Solace of Open Spaces*.

John McPhee, *Basin and Range; Annals of the Former World*.

George Greenstein, *Frozen Star*.

John Hay, *Nature's Year*.

John Graves, *Goodbye to a River; From a Limestone Ledge*.

Alan P. Lightman, *Time Travel and Papa Joe's Pipe*.

Loren Eiseley, *The Star Thrower*.

John K. Terres, *From Laurel Hill to Siler's Bog*.

Barry Lopez, *Desert Notes; Arctic Dreams*.

Gene Stratton Porter, *Moths of the Limberlost*.

Rutherford Platt, *The Great American Forest*.

Edwin Way Teale, the tetralogy: *The American Seasons: North with the Spring; Journey into Summer; Autumn Across America; Wandering North through Winter*.

James McConkey, *Court of Memory*.

Henry Beston, *The Outermost House*.

Laurens van der Post, *The Heart of the Hunter*.

Gerald Durrell, *The Whispering Land*.

Niko Tinbergen, *Curious Naturalists*.

Konrad Lorenz, *King Solomon's Ring*.

GRETEL EHRLICH

Lewis Thomas, *Lives of a Cell*. Dazzling insights based on surprising biological detail; Thomas reconnects modern, fragmentary man. His thoughts moved inexorably towards life. The book makes me know why I want to live. Also recommended: *The Medusa and the Snail* and *Late Night Thoughts on Listening to Mahler's Ninth Symphony*.

Henry David Thoreau, *Complete Works of* and *Journals*. The whole oeuvre constitutes a classic meditation; the *Journals* are springs we dip into and come away enlivened and refreshed.

John Muir, *My First Summer in the Sierra*. Muir's lush, rhapsodic, vivid account of his first season in the Sierra, mountains which would remain his spiritual home. He wrote: "Gazing awestricken, I might have left everything for it. Glad, endless work would then be mine, tracing the forces that have brought forth its features, its rocks and plants and animals and glorious weather. Beauty beyond thought everywhere, beneath, above, made and being made forever."

Ralph Waldo Emerson, *Collected Essays.* A seminal work that guides us in our thinking about the spectacle of life—nature, love, friendship, the natural and human condition.

The Kokinshu. One thousand, one hundred and eleven poems (mostly tankas) written in tenth-century Japan. A great many have to do with the changing seasons.

Japanese Poetic Diaries, ed. Earl Miner. Including Basho's *Journey to the Far North;* travel accounts in prose and poetry; nature as metaphor.

Annie Dillard, *Pilgrim at Tinker Creek* and *Teaching a Stone to Talk.* Brash, pious, rap-on-the-knuckles prose that throws up for speculation the routes and dramas of human meaning in the natural world.

Edward Hoagland, *Red Wolves and Black Bears.* Vivid, munificent prose; acute appraisals of what's left of our wild animals and the bedroll scientists who study them.

Loren Eiseley, *The Immense Journey.* Given to me by an aunt when I was thirteen, this book showed me the role of speculation and imagination in the natural history essay. After, I looked at the world with new eyes.

Joseph Wood Krutch, *The Desert Year* and *The Great Chain of Life.* Lovely, thoughtful essays.

Rockwell Kent, *N by E.* Ingenuous and charming account of a trip by boat to the coast of Greenland, wrecking there, living and loving like a native. Gorgeously illustrated with woodblock prints by the author. His illustrations, not his writings, were his forte.

Frank Craighead, *Track of the Grizzly.* An absorbing account of tracking, tagging, and living with the grizzlies of the Yellowstone by the two Craighead brothers, the experts in the field. Beautifully written, heartbreaking.

Karl Von Frisch, *The Dancing Bees; Man and the Living World;* and *Animal Architecture.* By the Nobel Prize-winner, each book is readable and chockful of fascinating detail.

Walt Whitman, *Leaves of Grass*. Inchoate, rhapsodic, erotic; the self in the cosmos — the cosmos in the self. Truly American verse.

Journals of Lewis and Clark. A daybook of the New World.

Margaret Murie, *Two in the Far North*. Married to Olaus Murie, who, with his brother, Adolph, pioneered in the ecology of the wolf, caribou, and elk, Murie describes in this lovely, gentle book her honeymoon behind a dogsled in Alaska.

Virgil, *Ecologues*. Memoirs of an agriculturalist and poet.

Herman Melville, *Moby-Dick*. In the words of Alfred Kazin: ". . . the most memorable confrontation we have had in America between Nature — as it was in the beginning, without man, God's world alone — and man, forever and uselessly dashing himself against it."

William Faulkner, *The Bear; Act II;* and *Requiem for a Nun*. Man and nature; and, Faulkner's version of the origins of the world.

HERE'S A LIST OF SOME I DON'T SEE ON ANY LIST, UNANNOTATED

Gregory Bateson, *Mind & Nature*.

Henry Nash Smith, *Virgin Land*.

Uwe George, *In the Deserts of This Earth*

Nigel Calder, *The Weather Machine*.

William Kauffman, *The Cosmic Frontier*.

JOHN HAY

Specimen Days, by Walt Whitman. Wonderful nature essays. I think "Song of Myself" also qualifies as a work of nature.

D. H. Lawrence's writings, especially those having to do with travel such as "Twilight in Italy" or "Mornings in Mexico"; they describe the surroundings with beautiful clarity.

The Winged Serpent, by Margot Astrov. An anthology of Indian prose and poetry, with an extremely sensitive introduction describing the poetic language of Native Americans.

Knud Rasmussen also collected native songs and tales of Greenland, which are quite extraordinary, but, alas, most have been translated into Danish, not English. However, something ought to be put into any list of the contribution of those who inhabited the continent before us and who knew the world of nature in a more completely experienced way than we do.

Animal Awareness and *Animal Thinking*, by Donald Griffin. A new contribution to the study of consciousness in the world of nature and nonhuman life.

Life on a Little-Known Planet, by Howard E. Evans. Essays by a Harvard biologist on the subject of insects—learned and readable enough to encourage any reader who wants to know more about these fascinating worlds of life.

The Dancing Bees, by Karl Von Frisch, discoverer of the language of bees and their means of communication.

The Herring Gull's World, by Niko Tinbergen. An important book about animal behavior by a trained observer, one of the pioneers in the science of ethology.

Four Masterworks of American Indian Literature, edited by John Pierhorst. This book includes the great ritual song of the Navajos, "The Night Chant," with its healing symbols of the earth.

It would be a mistake, I think, not to include Myth in any readings of this kind. A great deal of material has been written about it, but a classic treatment of world mythology can be found in Joseph Campbell's books, especially in the four volumes entitled *The Masks of God*.

A new book by David Abrams entitled *The Lure of the Sensuous* deals in a thoughtful way with the modern dismissal of myth sustaining cultures, and our disengagement from the animistic nature of the earth.

In recent years, a number of new naturalist-writers have published books which should not be overlooked. Of these the following stand out for me in their commitment to nature:

The Desert Smells Like Rain and *Gathering the Desert*, by Gary Paul Nabhan, are two careful, learned, and humane books about the desert plants of the Southwest and their interrelationship with the Papago Indians.

Richard K. Nelson's *Make Prayers to the Raven* which studies the language and close association with their wilderness world, has been followed by *The Island Within*, the author's sensitive account and defense of that world as it pertains to himself.

Bernd Heinrich's intense and dedicated book, *Ravens in Winter*, contains observation of a high order.

Barry Lopez, with his *Arctic Dreams*, opened up new windows on the vast range and beauty of the arctic, and some of its explorers and interpretors.

EDWARD HOAGLAND

The books that most excited and enlightened me as I acquired a love of nature and a bent for writing about it were not just the nonfiction masterpieces of observation like Thoreau's *Walden* and Darwin's *The Voyage of the Beagle*, or more recent books like Aldo Leopold's *A Sand County Almanac* and Loren Eiseley's *The Immense Journey*. Reading Ivan Turgenev's *A Sportsman's Notebook* and Tolstoy's country descriptions was probably a more significant experience because my ambition at first was to be a novelist. Other great works of fiction, like *Huckleberry Finn*, *Moby-Dick*, and Conrad's work, and some of Faulkner's and Thomas Hardy's, and even Flaubert's and Thomas Mann's *(Madame Bovary* and *Confessions of Felix Krull)* affected me powerfully in my responses to what I encountered out-of-doors. Nature was inherent in many master-novels of an earlier era. And there were American travel journals like William Bartram's, Lewis & Clark's, John Muir's, John Wesley Powell's, Josiah Gregg's, John James Audubon's, George Catlin's, and Mary Austin's *Land of Little Rain*, and Osborne Russell's *Jour-*

nal of a Trapper. In listing authors, one could go on and mention Willa Cather, W. H. Hudson, Jack London, Joshua Slocum, Rudyard Kipling, Rockwell Kent, Thomas Wolfe, Ernest Hemingway, and John Steinbeck. But, perhaps we should begin by saying that Aristotle was the first natural scientist in literature and Homer the first nature rhapsodist, once his words had been transcribed—though even Homer does not surpass God's cymbaling dithyramb on the animal kingdom to Job, out of the whirlwind, in the *Book of Job.*

A decent list could range from Aesop to the Russian writer Mikhail Prishvin (1873–1954), or our own Donald Culross Peattie on the subject of trees. Yet we shouldn't forget that the Montaigne of nature essayists was the Reverend Gilbert White, whose *The Natural History of Selborne* came out in 1789 and remains a nonpareil read. White's British heirs include Richard Jefferies (1848–1887) and John Fowles. Among my dead friends who have honored the genre were Edward Abbey and Wallace Stegner; and among living friends I would mention Annie Dillard, Gretel Ehrlich, and of course Peter Matthiessen. Diane Ackerman, Barry Lopez, Caroline Alexander, Richard Nelson and David Quammen are some of the younger crop. As wild nature dies, more and more elegists will materialize. Yet still contemporary nature writing tends to combine rhapsody with science and to connect science with rhapsody—in other words, to imply a belief finally in the radiance of God. Homer's purposes are thus linked with Darwin's, and for that reason it is a salient and a nourishing genre.

BARRY LOPEZ

Fine, thoughtfully prepared reading lists are now so readily available in this problematic field—problematic because its bounds are so amorphous—I thought I would limit myself here to a few works of nonfiction that seem unduly obscure.

The Desert, John C. Van Dyke. The author, an art historian and librarian, traveled extensively in the Mojave and Sonoran deserts between 1898 and 1901. He wrote with an extreme sensitivity to light and color, and his philosophical deliberations on the landscape have held up remarkably well.

Make Prayers to the Raven: A Koyukon View of the Northern Forest, Richard Nelson. A non-Cartesian field guide, grounded in historical research, on lengthy interviews, and the author's own experience. Nelson writes with deference toward the people and with an engaging enthusiasm.

The Peregrine, John Baker. An intensely observed, beautifully written account of "the bird, the watcher, and the place that holds them both." Baker's eye is sharply discriminating, his approach wild and unsentimental.

The Clam Lake Papers: A Winter in the North Woods, Edward Lueders. A graceful concatenation of ideas. The author builds a bridge between a particular winter landscape and the world of the mind, to illustrate the power of metaphor as a tool for human learning.

The Heart of the Hunter: Customs and Myths of the African Bushman, Laurens van der Post. One of several books based on van der Post's experiences with the native people of the Kalahari Desert. A compassionate, high-minded valediction, bearing, among other things, upon the role of story and the place of the individual in society.

The View from the Oak, Judith and Herbert Kohl. A lucid presentation of a fundamental idea in ethology — that different biological organisms perceive the same environment in different ways. Written for children, too.

If I could select a single annotated bibliography, it would be *Bringing the World Alive*, a list of nature stories for children ages 3–8 edited by Jennifer Sahn.

The general body of North American literature is rich in first-hand reports of encounters with the physical land, particularly landscapes startlingly new by virtue of their scale, their breadth, or their remarkable denizens. A representative book is William Brewer's *Up and Down California*, a vivid account of four years he spent in California with the first geological survey there (1860–1864), a series of very long letters, actually, ably edited by Francis Farquhar.

Brewer's book puts people squarely in the picture, especially their proprietary and perceptual attitudes toward the land. The inclusion of human history in the natural history of a region is also what makes John Graves's work, for example, stand out in a book like *Goodbye to a River*. In a vaguely related way, Rockwell Kent's *Wilderness*, about a soujourn in Alaska with his young son, is a wonderful example of how we project our romance with life onto certain landscapes. Isabella Bird is enthralled with a western landscape in *A Lady's Life in the Rocky Mountains*, but it functions as scenery for her. She is emotionally disengaged, and it is important to read her for that reason alone, for the difference and directness of her insight.

Fine but obscure animal books abound. For different reasons I think of Bernd Heinrich's *Bumblebee Economics;* Cynthia Moss's *Elephant Memories;* George Schaller's *The Last Panda;* Roderick L. Haig-Brown's book about steelhead fishing, *A River Never Sleeps;* Frans de Waal's *Peacemaking Among Primates;* and Laurence Klauber's *Rattlesnakes,* though its material on native American thought is, lamentably, slipshod.

An issue related to our curiosity about animals, troublesome but crucial to mention, is the tendency to romanticize their natures and their environments, to miss either the darker side of natural history or our own deep-seated differences with animals. Howard Norman's *Where the Chill Came From,* Donald Knowler's *The Falconer of Central Park,* Eugene Linden's *Silent Partners,* Jonathan Maslow's *Bird of Life, Bird of Death,* and a collection of John Haines's essays, *Stories We Listened To,* among recently published books, are skillful illuminations of different aspects of this problem.

Joseph Kastner's *A Species of Eternity* is a good introduction to the development of natural history writing in North America, and it underscores an important aspect of this kind of work—keenly observant writers have been out there in lightly-populated country for a long time. We are constantly turning up their unpublished papers in the archives of little-known historical societies. Some, who lacked a gift of language, have vision enough to make their work profound.

If I were to offer a reader any direction, places to explore, I would first suggest the large body of anthropological work that treats *other* visions of North America, those of native people, with respect and fidelity. And, second, the revitalized field of North American geography, work like Yi-Fu Tuan's *Space and Place,* for example, which deals with how we perceive (and develop separate feelings toward) undifferentiated lands and our home places.

In closing, I would like to put forth some thoughts that are obvious, but which perhaps need reiterating. Whatever term is used—nature writing, landscape writing, the literature of place—this tack in contemporary writing has clear historical antecedents. Indeed, the dynamic between human culture and physical place, exploring and settling these issues, might be what sets North American literature apart. A backward glance would include Melville, of course, Twain, Thoreau, Dickinson, and Whitman, certainly; but my eye is caught as well by, say Stephen Crane writing "The Open Boat" or, later, by the poems of Robinson Jeffers and essays of Mary Austin. The works of Cather and Steinbeck continue this tradition, reflected more recently in the novels, stories, poems, and essays of Merwin, Berry, Matthiessen, Clampitt, Stegner, Carson, and Snyder to quickly name a definitive handful.

It has occurred to many, probably, that the real subject here is not nature but restructuring the human community from which nature has so long been an outcast. The great casualties of modernism are nature, the diversity of human tradition, and the particularities of place. Much "nature writing," I think, can be approached as work both in opposition to modernism and as writing that emphasizes the issues of hope, of possibility, of *caritas* in postmodernism. Such a "literature of hope" might include writing that focuses on real or philosophical issues of human culture in a particular place, but also novels, say, that proceed out of a different awareness of human purpose or meaning than the pessimistic, modern understanding stretching from Copernicus through Darwin and Freud and culminating in a work like Sartre's *No Exit*.

I suppose this is a conceit, but by reincorporating nature into the meaning of human community, by including nature in that moral realm, I believe this sort of writing—landscape writing, nature writing—will one day be seen as part of a continuum in the mainstream of American letters and as work that will provide the foundation for a reorganization of American political thought.

I sense three things emerging in this kind of writing now. First, an ease, particularly on the part of women, in exploring relationships with nature that do not hinge on reason. Second, a willingness to address sanctity in a human relationship with place at a time of cultural cynicism and detachment. (In these areas, North American nature writing finds a kinship with postcolonial writing or "border writing" in Australia and other countries.)

Third, this is a tradition that can now call on several compelling bodies of new thought. Biological knowledge, which has grown exponentially since the 1950s and includes evolutionary theory, is an obvious example. Others include quantum physics, which has been so effective in questioning the primacy of science as the only path to "reality." And ecology. The anchor point in chaos that gave humanity its meaning, the mythic center that began to disintegrate with Copernicus, has been rediscovered in the science of ecology, the study of a center than can hold. It is the diffused center of a biological community, a center that does not depend on the fate of philosophies.

DAVID QUAMMEN

First, an admission: I don't read much of what's commonly thought of as "nature writing." My reason is an inherent impatience with the vicarious experiencing of landscape, natural beauty, or observational natural history. I'd rather lace up my boots and hike out into a snowy forest than read about someone else doing it; I'd rather watch a heron spearing fish, or a bear digging for corms, than "see" those phenomena through someone else's printed language, no matter how elegantly literary. Reading is the prototypic indoor activity and serves poorly, I think, as a substitute for being outdoors. So, call me a crank or a philistine, but when I read about the natural world, I'm generally reading for information, not for evocation. Mostly my tastes run to scientific and historical perspectives, and to the occasional authorial voice so peculiarly pungent that it would be worth reading on *any* subject.

The intention of my list is to alert readers to some leads they may not have already followed; there's no point in my reiterating titles that other advisory editors to this volume have mentioned. So I'll omit listing canonical classics (such as White's *Selborne*, *The Origin of the Species*, or the journals of Thoreau), more recent classics (such as *Desert Solitaire*), or well-known, important works by my colleagues (such as *Arctic Dreams*), and confine myself instead to some less obvious suggestions, dividing them between the scientific and the literary.

* * *

On the scientific side:

The Growth of Biological Thought, Ernst Mayr. A wise and authoritative survey of the history of biological science, from Aristotle through Linnaeus to James Watson. Mayr himself, besides being an important science historian and a good writer, is one of the great evolutionary biologists of this century.

The Formation of Vegetable Mould, through the Action of Worms, with Observations on Their Habits, Charles Darwin. His last and most charming book, eccentric but full of substance.

Nature's Economy, Donald Worster. A history of that particular branch of biological science we call *ecology*, from Gilbert White through Ernst Haeckel to Paul Ehrlich.

Modeling Nature, Sharon E. Kingsland. An episodic but deeply knowledgeable account of how scientists such as Alfred Lotka, G. Evelyn Hutchinson, and Robert MacArthur invented the field of population biology.

The Secular Ark, Janet Browne. A wonderful history of biogeography, the branch of biology that considers what species live where, and why.

The Ecology of Invasions by Animals and Plants, Charles S. Elton. A prescient little book, engagingly written and accessible, by a pioneer in the field of animal ecology. It elucidates one of the biggest threats facing the natural world as we presently know it.

Why Big Fierce Animals Are Rare, Paul Colinvaux. Important ecological insights, as explained by a personable expert.

Discordant Harmonies, Daniel B. Botkin. Scientific thinking about the ecological dynamics of the natural world is changing, and the changes are full of implications for how we regard, and how we treat, nature. This book describes the changes judiciously. Better to read about the new ideas here than to receive them, in distorted form, from gadfly commentators.

The Woman That Never Evolved, Sarah Blaffer Hardy. A fascinating discussion of the evolutionary bases of gender, by a primatologist.

A Feeling for the Organism, Evelyn Fox Keller. A fine biography of Barbara McClintock, the Mendel of maize.

Life Cycles, John Tyler Bonner. An intellectual memoir by a very eminent yet very humane evolutionary biologist. This book begins with the sentence: "I have devoted my life to slime molds." Who could resist that opening? Well, anyway, I couldn't.

Biophilia, Edward O. Wilson. Another intellectual memoir by another brilliant biologist and, also like Bonner's book, rich with both humanity and provocative thought.

* * *

Less scientific, more purely observational or literary:

The Soul of the White Ant, Eugène Marais. Marais, a South African lawyer and naturalist, a newspaperman, a morphine addict, an eventual suicide, was a remarkable person; and this is his most remarkable book, proposing the termite colony as metaorganism.

The Life of the Spider, J. Henri Fabre. My favorite among the Fabre samplings published in English. Even (especially?) arachnophobes can profit from it.

Charlotte's Web, E. B. White. Speaking of arachnophobia: This book, I think, offers a profoundly salubrious alternative worldview.

The Oysters of Locmariaquer, Eleanor Clark. Malacology and village culture in one tiny corner of the Brittany coast. It's really a travel book with an exquisitely fine sense of landscape (and seascape) and the little heartbeats of life.

Goatwalking, Jim Corbett. Corbett, a Quaker activist who helped found the Sanctuary movement in aid of Central American refugees in the early 1980s, offers a unique ethical and political vision, grounded on his experience living by goat-herding in a southwestern desert.

Great River, Paul Horgan. The subtitle says it: "The Rio Grande in North American History." A beautifully written epic, suitable reading for a *very* long river trip.

Blue Desert, Charles Bowden. Bowden, a former reporter for a Tucson newspaper, seems to have inherited two traits from Ed Abbey: a dark, dangerous wit, and a fierce, knowing passion for desert landscape.

Grizzly Years, Doug Peacock. Concerning *Ursus arctos horribilis*, and how a soul-seared Vietnam veteran healed himself during a decade of keeping company with the great bear.

Audubon: A Vision, Robert Penn Warren. A poem sequence, offered in meditation on the life of John James Audubon and his place in the American landscape.

The Theory & Practice of Rivers, Jim Harrison. Poems. The title work is one man's elegant love note to flowing, living water.

The Malay Archipelago, Alfred Russel Wallace. First published in 1869. Eight years studying insects and birds in the Malay Archipelago (now Indonesia) brought young Alfred Wallace to a world-shaking insight: that species evolve, through a process of natural selection. Unfortunately for him, a well-connected man named Darwin had thought of it earlier and was merely nursing the secret toward readiness. Wallace was arguably the greatest field biologist of the 19th century (far more of a field man than Darwin), and this chronicle of travels and observations is his greatest book. A neglected classic.

TERRY TEMPEST WILLIAMS

Sources of inspiration for natural history writing are often tangential, peripheral, to the subject at hand, yet central to the scaffolding of ideas present within the areas of ecological concern that I find myself writing. Here is a partial list of books and authors that I rely on repeatedly, call it my "baker's dozen":

Virginia Woolf: *The Waves.* I love the oscillations of thought in this novel, the stream of consciousness that is reflected in Woolf's narrative, how the ocean itself is the primary character. "The wave paused, and then drew out again, sighing like a sleeper whose breath comes and goes unconsciously. Imagery and the juxtaposition of seemingly unrelated ideas create a laminated text with depth and surprises. For me, Woolf is a literary naturalist, the natural world is the setting and atmosphere for her internal dialogues.

John Hersey: *Hiroshima.* This story of six human beings who survived the explosion of the atom bomb over Hiroshima is a story of human drama and compassion that is not separate from the land. Hersey shows us what it means to listen as a writer and the political implications of simply telling the story straight as he heard it from those who witnessed, "The Fundamental Project of Technology." Printed first in *The New Yorker* in 1946, the American public could no longer ignore the grim facts and horrific implications of our actions. Hersey wrote away the abstractions of World War II.

Simon Ortiz: *Woven Stone.* Simon Ortiz, an Acoma poet, is one of the most powerful American voices I know. He reminds us of true inhabitation, what native roots of this continent still mean and how far back they attach themselves to the land. This collection of Ortiz' poetry stretches back three decades including his works, *Going for the Rain; A Good Journey;* and *Fightin' Back.* His words, his stories speak to origins. Within these poems, Ortiz carries a sacred rage that cannot be ignored because of his eloquence and linguistic stamina. "Words yearn to be like wind, light, mountain, rain, love, because they are." When I think of survival, I think of Simon walking on the mesa, mindful of many worlds.

Mary Midgley: *Animals and Why They Matter.* Kant calls for responsible behavior with animals, even justice. "He who is cruel with animals becomes hard also in his dealings with men." Midgley, also a philosopher, makes the point that the ultimate act of anthropomorphism is to assume that animals don't feel. Her words are strong, brave, and brutally insightful regarding our relationship to Other. "When some portion of the biosphere is rather unpopular with the human race — a crocodile, a dandelion, a stony valley, a snowstorm, an odd-shaped flint — there are three sorts of human beings who are particularly likely still to see the point in it and befriend it. They are the poets, scientists, and children."

Breyten Breytenbach: *The Memory of Birds in Times of Revolution.* "The real revolutionary question is: What about the Other." In this collection of essays, Breytenbach reveals the candor, the cynicism, yet indomitable hope also found in his South African trilogy: *A Season in Paradise; The True Confessions of an Albino Terrorist;* and *Return to Paradise.* He is not afraid to confront the political nature of our lives and the realm it holds in the imagination. "It is important to take responsibility for the story. Imagination is politics." He has made the dangerous commitment "to plait my voice in the chorus of a national debate." Breytenbach reminds us there are consequences to writing and that in that paradox, "we must relearn silence."

Helene Cixous: *Coming to Writing and Other Essays.* "To look loss in the eye . . . " "To write out of the body. . . ." "I was outside, in a state of animal watchfulness. A desire was seeking its home. I was that desire. I was the question." Helene Cixous, a French writer and stylist, has saved my life. Her books have created a community of thought for me where I can question my own traditions and play with language in a way that can "break your heart with the magnificent calm of a beach safe from man." Cixous alerts me to the bodily pleasures and travails of narrative. She reminds me to speak the language women speak when there is no one there to correct us.

Octavio Paz: *Sor Juana.* I love this biography of Sor Juana Ines de la Cruz, one of the most striking figures in Spanish-American colonial literature. Her life reads like a novel. She was a charismatic poet and a nun in Hispanic seventeenth century. "May syllables be composed by the stars," she writes. She lived in a period of great prohibitions yet understood poetry as a form of rebellion, that her work inside and outside the constraints and freedoms within the convent were "utterances surrounded by silence: the silence of the things that cannot be said." We also see through the strength of her life the costs she paid in being a woman with a voice.

Emily Dickinson: *Collected Poems*. For me, Emily Dickinson defines "nature." The precision of her language, the elegance and clarity of her thoughts, her commitment to solitude and an interior life engaged, is sheer inspiration. "Life is a spell so exquisite everything conspires to break it." Word after word, poem after poem, Dickinson challenges us, how can we not respond?

John Steinbeck: *To A God Unknown*. This book illuminates the conflicts and reconciliations found within our own families with regard to the land. Steinbeck shows us how the power of ritual engages the power of reciprocity in the Earth's healing grace. I find this novella to be a metaphor for our time. We see how our ties to the land have been severed, the fear and pain we experience, the grief we hold, the healing we desire. Nothing less than our blood is required.

Terrence Des Pres: *Writing Into the World (Essays 1973–1987)*. Des Pres brings us to "a prose of witness," to see what is there, "imagination must have concrete points of entry." He goes on to say, "Worldly writing begins with fact, but relies on imagination to arrive at the heart of the matter." These right words "station the mind and hold the heart ready." It is the intensity of his mind that moves me. He accepts very little. The essay, "Self/Landscape/Grid" published in 1983, altered my perceptions of wildness, no matter where we live, we share our place on the nuclear grid. It is a political intrusion, a fact of our collective lives. How we live with this knowledge, this ambiguity drives art. Des Pres' hunger for a life of greater intention is evident on the page and he does not ignore history, our darkest history is his palette as a writer. It is the task of the poet to summon the tribe.

William Maxwell: *The Outermost Dream*. There is a grace and humanity in William Maxwell's work that supplies me with faith. There is a decency and a restraint in his prose, both in his stories and essays that creates an atmosphere of dignity that serves as a moral compass for me. His words are wise. I trust him and that is critical to me as a reader. His intelligence is provocative to the time we live. "Granted that one has to live in one's own Age or give up all contact with life . . ." And listen to these words regarding environmental degradation: "There was perhaps no stopping it, one thinks, and at the same time as one thinks that . . . it should never have been allowed to happen . . . with the terrible, heartbreaking impoverishment that is not confined to a single village in a remote valley of the Cotswolds, or to any one country. It is all but general, and very few of us know, at first hand, anything else. Like a fatal disease, it has now got into the bloodstream."

Walter P. Cottam: *Is Utah Sahara Bound?* Walter P. Cottam was a professor of botany at the University of Utah. On February 19, 1947, he delivered the eleventh annual Frederick William Reynolds Lecture. He questioned the land use practices of the state of Utah and asked if we could really afford the industrial exploitation and expansion we were engaged in regarding natural resources. He outlines through a systematic loss of Utah vegetation what the ecological consequences have been. In the tradition of Aldo Leopold, he not only raised biological and ethical questions but raised his voice in favor of a more comprehensive definition of community and stewardship. He confronted his own people with "the social wickedness of passing on to an unborn generation a land impaired by selfish exploitation." This scientific paper is a landmark piece of nature writing, a centennial examination of what had taken place from 1847 when the first Mormon pioneers came into the Great Salt Lake Valley to 1947. He suffers no illusions as a botanist, his science is interwoven with soul.

Nancy Newhall and Ansel Adams: *This Is The American Earth.* Perhaps it was my young age, perhaps it was the marriage of word to image that moved me, perhaps it was the fact that I was sitting in the old log library of the Teton Science School with a group of friends as each of us took turns reading paragraphs out loud—whatever the reasons, this large format Sierra Club book with text by Nancy Newhall and photographs by Ansel Adams serves as a national prayer in the name of our wildlands and the history of American conservation. It is a smart, lyrical incantation, the closest thing I know to "natural scriptures." Consider the closing lines, "Were all learning lost, all music stilled, Man, if these resources still remained to him, could again hear singing in himself and rebuild anew the habitations of his thought. Tenderly now let all men return to Earth."

JIM HARRISON

Of recent I have noted a troubling explosion in the arena of "nature writing," a watering down reminiscent of all the expansion teams in professional sports. I might feel different tomorrow and may have felt different yesterday, but I keep thinking of some comments by the Wyoming philosopher, Chip Rawlins, who pointed out bitingly that to say "nature writing" is to say "water swimming." We are nature, too, and the recent descension of this discipline into an academic genre is troubling, the evident distance between writer and subject rather too convenient.

But still I keep at it, this forced march through not so wondrous wondering, partly because the contemporary novel is a bourgeois morass of nifty people at loose but minimalist ends, and contemporary poetry enlivens the image of those miserable snow monkeys on their dirty little island of fake rock surrounded by shitty water at the Children's Zoo in Central Park. In a chilled building one of the penguins in the not quite living diorama would not turn from the trompe l'oeil arctic landscape to be fed. He stared at this back wall, and I thought, that's my favorite penguin.

Amid these private snits there's still a lot out there to be read and reread. I tend to favor the whole work of certain sensibilities: all of Loren Eiseley, Peter Matthiessen, Gary Snyder, Terry Tempest Williams, Barry Lopez, and David Quammen. These authors are essential, and the quality of writing is so high that one keeps reading when the stimuli of the information fades.

Separate books of a more recent vintage that are very good indeed include Jennifer Ackerman's "Notes from the Shore." Douglas Peacock's "The Grizzly Years" is a fine merging of the natural and unnatural worlds. David Petersen's "Racks," which is a natural history of antlered animals, continues to intrigue me and has been my "bathroom book" for years, waiting there among the pastel towels. David Abrams "The Spell of the Sensuous" is occasionally wrong headed but a marvelous tonic against the essential timidity of the imagination. Jack Turner's recent "The Abstract Wild" is sure to kick some well deserved ass, and is my favorite of late, combining as it does gorgeous observations of the natural world and the larger philosophical implications so readily avoided by others. A down to earth marvel is the recent "A Handful of Feathers" by Guy de la Valdéne who turned over the years a large Florida farm into a wild place.

I have noticed lately that hunting, tobacco, and wife beating are being lumped together in the feel good quadrant of yuppiedom, that ghastly, fluorescent hell of the professionally sincere that makes one long for the sixties. Not oddly, the hunter, who may even pause for a smoke, often has powers of observation that seem to escape the mandarin ethics of the observer. Turgenev's "Sportsman Sketches" comes to mind and so does Thomas

McGuane's "An Outside Chance." In both Turgenev and McGuane we have participants in the natural world and that adds the taste of the feral and incomprehensible, as does the very great "Dersu Ursula," which is as unforgettable as one's first coupling.

On thinking this all over I would have to add Bruce Chatwin's "Songlines," which is a flawless blend of landscape and the Natives who survived within it. Chatwin transcends all of the occidental presumptions we find so comfortable, as does Peter Nobokov's "As Testimony," a natural history of us by our own first citizens.

CONTRIBUTORS

Edward Abbey inspired a generation of environmentalists with his rage, his political incorrectness, and his sense of justice. Among his many books were the novels *The Monkey Wrench Gang* and *The Brave Country* and the memoir *Desert Solitaire*. He died in May, 1989.

David Abram's first book *The Spell of the Sensuous: Perception and Language in a More Than Human World* appeared in 1996. He lives in the Pacific Northwest.

Jennifer Ackerman is the author of *Notes from the Shore*. She lives in North Carolina.

Keith H. Basso is professor of anthropology at the University of New Mexico. He has conducted linguistic and ethnographic research in the Apache community at Cibecue since 1959. His most recent book, *Wisdom Sits In Places*, received the 1996 Western States Book Award for nonfiction.

John Berger lives in a small rural community in the French Alps. Among his novels are *G.*, winner of the Booker Prize, the trilogy *Into Their Labors (Pig Earth, Once in Europa and Lilac and Flag)*, and *To the Wedding.*

Elizabeth Bishop (1911–1979) received both the Pulitzer Prize and National Book Award for her poetry. Her correspondence, *One Act*, was published in 1995.

Julia Blackburn is the author of two works of nonfiction, *The Emperor's Last Island* and *Daisy Bates in the Desert. The Book of Color*, her most recent work, is a novel. She lives in Suffolk, England.

Paul Bowles studied music with Aaron Copeland in the 1920s, and first gained recognition as a composer. His numerous books include *The Sheltering Sky*, a novel; *The Delicate Prey*, stories; and *Too Far From Home*, a selection of his writings. He has lived in Tangier since 1947.

Italo Calvino (1923–1985) is the author of numerous books, including *Numbers in the Dark*, *Invisible Cities*, *The Baron in the Trees*, and *The Path to the Nest of Spiders*.

Bruce Chatwin's (1940–1989) books include *In Patagonia*, *The Victory of Oridah*, and the novels *On the Black Hill* and *Utz*.

Jim Crace's first novel *Continent* won the 1986 Whitbread First Novel prize. His other works include *The Gift of Stones*, *Arcadia*, and *Signals of Distress*. He lives in Birmingham, England.

Annie Dillard received a Pulitzer Prize for *Pilgrim at Turner Creek*. Her recent works include *An American Childhood*, a memoir, and *The Living*, a novel.

Gretel Ehrlich's books include her memoirs, *The Solace of Open Spaces*, and *A Match to the Heart*, and the novel *Heart Mountain*. She lives in Gaviota, California.

Richard Ford's books include *Rock Springs*, *Wildlife*, and the Pulitzer Prize-winning novel *Independence Day*.

John Fowles's books include *The French Lieutenant's Woman* and *The Magus*. He lives in England.

Louise Glück's most recent book of poems is *Meadowlands*. Among her previous books of poetry are *The Triumph of Achilles*, for which she won a National Book Critics Circle Award, and *The Wild Iris*, which received the Pulitzer Prize.

John Haines lives in his homestead in Fairbanks, Alaska. He is the author of a collection of essays titled *Stories We Listened To*.

Jim Harrison is a poet and novelist whose books include *The Woman Lit By Fireflies*, *Dalva*, *Legends of the Fall*, and *Just Before Dark*, his most recent collection of essays. He lives on a farm in northern Michigan.

Robert Hass, currently Poet Laureate of the United States, is the author of four books of poetry: *Field Guide*, *Praise*, *Human Wishes*, and most recently *Sun Under Wood*.

John Hay is a resident of Cape Cod but spends his summers in Maine "growing superior vegetables, boating between islands and watching seals and seabirds."

Seamus Heaney, who has published many collections of poetry and essays, won the 1995 Nobel Prize for Literature. He lives in Dublin.

Edward Hoagland's most recent collection of essays is *Balancing Acts*. He lives in Northern Vermont, and is currently completing a memoir.

Ted Hughes, the Poet Laureate of England, is the author of sixteen volumes of poetry, among them *Winter Pollen, Difficulties of a Bridegroom*, and *Spring Awakening*. He lives in Devon, England.

William Langewiesche's most recent book is *Sahara Unveiled: A Journey Across the Desert*. He writes frequently for the *Atlantic Monthly* and lives in California.

Barry Lopez is the author of *Artic Dreams*, winner of the 1986 National Book Award, and *Of Wolves and Men*, as well as several story collections. He lives in Finn Rock, Oregon.

Cormac McCarthy is the author of six novels, including *Blood Meridian* and *All the Pretty Horses*, for which he received the National Book Award, and *The Gardener's Son*, a screenplay.

John McPhee has written numerous books including *Coming Into the Country, Encounters With the Archdruids*, and *The Control of Nature*. He lives in Princeton, New Jersey.

David Malouf's most recent novel is *The Conversations at Curlow Creek*. Among his previous books are *Remembering Babylon* and *An Imaginary Life*. He lives in Sydney, Australia.

Gabriel García Márquez is the author of many novels and collections of stories, including *One Hundred Years of Solitude, Love in the Time of Cholera, Strange Pilgrims*, and *No One Writes to the Colonel Any More*. He lives in Mexico City and Bogota.

Peter Matthiessen's works of fiction include *At Play in the Fields of the Lord;* his books of nonfiction include, most prominently, *The Snow Leopard,* for which he received the National Book Award. He lives in Sagaponack, New York.

W.S. Merwin's many books of poetry include his *Selected Poems* and, most recently, *The Vixen.* He lives in Hawaii.

Gary Nabhan's most recent book is *Cultures of Habitat.* He lives in the Arizona Desert.

Richard K. Nelson is an anthropologist who has lived for extended periods in several Alaskan Eskimo and Athapaskan Indian villages. He is the author of several books, including *The Deer.*

Joyce Carol Oates's most recent books are *We Were the Mulvaneys* and *First Love.* She lives in New Jersey and teaches at Princeton University.

Noel Perrin has been tending 100 acres of land in Vermont for the last 35 years, and has taught at Dartmouth College for 37. His books include *First, Second,* and *Third Person Rural.*

David Quammen's most recent book is *The Song of the Dodo: Island Biography in the Age of Extinction.* Since 1981 his column, "Natural Acts," has appeared in *Outside* magazine. He lives with his wife in Bozeman, Montana.

Leslie Marmon Silko has written *Ceremony* and *Almanac of the Dead.* She lives in Tucson, Arizona.

Gary Snyder's most recent book of selected poems, *No Nature,* was nominated for a National Book Award. *A Place in Space* is a new collection of prose. He lives in the foothills of the Sierra Nevada in Northern California.

Guy de la Valdéne is the author of *For a Handful of Feathers.*

Derek Walcott's many works include *The Fortunate Traveller* and *American Without America.* He lives in Massachusetts.

Edward O. Wilson is Baird Professor of Science and Curator in Entomology at Harvard University. His most recent books include *Naturalist* and *Biodiversity II*.

Terry Tempest Williams is the author of *Refuge* and *An Unspoken Hunger*. Her most recent book, *Desert Quartet*, was a collaboration with the artist Mary Frank. The recipient of a Lannan Literary Fellowship in Creative Nonfiction, she is Naturalist-in-Residence at the Utah Museum of Natural History.

Ann Zwinger is the author of *The Mysterious Lands* and *Run, River, Run*. She spends part of the year in Colorado Springs and "the rest on the road in faraway places with strange-sounding names."

ACKNOWLEDGMENTS

"The Moon-Eyed Horse," from *Desert Solitaire,* first published 1968 by McGraw-Hill. Copyright © 1968 by Edward Abbey. Reprinted by permission. All rights reserved.

"The Ecology of Magic," from *The Spell of the Sensuous* by David Abrams, published by Pantheon. Copyright © 1991 by David Abrams. Reprinted by permission. All rights reserved.

"Five Fathoms," from *Notes from the Shore,* by Jennifer Ackerman, published by Viking. Copyright © 1995 by Jennifer Ackerman. Reprinted by permission. All rights reserved.

"Stalking with Stories: Names, Places, and Moral Narratives among the Western Apaches," by Keith H. Basso first appeared, in longer form, in *The Yale Review,* republished in *Antaeus.* Copyright © 1986 by Keith H. Basso.

"Goats," from *Pig Earth* by John Berger, first published by Pantheon. Copyright © 1979 by John Berger. Reprinted by permission. All rights reserved.

"The Map," from *The Complete Poems of Elizabeth Bishop,* first published by Farrar, Straus & Giroux, Inc. Copyright © 1984. Reprinted by permission. All rights reserved.

"St. Helena's," from *The Emperor's Last Island,* first published by Pantheon. Copyright © 1991 by Julia Blackburn. Reprinted by permission. All rights reserved.

"The New Day," from *The Sheltering Sky,* copyright © 1949, 1990 by Paul Bowles. Published by The Ecco Press.

"The Drought," from *The Viceroy of Quidah,* first published by Summit Books. Copyright © 1980 by Bruce Chatwin. Reprinted by permission. All rights reserved.